Prentice Hall Advanced Reference Series

Engineering

ANTOGNETTI AND MILUTINOVIC, EDS. *Neural Networks: Concepts, Applications, and Implementations, Volumes I, II, III, and IV*

DENNO *Power System Design and Applications for Alternative Energy Sources*

ESOGBUE, ED. *Dynamic Programming for Optimal Water Resources Systems Analysis*

FERRY, AKERS, AND GREENEICH *Ultra Large Scale Integrated Microelectronics*

GNADT AND LAWLER, EDS. *Automating Electric Utility Distribution Systems: The Athens Automation and Control Experiment*

HALL *Biosensors*

HAYKIN, ED. *Advances in Spectrum Analysis and Array Processing, Volumes I and II*

HAYKIN, ED. *Selected Topics in Signal Processing*

HENSEL *Inverse Theory and Applications for Engineers*

JOHNSON *Lectures on Adaptive Parameter Estimation*

MILUTINOVIC, ED. *Microprocessor Design for GaAs Technology*

QUACKENBUSH, BARNWELL III, AND CLEMENTS *Objective Measures of Speech Quality*

ROFFEL, VERMEER, AND CHIN *Simulation and Implementation of Self-Tuning Controllers*

SASTRY AND BODSON *Adaptive Control: Stability, Convergence, and Robustness*

SWAMINATHAN AND MACRANDER *Materials Aspects of GaAs and InP Based Structures*

TOMBS *Biotechnology in the Food Industry*

NEURAL NETWORKS
Concepts, Applications, and Implementations
Volume III

Paolo Antognetti and Veljko Milutinović
Editors

Prentice Hall, Englewood Cliffs, New Jersey 07632

Library of Congress Cataloging-in-Publication Data

(Revised for vol. 3)
Neural networks.

(Prentice Hall advanced reference series. Engineering)
Includes bibliographical references and indexes.
1. Neural networks (Computer science)
I. Antognetti, Paolo. II. Milutinović, Veljko.
III. Series.
QA76.87.N48 1991 006.3 90-7485
ISBN 0-13-612516-6
ISBN 0-13-612771-1 (v. 3)

Cover Design: *Karen A. Stephens*
Manufacturing buyer: *Kelly Behr/Susan Brunke*
Acquisitions Editor: *Bernard Goodwin*

Prentice Hall Advanced Reference Series

The publisher offers discounts on this book when ordered in bulk quantities. For more information, write:

Special Sales/College Marketing
Prentice-Hall, Inc.
College Technical and Reference Division
Englewood Cliffs, New Jersey 07632

ISBN 0-13-612771-1

Printed in the United States of America

10 9 8 7 6 5 4 3 2 1

ISBN 0-13-612771-1

PRENTICE-HALL INTERNATIONAL (UK) LIMITED, *London*
PRENTICE-HALL OF AUSTRALIA PTY. LIMITED, *Sydney*
PRENTICE-HALL CANADA INC., *Toronto*
PRENTICE-HALL HISPANOAMERICANA, S.A., *Mexico*
PRENTICE-HALL OF INDIA PRIVATE LIMITED, *New Delhi*
PRENTICE-HALL OF JAPAN, INC., *Tokyo*
SIMON & SCHUSTER ASIA PTE. LTD., *Singapore*
EDITORA PRENTICE-HALL DO BRASIL, LTDA., *Rio de Janeiro*

Contents

APPLICATIONS

IMPLEMENTATIONS

Foreword

When interest in neural networks revived some fifteen years ago, few people believed that such systems would ever be of any use. Computers worked too well; it was felt that they could be programmed to perform any desired task.

Clearly, fashion has changed. Now, limitations of current computers in solving many problems involving difficult to define rules or complex pattern recognition are widely recognized; if anything, expectations for neural networks may be too high. The problem is no longer to convince anyone that neural networks might be useful, but rather to actually incorporate such networks into systems that solve real-world problems economically.

Neural networks are inspired by biological systems where large numbers of neurons, that individually function rather slowly and imperfectly, collectively perform tasks that even the largest computers have not been able to match. They are made of many relatively simple processors connected to one another by variable memory elements whose weights are adjusted by experience. They differ from the now standard Von Neumann computer in that they characteristically process information in a manner that is highly parallel rather than serial, and that they learn (memory element weights and thresholds are adjusted by experience) so that to a certain extent they can be said to program themselves. They differ from the usual artificial intelligence systems in that (since neural networks learn) the solution of real-world problems requires much less of the expensive and elaborate programming and knowledge engineering required for such artificial intelligence products as rule-based expert systems.

In their current state, neural networks are probably best at problems related to pattern recognition. Some existing neural network systems can efficiently and rapidly learn to separate enormously complex decision spaces. The problem of coordinating many neural networks, each a specialist in dividing some portion of the decision space, has also been solved. It is in these areas, therefore, that the first commercial uses will appear. Products that recognize characters, assembly line parts or signatures, that make complex decisions mimicking or improving on human experts (such as underwriters) that can diagnose engine or assembly line problems are in the prototype stage and/or are already fielded. One expects, further, that the pattern recognition ability coupled with, and feeding back and forth to rule-based systems (as has already been done in some simple applications) will finally result in machines that share our ability to learn and duplicate our processes of reasoning—machines that might be said to think.

The question is not whether but when.

Predicting the future, as we all know, is risky. Predicting the evolution of new technology is downright hazardous. Who in the 1930's would have said that among the consequences of the uncertainty principle would be transistors, silicon chips, and all of the vast array of solid state devices on which all modern computers depend? Or that superconductors would lead to extraordinarily sensitive detectors of magnetic fields now carried on many naval ships? Or in the late 19th century, that among the consequences of the research of Maxwell, Lorentz and Einstein, would be all that we call modern communication: radio, radar, etc.?

Accepting this risk, I would predict that neural networks will become standard components of what we today call computers. This will likely occur in a somewhat evolutionary manner: they will encroach gradually—board by board, intelligent components, that can be trained by humans in a language humans understand, into dumb machines—somewhat like neo-cortex came to dominate the reptilean brain. And, just as the 20th century is the century of automobiles, airplanes, telephones and computers, the 21st will be the century of intelligent machines. We will not only learn to live with these machines but, indeed, will wonder, one day, how we ever lived without them.

Leon Cooper
1972 Nobel Laureate

Preface

Neural networks and neural engineering in the wide sense are among the most rapidly developing scientific fields today. The field is interdisciplinary in its nature, and the success formula is to combine expertise and experience from several scientific fields.

The basic idea behind this series of books is to combine expertise and experience of contributing authors from a number of different scientific disciplines.

The style and structure of the books are oriented to those who need to get a broad insight into the state-of-the-art developments in the field. Each book in the series includes three parts: Concepts, Applications, and Implementations.

We would like to thank all contributing authors for their efforts and enthusiasm. Most of them are also the major contributors to the field itself, and we feel honored to have had an opportunity to work with them.

We would also like to thank Professor Leon Cooper for his creative rôle during our meetings in Genoa, Italy. His foreword to this series sheds an important new light on the future development of the field.

Finally, we would like to thank our colleagues from Genoa Research, Italy (especially Dr. Marenco, Mrs. Arata, and Ms. Ponta), and the University of Belgrade, Yugoslavia (especially Professors Dujmovic, Djordjevic, Lazic, Jovanovic, Oklobdzija, and Velasevic), for their suggestions and encouragement.

Please note that the Appendix provides a complete listing of contents and contributing authors for all four volumes of *Neural Networks.*

Paolo Antognetti and Veljko Milutinović, Editors

1

DECISION MAKING AND PATTERN CLASSIFICATION BY STOCHASTIC AND DETERMINISTIC NEURAL NETWORKS

by Eyal Yair† and Allen Gersho,
Center for Information Processing Research,
University of California

1. Introduction

Decision-making and pattern classification tasks appear in many areas of engineering. Generally there are several, say M, possible decisions, and the problem is to make the best decision given that some information $\mathbf{x}$ is known. In terms of classification, the given information, $\mathbf{x}$, which is generally a sample vector from a random source, is to be assigned to the most appropriate class out of the M possible classes. Obviously, some quality criterion should be specified in order to quantify the appropriateness of each class.

A general way to perform the classification is to define a set of M decision functions $d_m(\mathbf{x})$, one for each class, and to choose the most appropriate class, m^*, for the information $\mathbf{x}$ as the class for which the decision function is maximal,

$$m^* = \underset{1 \le m \le M}{\operatorname{argmax}} \{ d_m(\mathbf{x}) \} \quad . \tag{1.1}$$

The type of classifier is determined by the choice of the decision functions. Generally, these functions are parametrized by a set of parameters, and the design of the classifier is made by determining the values of the parameters from a given set of examples called a *training set.*

The data $\mathbf{x}$ is assumed to be a real-valued vector in the Euclidean I-dimensional space drawn from a probability distribution $Q(\mathbf{x})$. When the decision functions are linear with $\mathbf{x}$, the classifier is called a *linear classifier*, and the decision functions are given in this case by

$$d_m(\mathbf{x}) = \mathbf{x}' \mathbf{w}_m + \gamma_m \qquad ; \qquad m = 1, \cdots, M \quad , \tag{1.2}$$

where the set of vectors $\{\mathbf{w}_m\}$ and scalars $\{\gamma_m\}$ are the classifier parameters, and $\mathbf{x}'$ denotes the transpose of the column vector $\mathbf{x}$. Using the criterion (1.1) for determining the most appropriate class for $\mathbf{x}$, it follows that for $m = m^*$ we get $d_{m^*}(\mathbf{x}) - d_n(\mathbf{x}) \ge 0$ for all

This work was supported by the Weizmann Foundation for scientific research, the University of California MICRO program, Bell-Northern Research, Rockwell International, and by Bell Communications Research.

† Eyal Yair is currently at the IBM Scientific Center in Haifa, Israel.

$n \in \{1, \cdots, M\}$, while for any $m \neq m^*$ the difference $d_m(\mathbf{x}) - d_n(\mathbf{x})$ will not be positive for all values of n. Therefore, by defining the hard-limiter function

$$f_H(x) = \begin{cases} 1 & \text{if } x \geq 0 \\ 0 & \text{otherwise} \end{cases} \quad , \tag{1.3}$$

we can write for the linear classifier

$$\begin{aligned} \sum_{n=1}^{M} f_H\,[\,d_m(\mathbf{x}) - d_n(\mathbf{x})\,] &\leq M-1 \quad ; \quad \text{for all } m \neq m^* \\ \sum_{n=1}^{M} f_H\,[\,d_m(\mathbf{x}) - d_n(\mathbf{x})\,] &= M \quad ; \quad \text{for } m = m^* \quad . \end{aligned} \tag{1.4}$$

Defining $\mathbf{w}_{mn} = \mathbf{w}_m - \mathbf{w}_n$ and $\gamma_{mn} = \gamma_m - \gamma_n$, the decision scheme for the linear classifier can be computed, using (1.2) and (1.4) by evaluating the vector $\mathbf{y} = (y_1, \cdots, y_M)'$ whose components are given by

$$y_m = f_H\,[\,(\tfrac{1}{2} - M) + \sum_{n=1}^{M} f_H\,(\mathbf{x}'\mathbf{w}_{mn} + \gamma_{mn})\,] \quad ; \quad m = 1, \cdots, M \ . \tag{1.5}$$

The *only* component of $\mathbf{y}$ which is 'on' (i.e., its value is one) will be the m^*-th component, while all the other components of $\mathbf{y}$ will be 'off' (i.e., will have a zero value). The above scheme can be implemented by a two-layer network as depicted schematically in Figure 1. Such a network is called a *perceptron* and was first suggested by Rosenblatt (1959) for solving a two-class classification problem with a linear classifier. Note that for a two-class classifier, only one layer is required and the value of the single output unit indicates what class was chosen. For the multi-class classifier, the two-layer perceptron of Figure 1 may be used.

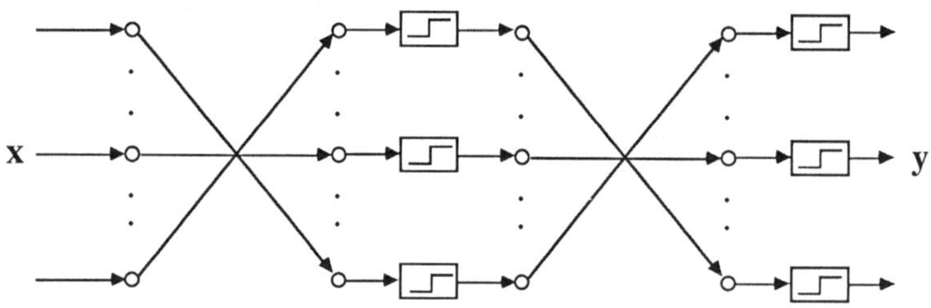

Figure 1: Schematic description of signal flow in a two-layer perceptron used for the multi-class linear classifier.

The presentation of the perceptron by Rosenblatt in 1959 marked the beginning of the appearance of new types of structures for pattern classification which are now known as *neural networks*. The name was associated with such types of nonlinear networks due to the study of McCulloch and Pitts (1943) which gave a schematic functional description to the biological neural cell as a summation element with weighted inputs followed by a hard-limiter type of nonlinear transformation, which can be 'on' (firing) or 'off' (not firing) depending on whether the sum of weighted inputs exceeds some internal voltage threshold of the cell. The perceptron is constructed by a hierarchical layered structure of such cells (also called neurons or network units).

The structure of the original perceptron, and in particular the non-differentiability of the hard-limiting functions, possessed some difficulties finding efficient learning algorithms to design the classifier parameters for general problems. Although a now classical learning algorithm was proposed by Rosenblatt, its use was limited to problems for which the classes were linearly separable. That is, the sets of training patterns representing two different classes could be separated by a hyperplane. This fact imposed a severe limitation on the usefulness of the perceptron for general classification problems, for which the linear separability property could not be guaranteed.

A "modern" type of perceptron, known as the *multi-layer perceptron* (MLP), which avoids most of the difficulties of the original perceptron, was recently proposed by several researchers (Rumelhart et. al., 1986; Parker, 1985; Werbos, 1974). The MLP has an arbitrary number of layers, and the hard-limiter nonlinearities are replaced by "soft", differentiable sigmoid functions, such as the logistic function given by

$$h_\beta(x) = \frac{1}{1+e^{-\beta x}} \quad , \tag{1.6}$$

where β controls the slope of the function. For an infinite value of β, the logistic function becomes the hard-limiter of (1.3) and the MLP then coincides with the original perceptron. A learning algorithm was also proposed for the MLP based on the gradient descent method and is known as the backpropagation algorithm. By using a multi-layered network, rather than a single-layer one, the linear separability requirement of the original perceptron is no longer required since the boundary between classes can be constructed by a union of hyperplanes. In fact, a three-layer perceptron can form any type of boundary between classes if the number of units is not limited (cf. Lippmann, 1987). However, in most applications where the boundaries are complicated, the number of network units required to approximate the boundaries by hyperplanes might be too large for practical use.

Other types of classifiers can be constructed by incorporating more complicated decision functions. In classical stochastic decision theory, it is common to consider the Bayes classifier as optimal, whereby the class chosen by the classifier for the given data $\mathbf{x}$ is the *most probable* class. Defining the decision functions to be $d_m(\mathbf{x}) = Pr(m \mid \mathbf{x})$, where $Pr(m \mid \mathbf{x})$ is the probability of choosing class m $(m \in \{1, \cdots, M\})$ given a specific information vector $\mathbf{x}$, the

Bayes classifier is obtained by evaluating the following maximization formula:

$$m^* = \underset{1 \le m \le M}{\operatorname{argmax}} \{ Pr(m \mid \mathbf{x}) \} \quad . \tag{1.7}$$

The probabilities $Pr(m \mid \mathbf{x})$ are known as the *a posteriori* probabilities, and the Bayes classifier thus supplies the *maximum a posteriori* (MAP) decision. To evaluate the a posteriori probabilities, the Bayes' Rule can be used as follows:

$$Pr(m \mid \mathbf{x}) = \frac{Pr(m)\, Pr(\mathbf{x} \mid m)}{Pr(\mathbf{x})} \quad , \tag{1.8}$$

and since the denominator is independent of m it can be omitted in the maximization formula of (1.7). The probability $Pr(m)$ is called the *prior* of the m-th class, and $Pr(\mathbf{x} \mid m)$ is the likelihood function of class m given $\mathbf{x}$. In many cases the priors are not known and the classification is performed by maximizing the likelihood functions over m. The resulting classifier is then known as the *maximum likelihood* classifier which coincides with the Bayes classifier if the priors are all equal.

The major drawback of using the Bayes classifier is that, unless the probabilistic model of the problem is known, the direct evaluation of the maximization in (1.7) cannot be performed. Generally, in such cases when the Bayes classifier is used, a probabilistic model for the given problem is assumed (e.g. Gaussian distributions are used) which limits the performance of the classifier to the stipulated model. Poor performance may be obtained if the real (or the "world") distributions are different than those of the model that is used.

When the probabilistic nature of the "world" is not known, a neural network which can learn the distributions of the problem from a training set, *without* any a priori assumptions of a probabilistic model, might be more powerful. By using a neural network instead of assuming a specific probabilistic model for the given problem, the limitations of the model are replaced by the capability of the network due to its architecture and mode of operation. In most cases, even a simple network which has a sufficient number of units can approximate complicated functions. The critical problem is really to construct a useful structure for the network along with an appropriate learning algorithm which can supply suitable values for the classifier parameters in a reasonable computation time.

In many applications one is interested not only in the most probable class, but also in the *probability* of each of the classes to be chosen for the given data. In such cases, the interest is to obtain an estimation of the *a posteriori* probabilities $Pr(m \mid \mathbf{x})$ for all the classes, while the decision of what class to use is postponed to a later stage of processing. This is generally the case when other information (such as context) is to be incorporated in higher levels of a hierarchical recognition procedure.

Since $Pr(\mathbf{x})$ can be expressed by

$$Pr(\mathbf{x}) = \sum_{m=1}^{M} Pr(m) Pr(\mathbf{x} \mid m) \quad , \tag{1.9}$$

the a posteriori probabilities of (1.8) can, in principle, be computed from the likelihood functions and the priors of the classes. However, generally theses quantities are not explicitly known and techniques other than the direct evaluation of (1.8) should be sought.

In this chapter we assume that the *a priori* knowledge consists of only a finite training set, and the objective is to devise a classifier that, after being trained on the given examples, can produce an estimate of the *a posteriori* probabilities for input vectors presented to it. No assumptions on the actual probabilistic nature of the problem are made, and thus, the classifier is universal in the sense that it is not restricted to an underlying probabilistic model. We will start by describing a stochastic type of classifier based on a Markov chain network, which is rather general but computationally expensive, and proceed by developing a deterministic classifier which eventually performs the same computation as the stochastic model with a substantially reduced complexity by a feed-forward deterministic network.

2. The Stochastic Classifier

The idea here is to define a stochastic network which, for a given data vector $\mathbf{x}$, chooses the classes stochastically, such that the probability of choosing each class will be that of the desired *a posteriori* probability. The stochastic network can be described by a network of interconnected binary-valued units which make random asynchronous changes between two possible values, zero and one, according to a probabilistic transition rule. Such a network can serve as a useful classifier if the network parameters (e.g., the connection weights between the network units) are suitably designed to yield a desired response of the network for the training patterns. Hence, in contrast to the Bayes classifier for which assumptions about the unknown probability distributions of the problem should be made, the above approach requires no a priori assumptions, and the network design is carried out by adjusting the classifier parameters to a known set of training patterns. The network is universal in the sense that it is not limited by a set of assumptions on the probabilistic model of the problem as in the case of the Bayes classifier, but rather, the "world" model is being learned from the training set via the learning (designing) procedure.

The classifier is described by a finite-state irreducible Markov model with a binary state vector $\mathbf{s}$ and a stationary probability distribution $Pr(\mathbf{s}\,|\,\mathbf{x})$. The notation indicates that $Pr(\mathbf{s}\,|\,\mathbf{x})$ is the probability of attaining a state $\mathbf{s}$ given a particular data vector $\mathbf{x}$. The network produces a Markov chain of binary vectors whose statistics are governed by the transition probabilities between the states. Assuming that all the states are attainable (i.e., there is a non-zero probability of reaching any state from any other state), the stationary probabilities of the states are strictly positive and therefore the stationary probability distribution can be represented by an exponential form as follows:

$$Pr(\mathbf{s}\,|\,\mathbf{x}) = \frac{1}{Z}\, e^{\beta H(\mathbf{s}|\mathbf{x})} \quad , \tag{2.1}$$

where $H(\mathbf{s}\,|\,\mathbf{x})$ is an arbitrary function of both $\mathbf{s}$ and $\mathbf{x}$, β is a non-negative number, and Z is a normalization factor given by

$$Z = \sum_{\mathbf{s}} e^{\beta H(\mathbf{s}|\mathbf{x})} \quad , \tag{2.2}$$

where the summation is over all possible values of the binary state vector $\mathbf{s}$.

The type of distribution given in (2.1) is known as the *Gibbs distribution*. The function $H(\mathbf{s}\,|\,\mathbf{x})$ is called the *Hamiltonian* function, and β represents the reciprocal of a physical temperature and is called, for reasons to be explained later, the *gain* of the classifier. The reason why a Gibbs distribution is used to represent the stationary state distribution is that while it is a general representation, it is easy to use analytically, and will be useful for constructing a learning algorithm and obtaining the deterministic scheme. Note that as long as $H(\mathbf{s}\,|\,\mathbf{x})$ is an arbitrary function, any positive $Pr(\mathbf{s}\,|\,\mathbf{x})$ can be represented by (2.1). However, it is practical to restrict $H(\mathbf{s}\,|\,\mathbf{x})$ to a certain type or class of functions in order to simplify the operation of the classifier and the learning algorithm. In this case, an arbitrary Markov chain will not necessarily yield a Gibbs distribution with the desired type of Hamiltonian. Therefore, before proceeding, we construct the necessary relationship between the transition probabilities and the Hamiltonian function required to guarantee a steady-state Gibbs distribution as given in (2.1).

A state transition, from state $\mathbf{s}_1$ to state $\mathbf{s}_2$, can be described by a succession of two stochastic operations: the proposal of a transition from $\mathbf{s}_1$ to $\mathbf{s}_2$ and the acceptance of the proposed transition. In the proposal stage, a target state $\mathbf{s}_2$ is generated stochastically according to a generating distribution $g(\cdot)$, which is also a function of the current state $\mathbf{s}_1$. In the acceptance stage, the proposed state $\mathbf{s}_2$ is either accepted or rejected according to an acceptance probability $w(\cdot)$. If the transition is accepted, the network moves from state $\mathbf{s}_1$ to state $\mathbf{s}_2$; otherwise, it remains in state $\mathbf{s}_1$. The probability of making a transition from state $\mathbf{s}_1$ to state $\mathbf{s}_2$, denoted by $p(\mathbf{s}_1,\mathbf{s}_2)$, can therefore be decomposed (for $\mathbf{s}_1 \neq \mathbf{s}_2$) as follows:

$$p(\mathbf{s}_1,\mathbf{s}_2) = g(\mathbf{s}_1,\mathbf{s}_2)\, w(\mathbf{s}_1,\mathbf{s}_2) \quad , \tag{2.3a}$$

where $g(\mathbf{s}_1,\mathbf{s}_2)$, the generation distribution, is the probability of proposing a transition from $\mathbf{s}_1$ to $\mathbf{s}_2$, and $w(\mathbf{s}_1,\mathbf{s}_2)$, the acceptance distribution, is the probability of accepting the transition from $\mathbf{s}_1$ to $\mathbf{s}_2$ given that it was proposed. The probability of remaining in the same state is accordingly given by

$$p(\mathbf{s}_1,\mathbf{s}_1) = g(\mathbf{s}_1,\mathbf{s}_1) + \sum_{\substack{\mathbf{s}_2 \\ \mathbf{s}_2 \neq \mathbf{s}_1}} g(\mathbf{s}_1,\mathbf{s}_2)\,[\,1 - w(\mathbf{s}_1,\mathbf{s}_2)\,] \quad , \tag{2.3b}$$

in which the first term expresses the probability of proposing the same state, and the second term expresses the total probability of proposing any other state but then rejecting the proposed transition. Note that $1 - w(\mathbf{s}_1,\mathbf{s}_2)$ is the probability of rejecting the proposed transition. The transition probability $p(\mathbf{s}_1,\mathbf{s}_2)$ also satisfies

$$\sum_{s_2} p(s_1,s_2) = 1 \quad , \tag{2.4}$$

where the left hand side of (2.4) is the probability of making a transition from s_1.

The steady-state distribution, $Pr(s|x)$, of the Markov model should satisfy for any arbitrary state s_1,

$$Pr(s_1|x) = \sum_{s_2} Pr(s_2|x)\, p(s_2,s_1) \quad , \tag{2.5}$$

which means that the probability of state s_1 is the sum of the probabilities of all possible transitions from any other state of the network to state s_1. Since we want the steady-state distribution to be given by the Gibbs distribution, (2.5) can be expressed, using (2.1), as

$$\sum_{s_2} p(s_2,s_1)\, e^{\beta[H(s_2|x)-H(s_1|x)]} = 1 \quad . \tag{2.6}$$

In order to enable implementation of the model by a neural network, it is useful to assume that each of the components of the binary state vector s is represented by an independent unit (or neuron) which can be in one of two possible positions. The neurons change their states asynchronously, and hence it may be assumed that in each state transition only one component of s is flipped. Mathematically, this can be described by letting

$$g(s_1,s_2) = 0 \qquad \text{for} \quad d_H(s_1,s_2) \geq 2 \quad , \tag{2.7}$$

where $d_H(s_1,s_2)$ is the Hamming distance between the two binary vectors s_1 and s_2 (which counts the number of components which are different in s_1 and s_2). That is, a state transition in which more than one neuron are flipped simultaneously will never be proposed. Denoting by $\eta(s_1)$ the neighborhood of the state s_1 defined by

$$\eta(s_1) = \{ s_2 \mid d_H(s_1,s_2) = 1 \} \quad , \tag{2.8}$$

condition (2.6) can be written by

$$p(s_1,s_1) + \sum_{s_2\in\eta(s_1)} p(s_2,s_1)\, e^{\beta[H(s_2|x)-H(s_1|x)]} = 1 \quad . \tag{2.9}$$

Suppose that the generation of the proposed state is carried out by choosing one component of s at random with uniform distribution. That is,

$$g(s_1,s_2) = \frac{1}{K} \qquad \text{for} \quad d_H(s_1,s_2) \leq 1 \quad , \tag{2.10}$$

where K is the dimension of s (the number of neurons). Then, by using (2.3), condition (2.9) can be expressed as

$$\sum_{s_2\in\eta(s_1)} [\ 1 - w(s_1,s_2) + w(s_2,s_1)\, e^{\beta[H(s_2|x)-H(s_1|x)]}\ ] = K-1 \quad . \tag{2.11}$$

For any Hamiltonian $H(\mathbf{s}|\mathbf{x})$, eq. (2.11) is a function of the acceptance probability distribution, and any solution will guarantee the Gibbs distribution for the network states. Note that the cardinality of $\eta(\mathbf{s}_1)$ (i.e., the number of its elements) is $K-1$, and thus (2.11) can be satisfied by setting each term in the summation to unity. This simplification leads to the following condition on the transition rule:

$$\frac{w(\mathbf{s}_1,\mathbf{s}_2)}{w(\mathbf{s}_2,\mathbf{s}_1)} = e^{\beta[H(\mathbf{s}_2|\mathbf{x})-H(\mathbf{s}_1|\mathbf{x})]} \qquad \text{for all } \mathbf{s}_1, \text{ and } \mathbf{s}_2 \in \eta(\mathbf{s}_1) \quad , \tag{2.12a}$$

which is accompanied by

$$0 \le w(\mathbf{s}_1,\mathbf{s}_2) \le 1 \qquad \text{for all } \mathbf{s}_1, \mathbf{s}_2 \quad , \tag{2.12b}$$

since $w(\mathbf{s}_1,\mathbf{s}_2)$ is a probability expression.

The simplification of (2.11) by (2.12a) is effectively equivalent to the *detail balance principle* of statistical mechanics given by the relation

$$Pr(\mathbf{s}_1|\mathbf{x})\, p(\mathbf{s}_1,\mathbf{s}_2) = Pr(\mathbf{s}_2|\mathbf{x})\, p(\mathbf{s}_2,\mathbf{s}_1) \quad , \tag{2.13}$$

for which any solution for the transition probabilities that satisfies (2.13) will also satisfy the general requirement (2.5), since by (2.4) it follows that

$$Pr(\mathbf{s}_1|\mathbf{x}) = Pr(\mathbf{s}_1|\mathbf{x}) \sum_{\mathbf{s}_2} p(\mathbf{s}_1,\mathbf{s}_2) = \sum_{\mathbf{s}_2} Pr(\mathbf{s}_2|\mathbf{x})\, p(\mathbf{s}_2,\mathbf{s}_1) \quad . \tag{2.14}$$

We therefore refer to (2.12) as the detail balance condition for the acceptance probability.

Two algorithms that comply with the detail balance condition of (2.12) have been suggested so far. The first one, known as the Metropolis algorithm, given by

$$w(\mathbf{s}_1,\mathbf{s}_2) = \begin{cases} 1 & \text{if } H(\mathbf{s}_1|\mathbf{x}) \le H(\mathbf{s}_2|\mathbf{x}) \\ e^{-\beta[H(\mathbf{s}_1|\mathbf{x})-H(\mathbf{s}_2|\mathbf{x})]} & \text{otherwise} \quad , \end{cases} \tag{2.15}$$

was originally proposed for simulating a melted substance in a heated bath (Metropolis et. al., 1953). The Metropolis algorithm is rather popular in simulated annealing algorithms (Kirkpatrick et. al., 1983; Laarhoven and Aarts, 1987) which are used in optimization schemes where the global minimum of a non-convex function is sought.

Another technique was suggested by Hinton et. al. (1984, 1986) for the Boltzmann machine where the acceptance probability is obtained by applying the logistic function of (1.6) to the Hamiltonian difference of the two states between which the transition is made. Specifically,

$$w(\mathbf{s}_1,\mathbf{s}_2) = h_\beta(H(\mathbf{s}_2|\mathbf{x}) - H(\mathbf{s}_1|\mathbf{x})) \quad . \tag{2.16}$$

In fact, it can be verified that if the acceptance distribution is assumed to be "symmetric" in the sense that

$$w(\mathbf{s}_2,\mathbf{s}_1) = 1 - w(\mathbf{s}_1,\mathbf{s}_2) \quad , \tag{2.17}$$

condition (2.11) is reduced to

$$\sum_{\mathbf{s}_2 \in \eta(\mathbf{s}_1)} \frac{w(\mathbf{s}_2,\mathbf{s}_1)}{h_\beta(H(\mathbf{s}_1|\mathbf{x}) - H(\mathbf{s}_2|\mathbf{x}))} = K-1 \quad , \tag{2.18}$$

for which the expression given in (2.16) is the unique solution. The transition rule of (2.16) is appealing for neural network architectures, particularly when the Hamiltonian is a quadratic function of the form

$$H(\mathbf{s}|\mathbf{x}) = \frac{1}{2}\mathbf{u}'\mathbf{W}\mathbf{u} + \mathbf{u}'\boldsymbol{\delta} \quad , \tag{2.19}$$

where $\mathbf{W}$ is a symmetric zero-diagonal matrix and $\mathbf{u}' = (\mathbf{x}',\mathbf{s}')$. The entries of $\mathbf{W}$ can then be regarded as the connection weights between the network units, and the components of $\boldsymbol{\delta}$ are their bias values. Since $\mathbf{s}_1$ and $\mathbf{s}_2$ differ only in one component, say the j-th component, the Hamiltonian difference $H(\mathbf{s}_2|\mathbf{x}) - H(\mathbf{s}_1|\mathbf{x})$ is given in this case by

$$H(\mathbf{s}_2|\mathbf{x}) - H(\mathbf{s}_1|\mathbf{x}) = \Delta s_j \left[\sum_{i=1}^{I+K} w(i,I+j)u(i) + \delta(j) \right] \quad ; \quad \Delta s_j \triangleq s_2(j) - s_1(j) \quad , \tag{2.20}$$

where $u(i)$ is the i-th component of $\mathbf{u}$, $\delta(j)$ is the j-th component of $\boldsymbol{\delta}$, $w(i,k)$ is the i,k-th entry of $\mathbf{W}$, and $s_1(j)$ and $s_2(j)$ are the j-th components of $\mathbf{s}_1$ and $\mathbf{s}_2$ respectively. Note that Δs_j can take only values of +1 or -1, and hence can only affect the sign of the Hamiltonian difference. The state transition rule can be simplified by evaluating the probability of $s_2(j)$ to be 1 (regardless of its current value):

$$\begin{aligned} Pr\{s_2(j)=1\} = Pr\{s_1(j)=0\} \cdot Pr\{\text{acceptance} \mid s_1(j)=0\} \; + \\ Pr\{s_1(j)=1\} \cdot Pr\{\text{rejection} \mid s_1(j)=1\} \; . \end{aligned} \tag{2.21}$$

Denote by H_0 the value of the Hamiltonian function evaluated for the state vector ($\mathbf{s}_1$ or $\mathbf{s}_2$) whose j-th component is "off" (i.e., equal to zero),

$$H_0 = \begin{cases} H(\mathbf{s}_1|\mathbf{x}) & \text{if } s_1(j)=0 \\ H(\mathbf{s}_2|\mathbf{x}) & \text{if } s_2(j)=0 \end{cases} \quad , \tag{2.22}$$

and by H_1 the value of the Hamiltonian evaluated for the state vector whose j-th component is "on" (i.e., equal to one). Then, by substituting (2.16) into (2.21), it follows that

$$Pr\{s_2(j)=1\} = h_\beta(H_1 - H_0) \quad , \tag{2.23a}$$

where the Hamiltonian difference $H_1 - H_0$ is given by

$$H_1 - H_0 = \sum_{i=1}^{I+K} w(i,I+j)u(i) + \delta(j) \quad . \tag{2.23b}$$

Eqs. (2.23), which constitutes the transition rule of the Boltzmann machine, can be implemented efficiently using a neural network since the computation of the transition rule based on these expressions can be carried out locally and independently by each unit of the network. The network operates by performing successive transitions. In each transition, a unit is chosen from a uniform distribution and its value is then set to unity with the probability specified in (2.23).

2.1. Mode of Operation and Learning

Having specified the conditions required from the state transitions to achieve the Gibbs distribution for the states of the model, we now define how the classification is carried out by such a network. The set of all 2^K possible states is partitioned into M distinct subsets of states which are associated with the M classes, and the probability of attaining a state in the m-th subset when the network is in steady-state is defined as the *a posteriori* probability of class m. A possible partition of the set of states is to dedicate M of the network units, say $y_1, \cdots, y_M$, to the M possible classes, and to associate class m with a state for which $y_m = 1$ and $y_n = 0$ for all $n \neq m$, while the values of the remaining components of **s** are arbitrary. These M units are called the *visible* units and they are the only units that should be observed for determining the network's output. All the other units need not be observed and they are therefore called the *hidden units.* Their role is to serve as internal auxiliary processors for the visible units. The classification is performed by first evaluating the probabilities of the above subsets of states by letting the network reach a steady-state for the given input data **x**, and then accumulating statistics regarding the relative frequency of occurrence of each of the classes by observing the random values of the visible units.

To design the classifier, all that is needed is to specify a certain type of Hamiltonian function and adjust it to get the best performance for the training set. The transition rule is obtained from the Hamiltonian by satisfying either the detail balance condition (2.12) or the more general condition (2.11), and the steady-state probability distribution is obtained by (2.1). It is convenient to parametrize the Hamiltonian by a set of parameters and the rule for adjusting these parameters is called a *learning algorithm.* The learning algorithm is performed by optimizing the classifier parameters through an iterative maximization of some similarity measure between the actual *a posteriori* distribution supplied by the classifier and the desired one. A meaningful similarity measure between two probability distributions $P(\mathbf{y}|\mathbf{x})$ and $Q(\mathbf{y}|\mathbf{x})$ was suggested by Kullback in 1959. In the literature of information theory, it is also known as the cross-entropy measure due to its close relation to the maximum entropy principle of statistical mechanics (cf. Shore and Johnson, 1981). The cross-entropy between the actual a posteriori probability $P(\mathbf{y}|\mathbf{x})$ for the visible vector $\mathbf{y}=(y_1, \cdots, y_M)'$ and the desired probability $Q(\mathbf{y}|\mathbf{x})$, denoted by $I(P,Q)$, is given by

$$I(P,Q) = \sum_{\mathbf{x}} Q(\mathbf{x}) \sum_{\mathbf{y}} Q(\mathbf{y}|\mathbf{x}) \ln[P(\mathbf{y}|\mathbf{x})] \quad . \tag{2.24}$$

Denoting by **v** the vector of all the $K-M$ hidden units, the actual probability $P(\mathbf{y}|\mathbf{x})$ for the visible vector $\mathbf{y}$ can be obtained from the joint probability $Pr(\mathbf{s}|\mathbf{x})$ by summing it over all possible values of the hidden units as follows:

$$P(\mathbf{y}|\mathbf{x}) = \frac{1}{Z} \sum_{\mathbf{v}} e^{\beta H(\mathbf{s}|\mathbf{x})} \quad . \tag{2.25}$$

Hence, the cross-entropy measure can be written as a function of the Hamiltonian by substituting (2.25) and (2.2) in (2.24). The learning algorithm is therefore a maximization procedure aimed at maximizing $\boldsymbol{I}(P,Q)$ as a function of the Hamiltonian parameters. The details of each learning algorithm depends on the specific type of Hamiltonian function and the maximization technique used.

A gradient ascent procedure for a quadratic Hamiltonian (such as given in (2.19)) was described by Hinton et. al. (1986) in which the network parameters are updated in the direction of the gradient of $\boldsymbol{I}(P,Q)$ in the parameter space. That is, the update formula of any parameter w, which expresses a weight between two network nodes, is given by

$$w \leftarrow w + \varepsilon \frac{\partial \boldsymbol{I}(P,Q)}{\partial H(\mathbf{s}|\mathbf{x})} \cdot \frac{\partial H(\mathbf{s}|\mathbf{x})}{\partial w} \quad . \tag{2.26}$$

The second term, obtained directly by differentiating (2.24) and (2.19), can be shown to be the difference of two quantities. The first quantity is the expected value of the product of the two nodes connected through the connection link w conditioned on $\mathbf{x}$, while the second quantity is an unconditional expected value of this product. The gradient of $\boldsymbol{I}(P,Q)$ is thus computed in a stochastic manner in two phases. In the first phase, patterns $\mathbf{x}$ drawn from the desired probability distribution (i.e., the training set) are clamped on the visible units and the desired conditional expected values are computed, whereas in the second phase the computation of the unconditional expectations are evaluated while no inputs are clamped on the network. In both cases, the evaluation of the expected values is obtained by accumulating statistics on the random values of the nodes and then computing the sample average of the observations.

Assuming that an uphill algorithm such as the gradient ascent, although converging into a local maximum, can provide a good solution for the classifier parameters, the above stochastic classifier seems to be the answer to the classification problem introduced in the previous section. It requires no assumptions on the probabilistic nature of the "world", it has a fairly general structure along with the capability of providing the *a posteriori* probabilities themselves, and it has a closed-form learning algorithm for designing its parameters. However, the above stochastic paradigm has one major drawback which severly limits its practical use, namely, its computational inefficiency. The Gibbs distribution for the network states is guaranteed only if the network was previously brought to a steady-state. Theoretically, this is achieved after an infinite execution time. The fastest way to achieve a steady-state in practice in to use a simulated annealing technique in which the gain β starts at a very low value and is gradually increased to its final value. Nevertheless, simulated annealing is itself a time-consuming procedure. Moreover, in the learning algorithm where expected values are approximated by sample averages over a finite period of time, a trade-off between accuracy and complexity is unavoidable.

3. The Deterministic Classifier

In order to overcome the computational difficulties of the stochastic model while maintaining its capability of supplying the *a posteriori* probabilities, a deterministic classifier, based on the same principles as the stochastic classifier, is developed in this section. In this case, the Hamiltonian function is defined to allow an explicit computation of the *a posteriori* probabilities by the network directly from the Gibbs distribution. This results in an efficient scheme in which the output probabilities are computed by a deterministic perceptron-like feed-forward network whose complexity is similar to that of a multi-layer perceptron.

Suppose, as before, that the state vector $\mathbf{s}$ is partitioned into two subvectors $\mathbf{v}$ and $\mathbf{y}$ with dimensions J and M respectively, and the Hamiltonian function takes the following quadratic form:

$$H(\mathbf{s}\,|\,\mathbf{x}) = \mathbf{v}'\mathbf{R}\mathbf{x} + \mathbf{y}'\mathbf{A}\mathbf{x} + \mathbf{v}'\mathbf{Q}\mathbf{y} + \mathbf{v}'\mathbf{c} + \mathbf{y}'\mathbf{t} \quad , \tag{3.1}$$

where the matrices $\mathbf{A}$, $\mathbf{R}$ and $\mathbf{Q}$ are of dimensions $M\times I$, $J\times I$ and $J\times M$ respectively, and $\mathbf{c}$ and $\mathbf{t}$ are vectors of length J and M respectively. The components of these quantities are the classifier parameters.

We now assume that the network is in steady-state, for which the Gibbs distribution may be used, and we will find an explicit expression for the m-th class probability, denoted hereafter by $P(m\,|\,\mathbf{x})$, which is given by the probability of attaining $\mathbf{y}=\mathbf{e}_m$ for the visible vector $\mathbf{y}$, where $\mathbf{e}_m$ is the m-th column of the $M\times M$ identity matrix. Since we are interested only in visible vectors of the type $\mathbf{y}=\mathbf{e}_m$, we can restrict attention to state vectors $\mathbf{s}=(\mathbf{v},\mathbf{e}_m)$, and thus the Gibbs distribution of (2.1) is normalized by

$$Z = \sum_{m=1}^{M} \sum_{\mathbf{v}} e^{\beta H(\mathbf{v},m\,|\,\mathbf{x})} \quad , \tag{3.2}$$

where $H(\mathbf{v},m\,|\,\mathbf{x})$ is the Hamiltonian function evaluated for an arbitrary value of $\mathbf{v}$ and $\mathbf{y}=\mathbf{e}_m$.

We define $L_m(\mathbf{x})$ to be

$$L_m(\mathbf{x}) = \frac{1}{\beta}\ln\,[\,\sum_{\mathbf{v}} e^{\beta H(\mathbf{v},m\,|\,\mathbf{x})}\,] \qquad ; \qquad \text{for } m=1,\cdots,M \quad , \tag{3.3}$$

which, by substituting the Hamiltonian from (3.1) with $\mathbf{y}=\mathbf{e}_m$, can be expressed as

$$L_m(\mathbf{x}) = \mathbf{a}'_m\mathbf{x}+t_m + \frac{1}{\beta}\ln\,[\,\sum_{v_1=0}^{1}\cdots\sum_{v_J=0}^{1} e^{\beta\mathbf{v}'(\mathbf{R}\mathbf{x}+\mathbf{q}_m+\mathbf{c})}\,] \quad , \tag{3.4}$$

where $\mathbf{a}'_m$ is the m-th row of $\mathbf{A}$, t_m is the m-th component of $\mathbf{t}$, $\mathbf{q}_m$ is the m-th column of $\mathbf{Q}$, and $v_1, \cdots, v_J$ are the components of the binary vector $\mathbf{v}$. The second term in (3.4) can be simplified by using the separability of the exponent with respect to the J components $v_1, \cdots, v_J$ yielding

$$L_m(\mathbf{x}) = \mathbf{a}'_m \mathbf{x} + t_m + \frac{1}{\beta} \sum_{j=1}^{J} \ln \left[1 + e^{\beta(\mathbf{r}'_j \mathbf{x} + c_j + q_{jm})} \right] \quad , \tag{3.5}$$

where $\mathbf{r}'_j$ is the j-th row of $\mathbf{R}$, c_j is the j-th component of $\mathbf{c}$, and q_{jm} is the j,m-th entry of $\mathbf{Q}$.

The class probabilities can be written using (2.25) and (3.2) as a function of the quantities $L_m(\mathbf{x})$ as follows:

$$P(m \mid \mathbf{x}) = \frac{e^{\beta L_m(\mathbf{x})}}{\sum_{n=1}^{M} e^{\beta L_n(\mathbf{x})}} = \frac{1}{1 + \sum_{\substack{n=1 \\ n \neq m}}^{M} e^{\beta L_{n,m}(\mathbf{x})}} \quad , \tag{3.6}$$

which is a generalization of the logistic function of (1.6) to the multi-dimensional case; where $L_{n,m}(\mathbf{x})$, defined by $L_{n,m}(\mathbf{x}) \triangleq L_n(\mathbf{x}) - L_m(\mathbf{x})$, is given, according to (3.5), by

$$L_{n,m}(\mathbf{x}) = \mathbf{a}'_{nm} \mathbf{x} + t_{nm} + \frac{1}{\beta} \sum_{j=1}^{J} \ln \left[\frac{1 + e^{\beta(\mathbf{r}'_j \mathbf{x} + c_j + q_{jn})}}{1 + e^{\beta(\mathbf{r}'_j \mathbf{x} + c_j + q_{jm})}} \right] \quad , \tag{3.7}$$

where $\mathbf{a}_{nm} = \mathbf{a}_n - \mathbf{a}_m$, and $t_{nm} = t_n - t_m$. Hence, according to (3.6), $P(m \mid \mathbf{x})$ is also a Gibbs distribution with $L_m(\mathbf{x})$ being its Hamiltonian function. Hereafter, we thus call $L_m(\mathbf{x})$ the *local Hamiltonian* of the class probability distribution $P(m \mid \mathbf{x})$.

We now define the following function, which will be the activation nonlinearity of the feed-forward network:

$$f_q(x) \triangleq \frac{1}{\beta q} \ln \left[\frac{1 + e^{\beta q (x + 1/2)}}{1 + e^{\beta q (x - 1/2)}} \right] \quad . \tag{3.8}$$

This is a sigmoid function as depicted in Figure 2 for several values of the gain β.

By defining $q_{jnm} = q_{jn} - q_{jm}$ and making the following transformation for the parameters of the stochastic network

$$\mathbf{u}_{jnm} = \frac{1}{|q_{jnm}|} \mathbf{r}_j \quad ; \quad l_{jnm} = \frac{1}{|q_{jnm}|} \left(c_j + \frac{q_{jn} + q_{jm}}{2} \right) \quad , \tag{3.9}$$

it can be verified that $L_{n,m}(\mathbf{x})$ can be computed for any $n \neq m$ by the following two-layer perceptron:

$$L_{n,m}(\mathbf{x}) = \mathbf{a}'_{nm} \mathbf{x} + t_{nm} + \sum_{j=1}^{J} q_{jnm} f_{|q_{jnm}|} (\mathbf{u}_{jnm}' \mathbf{x} + l_{jnm}) \quad , \tag{3.10}$$

and the classification is performed by evaluating eqs. (3.10) and (3.6), in which the class

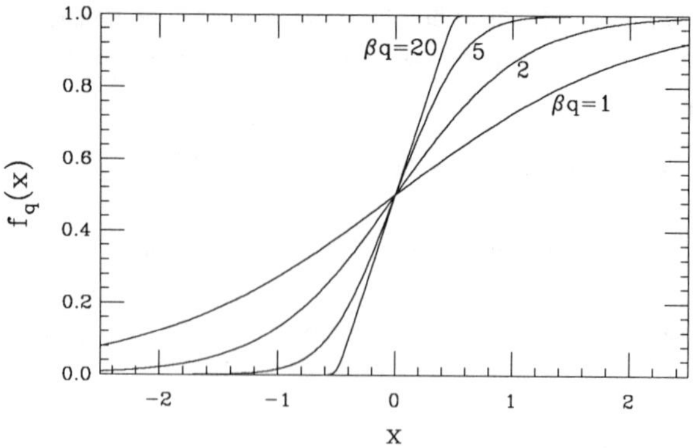

Figure 2: The activation function, $f_q(x)$, for several values of βq. For $|\beta q| > 20$, $f_q(x)$ becomes, practically, equal to its asymptote $\bar{f}(x)$ defined in (3.11).

probabilities $P(m \mid \mathbf{x})$ are computed by a three-layer feed-forward deterministic network. Since the evaluation of the class probabilities is equivalent to that performed by the Boltzmann machine while the architecture of this classifier is similar to the perceptron, we call this network the *Boltzmann Perceptron Classifier* (BPC), which can be efficiently implemented by a neural network.

The BPC can also be used as a MAP classifier if a high value is used for the gain β. The case where $\beta \to \infty$ corresponds to a zero temperature in a physical system for which the local Gibbs distribution of (3.6) becomes a delta function around the most probable class m^*, which has the highest value of the local Hamiltonian $L_m(\mathbf{x})$. In fact, the Gibbs distribution of (2.1) is also concentrated around the global maximum of the Hamiltonian $H(\mathbf{s} \mid \mathbf{x})$ yielding zero probability for all other states. A technique of gradually decreasing the temperature of a Gibbs distribution in order to find the global maximum of a Hamiltonian function is often used in simulated annealing schemes. However, in our case, no annealing is required since the derivation of the BPC was already done in steady-state and thus β can be *set* to any desired value. In order to use an infinite gain, the same scheme as the finite gain BPC can be used, where the non-linearities $f_q(x)$ of (3.8) used in (3.10) are replaced by their asymptotes $\bar{f}(x)$ for the high gain limit, given by

$$\bar{f}(x) = \begin{cases} 0 & \text{for} \quad x \le -\tfrac{1}{2} \\ x + \tfrac{1}{2} & \text{for} \quad -\tfrac{1}{2} < x < \tfrac{1}{2} \\ 1 & \text{for} \quad x \ge \tfrac{1}{2} \end{cases} \qquad (3.11)$$

which are linear-limiter functions (see Figure 2) replacing the soft sigmoid curves of lower values of β.

3.1. The Learning Algorithm

In principle, the BPC can be trained by using the learning algorithm of the Boltzmann machine discussed in Section 2, and then taking the transformations of (3.9) to obtain the BPC parameters. However, a direct learning algorithm for the BPC can be obtained which avoids the complexity of the stochastic learning algorithm and is similar in complexity to the backpropagation algorithm. The learning process described below is an iterative maximization of the cross-entropy measure of (2.24), carried out by the partial conjugate gradient (PCG) algorithm. The cross-entropy will be denoted hereafter by $\boldsymbol{I}(\omega)$ to indicate the dependency upon the classifier parameters ω. The PCG minimization algorithm (cf. Luenberger, 1984) is an iterative ascent procedure, similar to the gradient ascent of (2.26), in which, at the k-th iteration, the vector of parameters ω is updated in a direction $\mathbf{d}_k$, which is not necessarily the gradient direction, with a dynamic step-size α_k as follows:

$$\omega(k+1) = \omega(k) + \alpha_k \, \mathbf{d}_k \quad . \tag{3.12}$$

If $\mathbf{d}_k$ is taken as the gradient of $\boldsymbol{I}(\omega)$ computed at $\omega(k)$, the algorithm reduces to the gradient ascent of (2.26). However, in the PCG algorithm, the direction $\mathbf{d}_k$ is chosen as a combination of the gradient and the previous direction as follows:

$$\mathbf{d}_k = \mathbf{g}_k + \mu_k \, \mathbf{d}_{k-1} \quad ; \qquad k = 1, \cdots, R-1 \quad , \tag{3.13}$$

where $\mathbf{g}_k$ is the gradient at the k-th iteration, and R is called the restart parameter of the PCG. The iterations are initialized by the direction of the gradient with $\mathbf{d}_0 = \mathbf{g}_0$. Every R iterations the direction vector is restarted by resetting k to zero, $\mathbf{d}_0$ to $\mathbf{g}_0$, and by renaming $\omega(R)$ to be $\omega(0)$. Note that since the first step of the PCG is in the direction of the gradient, a PCG with $R = 1$ becomes the gradient ascent. If the function $\boldsymbol{I}(\omega)$ was quadratic, the PCG algorithm would converge in a finite number of steps (the number of parameters in ω). The restart mechanism is a remedy for a non-quadratic function and the value of R is problem dependent which is generally chosen by experience.†

In order to assure ascent, the step-size α_k should be optimally chosen as the argument of the scalar optimization (line search) along the current direction $\mathbf{d}_k$ as follows:

$$\alpha_k = \operatorname*{argmax}_{\lambda} \boldsymbol{I}(\, \omega(k) + \lambda \, \mathbf{d}_k \,) \quad . \tag{3.14}$$

It is known that accurate line searches do not enhance the convergence of the conjugate gradient algorithm (cf. Shanno, 1978) and thus it suffices to perform a crude line search which is computationally inexpensive. In similar minimization algorithms like the LMS or the backpropagation algorithm a fixed step-size is generally used for which the dynamic computation of the step-size is saved. It can also be used in the PCG algorithm, but generally, the number of

† For more details about the conjugate gradient method for optimization and how to choose μ in (3.13) the reader is referred to (Luenberger, 1984).

iterations required to converge will be larger, and it is also not clear how to choose the step-size in this case.

In order to perform a PCG search, we have to first compute the gradient $\mathbf{g}$ of $I(\omega)$. Assuming that w is some component of ω we can write

$$\frac{\partial I}{\partial w} = \sum_{\mathbf{x}} Q(\mathbf{x}) \sum_{m=1}^{M} \frac{Q(m\,|\mathbf{x})}{P(m\,|\mathbf{x})} \cdot \frac{\partial P(m\,|\mathbf{x})}{\partial w} \quad . \tag{3.15}$$

The above expression is the true gradient of the cross-entropy measure if the summation is carried out for all possible values of $\mathbf{x}$. Generally, a finite training set is given and the gradient can be estimated by averaging over the given training set. Such a technique is known as a *batch* learning algorithm. In many cases however, another technique, the *on-line* learning method, is successfully used, in which the training vectors are presented one at a time and after each such presentation the parameters are updated according to the instantaneous information about the gradient. This technique, known also as the *stochastic gradient* search, is used in learning algorithms like the LMS (Widrow, 1962), or the backpropagation algorithm for which a faster convergence for the on-line method over the batch method was found for applications of hand-written character recognition (Le-Cun, 1986). In the following discussion we omit the averaging over the training set in computing the gradient to describe the on-line learning scheme. For the batch scheme, an averaging of the stochastic gradients should be performed prior to each update of the classifier parameters.

For a presentation of a specific training vector $\mathbf{x}$ and by using (3.6) the derivative of $P(m\,|\mathbf{x})$ with respect to w can be written as

$$\frac{\partial P(m\,|\mathbf{x})}{\partial w} = P(m\,|\mathbf{x})\left[\frac{\partial L_m(\mathbf{x})}{\partial w} - \sum_{n=1}^{M} P(n\,|\mathbf{x})\frac{\partial L_n(\mathbf{x})}{\partial w}\right] \quad , \tag{3.16}$$

and since the sum of $Q(m\,|\mathbf{x})$ over the possible values of m is unity, the gradient of the cross-entropy measure becomes

$$\frac{\partial I}{\partial w} = \sum_{m=1}^{M} e(m\,|\mathbf{x})\frac{\partial L_m(\mathbf{x})}{\partial w} \quad ; \quad e(m\,|\mathbf{x}) \triangleq Q(m\,|\mathbf{x}) - P(m\,|\mathbf{x}) \quad . \tag{3.17}$$

The derivative of the cross-entropy measure with respect to some parameter w is therefore obtained by the inner product over m between the derivative of the local Hamiltonian functions $L_m(\mathbf{x})$ and the error vector $\mathbf{e}=(e(1\,|\mathbf{x}), \cdots, e(M\,|\mathbf{x}))'$. The gradient of the cross-entropy is thus obtained by the matrix operation

$$\mathbf{g} \triangleq \nabla_\omega I = \left[\nabla_\omega L_1(\mathbf{x}), \cdots, \nabla_\omega L_M(\mathbf{x})\right]\mathbf{e} \quad , \tag{3.18}$$

which can be easily implemented by a single feed-forward perceptron layer, given that the gradients of the local Hamiltonians, $\nabla_\omega L_m(\mathbf{x})$, are known.

From (3.5) we can express $L_m(\mathbf{x})$ as the output of a two-layer perceptron with the following nonlinear activation function in the hidden layer:

$$\rho(x) = \ln[1+e^{\beta x}] \quad . \tag{3.19}$$

Thus, the gradients $\nabla_{\omega} L_m(\mathbf{x})$ can be obtained by using the backpropagation algorithm for this two-layer perceptron, where the derivative of the activation function is given by the logistic function of (1.6),

$$\rho'(x) = \beta h_{\beta}(x) \quad , \tag{3.20}$$

and the desired gradient of the cross-entropy $\mathbf{g}$ is finally obtained by adding an additional layer as given in (3.18) to form a three-layer scheme similar to the backpropagation network. The complexity of evaluating the gradient of the BPC is thus equivalent to that of the backpropagation algorithm, which is computationally feasible for most applications.

3.2. Simulation Results

In this Section we will demonstrate the capability of the BPC in solving two simulated problems with a relatively moderate number of hidden units. In Figure 3a we have three Gaussian sources, two of them are associated with class 0 (dashed lines) and one is associated with class 1 (solid line). The sources are defined by their density function $Q_{i|x}$ and their prior probability $P(i)$. The true (Bayesian) a posteriori probability for class 1, denoted by $Q_{1|x}$, is computed by (1.8), and is depicted in Figure 3b to serve as a reference for the comparison with the actual a posteriori probability provided by the BPC. A BPC classifier with only three hidden units was trained on a training set of 20 examples drawn from the given problem with $\beta=1$. To test the classifier performance, the output probabilities computed by the BPC were evaluated for a dense grid of input patterns in the range [-6, 6] and were compared to the Bayesian curve in Figure 3b, in which the BPC output is marked by $\beta=1$. The two curves match almost perfectly, which means that the BPC could supply a Bayesian decision although no probabilistic model or other *a priori* assumptions were made. To demonstrate the MAP decision capability of the BPC a gain of $\beta=10$ was used for the same patterns (see Figure 3b) for which the input range was partitioned by the classifier (as desired) in accordance with the different classes defined in Figure 3a.

An example in a two dimensional space is given in Figure 4 for two overlapping Gaussian sources. The sources used are given in Figure 4a with the true boundary between the classes denoted by $Q_{1|x}=0.5$. In Figures 4b the boundary supplied by a BPC (marked by $P_{1|x}=0.5$) with 6 hidden units is given in comparison to the true boundary, demonstrating the high capability of the BPC to follow intricate boundaries even with a relatively small number of hidden units.

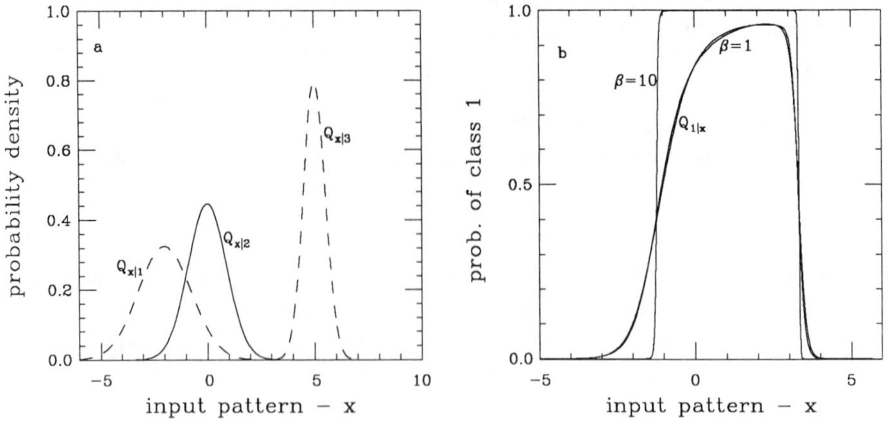

Figure 3: Classification results for Gaussian sources. (a) Problem presentation. (b) Classification using the BPC ($\beta = 1$) versus the Bayesian decision ($Q_{1|x}$), and the MAP decision ($\beta = 10$) for the high gain limit.

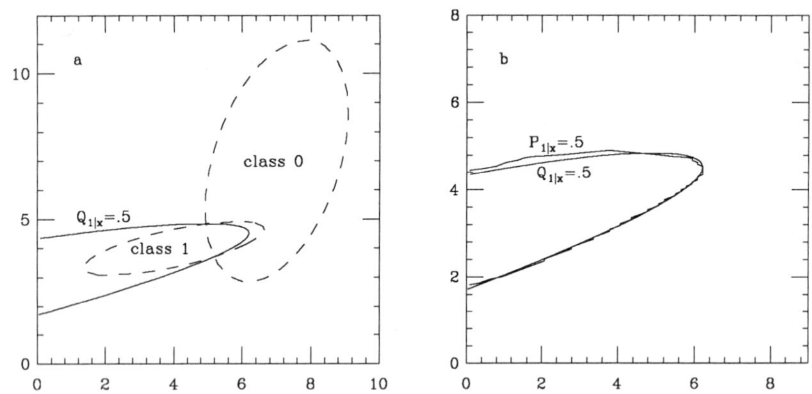

Figure 4: Classification in a 2D space (a) Problem presentation. (b) Boundary supplies by the BPC ($P_{1|x} = 0.5$) versus the true boundary ($Q_{1|x} = 0.5$).

Conclusions

Architectures and learning capabilities of neural networks can be used to perform classification without any a priori assumptions on the probabilistic nature of the problem. These classifiers can provide either the *a posteriori* probabilities of the classes or a MAP decision if designed properly. The classifier design is carried out by learning a Hamiltonian function for the given problem through the adjustment of its parameters by a learning algorithm. This learning algorithm is an iterative optimization procedure aimed at maximizing a performance measure on the training set. If the Hamiltonian function is allowed to have sufficient degrees of freedom (which roughly corresponds to sufficient number of parameters) almost any type of probability distribution can be obtained for the states of the network, and a Bayes classification can be approximated. In practice, for smooth probability distributions, a moderate number of parameters may be used for the Hamiltonian, which means a moderate number of units for the classifier.

In deriving the BPC classifier, the basic concepts underlying the evaluation of the class probabilities by a stochastic neural network were introduced first. This technique offers a powerful alternative to the Bayes classifier for problems in which the probabilistic nature is not known. In practice, however, this alternative is not very useful due to the heavy complexity burden. The BPC classifier, derived from the same concepts, maintains the same capabilities as the stochastic classifier but with a substantially reduced complexity. In fact, the complexity of both its operation and learning algorithm are similar to that of a multi-layer perceptron which is widely used in neural network applications. The BPC thus offers a useful alternative to the Bayes classifier in cases where *a priori* assumptions about the "world" should be avoided.

References

Hinton, G.E., Sejnowski T.R., & Ackley D.H. (1984). Boltzmann machines: constraint satisfaction networks that learn. *Carnegie-Melon Technical Report*, CMU-CS-84-119.

Hinton G.E., & Sejnowski T.J. (1986). Learning and Re-learning in Boltzmann Machines. In D.E. Rumelhart & J.L. McClelland (Eds.), *Parallel Distributed Processing: Explorations in the Microstructure of Cognition.* (Vol. 1, Chap. 7), MIT Press/Bradford Books.

Kirkpatrick, S., Gelatt, C.D., & Vecchi M.P. (1983). Optimization by simulated annealing. *Science*, **220**, 671-680.

Kullback, S. (1959). *Information Theory and Statistics*, New-York: Wiley.

Laarhoven, P.J.M., & Aarts, E.H.L. (1987). *Simulated Annealing: Theory and Applications.* D. Reidel Publishing Co., Dordrecht, Holland.

Le-Cun, Y. (1986). HLM: a multilayer learning network *Proceeding of the 1986 Connectionist Models Summer School.* 169-177, Carnegie-Mellon University, Pittsburgh, Penn.

Lippmann, R.P. (1987). An introduction to computing with neural networks. *IEEE Acoustic Speech and Signal Proc. Magazine.*, April, 4-22.

Luenberger, D.G. (1984). *Linear and nonlinear programming*, Addison-Wesley, Reading, Mass.

McCulloch, W.S. and Pitts, W. (1943). A logical calculus of the ideas imminent in nervous activity, *Bulletin of Mathematical Biophysics*, **5**, 115-133.

Metropolis, N., Rosenbluth, A.W., Rosenbluth, M.N., Teller, A.H., Teller, E. (1953). Equations of state calculations by fast computing machines, *J. Chem. Phys.*, **21**, 1087-1091.

Parker, D.B. (1985). Learning-Logic, TR-47, Center for Computational Research in Economics and Management Science, MIT.

Rosenblatt, R. (1959). *Principles of Neurodynamics*, New-York, Spartan Books.

Rumelhart, D.E., Hinton, G.E., & Williams R.J. (1986). Learning internal representations by error propagation. In D.E. Rumelhart & J.L. McClelland (Eds.), *Parallel Distributed Processing: Explorations in the Microstructure of Cognition.* (Vol. 1, Chap. 8), MIT Press/Bradford Books.

Shanno, D. (1978). Conjugate gradient methods with inexact searches. *Mathematics of operations research*, **3**, 244-256.

Shore J.E. and Johnson, R.W. (1981). Properties of cross-entropy minimization, *IEEE Trans. on Information Theory*, **27**, 472-482.

Werbos, P.J. (1974). Beyond regression: new tools for prediction and analysis in the behavioral sciences. Ph.D thesis in applied mathematics, Harvard university.

Widrow, B., & Hoff, M.E. (1960). Adaptive switching circuits, *1960 IRE WESCON Convention Record Part 4*, 96-104.

2

FIELD ADAPTATION IN VISUAL SYSTEMS IS A FUNCTION OF NONLINEAR LATERAL INHIBITION

by Robert P. Pinter and Bahram Nabet†*

1 Introduction

Lateral inhibition is the biological term for spatial difference operations among interneurons. Lateral inhibition has been studied in great detail and precision in the compound lateral eye of Limulus (Ratliff, et al., 1969; Brodie, et al., 1978). In these studies, electrical responses of eccentric cells of the compound eye were measured for various stimuli of specific spatio-temporal form, and the resulting systems models had considerable predictive power. Analyses of the mathematical forms of lateral inhibition have usually been on linear equations (e.g., Furman,1965; Ratliff, et al., 1969; Hadeler, 1974; Edwards, 1983), however, the study of Furman (1965) does include also a case of nonlinear shunting inhibition, but the results of the simulations are specific to certain input spatial waveforms. Poggio and Torre (1978) utilized conductance (but not voltage) as inputs in a neural network, and derived Volterra expansions for the voltages of a passive laterally interacting neural network without active feedback loops.

However, active feedback loops may be mediated by the voltage transfer characteristics of synapses. These voltage transfer characteristics may be mediated by the strong nonlinearity present in post-synaptic conductance or

*Departments of Electrical Engineering and Zoology; University of Washington, Seattle, WA 98195.

†Electrical and Computer Engineering Department; Drexel University; Philadelphia, PA 19104.

voltage as a function of pre-synaptic voltage, which is an important transduction in the nervous system, and relevant to the study of neural networks. The implications of this transduction for information processing in visual systems have been analyzed in (Pinter, 1983, 1984, 1985, 1987a,b).

An extensive experimental analysis of an excitatory synapse by Llinas et al., (1981a,b) indicates that a substantial factor in the steep rise of post-synaptic voltage as a function of pre-synaptic voltage is the function of sustained pre-synaptic calcium current on pre-synaptic voltage (in the experiments, pre-synaptic voltage was clamped to a steady level). If it is assumed that this calcium current function also plays a part for inhibitory synapses, such synaptic coupling nonlinearities may play an important part in lateral inhibition, especially for non-spiking networks. For spiking neurons, pre-synaptic inhibition may play a similar role in establishing multiplicative, active feedback.

Given such active,nonlinear inhibitory (negative) feedback loops, one possible analysis method for the nonlinear lateral inhibitory network is to then approximate the conductance as a function of voltage by a finite power series, and substitute these series into the M Volterra series for an M node network (Poggio and Torre, 1978) which would then yield a set of M coupled node equations each of which contains a Volterra series. That general case has not been analyzed, but the equations studied here are simplifications of that case in the following way: the synaptic dynamic relationships are assumed to be instantaneous, the nerve membrane cable properties are spatially discretized (lumped) and the lateral inhibition is spatially symmetrical and restricted to nearby neighbors. The biological bases for these assumptions rest on the spatially localized lateral inhibition found in some sensory systems (e.g., Brodie et al., 1978) and the need for a tractable set of network equations to analyze the effect of the nonlinear synaptic coupling in the most general manner possible.

For visual systems, the parameter of considerable interest for experimental and theoretical analyses is the mean level of the luminance input, for that parameter set the neuron response incremental gain and dynamics (e.g., Sakuranaga and Ando, 1985; Sakuranaga and Naka, 1985). This is often referred to as adaptation (light- or dark-) and occurs in photoreceptors and visual interneurons. In Limulus photoreceptors (retinular cells) this occurs and was accounted for by a nonlinear dynamic model (Fuortes-Hodgkin model) where the nonlinear coupling was presumed to have a molecular basis and accounted not only for Weber-Fechner type incremental sensitivity but also changes in photoreceptor dynamics (Fuortes and Hodgkin, 1964; Pinter, 1966; Borsellino and Fuortes, 1968) with the mean level of luminance. It should be noted that the nonlinear aspect of the Fuortes-Hodgkin model is parametric feedback, i.e.,the output of a chain of compartments is fed back to change the self-coupling parameter of each compartment. In nonlinear lateral inhibition there is similar parametric feedback, but more generally distributed among the compartments which have more parameters than in the Fuortes-Hodgkin model. The light- and dark-adaptation in visual interneurons can therefore be a function both of the nonlinear temporal properties of photoreceptors, and the nonlinear spatial and temporal properties of subsequent nonlinear lateral inhibition networks.

Experimentally, light adaptation occurs by changes of incremental sensitivity or gain functions and by changes of temporal and spatial input weighting functions in visual systems.[1] The term for this set of changes (in light adaptation of incremental sensitivity,and linear and nonlinear temporal and spatial weighting) produced by mean luminance changes (or illuminance or intensity in appropriate units) in a visual system or model of a visual system is ***spatial and temporal field adaptation,*** also known as the ***Rushtonian Transformation*** (Naka, 1985). This chapter describes field adaptation from several Volterra series properties derived from nonlinear lateral inhibition. It should be noted that if the lateral inhibition is linear, the field adaptation does not exist for the neural network and there is no adaptation in the neural network, if and only if the interneuron cell membrane properties are also linear. Since the photoreceptors are not within the feedback loops, their nonlinear properties will always cause adaptation of temporal properties, but not spatial field adaptation.

2 Nonlinear Lateral Inhibition

Under the assumptions of lumped nerve membrane cable properties and conductance dependence on neighboring cell or cell subunit voltages via a nonlinear no-memory relationship, the differential equations for the network of

[1]specific definitions are given by Sakuranaga and Naka, 1985.

nonlinear lateral inhibition will be,

$$\frac{dx_i}{dt} = L_i(t) - x_i\left(1 + \sum_{j\neq i} K_{ij} f_j(x_j)\right), \qquad i = 1, 2, \ldots \tag{1}$$

where x_i describes the variation of membrane potential from resting potential, L_i is the external input to each compartment or node, and K_{ij} is the coupling strength, also known as connection strength.

In Fig. 1 a circuit node described by one such equation is shown for inhibition limited to nearest and next-to-nearest neighbors. The network nodes are interconnected only via the nonlinear coupling of conductance modulation by voltage of neighboring cells, the neighbors extending to two in each direction on a one-dimensional space co-ordinate i. The electrophysiological basis of Fig. 1 which gives rise to the neural network model (1) is given by Pinter 1983).

The inputs $L_i(t) = L_0 + \alpha l_i(t)$, where L_0 represents the mean level of luminance and $0 \leq |l_i(t)| \leq L_0$. Taking this condition together with $x_i \geq 0$, and requiring symmetrical connection strengths, i.e., $K_{ij} = K_{ji}$, will give global stability of (1) since this system is a subset of the set of competitive equations for which Lyapunov functions have been derived and global stability proven, provided that the f_j functions are monotone nondecreasing (Cohen and Grossberg, 1983).

In order to apply the perturbation method to derive a Volterra series from the differential equation, it is necessary to specify a form for functions $f_j(x_j)$, and a polynomial in x_j is most useful and simple in constraints. In the development to follow, the functions f_j will be

$$f_j(x_j) = \sum_{r=1}^{m} c_{jr} x_j^r \tag{2}$$

with $c_{jr} \geq 0$ to satisfy the monotonicity constraint.

The polarity limitation on input to guarantee stability might at first glance appear a prohibitively strong constraint on a model of a neural network, until it is pointed out that in fact the description of the input L_i as a current source (see Fig. 1) is an approximation to simplify the bilinear aspect of input as conductance (Pinter, 1983). This means that in effect the L_i has a lower bound which is zero. and the lower bound limitation on $l_i(t)$ is

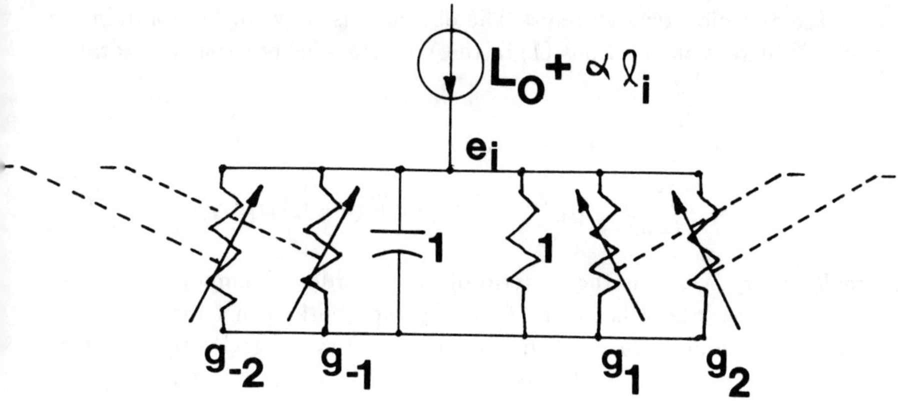

Figure 1: *A circuit diagram of the electrophysiological properties of an isopotential cell or cell subunit described by Eq. (1). Here the nonlinear lateral inhibition is symmetrical from the two nearest neighbors. Each voltage e_i in an array of cells each given by one such circuit represents the variation of transmembrane voltage of the cell i from resting potential in response to the input. The inputs are represented by current sources (from simplification of controlled conductance, see Pinter (1983)) which derive from luminance distributions in a visual space or voltages on an antecedent cell array. The controlled conductances have values of $g_j = f_j(e_j(t))$, and the dashed lines represent control of conductance g by neighboring cell voltage e_j.*

simply a consequence of the fact that the conductance, which is dependent on input, cannot be negative. Therefore, inputs $l_i(t)$ can certainly drive any network cell (or cell subunit) hyperpolarized from *resting,* i.e., a negative value of the *increment* of x_i, provided of course that $L_0 > 0$.

3 Volterra Series Representation

The nonlinear analysis technique of Volterra-Wiener expansions has been successfully applied to, among others, the analysis of wave propagation in random media, scattering by random surfaces, Brownian motion, theory of turbulence and biological systems. The objective is to write the solution to the set of differential equations (1) in the Volterra-Wiener expansion form

$$
\begin{aligned}
x_i = H_0 \;&+\; \int_{-\infty}^{\infty} H_{i1}(\tau) l_i(t-\tau) d\tau \\
&+\; \int_{-\infty}^{\infty}\int_{-\infty}^{\infty} H_{i2}(\tau_1, \tau_2) l_i(t-\tau_1) l_i(t-\tau_2) d\tau_1 d\tau_2 + \cdots,
\end{aligned}
\tag{3}
$$

where $H_{ij}(\tau_1, \tau_2, \cdots, \tau_i)$ is the ith term of the jth order of temporal Volterra kernel; the Wiener kernels can be found by the well-known Gram-Schmidt orthogonalization procedure. In equation (3) the first integral is the familiar convolution operator and the higher order terms show the inclusion of higher order nonlinearities in analysis and identification of nonlinear systems. A linear analysis technique is only capable of identifying the first two terms of (3).

The existence of the convergent Volterra series for a large class of systems is shown in Boyd and Chua (1985). For a single state variable differential equation, basic examples of kernels are given by Marmarelis and Marmarelis (1978) and general developments leading to a Volterra series of integral operators are given by Gilbert (1977) and Rugh (1981). These developments are basically perturbation methods (also called variational) and are a version of reversion of power series used by Poggio and Torre (1977) for the neural spike encoder integral equation and Schetzen (1980) for the pendulum nonlinear differential equation. However, the development of Gilbert (1977) is primarily a proof of existence, the development of Rugh (1981) is not readily used for the purposes here, and the pendulum problem treated by Schetzen (1980) is a two state variable problem.

Therefore the perturbation method is applied to the nonlinear lateral inhibition below, and further, in the simple form of an iteration or reversion. This technique leads immediately to identifiable forms of the Volterra series operators over the perturbational inputs $l_i(t)$. Simple examples of the perturbation method can be found in Andronov and Chaikin (1949), Cunningham (1958), Jordan and Smith (1979), Rugh (1981) and Pearson (1983). A further benefit of the perturbation method is to give the nonlinear system realization as an interconnected set of linear operators and multipliers, the latter being the only nonlinearity in that realization (as in Schetzen (1980), Ch.6).

The perturbation method requires a parameter which is in this case the α of $\alpha l_i(t)$ within the input $L_i(t) = L_0 + \alpha l_i(t)$. The parameter α then represents for inputs $|l_i(t)| < L_0$ the upper bound on the increment function on the background level L_0. While often the parameter resides in the dependent function terms in the perturbation method, here it is in the explicit time dependent portion (the input) which in effect similarly scales the nonlinear portion of (1).[2] The derivation of Volterra Kernels then proceeds according to the following outline:

1. Apply the input $L_i = L_0 + \alpha l_i$ where α is the perturbation parameter to the system.

2. Assume a solution of the form $\mathbf{x} = \mathbf{x}_0 + \alpha\mathbf{x}_1 + \alpha^2\mathbf{x}_2 + \cdots$, and differentiate it.

3. Insert this solution in the original differential equation.

4. Equate like powers of α in equations which result from steps 2 and 3 above, and extract the Volterra kernels by observing the resulting integral series.

Following the above procedure will, after step 3, result in

$$\dot{x}_i = L_0 + \alpha l_i - \left(\sum_r \alpha^r x_{ir}\right)\left[1 + \sum_{j \neq i} K_{ij} f_j\left(\sum_p \alpha^p x_{jp}\right)\right], \qquad r, p = 1, 2, 3, \ldots \tag{4}$$

where x_i is the ith component of the solution vector $\mathbf{x}$ and the second subscript of x_{ij} denotes the *order* of the term which is the order of approximation.

For the specific case of the polynomial form of f_j defined by Eq. (2), since

$$\dot{x}_i = \sum_j \alpha^j \dot{x}_{ij}, \tag{5}$$

equations (4) and (5) must hold for every value of the parameter α in the interval $\{0,1\}$ and hence the coefficients of powers of parameter α must balance,

[2]For an example of input scaling for specific input functions see the illustrations of shunting inhibition responses of Furman (1965).

and so for each power of α an equation is obtained as follows

$$\alpha^0: \quad 0 = L_0 - x_{i0}\left[1+\sum_j \sum_{r=1}^{m} c_{jr} x_{j0}^r\right], \quad c_{jr} = 0 \text{ for } r > m \tag{6}$$

$$\alpha^1: \quad \frac{dx_{i1}}{dt} = l_i(t) - x_{i1}\left[1+\sum_j \sum_{r=1}^{m} c_{jr} x_{j0}^r\right] - x_{i0}\left[\sum_j c_{j1} x_{j1}\right] \tag{7}$$

$$\alpha^n: \quad \frac{dx_{in}}{dt} = -x_{in} - \sum_j \Bigg[c_{j1} \sum_{r=0}^{n} x_{ir} x_{j(n-r)} + \cdots + c_{jq} \sum_{p_0=0}^{n} x_{ip_0} \sum_{p_1 \cdots p_q} \frac{q!}{p_1! p_2! \ldots p_q!} (x_{j0})^{p_1} (x_{j1})^{p_2} \cdots (x_{jk})^{p_q} + \cdots\Bigg] \tag{8}$$

$$\begin{aligned} n &\neq 0 \text{ or } 1; \quad p_1 + p_2 + \cdots + p_q = q \\ q &\neq 0 \text{ or } 1; \quad p_0 + p_2 + 2p_3 + 3p_4 + \cdots + kp_q = n \end{aligned}$$

Equation (6) is of zero order in parameter α and is algebraic, from which the constant or d-c components of x_i as a function of L_0, the background level, can be obtained. Here, these components will be uniform, $x_{i0} = \bar{x}_i$, except possibly for imposed spatial boundary conditions for a finite network, since the f_j do not vary with i. This is equivalent to stating that the response of the network to uniform input is uniform across the the network except at boundaries.

The positive real root of (6) which varies as $L_0^{1/(m+1)}$ asymptotically as $L_0 \to \infty$ is considered to be that which models the physiological process. Given the positivity of L_i and L_0, the form of the functions f_j, symmetricity of coefficient K_{ij}, and the theorem of Cohen and Grossberg (1983), that positive real root is part of the solution and is stable. It represents the positive deviation from resting potential caused by the positive L_0. Since the f_j do not depend on i, i.e., the lateral inhibition function over neighbors is uniform for every node, the same asymptotic relation prevails for each node. However, when L_0 is less than some number, which depends on the coefficients c_{jr}, the $\bar{x}_i$ can undergo non- monotonic variations as a function of L_0. In sum, it is clear that the x_{i0} depend implicitly on L_0 in nonlinear networks having coupling among the dependent variables, as here in eq. (2), and in the Fuortes-Hodgkin model.

This zero order response which is the solution to Eq. (6), is the zero order temporal Volterra kernel (Sakuranaga and Ando, 1985) as defined above in Eq. (3). For the special case of a linear function $f_j(x_j) = c_j x_j$, i.e., $m = 1$ in (2), the zero order kernel will be

$$H_0 = \bar{x}_i = \frac{-1 + \sqrt{1 + 4L_0 \sum_j K_{ij} c_j}}{2 \sum_j K_{ij} c_j} \tag{9}$$

which shows the square root compression of the input, as expected from the above discussion. This is the desired mean intensity dependence of the response which is captured by the Volterra series analysis. These results have been experimentally verified by analog electronic hardware implementation of Fig. 1 (Nabet et al. 1989). It will next be shown that the intensity dependence is also propagated through the higher order kernels.

3.1 First and Higher Order Kernels

The linear differential equation (7) has the incremental input time dependent function $l_i(t)$, and also rate constants dependent on the solution of (6), since x_{i0} depends on L_0 as discussed above. It is exactly this dependence which gives rise to the field adaptation. In perturbation methods, (7) is known as the generating equation, and its forced solution is the generating solution which determines the inputs of the higher order approximations ($n \geq 2$), as demonstrated in Eq. (8).

Each linear differential equation (8) possesses the same linear self-coupling and linear inhibitory terms, with time dependent input terms derived from the solutions of the previous, lower order n, linear differential equations. These input terms are sums of products of powers (the homogeneous functions) of the lower term solutions, all of which are products of the generating solution from (7). The generating solution which depends on L_0 and the forcing functions $l_i(t)$ then determine the input forcing functions for all orders n, and thereby propagates the input forcing functions to all order solutions.

By examining the formal solutions (by linear systems techniques) of the perturbation sequence of differential equations (elementary example in Pinter,1987a,b), and making one kind of variable of integration substitution, the $\mathbf{x}_n$ is obtained very simply as an nth order Volterra operator on the inputs

$l_i(t)$ (below). A further advantage of the form of equations (7),(8) is the reduction of the nonlinear system to a graph containing only the linear systems and multipliers with the given inputs and outputs.

Only the first differential equation (7) has input $l_i(t)$; the manner in which these n inputs appear formally in the higher term solution requires a Kronecker product notation such as applied by Rugh (1981). However, more simply, the solution of (7) has terms in the various $l_i(t)$ as single factors, and the solution of (8) has terms in the various $l_i(t)$ as products of n of the $l_i(t)$. Since there are w inputs $l_i(t)$, $i = 1, \ldots, w$, for a system of w nodes or compartments, the number of combinations of products of n inputs is w^n, and each of these combinations is integrated for the solution over w eigenfunctions. These eigenfunctions with their associated eigenvalues and eigenvectors are determined by the generating equation (7) for every order n, since the linear part of (8) is identical to that of (7). These eigenfunctions are also functions of L_0, which therefore determines the field adaptation for solutions of all orders.

In theoretical considerations of lateral inhibition, it is often useful to assume symmetrical lateral inhibition from neighbors. For this study, symmetrical lateral inhibition will be assumed, so that the summation over j in (1) is symmetrical and is over a symmetrical difference from i, and, as assumed above, f_j does not depend on i. This two-fold symmetry affects the linear differential equations (7), (8) such that the eigenvalues are real and if any eigenvalue is multiple (degeneracy) nevertheless the eigenfunctions for (7), (8) are all in simple real exponential form with coefficients, which are dependent on L_0, determined by eigenvector decomposition. This is due to the fact that in the linear system of Eq. (7) which is of the form $\dot{\mathbf{x}}_1 = \mathbf{A}\mathbf{x}_1 + \mathbf{l}$, the $\mathbf{A}$ matrix is Hermitian, therefore all eigenvalues are real, and if multiple, $\mathbf{A}$ is nevertheless diagonalizable and Jordan blocks are of order one (Franklin, 1968). The second aspect of the symmetry, that the f_j do not vary with i, is equivalent to assuming spatially invariant lateral inhibition functions, which simplifies the nature of resulting spatial steady-state receptive fields, as discussed below.

By linear system analysis methods (Kailath, 1980; Pinter, 1987a,b) applied to (7) the generating solution is obtained,[3] yielding the state transition

[3]Given the symmetry of nonlinear lateral inhibition the A matrix is diagonalizable and the state transition matrix has only entries of real exponential functions.

matrix which is the first order kernel in the Volterra series for this stable system of finite memory and inputs $l_i(t)$. These exponential functions propagate through all subsequent $n \geq 2$ solutions of (8) to give:

$$x_{in}(l_1 - l_n) = \int_0^t \cdots \int_0^t \sum_{k, c_{k1} \cdots c_{kn}} (c_{k1} \cdots c_{kn}) \Big[\frac{\prod_{l=1}^{n} e^{a_{kl}\tau_l}}{a_k - \sum_{i=1}^{n} a_{ki}} \times$$

$$\left(e^{(a_k - \sum_{i=1}^{n} a_{ki}) \min[\tau_1, \cdots, \tau_n]} - 1\right)\Big] l_{l_1}(t - \tau_1) l_{l_2}(t - \tau_2) \ldots l_{l_n}(t - \tau_n) d\tau_1 \ldots d\tau_n \quad (10)$$

For each of the $x_{in}(l_1 \ldots l_n)$ there are n^w possible combinations of inputs $l_{l_1} \ldots l_{l_w}$ for this w-input system, and for each such combination, there are $w^{(n+1)}$ terms in the summation shown by the $(n + 1)$ positions of the w eigenvalues a_{ki}. The coefficients $c_{k_1} \ldots c_{k_n}$ derive from eigenvector decomposition, and both $c_{k_1} \ldots c_{k_n}$ and a_{ki} depend on L_0 *via* $\mathbf{x}_0$ dependence on L_0 by Eq. (6) and the linear system analysis (**A** matrix inversion processes and characteristic equations, see (Pinter, 1987a,b)). This is the basis for the field adaptation and Rushtonian transformation defined above (Naka,1985) and illustrated below. It is necessary for the form of (10) that the **A** matrix, given by the (linear) last and next-to-last terms of (7) (which are also in (8) but less obvious) be diagonalizable, which is guaranteed by the symmetry of the nonlinear lateral inhibitory functions f_j around every i.

In many studies such as on directional properties, the nonlinear lateral inhibitory functions f_j are not symmetrical about i, and the **A** matrix may not be diagonalizable. In that case, one may preserve a useful form such as (10) by a theorem (Franklin, 1968) where, by continuity relations, adding to the non-diagonalizable **A** another matrix $\epsilon\mathbf{B}$ for an ϵ however small, the solutions for the system of $\mathbf{A} + \epsilon\mathbf{B}$ remain in a δ-space about the solutions for the system of **A**; the matrix $\mathbf{A} + \epsilon\mathbf{B}$ is diagonalizable, yielding the form of (10). Since the integrations of (10) are over the inputs $l_{l_1}(t-\tau_1) \ldots l_{l_n}(t-\tau_n)$, the nth order Volterra kernels are given by the indicated sums of the term in the brackets of (10).

4 Field Adaptation and the Rushtonian Transformation

The Rushtonian transformation for visual system response is the change in incremental sensitivity and spatial and temporal weighting factors (field adaptation) on change of mean luminance (Naka, 1985). Theories for Rushtonian transformations are necessarily nonlinear, such as the Fuortes-Hodgkin model for photoreceptors, conductance interaction (Poggio and Torre, 1978; Koch, Poggio and Torre, 1982), thresholds, presynaptic inhibition and nonlinear lateral inhibition. In the above section, the Volterra representation for nonlinear lateral inhibition has been developed from a discrete or ordinary differential equation description. In this section the Rushtonian transformation is illustrated on the basis of the above development, for a specific example of finite series, Eq. (2), nonlinear lateral inhibition.

The bases of the Rushtonian transformation are in the dependence of steady-state $\mathbf{x}_0$ on L_0 via (6) and the consequent dependence of the rate constants of (7) on L_0. It is unavoidable in this theory (as for example also in the Fuortes-Hodgkin model) to have an implicit relation, but it can be said that above some number, as the value of $L_0 \to \infty$, the values of all x_{i0} approach a dependence on L_0 determined by the inverse of the highest power term in the spatially uniform inhibitory conductance functions f_j. These functions are assumed here to be uniform across spatial dimension i, but this constraint can be relaxed to the effect that unless a given x_i becomes decoupled from the system ($c_{jr} = 0$ for every r) the inverse power relation will be determined approximately by the spatial distribution of the dominant highest power terms. Of course in the general case this problem becomes the classical one of polynomials in w variables, for which there is no known solution. Here, the constraints exist so that the Rushtonian transformation can be illustrated[4].

The solution of the steady-state nonlinear implicit relation (6) is then taken to the rate constants in (7) so that temporal kernels for all orders are functions of the eigenfunctions of (7). These eigenfunctions are sums of real exponentials, the eigenvalues of which are determined by the usual linear system techniques applied to (7). These methods involve matrix inverses, so that the dependence of the *rate constants* of (7) on L_0 propagates to the dependence of the *eigenvalues* of (7) on L_0. Assuming the spatially uniform lateral inhibition functions f_j as discussed above, as $L_0 \to \infty$ the eigenvalues of (7) $a_k \to L_0^{m/(m+1)}$ where m is the highest power relation (Eq. (2)) in the spatially uniform f_j (Pinter, 1987a,b). By a similar analysis, the co-

[4]In a later study the implications of distributions of powers (i.e., gradients of order, Pinter, 1985) and the approach to this general case will be considered.

efficients of the eigenfunctions, which are obtained by suitable eigenvector decomposition, depend on L_0 as $L_0^{-m/(m+1)}$. Since these eigenfunction coefficients multiply $(n+1)$ times in obtaining the nth order kernel from (8), the coefficients of the nth order kernel $(c_{k_1} c_{k_2} \dots c_{k_n})$ (10) are proportional to $L_0^{-(\frac{m}{m+1})(n+1)}$. The net effect of these two proportionalities of system properties on L_0 is that as $L_0 \to \infty$, the eigenvalues become larger, thus the kernels are faster, or in other words, move closer to the time origin, and the kernels become smaller in their impulse response magnitude. This is the basic temporal Rushtonian transformation. Of course, beginning from $L_0 = 0$, this transformation is not necessarily monotonic, but above some number for L_0 it will approach the given functions. To illustrate this, normalized terms of first and second order Volterra kernels are shown in Figures 2 and 3.

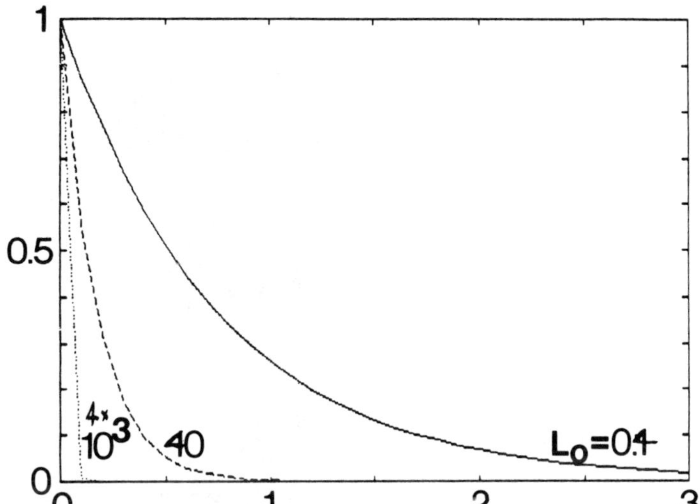

Figure 2: *Plots of the slowest decaying exponential function of the first order kernel from the linearized Equations (7). The respective curves give the function for the indicated values of mean input* L_0. *The coefficient* $c_{j1} = 1$, $c_{jr} = 0$ *for* $r > 1$, *calculation for* $w = 11$ *cells. Ordinate, normalized amplitude; abscissa, time in seconds.*

Here, nonlinear lateral inhibition extends only to nearest and next-to-nearest neighbors each side, and only c_{j1} is nonzero in the spatially uniform f_j. It can be seen that as L_0 increases, the kernel terms do move toward the origin; since $m = 1$, the inherent nonlinearity of this example is quadratic (see Eq. (9)), so then from (6) the response from resting is proportional to $L_0^{1/2}$. As discussed above, this proportionality from (6) controls the eigenvalues, and for that reason the kernel terms of Figs. 2 and 3 move toward the origin as shown. This means that in response to impulses or pairs of impulses, the temporal variations will be faster as L_0 increases. Higher order kernel terms will move similarly toward the origin, as shown by the form (10), and their magnitudes will be proportional to $L_0^{\frac{-(n+1)}{2}}$ for kernel of order n for this quadratic example.

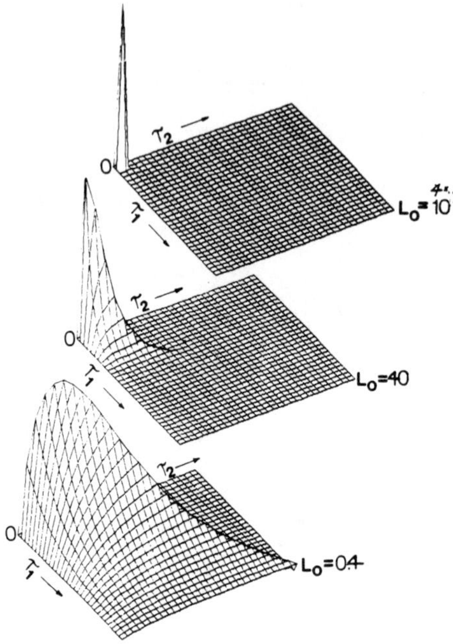

Figure 3: *Plots of the slowest decaying term of the second order kernel, given by Eq. (8) for n=2 , for the same three values of mean input* L_0 *and other conditions as for Fig. 2 . Ordinate, relative amplitude; abscissae, 0.1 second per division.*

The motivation for preserving w inputs here is to study the relative Rushtonian transformation in temporal versus spatial weighting. That topic is discussed next.

5 Adaptation of Spatial Kernels

The same perturbation technique as described above can be applied to the *steady state* solution of (1), the existence of which is due to the global stability of the network, to find the solution in the spatial Volterra-Wiener expansion form:

$$x_i = H_0 + \sum_j H_1(i,j)l_j + \sum_j \sum_k H_2(i,j,k)l_j l_k + \cdots \tag{11}$$

where the subscript denotes the order of the kernel which is the order of approximation and the kernels are written with spatial indices as argument to stress the spatial dependence.

Extraction of the spatial Volterra kernels, however, is simpler if Equations (6)–(8) are solved at steady state. The zeroth spatial kernel is then equivalent to the response of the network to (uniform) background intensity in steady state and is shown in equation (9). This response, as expected, is invariant to time and across the space as indexed by the cell number, assuming boundary effects are compensated by, for example, imposing periodic boundary condition by connecting the last elements of the array to the first ones.

5.1 First and Higher Order Spatial Kernels

The first order spatial response is found by solving the first order network equation (7), which is the linearized model of the network, in the steady state (Pinter 1987a). Thus

$$\mathbf{x}_1 = -\mathbf{A}^{-1}(L_0)\mathbf{l}, \tag{12}$$

where $\mathbf{A}$ and $\mathbf{l}$ are the linear coupling matrix and the input vector, respectively, and the dependence of matrix $\mathbf{A}$ on the mean intensity via the zero order kernel is shown above. The ith terms of the first order response is simply

$$x_{i1} = \sum_j b_{ij} l_j, \tag{13}$$

from which the ith term of the first order kernel is observed to be

$$H_1(i,j) = b_{ij} \tag{14}$$

where b_{ij} are the terms of the negative of the inverted matrix $\mathbf{A}^{-1}$, the existence of which is a result of the fact that since the network is globally stable, matrix **A** is positive definite.

Contrary to the temporal kernel case, a closed form expression for the response can not be written since that requires an analytical expression for elements of $\mathbf{A}^{-1}$.[5]

For the case where **A** is a Toeplitz matrix where along any diagonal the terms are identical, which is applicable here since the inhibitory functions f_j are spatially invariant, often the inverse of **A** is nearly Toeplitz, and in fact for a large number of cells the inverse of **A** not only is nearly Toeplitz, but a direct relationship between the rows (or columns) of **A** and its inverse is: the rows of A are the Fourier coefficients of a continuous function $B(\omega)$ on $\{-\pi, \pi\}$ and then the rows of the inverse of A are the Fourier coefficients of the continuous function $1/B(\omega)$ on $\{-\pi, \pi\}$ (from the Szëgo theorem; see Robinson and Treitel, 1980). This is useful especially for large number of cells and from the standpoint of deducing linearized lateral inhibition from given steady-state receptive fields (e.g., symmetrical Gabor functions), and also explains the inhibition-disinhibition pattern seen in Fig. 4. For finite number of cells, e.g., $w = 10$ and even small departures from Toeplitzness of **A** the result holds approximately. The functions $B(\omega)$ and $1/B(\omega)$ must be quadratically integrable.

From (12) it is seen that $\mathbf{A}^{-1}(L_0)$ specifies the receptive field of the network. A column of the inverted matrix is plotted in Fig. 4 for three different values of the mean intensity L_0. It should be emphasized that although the first order kernel is derived from a linearized system model, its intensity dependence is due to the shunting nonlinearity which gave rise to the intensity dependent zero order kernel. A model of a neural network without the multiplicative nonlinearity would not produce intensity dependent kernels.

[5]Common matrix inversion methods such as the cofactor method are *algorithms* rather than analytical expressions.

Similarly, higher-order spatial kernels are determined by finding the solution of Eq. (8) in steady state. The ith term of the mth order response can be written as (Nabet, 1989)

$$x_{im} = \sum_{j=1}^{w} b_{ij} p_{jm} \tag{15}$$

where b_{ij} are the terms of the inverse of matrix **A** and p_{jm} is a perturbation input term which depends on *all* the previous responses. The intensity dependence is thus propagated to all the higher order terms. Furthermore, the matrix inversion which is the most computationally intensive operation is performed only once and used recursively.

As mentioned previously an electronic hardware implementation of Eq. (1) has been reported (Nabet et. al, 1989). The results of the implementation confirm the theoretical analysis presented here and are shown in Figures 5 and 6. As seen in these figures, the on-center off-surround shape of the response to an impulse centered on cell 4 of a seven-cell implementation is similar to that shown in Fig. 4. The relative reduction of the inhibitory flanks versus the excitatory center as the mean intensity is reduced is clearly observable from Figures 5 and 6. The inset of the figures shows the adaptation of the receptive field of the LMC cell of the fly *Lucilia sericata* to variation of the background intensity. The insets were obtained (Pinter et. al 1989b) by curve fitting an analytical expression to the response of the fly to spatial gratings (reported in Dubs, 1982), and then Fourier transforming to produce the receptive fields.

Finally, the movement of temporal kernels towards the origin is much more pronounced than the increase of the relative inhibitory spatial flanks as the mean intensity increases. This is a straightforward result of the fact that the spatial kernel's dependence on L_0 is a power law dependence whereas the temporal kernels dependence is exponential.

6 Discussion

The temporal and spatial field adaptation (Rushtonian transformation) can be considered an approach to solving the gain-bandwidth interchange problem for visual scenes of different mean luminance. Since the biological visual systems demonstrate this adaptation or Rushtonian transformation, (human perception:Kelly,1975; cat retina:Derrington and Lennie,1982; catfish retina:Naka,1985;Sakuranaga and Naka,1985;insect retina LMC cells: Dubs, 1982; Pinter et al., 1989b; insect optic lobe visual interneurons:Srinivasan and Dvorak,1980;insect ventral nerve cord visual interneurons:Olberg and Pinter,1989;Pinter et al.,1989a) the circuitry for accomplishing this nonlinear transformation has somehow evolved via the behavior. The model of nonlinear lateral inhibition has been proposed on elemental physiological grounds, and shown to possess many of the Rushtonian transformation properties found in visual systems. Since the experimental results show this transformation among a great diversity of details, and the number of quanta needed for the given neural events is not usually known, the model presented here is quite general and the general aspects of the Rushtonian transformation are given, without attempting to state a specific optimality problem solution,a subject for further study. A striking feature of these aspects is the relatively greater adaptation or transformation on temporal kernels' characteristics than on spatial receptive fields in their relative sharpening and narrowing toward the origin as mean luminance increases. This is simply the result of the way eigenvalue transformation lies in the exponential functions of time, whereas the spatial receptive fields are controlled directly by the rate constants of the linear generating equation (7). But it is seen that if the spatial gradient of order of nonlinear lateral inhibition (the order is the highest nonzero term of $f_j(x_j)$ (eqn.2)) is substantial, the rate constants of the linearized generating equation (7) will have substantial spatial gradients dependent on the mean level L_0, and the adaptation or transformation of the receptive fields may approach that of the temporal characteristics (see also Pinter, 1984,1985). Note that under such spatial gradients of order, the A matrix is still symmetrical and Toeplitz, since c_{ji} does not depend on i. From this standpoint it is interesting to note that the steady-state (static) spatial receptive fields of catfish photoreceptors and horizontal cells adapt to mean luminance far less (almost not at all) than their temporal kernels whose peaks move to shorter times as mean luminance increases (Kawasaki,et al.,1984). Thus it may be said for this part of outer retina that the Rushtonian transformation on spatial and temporal kernels is primarily on the temporal, much like the nonlinear lateral inhibition model shown above in the example of Figs.2,3,4 which does not have substantial spatial gradient of order of nonlinear lateral inhibition. In psychophysical results for the human visual system, Kelly (1975) has proposed the adjustable Laplacian differentiator to account for implied spatial receptive field adaptation to mean luminance. That is a special case of the generating equation (7) above.

The compound eye possesses a unique spatial field adaptation which is not dependent on lateral inhibition. This is the narrowing of the retinular cells' angular acceptance characteristic as mean luminance is increased (Tunstall and Horridge, 1967). But higher order visual cells of the fly show much broader adaptation of spatial receptive fields (Srinivasan and Dvorak, 1980) so that the spatial adaptation may be a function both of the adaptation of retinular cells' angular acceptance characteristic and nonlinear lateral inhibition. Furthermore, the time course of photomechanical adaptation of angular acceptance characteristics is often slower than that which is likely due to nonlinear lateral inhibition so that one may separate the two causes of spatial field adaptation on a temporal basis via extended steady-state responses.

On the basis of spatial autocorrelation functions of visual scenes and inherent photon detection noise, optimal steady-state receptive fields for different mean luminances have been derived using linear prediction theory (Srinivasan, et al., 1982). These show narrowing and sharpening of form of inhibitory surrounds on increase of mean luminance very similar to those for nonlinear lateral inhibition having substantial spatial gradient of order negative away from center (Pinter, 1984,1985). A similar derivation for temporal impulse responses gives a (causal) result similar to the spatial case, so that for moving visual scenes the trend of the linear spatio-temporal impulse response is in the same direction with mean luminance: narrowing and sharpening as mean luminance increases. Since the spatial and temporal impulse responses from the statistical prediction theory are linear, and similar first order spatial and temporal kernels (impulse responses) are derived directly from the linearized nonlinear lateral inhibition (7), one may view the nonlinear lateral inhibition as a cellular mechanism for the statistically predicted shapes of impulse responses. But in addition, from (7) and (8) one obtains the higher order (Volterra series) nonlinear interactions over time, and as a function of mean luminance. In sum it can be said that nonlinear lateral inhibition may be a cellular mechanism for the parametric changes exhibited by the application of linear prediction theory. Such nonlinear neural circuitry may have evolved by organisms' predictions based on imperfect vision.[6]

[6]This study has been supported in part by grants from the NSF, BNS-8510188 and

References

[1] Andronow, A.A. and Chaikin, C.E.: *Theory of oscillations.* (English translation), Reprinted Princeton: Princeton University Press 1949.(Dover Press,1987)

[2] Borsellino, A. and Fuortes, M.G.F.: "Responses to single photons in visual cells of Limulus." *J. Physiol.(Lond.)* **196,** 507–539 (1968).

[3] Boyd,S. and Chua,L O: "Fading memories and the problem of approximating non-linear operators with Volterra series," *IEEE Trans. on Circ. and Sys.,***32** 1150–1160, (1985).

[4] Brodie, S.E.,Knight, B.W. and Ratliff, F.: The "spatio-temporal transfer function of the Limulus lateral eye." *J. Gen. Physiol.* **72,** 167–202 (1978).

[5] Cohen, M.A. and Grossberg, S.: "Absolute stability of global pattern formation and parallel memory storage by competitive neural networks." *IEEE Trans. on Syst.,Man and Cybern.* **SMC-13,** 815–826 (1983).

[6] Cunningham,W.J.: *Introduction to nonlinear analysis.* New York: McGraw-Hill, 1958.

[7] Derrington,A.M. and Lennie,P.: "The influence of temporal frequency and adaptation level on receptive field organization of retinal ganglion cells in cat." *J. Physiol.(Lond.)* **333,** 343–366 (1982).

[8] Dubs,A. "The spatial integration of signals in the retina and lamina of the fly compound eye under different conditions of luminance." *J. Comp. Physiol.* **146,** 321-343 (1982).

[9] Edwards, D.H.: "Response vs. excitation in response-dependent and stimulus-dependent lateral inhibitory networks." *Vision Res.* **23,** 469–472 (1983).

[10] Franklin,J.N.: *Matrix theory.* Englewood Cliffs: Prentice-Hall (1968).

MIP-8822121.

[11] Fuortes, M.G.F. and Hodgkin, A.L.: "Changes in time scale and sensitivity in the ommatidia of Limulus." *J. Physiol. (Lond.)* **172,** 239–263 (1964).

[12] Furman, G.G.: *Comparison of models for subtractive and shunting lateral inhibition in receptor-neuron fields." Kybernetik* **2,** *257–274 (1965).*

[13] Gilbert, E.G.: "Functional expansions for the response of nonlinear differential systems. IEEE Trans. on Aut. Contr. **AC-22,** 909–921 (1977).

[14] Hadeler,K.P.: "On the theory of lateral inhibition." *Kybernetik* **14,** 161–165 (1974).

[15] Jordan, D.W. and Smith, P.: *Nonlinear ordinary differential equations.* Oxford: Clarendon Press 1979.

[16] Kailath, T.: *Linear Systems.* Englewood Cliffs: Prentice-Hall 1980.

[17] Kawasaki,M. , Aoki, K. and Naka, K.-I.: "Effects of background and spatial pattern on incremental sensitivity of catfish horizontal cells." *Vision Res.* **24,** 1197–1204 (1984).

[18] Kelly, D.H.: "Spatial frequency selectivity in the retina." *Vision Res.* **15,** 665–672 (1975).

[19] Koch,C., Poggio,T. and Torre, V.: "Retinal ganglion cells: a functional interpretation of dendritic morphology." *Phil. Trans. R. Soc. Lond.* **B298,** 227–264 (1982).

[20] Llinas,R.,Steinberg,I.Z. and Walton,K.: "Presynaptic calcium currents in squid giant synapse." *Biophys.* **J.33,** 289–322, (1981a).

[21] Llinas, R., Steinberg,I.Z. and Walton,K.: "Relationship between presynaptic calcium current and postsynaptic potential in squid giant synapse." *Biophys.* **J.33,** 3223–352 (1981b).

[22] Marmarelis, P.Z.and Marmarelis,V.Z.: *Analysis of physiological systems-the white noise approach.* New York: Plenum Press 1978.

[23] Nabet, B. "Design, anlysis, and gallium arsenide based implementation of a class of neural networks wit application to vision and optoelectronics," Ph.D. dissertation, Electrical Engineering, University of Washington, 1989.

[24] Nabet, B., Darling, R. B. and Pinter, R. B.: "Analog implementation of shunting neural networks" in *Advances in Neural Information Processing Systems,* (NIPS 88) D. S. Touretzky ed., Morgan Kauffman Publishers Inc., 695–702, 1989.

[25] Naka, K.-I.: "Field adaptation in horizontal cells; Rushtonian transformation." *J. Nippon Med. Sch.* **52,** 251–262 1985.

[26] Olberg,R.M. and Pinter,R.B.: "The effect of mean luminance on the size selectivity of identified target interneurons in the dragonfly." *J. Comp. Physiol.* submitted, 1989.

[27] Pearson, C.E.(ed.): *Handbook of applied mathematics. 2nd Ed.* New York: Van Nostrand Reinhold 1983.

[28] Pinter, R.B.: "Sinusoidal and delta function responses of visual cells of the Limulus eye." *J. Gen. Physiol.* **49,** 565–593 (1966).

[29] Pinter,R.B.: "The electrophysiological bases for linear and for nonlinear product-term lateral inhibition and the consequences for wide-field textured stimuli." *J. Theor. Biol.* **105,** 233–243 (1983).

[30] Pinter,R.B.: "Adaptation of receptive field spatial organization via multiplicative lateral inhibition." *J. Theor. Biol.* **110,** 434–444 (1984).

[31] Pinter, R.B.: "Adaptation of spatial modulation transfer functions via nonlinear lateral inhibition." *Biol.Cybern.* **51,** 285–291 (1985).

[32] Pinter, R.B.: "Kernel synthesis from nonlinear multiplicative lateral inhibition." In: *Advanced Methods of Physiological System Modeling.* (ed.V. Z. Marmarelis). Los Angeles: Biomedical Simulations Resource, University of Southern California. vol.I, 258–277 (1987a).

[33] Pinter,R.B.: "Adaptation of temporal and spatial kernels of nonlinear lateral inhibition." *Proceedings, International conference on modeling*

and simulation. Melbourne: AMSE, Swinburne Inst. of Technology. 460–472 (1987b)

[34] Pinter, R.B., Olberg, R.M., and Warrant, E.J.: "Luminance adaptation of preferred object size in identified dragonfly movement detectors." In: *Proceedings, Annual International Conf. on Systems, Man and Cybernetics;* IEEE Systems, Man and Cybernetics Soc.. in press,1989a

[35] Pinter, R.B., Osorio,D., and Srinivasan, M.V.: "Matched filter theory applied to responses of fly lamina cells predicts loss of edge-preference on lowering luminance." In: *Proceedings of 11th Annual International Conf. IEEE Engineering in Medicine and Biology Soc.*. In press, 1989b

[36] Poggio, T. and Torre, V.: "A Volterra representation for some neuron models." *Biol. Cybern.* **27,** 113–124 (1977).

[37] Poggio, T. and Torre, V.: "A new approach to synaptic interactions." *Proceedings, symposium on theoretical approaches to complex systems,* 89–115 : *Lecture notes in biomathematics* (eds. Heim, R. and Palm, G.) Berlin: Springer-Verlag, 1978.

[38] Ratliff, F., Knight,B.W. and Graham, N.: "On tuning and amplification by lateral inhibition." *Proc. U.S. Nat. Acad. Sci.* **62,** 733–740 (1969).

[39] Robinson, E. A. and Treitel, S.: *Geophysical signal analysis.* Englewood Cliffs: Prentice-Hall 1980

[40] Rugh, W.J.: *Nonlinear system theory-the Volterra/ Wiener approach.* Baltimore: Johns Hopkins University Press 1981.

[41] Sakuranaga, M. and Ando, Y.-I.: "Visual sensitivity and Wiener kernels." *Vision Res. 25*, 507–510 (1985).

[42] Sakuranaga, M. and Naka, K.-I.: "Signal transmission in the Catfish retina. II. Transmission to type-N cell." *J. Neurophys.* **53,** 390–410 (1985).

[43] Rugh, W.J.: *Nonlinear system theory-the Volterra/ Wiener approach.* Baltimore: Johns Hopkins University Press 1981.

[44] Sakuranaga, M. and Ando, Y.-I.: "Visual sensitivity and Wiener kernels." *Vision Res. 25,* 507–510 (1985).

[45] Sakuranaga, M. and Naka, K.-I.: "Signal transmission in the Catfish retina. II. Transmission to type-N cell." *J. Neurophys.* **53,** 390–410 (1985).

[46] Schetzen,M.: *The Volterra and Wiener theories of nonlinear systems.* New York: Wiley and Sons 1980.

[47] Srinivasan, M.V., and Dvorak, D.R.: "Spatial processing of visual information in the movement detecting pathway of the fly." *J. Comp. Physiol.* **140,** 1–23 (1980).

[48] Srinivasan, M.V., Laughlin, S.B., and Dubs,A.: "Predictive coding: a fresh view of inhibition in the retina." *Proc. R. Soc. Lond.* **B216,** 427–459 (1982).

[49] Tunstall,J. and Horridge, G.A.: "Electrophysiological investigation of the optics of the locust retina." *Z.vergl. Physiol.* **55,** 167–182 (1967).

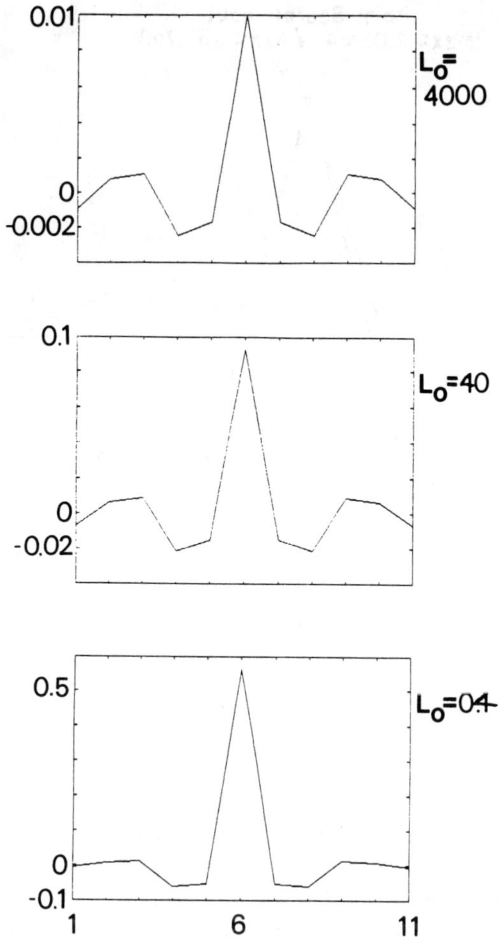

Figure 4: *The spatial first order kernel of Eq. (11) calculated for 11 cells for a unit pulse centered on the input array at cell 6. The spatial first order kernel is shown for the same three values of mean input L_0 of Figs. 2 and 3. Ordinate, value of kernel; abscissa, cell number which is equivalent to spatial dimension. The graph interpolates a linear function between points for visual consistency only.*

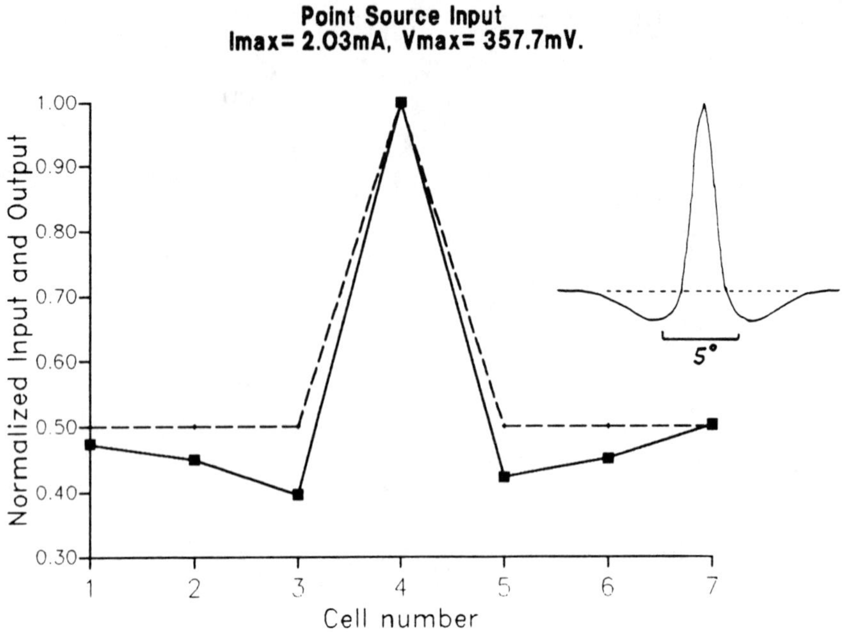

Figure 5: *Response of an analog hardware implementation of Fig. 1 to a point source input. Dotted line is the input and solid line is output of a seven cell array with nearest neighbor interconnections. The inset shows the receptive field of the LMC cell of the fly Lucilia sericata. Inset from Pinter et al., 1989b.*

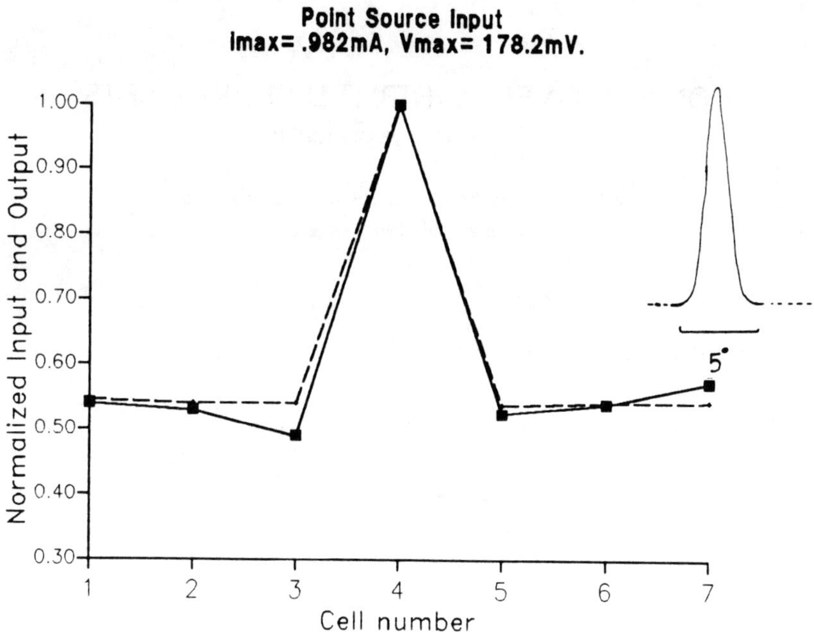

Figure 6: *Response of an electronic hardware implementation of Fig. 1 to a point source input of similar reflectance but less mean intensity than figure 5. The Rushtonian transformation is obvious. Inset shows similar effect in the LMC cell of the fly Lucilia sericata. Inset from Pinter et. al 1989.*

3

COMPETITIVELY INHIBITED NEURAL NETS: Analysis and Applications[1]

by Michael Lemmon and B.V.K. Vijaya Kumar, Carnegie Mellon University

1 Introduction

Recent years have witnessed a resurgence of interest in the artificial neural network (ANN) computing paradigm. To a great extent this interest stems from the realization that biological neural networks (i.e., brains) are better adapted to solving certain problems than their artificial counterparts (i.e., computers)[8]. These problems may be found in a variety of current and proposed engineering systems for computer vision [1] and robotics applications[19]. An example of the biological system's processing power may be found in figure 1. It takes only a half second for the human observer to notice that the car in this picture is missing a headlight and is parked in a "NO PARKING" zone. If this same picture were viewed by a computer vision system, the correct percept may have formed after several thousand or tens of thousand of inferences. The difference between the biological and computer systems is more striking when we recall that the average time constant of the brain's elemental processing unit, the neuron, is 5 milliseconds. This means that the brain formed the percept in no more than 100 processing steps whereas the computer required several thousand processing steps[8]. Clearly the biological system is doing something intrinsically different than the computer.

The performance differences between the biological system and the computer are generally attributed to architectural differences. This conjecture nourishes the hope that if the biological system's architectural principles can be transplanted into an artifical device, the resulting machines will be better able to handle complex vision and robotic tasks. Succinctly stated, the goal of ANN research is to draw upon the organizational principles of biological systems to improve our existing devices. To achieve this goal, researchers often concentrate in one or more of the following areas.

[1]This research was supported in part by the Air Force Office of Scientific Research (AFOSR) under grant AFOSR-89-0551

Figure 1: NO PARKING

- Identify the architectural principles giving the biological system its capabilities.
- Analyze those principles to understand why they work.
- Implement those principles in devices we can build.
- Apply the networks to specific problems.

This chapter addresses the preceding four areas for a class of neural net where neurons mutually inhibit each other. We first identify the principle of competitive interaction and then formulate a neural network embodying this principle. The resulting network's dynamics are analyzed and those analyses are used to suggest applications for and implementations of the net.

The following sections present this four step development in more detail. The notion of competition and how it might be incorporated into a neural network is discussed in section 2. This discussion leads to a special neural net which we call the **competitively inhibited neural net** or CINN. The dynamics of this network are analyzed in section 3 and these analyses lead to the formulation of an algorithm characterizing the input-output properties of the net. This algorithm is called the **CINN algorithm.** The CINN algorithm has two implications which are explored in section 4 and 5. The first implication is that the algorithm suggests efficient methods for using parallel computers to host the CINN (section 4). The second implication is that the algorithm allows the development of a **continuum model** describing how a CINN "learns" (section 5). This continuum model can make quantitative predictions about the CINN's long run behaviour (section 6) and thereby identifies applications for which the network is well suited (section 7). The principle themes of this chapter are then summarized in section 8.

2 CINN Equations

Competitive interactions constitute an important organizational principle in many biological networks, not just neural nets. In ecological systems, competitive interactions between species in a nonpredating ecology can give rise to niche selection[3]. In neural systems, competition between neurons of the sensory cortex is generally attributed to assist with the early self-organization of sensory receptor fields[5]. We therefore concentrate on competition as an organizational principle for large scale computation. To effectively study competition, we introduce a special class of neural network in which the competition level has been parameterized. We call this network the competitively inhibited neural net (CINN). The following section introduces the CINN equations and briefly points out its relationship to other prominent neural net models.

An artificial neural network (ANN) is a collection of processing elements whose dynamics are patterned after the dynamics of biological **neurons**. The biological neuron[14] (see figure 2) consists of four parts. There is an input fiber called a **dendrite**. The **cell body** processes the signals from the dendrite to produce an output pulse that propagates down an output fiber called the **axon**. The axon connects to the dendrites of other neurons at a **synapse**. The synapse is a specialization of the neuron's membrane which allows the output pulse from the axon to induce a voltage over the receiving dendrite's cell membrane. Figure 2 shows how these four parts can be schematized into an "artificial neuron".

A neural network arises when we interconnect these neurons together as shown in figure 3. Let the network have N_t neurons. Figure 3 shows that each neuron is characterized by two states. The **short term memory** or STM state for the ith neuron of the network is a real scalar, x_i. The STM state models the neuron's local activity level. The **long term memory** or LTM state for the ith neuron is a real m-vector, $\bar{z}_i$. The LTM state models the synaptic weights associated with the ith neuron.

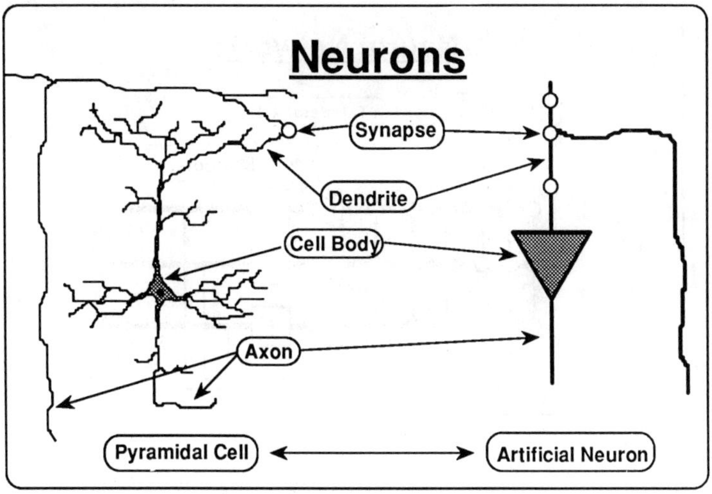

Figure 2: Neurons: biological versus artificial

The **inputs** to the network are generated by an external source. This source is represented by the ordered triple, (Y, p, T). The input vectors, $\bar{y}$, are drawn from the "alphabet", $Y = \Re^m$ with respect to a density function p which we sometimes call the **source density**. Input vectors are generated at regular intervals of length T such that the resulting sequence is statistically independent and distribution-ergodic[20]. The LTM state vector and input lie in the same set, $\Re^m$, which we sometimes call the **LTM space**.

In response to the applied input vector, each neuron produces an **output**. The ith neuron's output is a sigmoid function of the STM state, $f(x_i)$. In this chapter, we assume that the output function is simply a step function which is unity for positive STM states and zero otherwise. We say a neuron is **active** if it has a nonzero output, otherwise it is **inactive**.

Precisely how the outputs are generated depends on the dynamics of the STM and LTM states. The ith neuron's states satisfy the following ordinary differential equations. These equations are based on models for large scale neuronal signaling[7] as well as conjectures about synaptic modification in biological neurons[25] [12].

$$\dot{x}_i = -x_i + E(\bar{y}, \bar{z}_i) + I_i \quad , \tag{1}$$

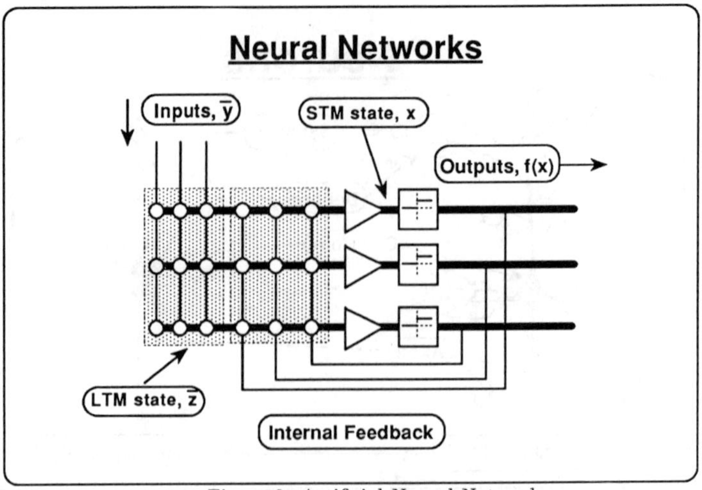

Figure 3: Artificial Neural Network

$$\dot{\bar{z}}_i = f(x_i)(\bar{y} - \bar{z}_i) \quad . \tag{2}$$

Equations 1 and 2 are called the STM and LTM state equations, respectively.

The function $E(\bar{y}, \bar{z}_i)$ seen in equation 1 is called the **external stimulus function**. It models the way in which the applied input $\bar{y}$ is coupled through the LTM state, $\bar{z}_i$, to drive the neurons. In general, the external stimulus represents a generalized inner product over the LTM space. One popular choice is to simply use the usual vector inner product. For our purposes, we assume that the external stimulus is a bounded positive function which is decreasing in $|\bar{y} - \bar{z}|$.

The function I_i seen in equation 1 is called the **internal stimulus function**. It models feedback effects and represents the way in which competition can be parameterized in the network. A **competitively inhibited neural net** or **CINN** results when we let the internal stimulus be

$$I_i = \alpha f(x_i) - \beta \sum_{j=1, j \neq i}^{N_t} f(x_j) \quad , \tag{3}$$

where α and β are positive constants. From equation 3, we see that when the ith neuron is active, it provides a positive component to I_i. Therefore the neuron is "self-stimulating".

On the other hand if any other neuron fires, it contributes a negative component of strength β to I_i. This means that neurons are mutually inhibiting. Equation 3 provides the means for parameterizing competitive interactions in the CINN. In particular, the strength of the constant β controls the amount of competition in the network.

The CINN is closely related to two other neural net models. These networks are S. Grossberg's adaptive resonance theory (ART) network[9] [1] and T. Kohonen's adaptive vector quantization (AVQ) algorithm (also called the self-organizing feature map)[13]. The CINN can be identified with a subnet of Grossberg's ART1 system. The differences between the ART1 subnet and the CINN are that our model explicitly parameterizes the competition level by β and uses a generalized inner product to couple the input into the network. In section 4, we will see that the CINN can be described by an algorithm. This algorithm has striking similarities to Kohonen AVQ algorithm. The difference between the AVQ algorithm and the CINN algorithm lies in the set of neurons which are free to adapt when an input is presented. The differences and similarities between the CINN and these two other nets are detailed elsewhere [17].

3 CINN Algorithm

This section analyzes the CINN's behaviour when driven by a constant input vector. In this situation, we are able to make precise statements about the stability and steady states of the system. These theorems provide a parametric characterization of the CINN's steady state. The characterization allows us to predict the network's STM and LTM states given the input vector. We can fashion these results into a so-called **CINN Algorithm**.

3.1 Dynamics

Let us assume that the CINN is globally stable to a point attractor. This assertion is proved in detail in references [18] and [17] using the properties of monotone mappings[11] [24]. We perform a local stability analysis of the network's critical points to characterize the net's steady states. This analysis yields the following two results.

Theorem 1 *The number of activated neurons, p, which can be supported by a CINN is*

$$p < 1 + \frac{\alpha}{\beta} + \frac{E(\bar{y}, \bar{y})}{\beta} - p_{max} \quad . \tag{4}$$

Proof: Let p be the number of activated neurons. It can be readily shown that the steady state LTM states of activated neurons will be equal to the applied input vector. Therefore, any activated neuron at steady state must have a positive STM state satisfying

$$0 < \alpha + \beta - p\beta + E(\bar{y}, \bar{y}) \quad , \tag{5}$$

which rearranged yields equation 4. **QED**

The right hand side of equation 4 is an upper bound on the number of activated neurons. We denoted this bound as p_{max}. The following theorem provides a sufficient condition for inactive neurons to turn active. This condition represents a "sliding threshold test" on the initial external stimulus levels. The theorem is therefore called the **sliding threshold theorem.**

Theorem 2 *Assume that there are p active neurons in the network. Then the next neuron to turn active will remain active if its initial stimulus level exceeds the following threshold*

$$E(\bar{z}_j(0), \bar{y}) > p\beta \quad . \tag{6}$$

Proof: Assume that there are p active neurons, the STM state's time rate of change for the next inactive neuron to turn active is

$$\dot{x}_j = E(\bar{y}, \bar{z}_j(0)) - p\beta - x_j \quad . \tag{7}$$

To become active, this neuron's dx/dt must be positive in a small neighborhood about the origin. This consideration implies that

$$E(\bar{y}, \bar{z}_j(0)) - p\beta > \dot{x}_j \geq 0 \quad , \tag{8}$$

which can be rewritten to obtain the threshold in equation 6. In [17] it is shown that such a neuron must remain active. **QED**

Theorem 2 allows us to predict which neurons of the network will turn active for a given input vector. The LTM state equation (Eq. 2) shows that only the LTM states of an activated neuron can be changed by the applied input. This fact becomes apparent when we recall that $f(x)$ is unity for an active neuron and zero for an inactive neuron. Therefore, when a neuron is active the LTM state equation becomes a linear differential equation whose solution is given below,

$$\bar{z}_j(t) = \bar{z}_j(0)e^{-t} + (1 - e^{-t})\bar{y} \quad . \tag{9}$$

The LTM states of inactive neurons will simply be, $\bar{z}_j(0)$. If we assume that the initial STM states are "small" and negative, then those neurons which are going to turn active will do so quickly. Therefore, soon after the input is applied we know which neurons are active and which are not. This means that the LTM states of the active neurons will have been adapting (learning) for approximately the same length of time. As a result, equation 9 represents a good approximation for the LTM states of all active neurons.

3.2 Algorithm

The preceding results allow the formulation of a method for predicting which neurons will turn active when a given input vector, $\bar{y}$, is applied. Let $E_j = E(\bar{y}, \bar{z}_j(0))$ be the initial external stimulus for the jth neuron. The set of all initial external stimulus levels can be sorted into a monotonically decreasing sequence as shown below,

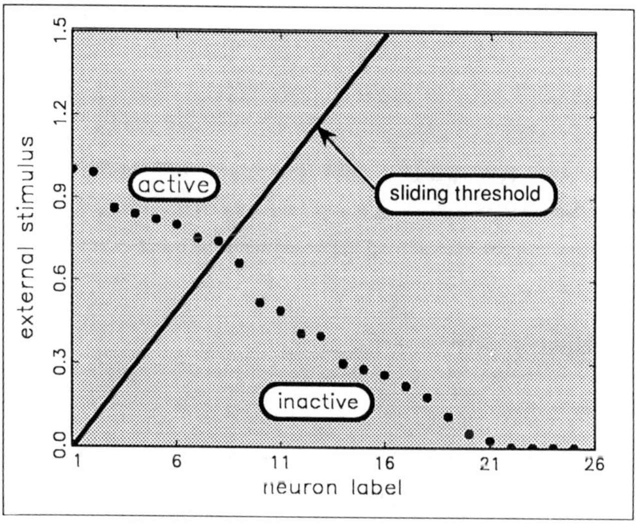

Figure 4: Sliding Threshold Test

$$E_{j1} \geq E_{j2} \geq E_{j3} \geq \ldots \geq E_{jN_t} \quad , \tag{10}$$

where $j1, \ldots, jN_t$ are integers labeling the neurons. Theorem 2 yields a sliding threshold conditions for each neuron entering activity. We form a monotonically increasing sequence of these thresholds,

$$0 < \beta < 2\beta < \ldots < (N_t - 1)\beta \quad . \tag{11}$$

The sequences in equations 10 and 11 are graphically illustrated in figure 4, where the stimulus levels are plotted as a decreasing sequence of points and the sliding threshold is a solid line. The sliding threshold theorem (Eq. 6) states that all neurons above this threshold line will turn active and remain active. The LTM states of these activated neurons will then be updated using equation 9.

Figure 4 suggests a methodology for predicting the short term steady states of the network. This methodology can be restated as an algorithmic procedure whose heart is the sliding threshold test of theorem 2. This algorithm consists of four steps which are itemized below. A more complicated version of this algorithm presented in reference [18], accounts for situations when multiple neurons can enter activity simultaneously. The algorithm shown below is a special case of the more general algorithm.

CINN Algorithm

1. Compute external stimuli, E_j, for each neuron.
2. Determine which neurons satisfy the sliding threshold test (eq. 6).
3. Designate at most $p_{\max}$ (Eq. 4) of the neurons satisfying the sliding threshold test as active.
4. Update the LTM states of all activated neurons using equation 9.

4 CINN Emulation

As presented to this point, the CINN is only a paradigm for parallel computation. This model must be transformed into an actual device before it can be used in applications. The following section shows how fine-grained parallel computers can efficiently host the CINN.

The CINN algorithm possesses sufficient regularity to be hosted by bit serial processors (BSPs) arranged in a rectangular array with nearest neighbor connections. Each processing element (PE) works on one bit of data per clock cycle. In this parallel implementation, $m + 1$ processors are associated with each neuron, see figure 5. One PE is committed to the computation of the STM state while the other m PEs are committed to computation of the LTM state. When an input enters the network, it is broadcast to the LTM PEs. A given LTM PE contains one element of a neuron's LTM state vector and that PE computes

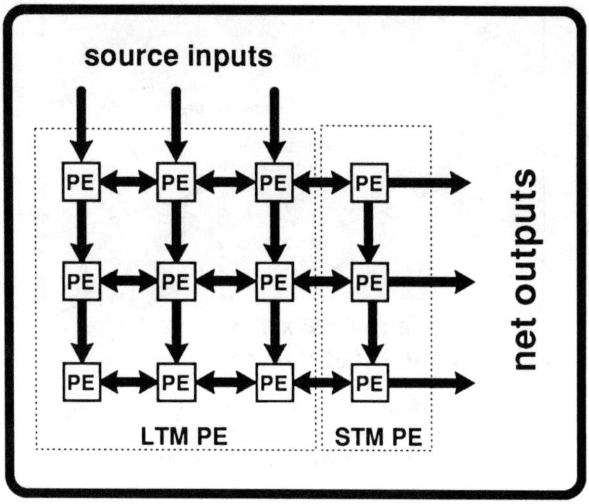

1) Input is broadcast to LTM PEs which compute components of external stimulus.

2) External stimulus components are accumulated in STM PEs.

3) STM PEs perform sliding threshold test.

4) Threshold test decision is broadcast back to LTM PEs who then update their LTM states.

Figure 5: BSP Array Hosting the CINN Algorithm

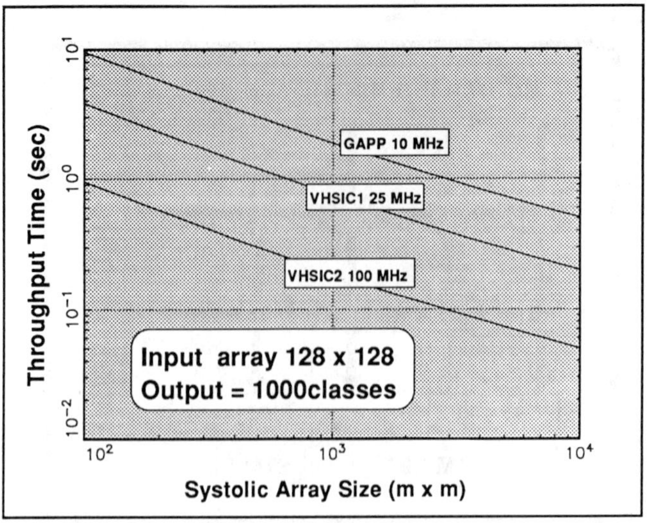

Figure 6: BSP Host Throughput Rates

the portion of the external stimulus associated with that one compnent of the LTM state vector. After computing a portion of the stimulus level, all LTM PEs forward their results to the STM PEs. The STM PE combines all received results to form the external stimulus level, E_j, in the STM processor. A sorting algorithm is then used among the STM PEs to determine which PEs have external stimulus levels satisfying the sliding threshold test of theorem 2. The "winning" PEs broadcast news of their victory back to all of their associated LTM PEs who then proceed to update their LTM states using equation 9. Figure 5 shows the BSP array and the flow of information through it.

We have done preliminary timing estimates for a hypothetical BSP host assuming clock speeds consistent with the GAPP chip[4], and hypothetical VHSIC phase 1 and phase 2[15] versions of the GAPP chip[18]. These estimates are shown in figure 6 as a function of array size (number of PEs) for a hypothetical problem involving 128^2 dimensional input vectors and 10^3 neurons. They indicate that for large arrays of PEs, the GAPP-like processors could exhibit throughput times of less than one second (for the hypothetical problem of classifying 128^2 dimensional inputs into one of 10^3 classes). For VHSIC phase 2 chips with projected clock rates of 100 MHz, these throughput times would be 50 milliseconds. These times are fast enough for many real-time applications, thereby suggesting that existing VLSI technologies are capable of hosting CINNs.

In figure 6, we note a slower than linear increase in throughput performance as we increase array size. This phenomenon is due to the overhead associated with pipelining in a nearest neighbor processor topology. To reduce the performance degradation associated with pipelining, we must shorten the pipe. In other words, LTM PEs must have more direct access to their associated STM PEs. This may be accomplished by resorting to different PE interconnection topologies. The n-cube architecture used by the Connection Machine[10] appears to be a perfect candidate for the job. In the Connection Machine implementation, we continue to associate a single PE with each LTM and STM state, but now the interconnection topology allows shorter communication delays between PEs.

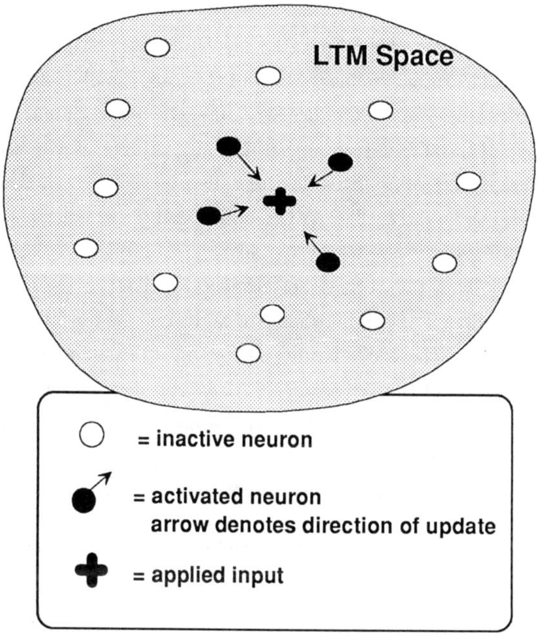

Figure 7: Applied inputs activate neurons which then move in the direction of the input.

5 Continuum Model

The CINN algorithm presents a simplified view of network dynamics. Figure 7 illustrates this viewpoint by showing position of inputs and neurons in the LTM space. The ith neuron is represented by a point in the LTM space, whose position is determined by the neuron's LTM state vector, $\bar{z}_i$. The input, $\bar{y}$, also lies in the LTM space and is represented by another point in the LTM space. The CINN algorithm asserts that all neurons lying within a specified distance of the applied input will be activated and begin moving toward the applied input. Figure 7 shows the activated neurons as filled circles and the inactive neurons as open circles. The activated neurons move in the direction indicated by the arrows which is in the direction of the applied input.

The situation outlined above constitutes a "competitive learning paradigm"[22]. There are numerous competitive learning schemes. Many of these are usually defined as algorithms such as the CINN algorithm[13] [22]. The primary difference between our formulation and that of others is our use of the sliding threshold test. This test determines the neighborhood of activated neurons. In other competitive learning algorithms, the neighborhood of activated neurons is defined differently. The AVQ algorithm of T. Kohonen[13], for instance, activates a neighborhood of neurons whose topology is determined by the actual spatial relationship of neurons within the net. Other schemes involve the use of winner-take-all (WTA) rules for determining the neighborhood of activated neurons[9] [22]. The CINN algorithm is closely related to these WTA-rule schemes since the sliding threshold test may be viewed as a generalization of the WTA-rule. Unlike other networks where the specification of the "activation" neighborhood is somewhat ad hoc, the CINN algorithm has been rigorously derived from the actual graded network's dynamics. In this respect, the CINN algorithm has a more solid theoretical foundation than its WTA counterparts.

Each time the network is stimulated by an applied input, the LTM states (i.e. neurons) move in the LTM space. If we stimulate the network with a sequence of inputs, it then makes sense to talk about the "collective" movement of the neurons through the LTM space. This realization leads to the development of a **continuum model** which describes the evolution of the distribution of neurons throughout the LTM space. The following discussion introduces this continuum model. A more detailed development of the model may be found elsewhere [17].

5.1 Assumptions

The continuum model's development requires some initial assumptions on the nature of the stimulating source, the reset of STM parameters, and constraints on network parameters.

We assume that the CINN is driven by an **ergodic source**. The source is represented by the ordered triple (Y, p, T). Input vectors, $\bar{y}$, are generated at regular time intervals, T, by randomly drawing vectors out of $Y = \Re^m$ with respect to a probability density function, $p(\bar{y})$, which we call the **source density**. The length of time an input is presented to the net is called the **presentation interval**, T. It is assumed that the resulting sequence of random vectors is distribution-ergodic[20].

We will assume that the CINN satisfies the **STM Reset Assumption**. This assumption means that prior to each new input vector, the STM states are all reset to small negative values. This assumption guarantees two things. First, it guarantees that the network is inactive at the start of each presentation interval. In the second place, the assumption guarantees that all neurons start off with the same level of inactivity. In this way, all neurons firing at the end of the presentation interval will be firing as a direct consequence of the input vector generated during that interval. The initialization strategy therefore insures that the STM states are only influenced by short term inputs (i.e., over a single presentation interval) and that LTM states arise as a result of long term stimulation (i.e., over several presentation intervals).

We will place some restrictions on the network parameters in order to facilitate the model's development. The network parameter α will be chosen large enough so that $p_{max} \geq N_t$ (see equation 4). This assumption insures that all neurons whose LTM states satisfy the sliding threshold test will be activated.

5.2 Conservation Law

The continuum model describes the evolution of the distribution of neurons in the LTM space. This distribution will obey a conservation principle whose mathematical formulation constitutes the heart of the continuum model.

We can formally define the notion of "neural density" to make this concept more precise.

Definition 1 *The* **neural density** *is a generalized function,* $n(\bar{\omega}) \mid \Re^m \rightarrow \Re$, *such that* *for any bounded region R in the LTM space,*

$$N_R = \int_R n(\bar{\omega}) d\bar{\omega} \quad , \tag{12}$$

where N_R is the number of neurons whose LTM states lies in the set R.

Heuristically speaking, $n(\bar{\omega})$ represents the "concentration" of LTM states about the point $\bar{\omega}$.

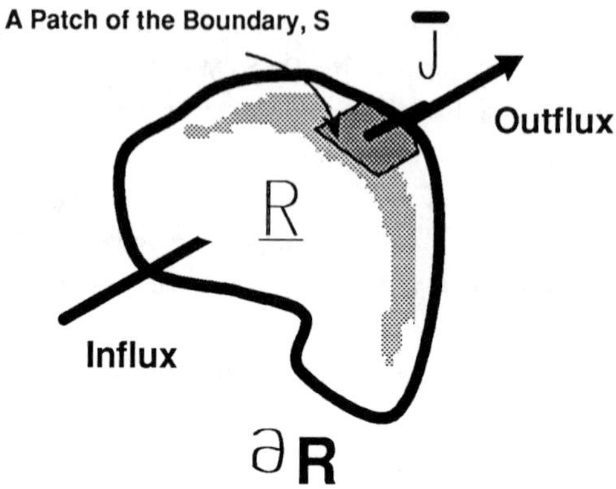

Figure 8: Neural Density

Figure 8 shows the set R introduced in definition 1. Since neurons are moving about in the LTM space it makes sense to talk of the "rate" at which neurons cross over R's boundary, ∂R. In figure 8 we show a patch of this boundary, S, centered at the point $\bar{\omega}$. The rate at which neurons cross this patch is called the **neural flux** across $\bar{\omega}$. It is denoted as $\bar{J}(\bar{\omega})$. Formal definition of the neural flux is somewhat involved. A complete statement of these concepts can be found elsewhere [17].

The rate at which neurons cross the patch of border in figure 8 is determined by neurons going in two different directions. Figure 9 shows this patch in more detail. A neuron can either cross from the righthand side of S to the left or vice versa. These two possibilities can be interpreted as a positive and a negative **subflux**, which we denote as $\bar{J}^+(\bar{\omega})$ and

$\bar{J}^-(\bar{\omega})$, respectively. Under this development the total flux can be written as

$$\bar{J}(\bar{\omega}) = \bar{J}^+(\bar{\omega}) - \bar{J}^-(\bar{\omega}) \quad . \tag{13}$$

Figure 9 explicitly shows the positive subflux. In this figure we look more closely at the patch of border, S, shown in figure 8. We denote this patch as the "border". The positive subflux arises when inputs to the right of the border activate neurons to the left of the border and these activated neurons subsequently cross the border in a single presentation interval. The set of inputs capable of contributing to the positive subflux form a boundary layer to the right of the border (see figure 9). The set of activated neurons forms another boundary layer to the left of the border. It is the interaction between inputs and neurons in these two boundary layers that give rise to the positive subflux. The width of these boundary layers is called the activation width.

With the preceding definitions, the flux conservation law modeling LTM state redistribution can be developed. It will be taken as axiomatic that the time rate of change in the number of LTM states contained within the bounded region R equals the total flux into this region over its boundary. This statement can be expressed as the integral relation

$$\frac{d}{dt}\int_R n(\bar{\omega})d\bar{\omega} = -\int_{\partial R} \bar{J}(\bar{\omega})\cdot d\bar{s} \quad , \tag{14}$$

where ∂R is the boundary of R and $d\bar{s}$ is a vector representing an infinitesimal patch of the boundary. Application of the Divergence Theorem and taking the time derivative inside the integral yields[16] [2],

$$0 = \int_R (n_t + \nabla \cdot \bar{J})d\bar{\omega} \quad , \tag{15}$$

where n_t is the partial derivative of the neural density with respect to time and $\nabla \cdot \bar{J}$ is the divergence of the flux vector field. Equation 15 can often be interpreted as a partial differential equation of the following form.

$$n_t + \nabla \cdot \bar{J} = 0 \quad . \tag{16}$$

Equation 16 represents a mathematical model for the time rate of change in the neural density.

5.3 Flux Approximation

The utility of equation 16 rests upon our ability to find an expression for the neural flux vector. This section describes such an approximation for 1-dimensional LTM spaces. In reference [17] it is shown that this 1-d approximation adequately models a single component of the flux vector in multi-dimensional LTM spaces. Therefore any results obtained for the 1-d case can be extended to the multidimensional case.

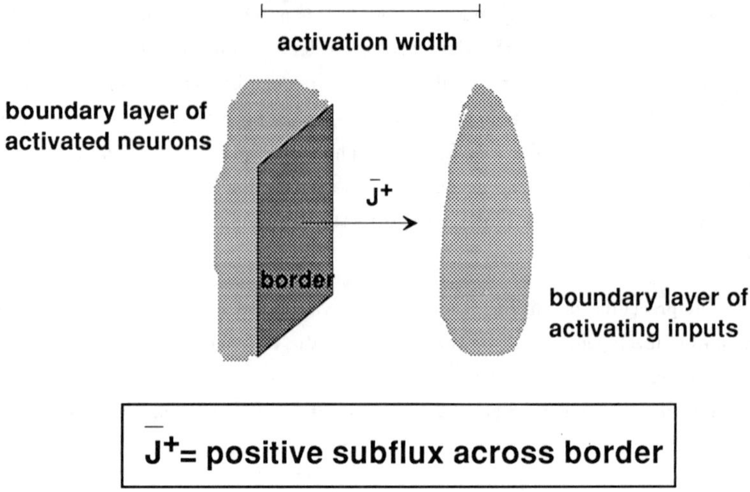

Figure 9: Neural Flux

By referring to figure 9, we saw that the positive subflux exists when inputs to the right side of border activate neurons to the left side of ω. These two set of inputs and neurons form boundary layers on either side of ω. The location and extent of these boundary layers is graphically portrayed in figure 9. It can be shown that under certain conditions[17] the width of the lefthand boundary layer is $\delta(e^T - 1)$ and the width of the righthand boundary layer is δ. The quantity δ is called the **activation width** and is an implicit function which varies inversely with the neural density as below,

$$\delta = \frac{E(\omega, \omega + \delta)}{2\beta N_t n(\omega)} \quad . \tag{17}$$

The extent of this width is shown in figure 9.

Figure 9 suggests that the rate at which neurons cross S from left to right will be proportional to the product of the number of neurons in the left hand boundary layer and the number (rate) of inputs in the right hand boundary layer. This principle is essentially the "law of mass action" found in chemical kinetic reaction theory[23]. This principle means that the positive flux can be written as the following integral.

$$J^{+}(\omega) = \int_0^{\delta} \left\{ \int_{\eta(e^T-1)}^{0} n(\omega - x)dx \right\} p(\omega + \eta)d\eta \quad . \tag{18}$$

Dual considerations lead to the following equation for the negative subflux.

$$J^{-}(\omega) = \int_0^{\delta} \left\{ \int_{0}^{\eta(e^T-1)} n(\omega + x)dx \right\} p(\omega - \eta)d\eta \quad . \tag{19}$$

Formal development of these equations will be found elsewhere [17].

Equation 18 and 19 are essentially Chapman-Kolmogorov relations[20]. We can use them to derive several expressions for the total flux across ω. Many such results are presented in [17]. A particularly useful such expression is the **first order flux approximation**. This expression asserts that a good first order approximation of the neural flux is

$$J(\omega) \approx n(\omega)(e^T - 1)\delta^3 \left(\psi\left(\frac{\omega}{\delta}\right) * p_\omega(\omega) \right) \quad , \tag{20}$$

where

$$\psi\left(\frac{\omega}{\delta}\right) = \left(1 - \frac{\omega^2}{\delta^2}\right) \mathrm{B}\left(\frac{\omega}{\delta}\right) \quad . \tag{21}$$

In equation 21, the "box" function, $B(\omega)$, is defined to be unity for arguments between plus and minus one and zero otherwise. The function p_ω is the slope of the source density and $f * g$ denotes the convolution of functions f and g. This approximation arises out of first order Taylor series approximations for the distribution of neurons about ω. Equation 20 along with equation 17 and 16 constitute the CINN's continuum model.

6 CINN Learning

This section describes the continuum model's implications. The results presented below specifically apply to 1-dimensional LTM spaces, but they can be easily extended to multi-dimensional cases[17]. The "method of characteristics"[2] is used to study trajectories of constant neural density in the Cartesian product of the LTM space and time axis. It will be shown that under certain constraints, which we call the "clustering constraints", these trajectories ascend the gradient of a smoothed version of the source density. This gradient ascending property means that, in the long run, neurons will "cluster" about the modes of this smoothed density function. These clusters comprise an invariant density function which can be interpreted as a nonparametric representation of the source density. Density estimation is essential to machine learning[6] and so the continuum model becomes a useful tool for studying "CINN learning".

6.1 Characteristics and Clustering

Solving the continuum model for $n(\omega, t)$ provides a complete picture of the neural density's evolution. The continuum model's solution will be obtained by solving the highly nonlinear partial differential equation embodied by the flux conservation law, $n_t = -\nabla \cdot \bar{J}$. One approach to such problems is the **method of characteristics**[2]. A **characteristic** is a trajectory through the Cartesian product of the LTM space, ω, and time axis, t, along which the neural density, $n(\omega, t)$, is constant. We denote this trajectory by the parameterized curve $c(t) = 0$. It is a standard result[2] [16] that the characteristic's slope, for nonlinear diffusions satisfying a conservation law, will satisfy the following differential equation

$$c_t = J_n \quad , \tag{22}$$

where subscripts denote the partial derivatives of that function.

By inserting the first order flux approximation (Eq. 20) into Equation 22, an expression is obtained for the CINN's "first order" characteristics. This expression is shown below,

$$c_t = \frac{2}{3}(e^T - 1)\delta^3 \left(\frac{|E_\delta| - 3E/\delta}{|E_\delta| + E/\delta} \right) \left[B\left(\frac{\omega}{\delta}\right) * p(\omega) \right]_\omega \quad . \tag{23}$$

where E is the external stimulus function, $E(\omega, \omega + \delta)$, and $[f * g]_\omega$ denotes the partial derivative of the convolution of functions f and g. These first order approximations to the actual CINN's characteristics are exact at certain points in the LTM space and provide considerable insight into the continuum model's behaviour[17].

The characteristic's slope (Eq. 23) will be proportional to either the positive or the negative gradient of the smoothed density function $B * p$. If the proportionality is positive, then the characteristics follow a gradient ascent of the smoothed source density and we expect neurons to eventually "cluster" about the modes of this density function. If the proportionality is negative, then the characteristics follow a gradient descent away from the smoothed density's modes. For application purposes, we usually prefer that the former case hold. This means that we must find constraints on the external stimulus function and competition constant which insure that the characteristics are always ascending the smoothed density's gradient.

These constraints are called the **clustering constraints.** They assume that the network uses a **standard external stimulus function** of the form

$$E_{\gamma}^{\theta}(\delta) = \begin{cases} 1 & \text{if } \delta < \gamma \\ \left|\frac{\gamma}{\delta}\right|^{\theta} & \text{if } \delta \geq \gamma \end{cases} \tag{24}$$

where θ and γ are positive constants. The clustering constraints consist of the following restrictions on the parameters θ and β. The first "clustering constraint" is that $\theta \gg 3$ and the second constraint is that $\beta < \frac{1}{N_t}$. Under these conditions, it can be shown [17] that the first order characteristics are always ascending the gradient of the smoothed source density and that the slope of the characteristics will be approximated by

$$c_t \approx \frac{2}{3}(e^T - 1)\delta^3 \left[B\left(\frac{\omega}{\delta}\right) * p(\omega)\right]_{\omega} \quad , \tag{25}$$

where δ is the activation width (see equation 17). For the standard external stimulus function (Eq. 24), it can be shown [17] that this width is bounded below by γ.

Equation 25 implies that the characteristics are ascending the gradient of the smoothed source density. This means that in the long run the characteristics should converge to the modes of the smoothed source density. Because of the box function, $B(\omega/\delta)$, the amount of source density smoothing is a function of the density along that characteristic. Two different characteristics might conceivably converge to two different modes since they are ascending the gradient of two different smoothed versions of the source density. It can be shown [17] that after a large number of presentation intervals, all of these different smoothed versions become the same. Since the activation width is bounded below by γ, the characteristics of the CINN will **eventually** attempt to locate the modes of the following smoothed version of the source density.

$$p_s(\omega) = B\left(\frac{\omega}{\gamma}\right) * p(\omega) \; . \tag{26}$$

We therefore expect the neurons to form clusters about the modes of the smoothed objective function (Eq. 26). It can be shown[17] that the "formation rate" of these clusters will vary inversely with γ^3.

6.2 Simulation Experiments

The preceding predictions concerning LTM clustering have been corroborated by simulation experiments. In the following experiments, we consider a 100 neuron network with a 1-d LTM space whose parameters satisfy the clustering constraints. Our first simulation experiments assume that the source's density function is zero mean and Gaussian with unit variance. At time zero, we assume that all neurons have LTM states uniformly distributed over the region -3 to 3 in the LTM space. We can integrate equation 25 numerically to obtain a graphic picture of the system's characteristics. The resulting characteristic trajectories are plotted in figure 10.

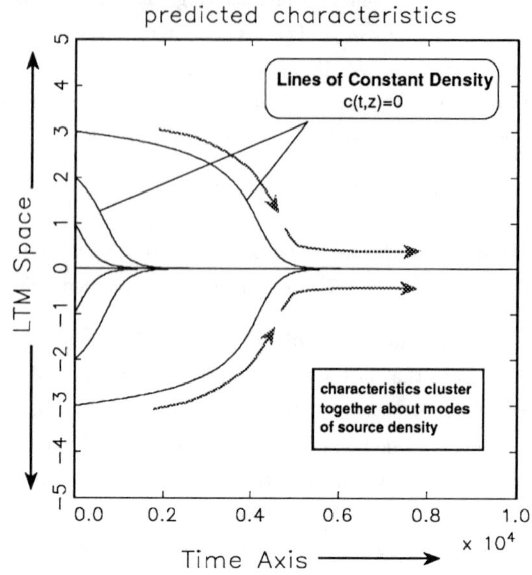

Figure 10: Predicted Characteristics for Simulation Experiment

A computer simulation for the CINN was implemented using the CINN algorithm. At each time point, the network's LTM states were used to generate a kernel-based estimate of the neural density[26]. This approach to density estimation is often referred to as "generalized histogramming". The estimated neural densities at each time point were combined to form a halftone image illustrating the neural density's evolution over the simulation run. Figure 11 shows the resulting halftone image for the problem whose predicted characteristics are shown in figure 10. In this figure, light regions correspond to high neural density and dark regions correspond to low neural density. As can be seen in the figure, neurons are clustering about the mode of the source density. Furthermore the rate of this clustering appears to be consistent with the predictions of figure 10.

The "formation rate" of these LTM clusters varies inversely as γ^3. Simulation experiments corroborate this prediction. Define the "entry time" as the length of time it takes for all neurons to enter a neighborhood of width γ about the source mode. Figure 12 shows the

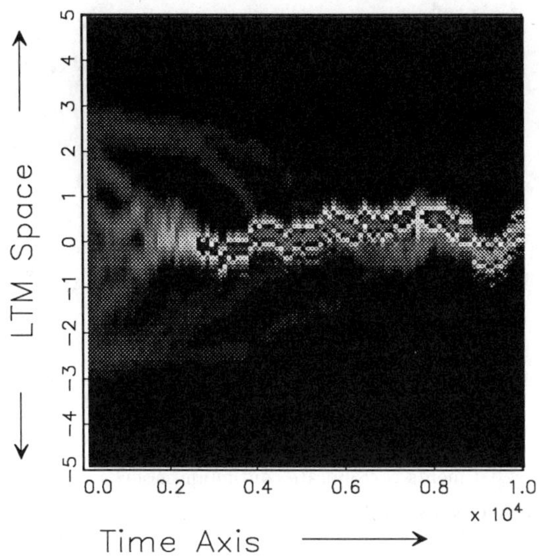

Figure 11: Estimated neural density for CINN simulation.

variation in entry time versus the parameter γ. Our analyses predict that this entry time should vary inversely with the cube of γ[17]. This figure plots the logarithm of the predicted entry times (normalized by the actual entry time for $\gamma = 1.0$) along with the logarithm of the observed entry times (once again normalized by observed entry times for $\gamma = 1.0$). The observed data (for two separate runs) are shown by the squares while the solid line shows the predicted entry times. As can be seen there is close agreement between predicted and observed entry times.

The continuum model predicts that clusters will be located at the modes of the smoothed source density. This means that in cases where the source density is asymmetric about the mode, the clusters will be biased off of the modes of the source by a predictable amount. A simulation experiment was designed to test our bias predictions. The CINN described above was used, but this time it was driven by a one-sided exponential source density. The

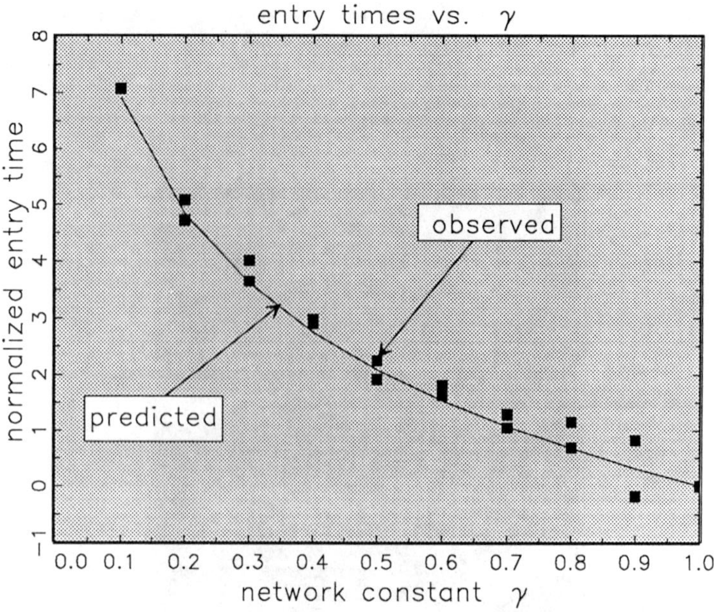

Figure 12: Simulation experiments corroborate continuum model's prediction that the formation rate of LTM clusters varies as $1/\gamma^3$.

predicted biases were computed for various network constants, γ,and are shown by the solid line in figure 13. The simulations were run till the network formed an impulsive distribution of LTM states. The location of this impulse was then observed over several presentation intervals to obtain a mean observed bias and its associated variance. In figure 13, the mean biases plus or minus one sample standard deviation are shown by the dashed error bars. These results indicate close agreement between the observed and predicted biases.

6.3 Competition's Role in CINN Learning

The continuum model showed that the CINN exhibits clustering provided the clustering constraints are satisfied. The astute reader will note, however, that the clustering constraints are also satisfied if $\beta = 0$, i.e. no competitive interaction. If this is so, then what is the significance, if any, of including competition into the CINN?

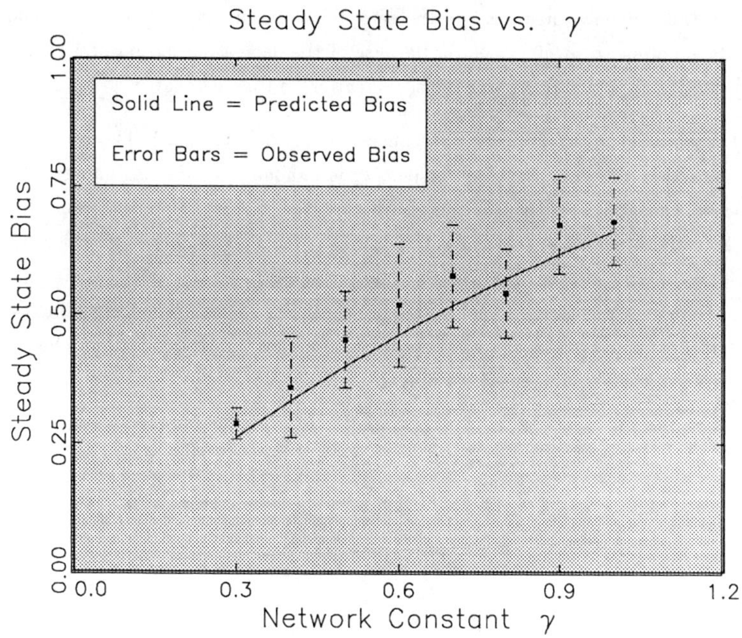

Figure 13: Simulation experiments corroborate continuum model's predictions concerning the LTM clusters location.

To answer this question, we return to section 6.1 where it was established that characteristics ascend the gradient of $B(\omega/\delta) * p(\omega)$. This function is a smoothed version of the source density where the degree of smoothing is controlled by the activation width, δ. The activation width, however, is inversely proportional to the neural density along that characteristic (equation 17). Therefore, characteristics with different neural densities will be attempting to maximize different smoothed density functions. This family of smoothed densities, $B(\omega/\delta) * p(\omega)$, is parameterized by the activation width, δ.

Now consider a point where neurons are clustering together. It can be shown[17] that the neural density at this cluster will be an increasing function of time. Since the activation width (Eq. 17) is inversely proportional to the neural density, it can be concluded that the activation width for this cluster is a decreasing function of time, $\delta(t)$. The characteristics associated with this cluster of neurons will therefore be ascending the gradient of a time-varying density function, $B(\omega/\delta(t)) * p(\omega)$. Because of the decreasing nature of $\delta(t)$, this time-varying density approaches the true density function as time gets large.

Figure 14 shows an example of the time varying density, $B(\omega/\delta(t)) * p(\omega)$. This particular example assumes that the underlying source density is bimodal. At the beginning of the learning process, the activation width is large so that the smoothed density, $p(\omega, \delta(0))$ is unimodal. As time increases, the amount of source smoothing decreases (because the activation width shrinks) so that after a given time the smoothed density is also bimodal. Since the LTM clusters are forming about the modes of the smoothed density function, this means that after a given time the LTM cluster will bifurcate into two distinct clusters centered about each of the source density's modes.

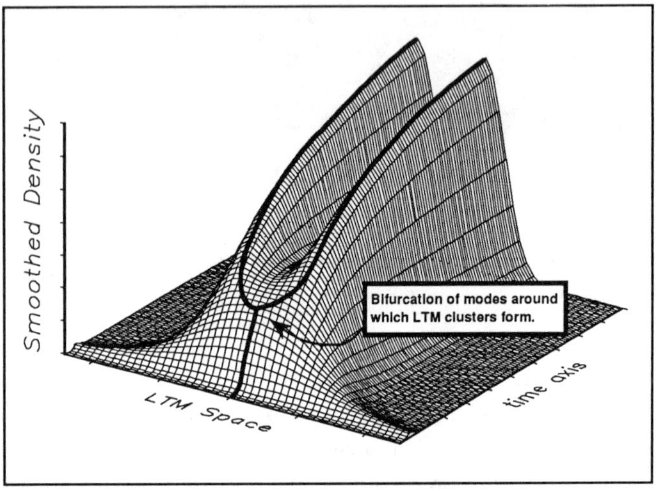

Figure 14: Global Search Property of CINN

Figure 15 shows a halftone image of the estimated neural density for a simulation experiment exhibiting this predicted behaviour. In this experiment the source is a bimodal Gaussian density. The initial neural density is uniformly distributed about one of these modes. For the appropriate choice of parameters β and θ the neural density evolves so that two clusters of LTM states form, one located at each mode.

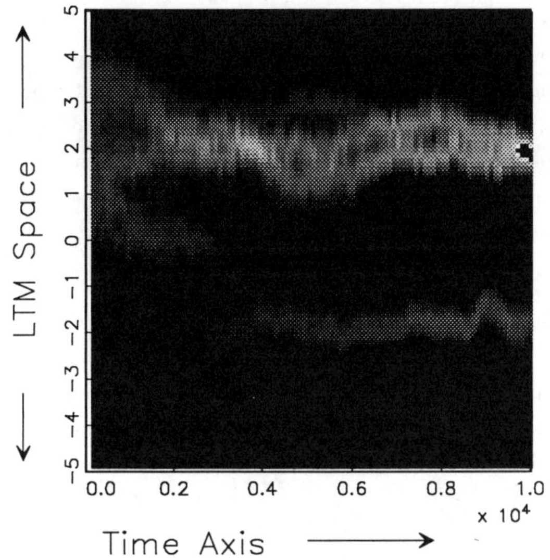

Figure 15: Simulation Example of Global Search Property

The behaviour observed in figure 15 has important consequences. It means that a CINN with nonzero competition levels has a chance of locating **all** the modes of the source density. We denote this property of the CINN as the **global search** property. It is a direct consequence of competitive interaction and therefore represents the primary role of competition in CINN learning.

7 CINN Applications

The preceding analyses and simulation examples showed that a CINN, driven by an ergodic source, will "cluster" its LTM state vectors about the modes of a smoothed version of the source's pdf. This clustering property suggests that, from a narrow point of view, the

LTM state vectors can be interpreted as estimates of the source density's modes. From a broader perspective, however, the entire distribution of LTM states can be treated as a **nonparametric** representation of the source's probabilistic structure.

Parameter estimation problems are often solved by finding the maximum mode of a performance function or suitable probability density function[20]. It is therefore logical to see if a CINN can be used as a parameter estimator. In particular, since the CINN forms a nonparametric representation of the source density we might expect such a CINN parameter estimator (CINNPE) to work on a wider class of estimation problems than any single existing technique can address today. This section shows how the CINN might be applied to parameter estimation problems and presents simulation results demonstrating a CINNPE being used for multitarget track initiation.

7.1 Parameter Estimation

The parameter estimation problem to be studied will be of the following form. Let $\bar{v}$ be a random p-dimensional vector called a **parameter.** Let $\bar{y}$ be an m-dimensional real ergodic process (also called the **observation process**) such that

$$\bar{y} = A(\bar{v}) + \bar{q} \quad , \tag{27}$$

where $A(\cdot)$ is a potentially nonlinear differentiable operator (called the **observation operator**) mapping the **parameter space,** $\Re^p$, onto the **observation space,** $\Re^m$, and where $\bar{q}$ is an m-dimensional white noise process with primary mode at zero (also called the **observation noise**).

Assume that the observation operator, $A(\cdot)$, is known and assume no prior statistical knowledge of the unknown parameter, $\bar{v}$, or the observation noise, $\bar{q}$. Finally assume that we have N sample outcomes, $(\bar{y}_1, \ldots, \bar{y}_N)$, of the observation process. The **parameter estimation problem** is to estimate the unknown parameter, $\bar{v}$, from the known sample outcomes.

A modified CINN can be used to solve the parameter estimation problem. This network is called the CINNPE. The CINNPE is a large scale nonautonomous dynamic system consisting of N_t neurons. The ith neuron's state is the ordered pair, $(x_i, \bar{z}_i)$, where x_i is the STM state and $\bar{z}_i$ is the LTM state vector. These states are dynamically modified by an applied input vector, $\bar{y}$. For our discussion, $\bar{y}$ is generated by an ergodic source and there exists a parameter, $\bar{v}$, such that equation 27 holds. The dynamics for the ith neuron are generated by the following ordinary differential equations.

$$\dot{x}_i = -x_i + E(\bar{y}, \bar{z}_i) + I_i \quad , \tag{28}$$

$$\dot{\bar{z}}_i = f(x_i)B(\bar{y} - A(\bar{z}_i)) \quad , \tag{29}$$

where $E(\bar{y}, \bar{z}_i)$ is the standard external stimulus function (Eq. 24) and I_i is the internal stimulus of equation 3. The network is assumed to satisfy the clustering constraints of section 6. The matrix, B, maps the observation space onto the parameter space, and $A(\cdot)$ is the known observation operator in equation 27.

The LTM state equation 29 establishes a relationship between the parameter, $\bar{v}$, and the LTM state vectors. The exact nature of this relationship will be discussed below. For now, however, we will define the **estimate**, $\hat{v}$, generated by the CINNPE as the LTM state of the neuron which was most stimulated by the current input vector. The reason for this definition will become clear in the discussion surrounding equation 31 This definition for the estimate means that the CINN must have some post-processing capabilities capable of extracting the LTM state of the most active neuron and passing that information to the user. Within the context of the original system equations, this output capability would be difficult to realize. If the network's state equations were implemented directly using analog circuitry, the extraction of a specific neuron's LTM state would require additional circuitry thereby adding a great deal of unnecessary complexity to the CINN implementation. This complexity is unnecessary because the CINN can be implemented on a fine-grained parallel machine using the CINN algorithm (see section 4). In this case, the post-processing function becomes very easy to implement. To extract the LTM states, the most active STM processing element (PE) will broadcast its status back to its associated LTM PEs who then output their LTM states over the computer's I/O bus.

The CINNPE is a generalization of the original CINN equations. If B and A are identity matrices and the parameter β is constant, then the CINNPE simplifies to the original CINN equations. One difference between the CINN and CINNPE lies in the generalization of the LTM state equation (Eq. 29). The modified LTM state dynamics represented in equation 29 were developed to account for dimensionality differences between the observation vectors, $\bar{y}$, and the parameter vector, $\bar{v}$. If there is no dimensional disparity, the CINNPE is a CINN and therefore admits a continuum model which predicts the clustering of LTM states about the source density's modes.

The same basic arguments can be used to prove that the CINNPE clusters LTM states even when the observation and parameter spaces have a dimensional disparity. Recall that the development of the continuum model relied on the fact that the LTM states of activated neurons would satisfy the following equation.

$$\begin{aligned} \bar{z}_j(T) &= e^{-T}\bar{z}_j(0) + (1-e^{-T})\bar{y} \\ &= (1-\epsilon)\bar{z}_j(0) + \epsilon\bar{y} \quad , \end{aligned} \tag{30}$$

where $\epsilon = 1 - e^{-T}$. Provided, $0 < 1 - \epsilon < 1$, then the continuum model's development follows as before and the network begins clustering LTM states about the source modes.

The CINNPE's LTM states also satisfy a relation similar to equation 30. If the CINNPE's LTM state update equation is expanded using a first order Taylor series[17], then the update can be rewritten as

$$\bar{z}_j(T) = (I - \epsilon BJ)\bar{z}_j(0) + \epsilon BJ\hat{v} + \hat{q} + o(|\bar{v} - \bar{z}_j|^2) \quad , \tag{31}$$

where $\epsilon = 1 - e^{-T}$, $\hat{v} = \bar{v} + \epsilon B\bar{q}$, $\hat{q} = \epsilon(I - \epsilon BJ)B\bar{q}$, $o(|\bar{v} - \bar{z}_j|^2)$ represents terms which are second order or higher, and J is the Jacobian matrix of A evaluated in the neighborhood of $\bar{z}_j(0)$. In equation 31, the stochastic process $\hat{v}$ is called the "associated parameter process". The associated parameter process has its primary mode at the unknown parameter we wish to estimate, $\bar{v}$. Since equation 31 has the same form as equation 30, we can think of the CINNPE as being a CINN driven by the associated parameter process $\hat{v}$. Under this viewpoint, if we can show that the CINNPE admits a continuum model, then we expect the LTM states to cluster about the modes of the associated parameter process (i.e. the unknown parameter).

The CINNPE admits a continuum model provided the matrix, ϵBJ, is diagonalizable with eigenvalues λ_i between zero and one[17] The trick, of course, is finding a matrix B such that this condition always holds. One choice is to let $B = J^t$. In this case the matrix factor becomes $I - \epsilon J^t J$. Since $J^t J$ is positive semidefinite, it has eigenvalues, $d_i \geq 0$, for $i = 1, \ldots, p$. We can therefore choose ϵ such that $0 < 1 - \epsilon d_i \leq 1$. If J has full rank then the right hand inequality becomes strict (i.e., $1 - \epsilon d_i < 1$) so that the LTM update becomes a contraction mapping. This condition is sufficient for the CINNPE to admit a continuum model predicting the clustering of LTM states.

7.2 Sample Application : Multitarget Track Initiation

The remainder of this section presents simulation results illustrating the application of a CINN. The particular example to be treated is the **multitarget track initiation problem** (MTIP).

Multitarget track initiation involves the estimation of target parameters when high target densities generate considerable ambiguity in the association of measurements and track hypotheses. Consider the following situation. A geosynchronous satellite (S/C) is designed to detect and track intercontinental ballistic missiles (ICBMs). Define a "frame" as the time interval over which missile "sightings" are gathered by the S/C sensor. A collection of sightings, gathered in a given frame, are output at the end of that frame. The ith sighting in the jth frame is characterized by a detection time t_{ij} and line of sight (LOS) measurement, (θ_{ij}, ϕ_{ij}), relative to the S/C field of view. The S/C's mission is to correlate the sightings in different frames to infer LOS, (θ, ϕ), and LOS rates, $(\dot{\theta}, \dot{\phi})$, for all observed missiles. An example of such a simulated scenario is shown in figure 16.

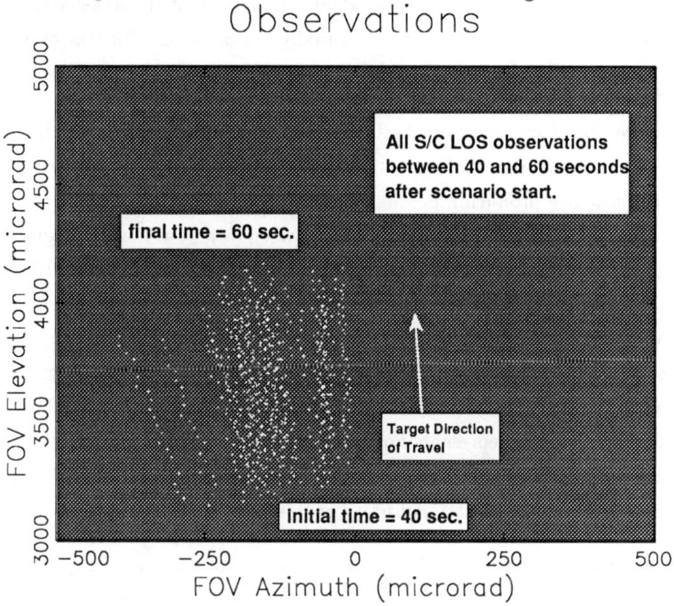

Figure 16: All S/C sightings between 40 and 60 seconds after scenario start

Inference of LOS rates requires correlating sightings from separate frame times with the same missile and then performing a linear regression. The difficulty with the MTIP is that the relative spacing of sightings in a single frame is too small to allow unambiguous interframe correlations. Standard approaches such as "Scan to Scan Correlation" (SSC) algorithms [21], involve splitting Kalman filter track hypotheses when ambiguity exists.

In dense target scenarios, however, this strategy leads to the uncontrolled proliferation of Kalman filter tracking hypotheses. The combinatorial explosion resulting from the proliferating filters can quickly overburden the S/C's computational resources.

How to use the CINN as a track initiator can be readily appreciated once we interpret the network as a prediction filter bank. In this interpretation, each neuron corresponds to a different prediction filter, (i.e., Kalman filter). Since the filter bank (i.e., network) is of fixed size we need not worry about overloading our computing resources. The association of observations with a given prediction filter (i.e., neuron) will be decided by competitive interactions between all filters. The continuum model for the CINN implies that this system must eventually cluster neural LTM states about the modes of the associated parameter process. In other words, the LTM states eventually converge to estimates of all the true target states.

Simulation results demonstrating the CINN track initiator are shown in figure 17 and 18. In this example, we simulated the tracking of thirty closely spaced targets from a geosynchronous satellite producing missile sightings once every half second. The assumed measurement noise was a quarter of the distance between targets at launch. Figure 17 shows the true targets and estimated target tracks at 30 and 60 seconds into flight. In this figure, the true target's position is denoted by a cross with a protruding straight solid line denoting the target's velocity vector. The length of this line represents the distance the target would travel over one second. The tracking filter estimates are represented in a similar manner, except that now the line is dashed and the estimated position is represented by an unfilled circle. The size of this circle represents how well the target is being tracked with respect to a figure of merit (FOM). The FOM shown in figure 17 is defined with respect to the tracking system's design requirements. FOM's of unity or less satisfy the tracking requirements.

Performance requirements for MTIP systems can be stated in a variety of ways. One common method is to require that the system track a given percentage of targets by a given time with a given degree of accuracy in both position and velocity. An example of such a requirement would be for the system to track 85 percent of all targets by 100 seconds after first launch with an LOS accuracy of 4 μradians and LOS rate accuracy of 2 μradians per second. These requirements will be used to assess the CINN track initiator's performance.

The CINN track initiator was designed so that a given input only generates an estimate if it lies within a specifed distance of one of the track filter's position estimates. This position gate was chosen to be 5 μrad. The number of estimates generated per frame represented the number of tracked targets. For each of these track estimates a "figure of merit" (FOM)

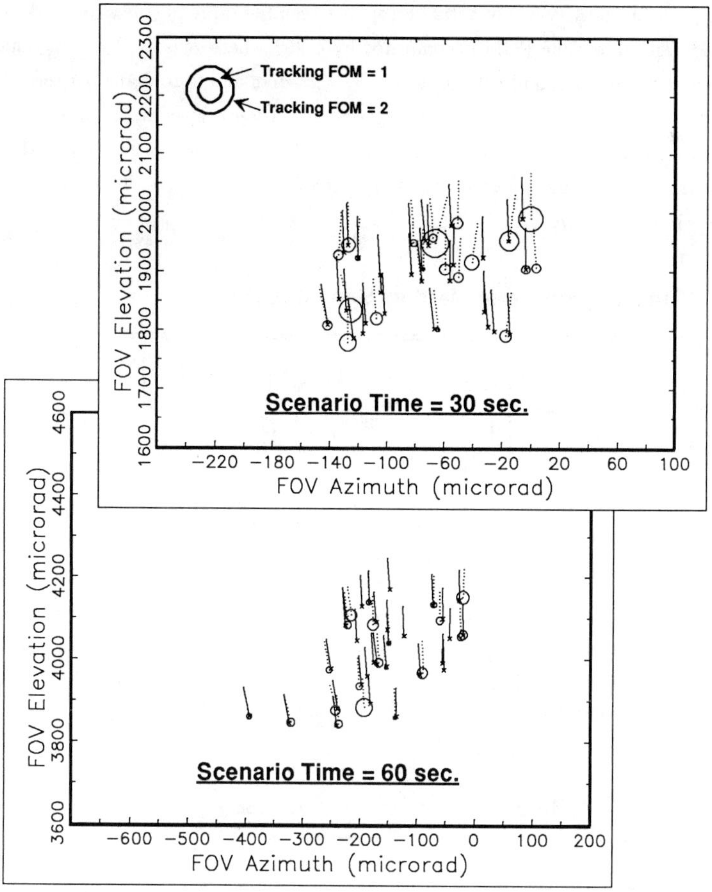

Figure 17: Simulation Example: True and estimated target tracks at 30 and 60 seconds after scenario start

was computed. Let ϵ be the 4-vector of actual errors between the target's true state and the track filter's state estimate. The FOM is computed by $\frac{1}{4}\epsilon R\epsilon^t$ where R is a 4 by 4 diagonal matrix normalizing the position and velocity errors by 4 μradian and 2 μradians per second, respectively. This means that the FOM is unity if the velocity error equals 2 μradian/sec and the position error equals 4 μradians. If a target track has a figure of merit less than unity then that track is meeting the accuracy requirements assumed above. This FOM was used to size the circles in figure 17.

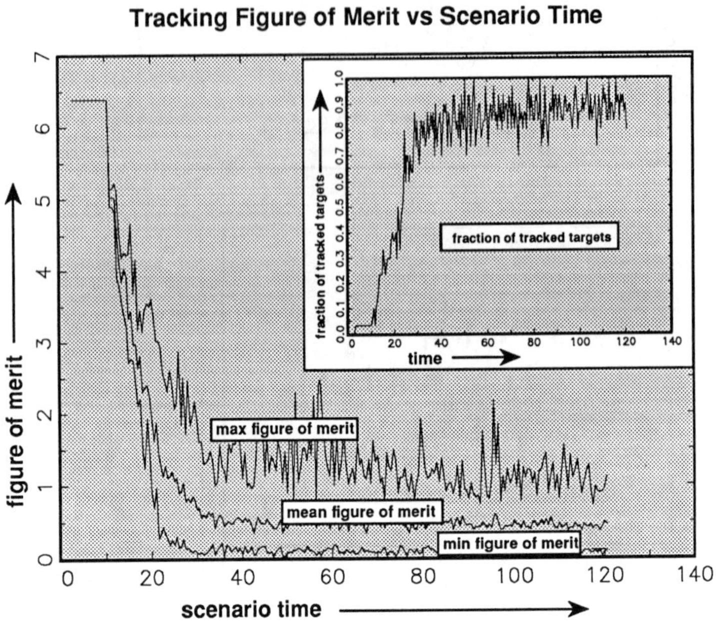

Figure 18: Simulation Example: Percentage of Tracked targets versus scenario time, Figure of Merit (max, mean, and min) versus scenario time

While figure 17 provides a snapshot of the CINN track initiator's performance at a specific time. The overall behaviour of the network is shown in figure 18. In this figure we have plotted the fraction of tracked targets (see insert) versus scenario time. The results show that by 100 seconds essentially 85 percent of the targets are being tracked. The accuracy of these tracking estimates is also shown in figure 18. We have plotted the figure of merit, defined above, versus scenario time. In particular, the maximum, minimum, and mean FOM over all tracks is shown. The results indicate that by 100 seconds after launch, the mean FOM is about .5 while the maximum FOM is a little greater than one.

The simulation results shown above indicate that the CINN track initiator is tracking an increasing percentage of targets with increasing accuracy. The tracker appears to meet the previously assumed performance requirements by finding 85 percent of the targets within 100 seconds after launch with a mean tracking figure of merit of less than 1.

8 Summary

One pervasive theme in biology is that of competitive interaction. This chapter has examined the role of competition in large scale computation by examining an artificial neural net where competition has been explicitly parameterized. For convenience, we have christened this net a "competitively inhibited neural net" or CINN. The principle results of this paper are itemized below

- The formulation of an input-output (I/O) characterization of the CINN's response to a constant input (the sliding threshold test). The reformulation of this characterization as an algorithmic procedure (CINN algorithm).
- The mapping of the CINN algorithm onto fine-grained parallel machines. The estimation of throughput rates for this implementation.
- The development of a continuum model characterizing the CINN's response to a random sequence of inputs. The analysis of this model and the subsequent formulation of the CINN clustering constraints.
- The quantitative predictions concerning the long run neural density for CINN satisfying the clustering constraints. The determination of competition's role in the learning process (global search property).
- The extension of the CINN to parameter estimation problems. The demonstration of a CINN parameter estimator application.

These accomplishments show that large scale systems like the CINN are amenable to formal analysis and that this analysis can provide important insight into the implementation and applications of neural nets.

References

[1] G. Carpenter and S. Grossberg. A massively parallel architecture for a self-organizing neural pattern recognition machine. *Computer Vision, Graphics, and Image Processing*, 37:54–115, 1987.

[2] G. Carrier and C. Pearson. *Partial Differential Equations, theory and technique.* Academic Press, New York, 1976.

[3] F.B. Christiansen and T.M. Fenchel. *Theories of Populations in Biological Communities.* Springer-Verlag, Berlin, 1977.

[4] R. Davis and D. Thomas. Systolic array chip matches the pace of high speed processing. *Electronic Design*, 32:207–218, 1984.

[5] Chr. Von der Malsburg. Self-organization of orientation sensitive cells in the striate cortex. *Kybernetik*, 14:85–100, 1973.

[6] R. Duda and P. Hart. *Pattern Classification and Scene Analysis.* John Wiley, New York, 1973.

[7] G. Ermentrout and J. Cowan. Large scale spatially organized activity in neural nets. *SIAM Journal of Applied Mathematics*, 38:1–21, 1980.

[8] J.A. Feldman and D.H. Ballard. Connectionist models and their properties. *Cognitive Science*, 6:141–152, 1985.

[9] S. Grossberg. Adaptive pattern classification and universal recoding: Ii. feedback, expectation, olfaction, illusion. *Biological Cybernetics*, 23:187–202, 1976.

[10] D. Hillis. *The Connection Machine.* MIT Press, 1985.

[11] M. Hirsch. Systems of differential equations that are competitive or cooperative ii: Convergence almost everywhere. *SIAM Journal of Mathematical Analysis*, 16:423–439, 1985.

[12] E. Kandel and J. Schwartz. Molecular biology of learning: Modulation of transmitte release. *Science*, 218:433–443, 1982.

[13] T. Kohonen. *Self-organization and Associative Memory.* Springer-Verlag, 1984.

[14] S. Kuffler and J. Nicholls. *From neuron to brain: a cellular approach to the function of the nervous system.* Sinauer Associates, Sunderland, MA, 1976.

[15] S.Y. Kung. *VLSI array processors.* Prentice Hall, Englewood Cliffs, NJ, 1988.

[16] P. Lax. *Hyperbolic Systems of Conservation Laws and the Mathematical Theory of Shock Waves*, volume 11 of *Regional Conference Series in Applied Mathematics.* SIAM, Philadelphia, 1973.

[17] M. Lemmon. *Parameter Estimation using Competitively Inhibited Neural Nets.* PhD thesis, Carnegie Mellon University, Pittsburgh PA 15213, April 1990.

[18] M. Lemmon and B.V.K. Vijaya Kumar. Emulating the dynamics for a class of laterally inhibited neural networks. *Neural Networks*, 2(3):193–214, 1989.

[19] B.W. Mel. *Murphy: A Neurally-Inspired Connectionist Approach to Learning and Performance in Vision-Based Robot Motion Planning.* Technical Report CCSR-89-17, Center for Complex Systems Research, University of Illinois at Urbana-Champaign, Feb 1989.

[20] A. Papoulis. *Probability, Random Variables, and Stochastic Processes.* McGraw-Hill, 2 edition, 1984.

[21] D. Reid. Tbd. *IEEE Trans. on Automatic Control*, AC-29(6), 1979.

[22] D. Rumelhart and D. Zipser. Feature discovery by competitive learning. In Rumelhart and McClelland, editors, *Parallel Distributed Processing: explorations in the microstructure of cognition.* MIT Press, 1986.

[23] L. Segel. *Mathematical Models in Molecular and Cellular Biology.* Cambridge University Press, 1980.

[24] H. Smith. Systems of ordinary differential equations which generate an order preserving flow. *SIAM Review*, 30:87–113, 1988.

[25] R. Sutton and A. Barto. Toward a modern theory of adaptive networks: expectation and prediction. *Psychological Review*, 88(2):135–170, 1981.

[26] J. Tapia. *Nonparametric Probability Density Estimation.* Johns Hopkins University Press, 1983.

4

HARMONIC ANALYSIS OF NEURAL NETWORKS

Jehoshua Bruck

Abstract

Neural networks models can be described as a network in which every node computes a linear threshold function. One of the main difficulties in analyzing the properties of these networks is the fact that they consist of nonlinear elements. However, it is well known that, when we consider linear systems, Fourier analysis is a very powerful tool. Are those tools useful for analyzing neural networks (which are nonlinear)? The main theme in this chapter is to show (via many interesting results) that harmonic analysis is a useful tool when we deal with neural networks. In particular, I will show how this technique can be applied to answer the following two fundamental questions (i) what is the computational power of a polynomial threshold element with respect to linear threshold elements? (ii) Is it possible to get exponentially many spurious memories when we use the outer-product method for programming the Hopfield model?

1 Introduction

The main purpose of this chapter is to introduce a useful tool for the analysis of discrete neural networks in which every node is a Boolean threshold gate. The difficulty in the analysis of neural networks arises from the fact that the basic processing elements (linear threshold gates) are nonlinear. The key idea in harmonic analysis of threshold functions is to represent the functions as polynomials over the field of real numbers. Answering different questions regarding neural networks becomes equivalent to answering questions related to the coefficients of these polynomials.

We will introduce the basic concepts of harmonic analysis of Boolean functions and mention two applications to neural networks. The first application is related to feedforward networks—we prove that a two layer feedforward network of linear threshold gates can compute strictly more than a single polynomial threshold gate [2]. The second application is related to the Hopfield model—we prove that the outer-product method for programming the Hopfield model can result in many spurious stable states(exponential in the number of vectors that we want to store) [4]. Also, we describe applications of harmonic analysis for proving that a given function is not linear threshold and for getting upper bounds on the number of polynomial threshold functions.

The chapter is organized as follows, in the next section we prove the representation theorem. In Section 3 we describe a few basic properties of the polynomial representation. In Section 4 and 5 we present the necessary and sufficient condition for a function to be polynomial threshold and its applications to counting and to proving that a given function is not polynomial threshold. In Section 6 we describe the application to getting lower bounds on the number of spurious memories in the Hopfield model.

2 The Representation Theorem

In this section the representation of Boolean functions as polynomials over the field of rational numbers is presented. This representation was first suggested by Muller [16] and then was used by Ninomiya [18] and Golomb [8] to get results on counting the number of equivalent Boolean functions. See [13] for an excellent presentation of the subject.

In what follows we present a novel derivation of the representation theorem. Throughout this chapter a Boolean function f of n variables is a mapping,

$$f : \{1, -1\}^n \mapsto \{1, -1\}.$$

Note that we use the multiplicative representation of $\{0, 1\}$ via the transformation $a \mapsto (-1)^a$.

Definition: Given a Boolean function f of order n, p is a polynomial (with coefficients over the field of rational numbers) *equivalent* to f iff for all $X \in \{1, -1\}^n$:

$$f(X) = p(X).$$

As an example, let $f = x_1 \oplus x_2$; that is, f is the XOR function of two variables. It is easy to check that in the $\{1, -1\}$ representation $p(x_1, x_2) = x_1 x_2$.

Notice that for every Boolean function f, the polynomial p is linear in each of its variables because $x^2 = 1$ for $x \in \{-1, 1\}$. It is known that every Boolean function has a unique representation as a polynomial [13] . This representation is derived by using the Hadamard matrix, as described by Theorem 1 below. Let's start by defining Hadamard matrices,

Definition: A *Hadamard matrix* of order m, to be denoted by H_m, is an $m \times m$ matrix of +1's and -1's such that

$$H_m H_m^T = mI_m \tag{1}$$

where I_m is the $m \times m$ identity matrix. The above definition is equivalent to saying that any two rows of H are orthogonal.

Hadamard matrices of order 2^k exist for all $k \geq 0$. The so called Sylvester construction is as follows [14]:

$$\begin{aligned} H_1 &= [1] \\ H_2 &= \begin{bmatrix} 1 & 1 \\ 1 & -1 \end{bmatrix} \\ H_{2^{n+1}} &= \begin{bmatrix} H_{2^n} & H_{2^n} \\ H_{2^n} & -H_{2^n} \end{bmatrix} \end{aligned} \tag{2}$$

Theorem 1 *Let f be a Boolean function of order n. Let p be a polynomial equivalent to f. Let A_{2^n} denote the vector of coefficients of p. Let P_{2^n} denote the vector of the 2^n values of p (and f). Then:*

1. *The polynomial p always exists and is unique.*

2. *The coefficients of p are computed as follows,*

$$A_{2^n} = \frac{1}{2^n} H_{2^n} P_{2^n}.$$

Proof: The proof is constructive. The idea is to compute A_{2^n} by solving a system of linear equations. Let us start by computing the coefficients of p, for f being a function of one variable:

$$p(x_1) = a_0 + a_1 x_1$$

and,

$$\begin{aligned} p(1) &= a_0 + a_1 \\ p(-1) &= a_0 - a_1. \end{aligned}$$

Clearly,

$$P_2 = H_2 A_2 \tag{3}$$

and by (1),

$$A_2 = \frac{1}{2} H_2 P_2. \tag{4}$$

The above can be generalized to n variables by induction on n. Assume it is true for n

$$P_{2^n} = H_{2^n} A_{2^n}.$$

For (n+1), consider the different values of x_{n+1} and get

$$\begin{aligned} P_{2^{n+1}} &= \begin{bmatrix} H_{2^n} & H_{2^n} \\ H_{2^n} & -H_{2^n} \end{bmatrix} A_{2^{n+1}} \\ &= H_{2^{n+1}} A_{2^{n+1}}. \end{aligned}$$

Hadamard matrices are nonsingular; thus, for any given f a unique p (defined by the vector of coefficients A_{2^n}) always exists. □

Example: Consider the function $f(x_1, x_2) = x_1 \wedge x_2$. Then
$f(1,1) = 1$, $f(1,-1) = 1$, $f(-1,1) = 1$ and $f(-1,-1) = -1$.
By Theorem 1:

$$\frac{1}{4} \begin{bmatrix} 1 & 1 & 1 & 1 \\ 1 & -1 & 1 & -1 \\ 1 & 1 & -1 & -1 \\ 1 & -1 & -1 & 1 \end{bmatrix} \begin{bmatrix} 1 \\ 1 \\ 1 \\ -1 \end{bmatrix} = \begin{bmatrix} 0.5 \\ 0.5 \\ 0.5 \\ -0.5 \end{bmatrix}. \tag{5}$$

Hence,

$$f(x_1, x_2) = \frac{1}{2}(1 + x_1 + x_2 - x_1 x_2).$$

Notation: The entries of the vector A are denoted by $\{a_\alpha \mid \alpha \in \{0,1\}^n\}$ and are called the spectral representation of a function. Note that a_α is the coefficient of X^α in the polynomial representation where $X^\alpha = x_1^{\alpha_1} x_2^{\alpha_2} \ldots x_n^{\alpha_n}$. Hence, every Boolean function can be written as:

$$f(X) = \sum_{\alpha \in \{0,1\}^n} a_\alpha X^\alpha.$$

The above method is applicable not only to Boolean functions but also to any function of the form $f : \{1,-1\}^n \longrightarrow \Re$.

3 Basic Properties

Here we give some very basic properties of the representation, in all the lemmas below, f denotes a Boolean function and $\{a_\alpha \mid \alpha \in \{0,1\}^n\}$ is its spectral representation:

Lemma 1 Orthogonalty:

$$\sum_{X \in \{1,-1\}^n} X^\alpha = \begin{cases} 2^n & \textit{if } \alpha = \textit{all-0 vector} \\ 0 & \textit{else.} \end{cases}$$

Proof: The result follows from the fact that every X^α corresponds to a row in a Sylvester type Hadamard matrix. Every row, but the first, has the same number of 1's and -1's (proved by induction). □

Lemma 2 Zero-Value:

$$\sum_{\alpha \in \{0,1\}^n} a_\alpha = f(1,1,\ldots,1) \in \{1,,-1\}.$$

Proof: Let $f(X) = \sum_{\alpha \in \{0,1\}^n} a_\alpha X^\alpha$, the result is obtained by plugging $X = (1,1,\ldots,1)$.□

Lemma 3 Moments:

$$\sum_{X \in \{1,-1\}^n} f(X) X^\alpha = 2^n a_\alpha$$

for all $\alpha \in \{0,1\}^n$.

Proof: The result follows from the Orthogonality Lemma, by considering the terms of $f(X)X^\alpha$. □

Lemma 4 Correlation:

$$\sum_{X\in\{1,-1\}^n} f(X)\hat{f}(X) = 2^n \sum_{\alpha\in\{0,1\}^n} a_\alpha \hat{a}_\alpha.$$

Proof: The result follows by application of the Moments Lemma. □

Lemma 5 a special case of Parseval's Theorem:

$$\sum_{X\in\{1,-1\}^n} f^2(X) = 2^n \sum_{\alpha\in\{0,1\}^n} a_\alpha^2 = 2^n.$$

Proof: Since $f(X) \in \{1,-1\}$ one identity is trivial. The second is a special case of the Correlation Lemma. □

Hence, $\sum_{\alpha\in\{0,1\}^n} a_\alpha^2 = 1$. The power spectrum of a Boolean function sums to 1.

4 Necessary and Sufficient Condition for Threshold Functions and their Applications

We use the polynomial representation of Boolean functions presented in the previous section to derive a necessary and sufficient condition for a function to be an S-threshold function, for arbitrary S. A Boolean function $f(X)$ is S-threshold, for a given set $S \subset \{0,1\}^n$, iff there exist weights such that $f(X) = sgn(\sum_{\alpha\in S} w_\alpha X^\alpha)$. This result turned out to be a generalization of a known result for linear threshold functions [6,11,17]. The results in this section and in the next section are based on [2] were more details can be found.

Let $f(X) = sgn(F(X))$ be a threshold function. Without loss of generality, assume that $F(X) \neq 0$ for all $X \in \{1,-1\}^n$. The following simple lemma enables us to express the relation between $f(X)$ and $F(X)$ in a global way. That is, instead of having 2^n conditions we have only one.

Lemma 6 *Let $f(X)$ be a Boolean function and let $F(X) \neq 0$ for all $X \in \{1,-1\}^n$; then*

$$f(X) = sgn(F(X)) \qquad \forall X \in \{1,-1\}^n \tag{6}$$

iff

$$\sum_{X\in\{1,-1\}^n} | F(X) | = \sum_{X\in\{1,-1\}^n} f(X)F(X). \tag{7}$$

Proof: Suppose there exists an X_1 that violates (6); that implies ($F(X) \neq 0$ for all X) that

$$| F(X_1) | > f(X_1)F(X_1).$$

Hence, (7) is also not true because violation in equation (6) can only decrease the value on the right hand side of (7). Clearly, if (6) is true so is (7). □

The necessary and sufficient condition follows from (7) by using the polynomial representation of a Boolean function.

Theorem 2 *Fix $S \subseteq \{0,1\}^n$. Let $F(X) = \sum_{\alpha\in S} w_\alpha X^\alpha$. Let $f(X)$, $X \in \{-1,1\}^n$, be a Boolean function with spectral representation $\{a_\alpha \mid \alpha \in \{0,1\}^n\}$. Then:*

$$f(X) = sgn(F(X)) \qquad \forall X \in \{1,-1\}^n$$

iff

$$\sum_{X\in\{1,-1\}^n} | F(X) | = 2^n \sum_{\alpha\in S} w_\alpha a_\alpha. \tag{8}$$

Proof: By the Lemma 6 it is enough to show that

$$\sum_{X\in\{1,-1\}^n} f(X)F(X) = 2^n \sum_{\alpha\in S} w_\alpha a_\alpha.$$

We write $f(X)$ as a polynomial:

$$f(X) = \sum_{\alpha\in\{0,1\}^n} a_\alpha X^\alpha$$

and find that the constant term of $f(X)F(X)$ is $\sum_{\alpha\in S} w_\alpha a_\alpha$. Hence, the result follows from the Orthogonality Lemma. □

Theorem 2 is interesting because it suggests that an S-threshold function is fully characterized by the set of spectral coefficients that correspond to S. To see the power of the condition we present two applications. The first application (Theorem 3) is a generalization of the known result that PARITY is not in LT_1 and the second application (Theorem 4) is an upper bound on the number of S-threshold functions.

Theorem 3 *Let*

$$PARITY(X) = \begin{cases} -1 & \text{odd number of } -1\text{'s in } X \\ 1 & \text{otherwise.} \end{cases}$$

Then PARITY is not an S-threshold function for any S such that the all-1 vector is not in S, i.e., $(1,1,\ldots,1) \notin S$.

Proof: Note that PARITY$(X) = x_1 x_2 \cdots x_n$; hence, for a set S that does not include the all-1 vector we have

$$\sum_{X\in\{1,-1\}^n} | F(X) | \neq 2^n \sum_{\alpha\in S} w_\alpha a_\alpha = 0.$$

Thus, the condition cannot be satisfied ($F(X) \neq 0$). □

A nice interpretation of this result is as follows: the X^α form a basis for the space of Boolean functions. Hence, by the definition of a basis, an element of the basis cannot be represented as a linear combination of the other elements in the basis. What Theorem 3 is saying is that it is also impossible to represent an element of the basis as the *sign* of a linear combination of the other elements in the basis.

Lemma 7 *Let f_1 and f_2 be Boolean functions with $\{a^i_\alpha \mid \alpha \in \{0,1\}^n\}$, $i = 1,2$, as their spectral representation, respectively. Assume that at least one of the functions is an S-threshold function. Then $f_1(X) = f_2(X)$ for all $X \in \{1,-1\}^n$ iff $a^1_\alpha = a^2_\alpha$ for all $\alpha \in S$.*

Proof: Suppose $f_1 = f_2$. By the uniqueness of the spectral representation (Theorem 1) we get the 'only if'. Assume with loss of generality that f_1 is an S-threshold function. Now suppose $a^1_\alpha = a^2_\alpha$ for all $\alpha \in S$. By Theorem 2 and the assumption that f_1 is S-threshold we get that there exists a set of weights that satisfies (8) for both f_1 and f_2. Hence, f_2 is also S-threshold and $F_1(X) = F_2(X)$ for all $X \in \{1, -1\}^n$. Thus, $f_1 = f_2$. □

Corollary 1 *Consider the set $S \subseteq \{0,1\}^n$. Let f_1 and f_2 be Boolean functions of n variables. If $a^1_\alpha = a^2_\alpha$ for all $\alpha \in S$, then either both f_1 and f_2 are S-threshold or both are not S-threshold.*

One application of the above is counting the number of different S-threshold functions.

Theorem 4 *Fix $S \subseteq \{0,1\}^n$. There are at most $2^{(n+1)|S|}$ different S-threshold functions.*

Proof: It can be shown that for all $\alpha \in \{0,1\}$, a_α can assume at most $(2^n + 1)$ different values. Hence, there are at most $2^{(n+1)|S|}$ different sets of $|S|$ spectral coefficients. Thus, the result follows from Corollary 1 . □

The above turned out to be a generalization of a known [11,17] upper bound on the number of linear threshold functions for which $|S| = n + 1$.

5 Characterization of Polynomial Threshold Functions

The necessary and sufficient condition that is derived above is used to derive lower bounds on the number of monomials in a threshold function, again, by using the spectral representation.

Let $f(X) = sgn(F(X))$ be an S-threshold function, namely,

$$F(X) = \sum_{\alpha \in S} w_\alpha X^\alpha.$$

We want to find lower bounds for $|S|$ as a function of the spectral representation of $f(X)$.

Lemma 8 *For all $\alpha \in S$:*

$$2^n \mid w_\alpha \mid \leq \sum_{X \in \{1,-1\}^n} \mid F(X) \mid .$$

Proof: First we prove the statement for α being the all-0 vector:

$$\begin{aligned}\sum_{X\in\{1,-1\}^n} |F(X)| &= \sum_{F(X)>0} F(X) - \sum_{F(X)<0} F(X) \\ &= \sum_{X\in\{1,-1\}^n} F(X) - 2\sum_{F(X)<0} F(X) \\ &\overset{(a)}{=} 2^n w_{00\ldots00} - 2\sum_{F(X)<0} F(X) \\ &\geq 2^n w_{00\ldots00}.\end{aligned}$$

Note that (a) follows from the Orthogonality Lemma. The proof for arbitrary α follows from the fact that $| X^\alpha | = 1$, hence:

$$| F(X) | = | X^\alpha || F(X) | = | X^\alpha F(X) | .$$

Hence, we can make any w_α be the constant term without changing the value of $|F(X)|$. If $w_\alpha < 0$ we take $-F(X)$ and get the result. □

Theorem 5 *Let $f(X) = sgn(\sum_{\alpha\in S} w_\alpha X^\alpha)$ be an S-threshold function and let $\{a_\alpha \mid \alpha \in \{0,1\}^n\}$ be its spectral representation; then*

$$\begin{aligned}|S| &\overset{(i)}{\geq} (\sum_{\alpha\in S} p_\alpha | a_\alpha |)^{-1} \\ &\overset{(ii)}{\geq} \hat{a}^{-1}\end{aligned}$$

where

$$p_\alpha = \frac{| w_\alpha |}{\sum_{\alpha\in S} | w_\alpha |}$$

and

$$\hat{a} = \max_{\alpha\in S} | a_\alpha | .$$

Proof: We first prove (i). By Theorem 2 and Lemma 8, for all $\alpha \in S$:

$$| w_\alpha | \leq \sum_{\alpha\in S} w_\alpha a_\alpha .$$

We sum the above inequality over all $\alpha \in S$ and get:

$$\begin{aligned}\sum_{\alpha\in S} | w_\alpha | &\leq | S | \sum_{\alpha\in S} w_\alpha a_\alpha \\ &\leq | S | \sum_{\alpha\in S} | w_\alpha || a_\alpha | .\end{aligned}$$

So we get (i). For (ii), just notice that $p_\alpha \geq 0$ and $\sum p_\alpha = 1$. □

Notice that using the same approach we can get even a better lower bound,

Theorem 6 *Let $f(X) = sgn(\sum_{\alpha\in S} w_\alpha X^\alpha)$ be an S-threshold function and let $\{a_\alpha \mid \alpha \in \{0,1\}^n\}$ be its spectral representation; then $\sum_{\alpha\in S} |a_\alpha| \geq 1$.*

Based on Theorem 5 we can prove the following fundamental result [2]: Every Boolean function that can be computed as a sign of a polynomial with a polynomial number of terms can be computed by a 2-layer, polynomial size circuit of linear threshold elements. On the other hand, there are Boolean functions that can be computed by a polynomial size 2-layer circuit of linear threshold elements that *cannot* be computed as a sign of a polynomial with only a polynomial number of terms. One of the conclusions of this result is that it is better to use linear threshold elements than to use polynomial threshold elements.

6 Spurious Memories in the Hopfield Model

This section is based on [4] were more details can be found. Here we consider the neural network model that was suggested by Hopfield in 1982 [10]. It is a discrete time system that can be represented by a weighted graph. There is a weight attached to each edge of the graph and a threshold value attached to each node (neuron) of the graph. The *order* of the network is the number of nodes in the corresponding graph. Let N be a neural network of order n; then N is uniquely defined by (W, T) where:

- W is an $n \times n$ matrix, with element w_{ij} equal to the weight attached to edge (i, j);

- T is a vector of dimension n, where element t_i denotes the threshold attached to node i.

Every node (neuron) can be in one of two possible states, either 1 or -1. The state of node i at time t is denoted by $v_i(t)$. The *state* of the neural network at time t is the vector $V(t) = (v_1(t), v_2(t), \ldots, v_n(t))$.

The state of a node at time $(t+1)$ is computed by:

$$v_i(t+1) = sgn(H_i(t)) = \begin{cases} 1 & \text{if } H_i(t) \geq 0 \\ -1 & \text{otherwise} \end{cases} \tag{9}$$

where

$$H_i(t) = \sum_{j=1}^{n} w_{j,i} v_j(t) - t_i.$$

The next state of the network, i.e. $V(t+1)$, is computed from the current state by performing the evaluation (9) at a single node of the network. This mode of operation is known as serial or asynchronous mode. The node at which the computation is performed can be chosen at random or according to some deterministic rule.

A state $V(t)$ is called *stable* iff $V(t) = sgn(WV(t) - T)$, i.e., the state of the network is not changing as a result of computation. The set of stable states of a network N is denoted by M_N.

One of the most important properties of the model is the fact that when it operates in a serial mode it will always get to a stable state (provided W is a symmetric matrix with nonnegative diagonal); see [3,7,10] for more details on convergence properties. This property suggests the use of the model as an associative memory device. An associative memory is a device which "memorizes" a set M of distinct n-bit vectors. It gets as an input an n-bit vector and its output is a vector which belongs to M and is the closest (e.g. in Hamming distance) to the input vector. The idea is that a network N can implement an associative memory with $M \subseteq M_N$ and the association done by convergence to the closest stable state. There are many interesting questions related to this idea—see for example [1,5,12,15].

One of the interesting issues concerning the use of the network as an associative memory is: how should one *program the network?*

Programming of a network can be defined as follows: Consider the set $M = \{V_1, V_2, \ldots, V_s\}$ that consists of s vectors over $\{1, -1\}^n$. Construct a network $N = (W, T)$ such that $M \subseteq M_N$, i.e. the set M is a subset of the set of stable states of N. Hopfield [10] suggested computing W by the *outer-product* method (which is a Hebb-type of rule [9]). Namely,

$$W = \sum_{i=1}^{s}(V_i V_i^T - I_n)$$

where I_n is the $n \times n$ identity matrix. Using this method, T is chosen to be the all-zero vector. Note that if the V_i's are orthogonal then

$$WV_1 = (n - s)V_1.$$

Since $n > s$, every one of the V_i's is stored. Hence, a natural question is: are there any other (spurious) stable states? Namely, what can be said about the number of stable states that are not in M?

The main contribution reported in this section is that in certain cases the number of spurious memories (vectors which are in M_N but not in M) can be exponentially (in s) big. Our results hold for the three following cases which cover all the possibilities for s:

1. s is "small" : $1 \leq s \leq \log n$.

2. s is "big" : $n - \log n \leq s < n$.

3. The intermediate cases: $s = 2^k$, where $0 \leq k < \log n$.

The results are the first constructive evidence for the results in [1,15,19] where such a phenomenon was suggested based on probabilistic arguments.

We include here a detailed description of the result for "small" s, namely, for $1 \leq s \leq \log n$. For more details the reader can refer to [4].

Theorem 7 *Let $s \geq 1$ be odd. Let $n = 2^s$. Consider the s vectors $X_1, X_2, \ldots X_s$ over $\{1,-1\}^n$ that correspond to the Boolean functions defined by the x_i's. Let W be the matrix that is computed by the outer-product method, i.e.*

$$W = \sum_{i=1}^{s}(X_iX_i^T - I_n).$$

Consider the vectors of the form

$$U_\beta = sgn(\sum_{i=1}^{s} \beta_i X_i)$$

where $\beta = (\beta_1, \beta_2, \ldots, \beta_s)$. Then: (i) For all $\beta \in \{1,0,-1\}^s$, such that the support of β (number of nonzero entries in β) is odd, the vector U_β is stable in the network $N = (W,T)$ (T is the all-zero vector). (ii) All the $\frac{3^s+1}{2}$ U_β's that correspond to β with odd support are distinct.

Proof: The idea in the proof is to compute WU_β and to show that $sgn(WU_\beta) = U_\beta$. First we prove that for β being the all-1 vector and for all $1 \leq i \leq s$ we have

$$X_i^T U_\beta = 2\binom{s-1}{\frac{s-1}{2}}.$$

Using the notation related to the polynomial representaion, $X_1^T U_\beta = 2^s a_{1,0,\ldots 0}$. Namely, the inner product of U_β with X_1 is just the corresponding spectral coefficient times 2^s. Without loss of generality we prove the result for $i = 1$. Notice that for β being the all-1 vector the vector U_β corresponds to the MAJORITY function of s variables. To compute the spectral coefficient that corresponds to X_1 consider the vector

$$V = X_2 + X_3 + \cdots + X_s.$$

Clearly, V is zero in $2\binom{s-1}{\frac{s-1}{2}}$ entries. For example, for s=3, $X_2 + X_3$ is zero in 4 entries. There is a symmetry in the values of the other entries, half of them being negative and half positive. Hence, in $X_1^T sgn(X_1 + V)$, the positive and negative entries cancel each other and we get as a result $2\binom{s-1}{\frac{s-1}{2}}$. By similar arguments we get the result for general β with odd support w:

$$X_i^T U_\beta = \beta_i 2^{s-w+1}\binom{w-1}{\frac{w-1}{2}}.$$

Hence for β with odd support w we have

$$WU_\beta = 2^{s-w+1}\binom{w-1}{\frac{w-1}{2}}\sum_{i=1}^{s}\beta_i X_i - sU_\beta.$$

From the foregoing equation it follows that the sign of WU_β is dominated by the sign of

$$\sum_{i=1}^{s}\beta_i X_i.$$

Thus, for all odd $s \geq 1$ and $\beta \in \{1, 0, -1\}^s$, such that the support of β is odd, we have $sgn(WU_\beta) = U_\beta$. The U_β's are distinct because they all have a distinct polynomial representation. □

7 Concluding Remarks

We have introduced the tool of harmonic analysis in the framework of neural networks. Doing that we were able to obtain a few interesting results related to the computational capabilities of feedforward networks as well as results related to the dynamics of the Hopfied model. It will be interesting to find out whether those tools are useful in the framework of learning with neural networks.

References

[1] Y. S. Abu-Mostafa and J. M. St. Jacques. Information capacity of the Hopfield model. *IEEE Transactions on Information Theory*, 31(4):461–464, 1985.

[2] J. Bruck. Harmonic analysis of polynomial threshold functions. *SIAM Journal on Discrete Mathematics*, February 1990. To Appear.

[3] J. Bruck and J. W. Goodman. A generalized convergence theorem for neural networks. *IEEE Transactions on Information Theory*, 34:1089–1092, September 1988.

[4] J. Bruck and V. Roychowdhury. On the number of spurious memories in the hopfield model. *IEEE Transactions on Information Theory*, 1989. To appear.

[5] J. Bruck and J. Sanz. A study on neural networks. *International Journal of Intelligent Systems*, 3:59–75, 1988.

[6] C. K. Chow. On the characterization of threshold functions. In *Proc. Symp. on Switching Circuit Theory and Logical Design*, pages 34–38, 1961.

[7] E. Goles, F. Fogelman, and D. Pellegrin. Decreasing energy functions as a tool for studying threshold networks. *Discrete Applied Mathematics*, 12:261–277, 1985.

[8] S. W. Golomb. *Shift Register Sequences.* Aegean Park Press, California, 1982.

[9] D. O. Hebb. *The Organization of Behavior.* John Wiley & Sons, New York, 1949.

[10] J. J. Hopfield. Neural networks and physical systems with emergent collective computational abilities. *Proceedings of the National Academy of Sciences USA*, 79:2554–2558, 1982.

[11] S. Hu. *Threshold Logic.* University of California Press, 1965.

[12] J. Komolós and R. Paturi. Effect of connectivity in associative memory models. In *29th FOCS*, pages 138–149, 1988.

[13] R. J. Lechner. Harmonic analysis of switching functions. In A. Mukhopadhyay, editor, *Recent Development in Switching Theory*, Academic Press, 1971.

[14] F. J. MacWilliams and N. J. A. Sloane. *The Theory of Error-Correcting Codes.* North-Holland, New York, 1977.

[15] R. J. McEliece, E. C. Posner, E. R. Rodemich, and S. S. Venkatesh. The capacity of the Hopfield associative memory. *IEEE Transactions on Information Theory*, 33(4):461–482, 1987.

[16] D. E. Muller. Application of Boolean algebra to switching circuit design and to error detection. *IRE Trans. on Elect. Computers*, 3:6–12, 1954.

[17] S. Muroga. *Threshold Logic and its Application.* John Wiley & Sons Inc., 1971.

[18] I. Ninomiya. A theory of coordinate representation of switching functions. *Memoirs of the Faculty of Engineering, Nagoya University*, 10:175–190, 1958.

[19] F. Tanaka and S. F. Edwards. Analytic theory of ground state properties of a spin glass: I. ising spin glass. *J. Phys. F: Metal Phys.*, 10:2769–2778, 1980.

5

NEURAL TRANSFORMS OF SENSORY STIMULI
Neural Networks in Explanations of Perceputal Phenomena

by Dejan Todorovic,
Laboratory of Experimental Psychology,
University of Belgrade

In this paper I will discuss how the conceptual framework of neural networks, based on data from sensory physiology, can be applied in the construction of theories of perception. The discussion will be limited to the visual and somatic modalities, which are endowed with extended sensory surfaces specialized for spatial processing. The paper has five parts. Part One presents some classical perceptual issues and gives an outline of three theoretical approaches. Part Two discusses some basic aspects of the structure and function of neurosensory systems, and introduces several concepts which are useful in the study of such systems. Parts Three and Four illustrate the application of these concepts in a model of spatial somatosensory discrimination, and a model of brightness perception. Part Five contains some further comments on the approach outlined in the paper.

1. Perception

Perception relates organisms to the world around them. Experimental studies of perception provide information on how various constellations of environmental conditions are linked to perceptual reactions of organisms. Two classes of phenomena involving perception can be distinguished, depending on the explanatory role of memory and experience. The first class, which will not be further considered, comprises various phenomena that by definition involve memory and experience, such as pattern recognition, object identification, reading, and the like. The second class is comprised by phenomena for whose explanation memory and experience are not strictly necessary, although such explanations can be and have been invoked. They include modality-specific phenomena such as color and brightness in vision, or touch, heat, cold and pain in somatic perception, as well as multi-modal phenomena such as form, texture, space and motion perception.

Organisms have extraordinary capacities for the veridical detection of structure and variations of the environment. The explanation of this faithful reflection of environmental aspects in organismic percepts is a crucial task for perceptual theories. However, in the history of perception enormous attention has been devoted to cases in which stimulus attributes (properties and relations of stimuli) are not reflected in analogous perceptual attributes. Examples of mismatch of stimuli and percepts provide important constraints for perceptual theories, because cases where perception 'goes wrong' can shed light on the manner in which it 'goes right', as it usually does.

To analyze these phenomena it is important to distinguish the concepts of the distal stimulus, the proximal stimulus, and the percept. The **distal stimulus** consists of intrinsic spatial, temporal, qualitative and intensive characteristics of the environment, which can affect a perceiving organism.

The **proximal stimulus**, is defined by the characteristics that the environmental features take on when they make contact with the sensory organs of the perceiver. The **percept** is the conscious apprehension of the environment by the perceiver. The study of perception is, in large part, the study of how distal stimulus attributes are transformed into proximal stimulus attributes, and how the proximal attributes are, in turn, reflected in the perceptual attributes.

These issues can be illustrated by simple examples from size perception. Two identical objects, say two rods, have by definition the same distal size. If they are at the same distance from the observer, their projected images will have the same proximal size. However, if one is further from the observer than the other, their proximal sizes will be different, although their intrinsic, distal sizes will of course stay the same. Conversely, if one object has twice the distal size of the other, but is located at twice the distance from the observer, then their distal sizes will be different but the proximal sizes will be equal. These discrepancies between distal and proximal attributes are trivial consequences of projective geometry. In general, relations between distal and proximal stimuli fall within the province of physics of perception. The psychology of perception deals with the relations between stimuli (distal or proximal) and percepts. A classical issue of psychology of perception is the fact that perceptual attributes often cannot be predicted from apparently plausible stimulus attributes. For example, stimuli of equal distal or proximal sizes may have different perceptual sizes, and vice versa.

There are two classes of such stimulus - percept discrepancies: perceptual illusions and perceptual constancies. **Perceptual illusions** are phenomena in which there is no discrepancy between distal and proximal stimuli, but there are discrepancies between attributes of stimuli and corresponding attributes of percepts (Coren & Girgus, 1978; Robinson, 1972). For example, in visual perception, lines of equal distal and proximal length may have different perceived length (Mueller-Lyer illusion, Ponzo illusion). Other examples of such so-called geometrical-optical illusions involve misperceptions of orientation, colinearity, parallelism, and shape distortions (Poggendorff illusion, Zoelner illusion, Orbison illusion, etc). Similar effects exist in tactual perception. Stimulus configurations similar to those involved in geometrical - optical illusions may also induce analogous tactile phenomena (Revesz, 1934). Another example is the phenomenon of orientation anisotropy in size perception: equal tactile distances are perceived as longer when they are applied transversely, that is, across a limb, than when they are applied longitudinally, that is, along the limb (Green, 1982; Todorovic, 1989).

Another group of phenomena of this class involve color and brightness perception. In achromatic (black-grey-white scale) perception, the distal attribute of a surface is its reflectance (ratio of reflected to incoming light), the proximal attribute is luminance (amount of light coming from a surface into the eye) and the perceptual attribute is brightness (perceived achromatic color of a surface). These definitions involve some simplifications, and more complex classifications are possible. The illusions in this domain involve cases in which surfaces of equal reflectance and luminance look differently bright, and vice versa. These phenomena include brightness contrast, brightness assimilation, Mach bands, the Craik-O'Brien-Cornsweet effect, and many others (Cornsweet, 1970). Analogous effects exist in the chromatic color domain (Hurvich, 1982).

Perceptual constancies involve cases of veridical perception, that is, the perceptual attributes are in accordance with the distal stimulus attributes; however, there are discrepancies between these attributes and the attributes of the proximal stimulus, which makes the veridicality of the percept puzzling (see Rock, 1975). For example, in size constancy, objects of equal distal size but at different distances from the observer, are, veridically, perceived to be equal, although their projected (proximal) sizes are different. In shape constancy, the paradigm example is that tilted circles continue to look circular, although they project as elliptical proximal stimuli. In brightness constancy, surfaces of the same reflectance are often perceived to look equally bright in spite of different illumination conditions, which makes them differently luminant. For example, a piece of paper continues to look white both under a lamp and in shadow, and a piece of coal looks black both in the cellar and in daylight.

What is the source of the mismatch between the stimulus (distal or proximal) and the percept? Three approaches to this question can be distinguished. In the **ecological approach** the stimulus - percept discrepancy is denied (Gibson, 1966, 1979). If an attribute of the percept does not agree with a putatively corresponding attribute of the stimulus, the recommended strategy is to reconsider the stimulus, and look for other, generally more complex attributes of the environment. Then a 'higher-order variable' may be found which unambiguously determines the percept, so that perfect environment - organism co-ordination is re-instated, but with the relevant stimulus aspect other than the classically assumed one. For example, size constancy may be explained if one assumes that the relevant aspect of the stimulus is not the proximal visual angle, but the number of visual array elements an object covers, a stimulus attribute which does not change with the distance of the observer (Gibson 1950). Another example is the notion that the brightness of a surface does not depend on its luminance, but on the ratio of its luminance to the luminance of the surrounding surface (Wallach, 1948, 1976). This ratio does not change with the change of overall illumination, although the absolute values of luminance do change. The ecological approach exhibits an important focus on the properties of the environment. However, it does not generally deal with the way the stimulus attributes are processed by the organism.

Another strategy, contrary to the ecological approach, is to acknowledge the possibility of cases of stimulus - percept discrepancies, and to seek their explanation in processes postulated to occur between the reception of the stimulus and the constitution of the percept. Two different approaches have been considered. In the first, **cognitive approach**, these intervening processes have been conceived to be similar to those involved in thinking and reasoning, involving hypothesis formation and testing, inference, engagement of previous experience and knowledge, and the like (Rock, 1983). For example, the perceived black color of the piece of coal, even under high illumination, may be explained by the general strategy that perceivers first recognize the object, and then draw from memory the information about its real, that is, usual color, which then influences the current percept. Similar explanations are sometimes offered for size and shape constancy. A problem with such explanations is that these constancies work just as well with novel objects (for example, pieces of grey paper) whose color, size or shape is not known to the observer.

In the second, **physiological approach**, the processes assumed to intervene between the stimulus and the percept are the transformations of the incoming information through the network composed of sensory receptors, other sensory neurons, afferent nerves, subcortical centers, and various cortical sensory regions. This approach will be considered here.

Up until about the middle of this century detailed knowledge about the properties of neural sensory pathways, other than gross anatomy, was scant. Psychological textbooks around the turn of the century depicted the connection between the neurons of the sensory surface and the neurons of the corresponding cortical area as a simple one-to-one affair. Excitation of a receptor was thought to cause an analogous excitation of the single corresponding cortical neuron. Thus the profile of the neural activity at the sense organ would be relatively faithfully preserved at the higher center. Given this assumption, it is understandable why cognitive operations were invoked to explain constancies and illusions: if all the brain can do is transmit the structure of the proximal stimulus, then only 'mind' is left to step in and explain the stimulus - percept inconsistencies. A different approach was taken by Gestalt theory (Koehler, 1920, 1947, Koffka, 1935). In order to explain perceptual phenomena, they postulated the existence of electrical fields in the brain, whose attributes would correspond to the attributes of the percept. Such fields had no basis in the physiology of their time, nor could be substantiated by later research. Nevertheless, the idea that nervous activity is isomorphic with the percept is still a fruitful heuristic, and will be elaborated in the following.

2. Structure and function of neurosensory systems

To set the perceptually relevant aspects of the neurosensory apparatus in perspective, consider again the notion of this apparatus as a simple stimulus transducer. As described in the previous section, an 'ideal' but imaginary system of this type consists of three components. The first level of the system is the sensory surface, comprised of punctate isolated elements of identical sensitivity, homogeneously distributed over the surface. The second level is the cortical receiving area, with a structure completely analogous to the sensory surface. The third component is the set of isolated transducing fibers connecting each single element of the first level to a single element of the second level in a topographical (neighborhood-preserving) manner. Such a system will be called 'the simple neurosensory system' in the following.

Compared to the simple neurosensory system, the biological sensory systems show tremendous differences. Three sources of complexity will be noted. First, the receptors in both the visual and the somatosensory mammalian system have neither homogeneous sensitivity nor homogeneous spatial distribution. With regard to sensitivity, as is well known, the visual system contains two classes of receptors, the rods (the achromatic system) and the cones (the chromatic system). The cones are further subdivided into three classes (S, M, and L), distinguished by the locus of the peak of spectral sensitivity. The somatosensory system contains at least three classes of receptors, transmitting information about touch, temperature variation, and painful stimuli. There are further subdivisions within these classes. For example, there are slow adapting and fast adapting tactile neurons, sensitive to sustained and transient stimulation (Iggo, 1982).

These receptors are not homogeneously distributed over the sensory surface. The cones are concentrated in the fovea (the center of the retina), and their density falls off rapidly towards the periphery. Furthermore, the S-cones are far outnumbered by the L- and M-cones. In contrast, the rods are absent from the fovea; they are most numerous in a ring around the center, and their density also declines toward the periphery. On the skin, there are also drastic absolute differences in receptor density, as well as receptor class differences (Johansson & Vallbo, 1979). The receptors are most numerous on the tips of the fingers and of the tongue, and their density declines over other parts of the body.

Second, the receptor surface is only the first out of many subsequent levels, that is, anatomically defined layers of a neurosensory system. In the visual system the retina contains, in addition to the receptor layer, four classes of cells (horizontal, bipolar, amacrine and ganglion cells), arranged in two-dimensional layers. The axons of the ganglion cells form the optic nerve, which mainly ends in the next station in the visual system, the lateral geniculate nucleus, which contains six anatomical layers. The next station is area 17, the striate cortex, from which information is distributed to a dozen or so extrastriate cortical visual areas, that all have six anatomical layers, which can be further subdivided (van Essen, 1985). Like the receptor layer, many of these post-receptor layers usually contain several cell types, with different characteristics.

Third, the connections between the anatomical levels, although generally local and topographical, are only exceptionally one-to-one, and often neither unidirectional nor hierarchical. For example, influence (excitation or inhibition) from a neuron at a lower level can diverge to several neurons at the higher level; conversely, neurons at the higher level may receive converging influence from several neurons at the lower level. Units at the higher level may feed back information to the lower level, thus upsetting the notion of sequential processing. Furthermore, in addition to the feed-forward and feed-back between-level relations, there may also be within-level lateral influences between units at the same level.

Thus, instead of the imaginary homogeneous, two-level, simply connected simple neurosensory system, we have to deal with biologically real inhomogeneous, multi-level, multiply connected systems. The complexity of the structure of such systems is necessarily reflected in the complexity of their functioning. For example, in the simple system, the stimulation of a single receptor induces an analogous excitation of a single neuron at the second level; conversely, activity of a neuron at the second level can only be induced by a single receptor at the first level. In real system, the situation is much more complex. The consequences of the three sources of complexity will be discussed in turn.

First, consider the consequences of multiple connectivity (divergence, convergence, feedback, lateral influences). They are reflected in the notions of 'point image' (Mallot, 1987; McIlwain, 1986) and 'receptive field'. These are dual concepts. The point image involves a single locus (a 'point' on the sensory surface) affecting an extended region of neurons at a subsequent level of the sensory system. The receptive field involves an extended region of the sensory surface affecting a single locus (a neuron at some subsequent level of the system). Whereas the point image has received only moderate attention, receptive fields have been studied in a large number of experiments since this notion was introduced by Kuffler (1953). In contrast to the simple neurosensory system, receptive fields of real neurons are not punctate, but consist of an extended portion of the sensory surface, they may involve inhibitory and not only excitatory influences, and they are not homogeneous, but have a spatial sensitivity profile.

The next source of complexity is the multiplicity of levels of real neurosensory systems. The consequence is the multiplicity of point images and receptive fields. Thus, in a simple extension of the concept of receptive field, one may allow that the receptive field of a neuron be located not only at the sensory surface, but at any other anatomically defined level. For example, one may study what portion of the LGN can influence a cortical neuron, and in what way. This area would be the LGN receptive field of that neuron. More generally, for each neuron one can define its 'complex receptive field' as the union of its receptive fields from all levels of the system.

The concept of the point image can also be extended in an analogous manner. As an example of the complex point image, take the case of an observer looking at a star, involving stimulation of a relatively small retinal area, approximating a point stimulus. This stimulus affects an increasingly diverging mass of foveal horizontal, bipolar, amacrine and ganglion cells, generating a point image at each of these levels. Next, the appropriate portions at all 6 LGN and striate cortical layers are activated, and finally the corresponding portions of the extrastriate areas are also affected. Note that this multi-level interconnected activity pattern, that is, the complex point image, is initiated by the activation of only a small portion of the sensory surface. In a further generalization, one may study point images of neurons which do not belong to the sensory surface, but may be located at any level of the neurosensory system. Related concepts were discussed by Grossberg & Mingolla (1985).

The third source of complexity of real neurosensory systems is the inhomogeneity of neuronal sensitivity and distribution. To appreciate the role of this factor, let us first define the structure of a neurosensory system as the totality of neural layers, and the way they are interconnected. The function of the system is defined by the activity pattern generated by the structural units. An anatomically defined neural layer can be conceptually subdivided into several **structural sublayers**, comprised of neurons with similar sensitivity or processing characteristics. Each sublayer is a two-dimensional array of processing units. Units belonging to several sublayers may be intermingled within a single neural layer. For example, the receptor layer can be subdivided into four structural sublayers: the rod sublayer, the S-cone sublayer, the M-cone sublayer, and the L-cone sublayer. A sublayer may be further subdivided. For example, the sublayer of simple cells may be subdivided into sublayers according to orientation tuning, as shown later on.

The spatial activity distribution of the sublayer units is a **functional subimage**. For example, a visual stimulus generates four functional subimages on the receptor layer: the rod-image, the S-cone image, the M-cone image, and the L-cone image. These functional subimages are physically superimposed, but they can be conceptually distinguished. Because the sensitivity characteristics of each sublayer are different, each subimage constitutes a different transformation of the input stimulus. Thus a single proximal stimulus generates, in parallel, a number of functional subimages, one for each structural sublayer. If this stimulus is a point stimulus, the consequent neurosensory activity is already considerable. However, the point stimulus is only a degenerate example of a stimulus. The neural effect of an everyday visual situation is much more complex. It involves the action of the corresponding spatially extended proximal stimulus upon the sensory surface, which induces a widespread variety of activity patterns throughout all levels of the neurosensory system. The perceptual image, that is, the conscious apprehension of the environment, somehow emerges as an aspect of the sum-total of this activity.

In sum, the neurosensory system may be structurally parsed into a number of interconnected structural sublayers, and the activity of the system may be functionally parsed into a number of superimposed functional subimages. The application of these concepts in the study of perception can be simply put. To explain an attribute of a perceptual image, the recommended strategy is to inspect the activity distributions in one or more functional subimages. Then an attribute of a subimage may be found which behaves analogously to an attribute of the percept. This strategy is an elaboration of the view that 'things look as they do because of the field organization [in the neurosensory system] to which the proximal stimulus distribution gives rise' (Koffka, 1935, p. 98). For example, if two surfaces have equal perceived brightness, than the corresponding two portions in a subimage may show equal activity levels. Thus a perceptual intensity attribute (level of perceived brightness) would correspond to a neural intensity attribute (level of activity). Or, if two stimuli have equal perceived length, then one should look for equality in a neural attribute which corresponds to perceived length. Both of these examples will be dealt with in more detail in the following two sections.

The main problem with this strategy is empirical testability. The large majority of neurosensory studies are multiple stimuli / single neuron experiments. That is, one neuron is recorded from, and it is studied how various properties of stimuli affect the activity of the neuron. In contrast, the present strategy calls for single stimulus / multiple neuron studies. In other words, what we want to know are the functional subimages induced by a stimulus upon sets of neurons comprising structural sublayers. There are three ways to fulfill this strategy. First, there are physiological procedures for multi-unit recording. In addition to multi-electrode studies, ingenious techniques are being introduce to visualize the concurrent activity of many neurons (Blasdel & Salama, 1986; Grinvald et al., 1986). Second, it is possible to record continually from one neuron, but systematically displace the stimulus in successive points in time, so that the neuron samples the whole stimulus image. Then one can reconstruct the activity distribution that would be induced by the stationary stimulus in a layer of identical neurons (De Valois & Pease, 1971; Nothdurft & Lee, 1982). The third possibility, which will be presented in the next two sections, is to simulate the functional subimage by computer. In this approach, one constructs a mathematical model of structural and functional properties of sensory neurons, based on available physiological data. The implementation of such a model on the computer allows the comparison of predicted functional subimages with data from perceptual experiments, which yield information on the attributes of perceptual images. Two such models from previous work will be presented here. Note that the conceptual vocabulary from this paper was not used in the original publications.

3. Somatosensory discrimination

The first example is a very simple but perceptually relevant model of a sensory system (Todorovic, 1989). The model has only two homogeneous levels, with a feed-forward connection from the first to the second level. This is a model of somatosensory spatial discrimination, where the first level models the skin, and the second level models a cortical somatosensory region, such as area 3a. The cortical units are assumed to have receptive fields whose sensitivity profiles are bivariate gaussians. These are simply structured receptive fields, with a central region of peak sensitivity, radial fall-off, and no inhibitory subregions. Initially, the shape of the receptive fields is assumed to be circular, that is, the radial fall-off is isotropic.

Figure 1a represents the way the sensory surface is covered with overlapping receptive fields. The radii of the circles correspond to receptive field sensitivity at half strength. A simple two-point

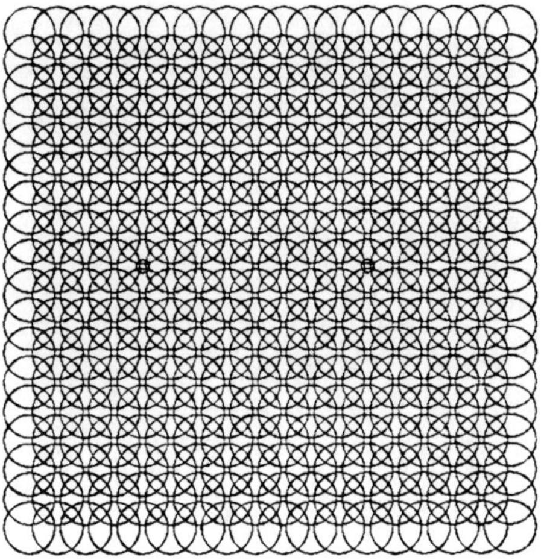

a

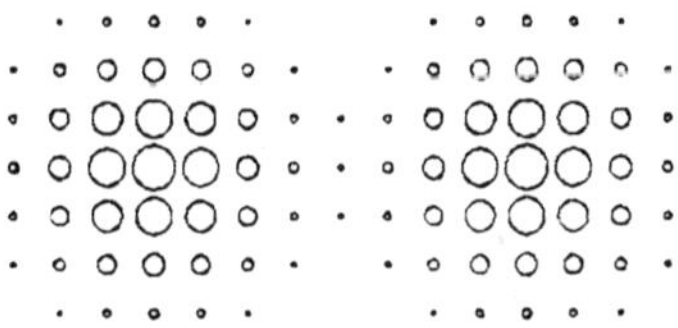

b

Figure 1

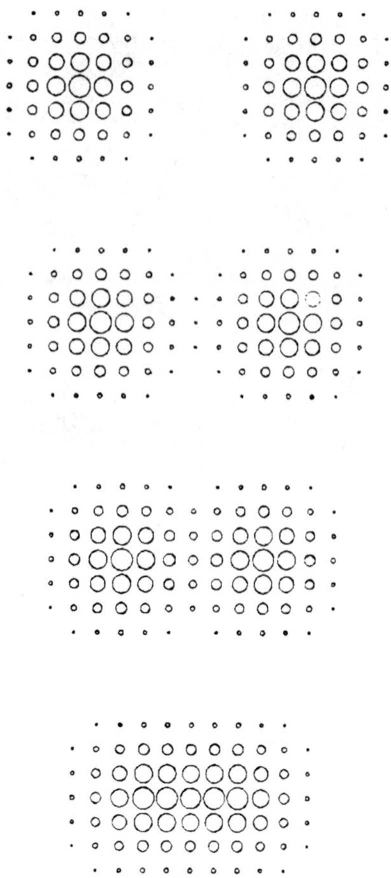

Figure 2

stimulus is indicated with two small circles, depicting a situation in which the skin is being simultaneously pricked with two needles. The effect that such a stimulus exerts at the second level is shown in Figure 1b. This is the depiction of the functional subimage. The circles denote the neural units, and their size codes excitation level. There are two neurons with maximal excitation, while the excitation of the neighboring neurons falls off radially. Each of the two clusters of excitation is a point image. Note that the intensity structure of the point images mirrors the gaussian structure of the sensitivity profile of the receptive fields. This is a consequence of the circular symmetry of the receptive fields and their isotropic overlap.

Figure 2 depicts the predicted changes in the functional subimage due to the change of distance between the two stimuli. The initially separate clusters begin to interpenetrate and finally form a single cluster, although the distance between the stimuli is greater than zero. This behavior of the model is in qualitative accord with experimental data on the two-point spatial threshold on the skin. In such studies subjects are treated with two-point stimuli and are asked whether they feel one indentation or two (Weinstein, 1968). The perceived attribute of 'two-ness' is assumed to correspond with the neural attribute of separateness of the two clusters. The threshold varies enormously over the various regions of the skin, from less than 1 mm on the tongue or finger-tips, up to 70 mm on the back. This can be explained by the changing size of the receptive field: the larger the size, the larger each cluster, and the sooner the two clusters begin to interpenetrate and become non-separable. If subjects are asked to describe the shape of the stimulus with decreasing needle separation, they report, in order, two indentations, a paddle or dumbbell shape, and an elongated line (Friedline, 1918). Thus the perceived attribute of shape corresponds well with the shape of the profile in the image.

On some parts of the body, such as on the limbs, the threshold is larger in the transversal orientation, that is, across the limb, than in the longitudinal orientation, that is, along the limb (Todorovic, 1989). This can be explained by the fact that the receptive fields on the limbs have elongated shape, with the longer axis aligned with the limb (Pons et al., 1987; Sur, Nelson & Kaas, 1982). Elongated receptive fields are presented in Figure 3a. Figure 3b shows that the two clusters formed by stimuli in the longitudinal orientation interpenetrate more than if the stimuli are transversely oriented. Thus transversely oriented stimuli are more likely to be perceived as 'two' than longitudinally oriented stimuli.

What is the neural attribute corresponding to perceived length? One candidate is the distance between cluster peaks generated by the ends. If so, then the model in this form cannot explain orientation anisotropy in tactile size perception, mentioned in Part One. This is because the distance between cluster peaks of activity is the same for both orientations in Figure 3b. One possible explanation is anisotropy in receptive field distribution and overlap. In Figure 4a the density of receptive fields as well as their overlap is greater in the transversal orientation. In consequence, the peak separation in Figure 4b is larger in the transversal orientation than in the longitudinal orientation, explaining why transversal distances are perceived to be larger.

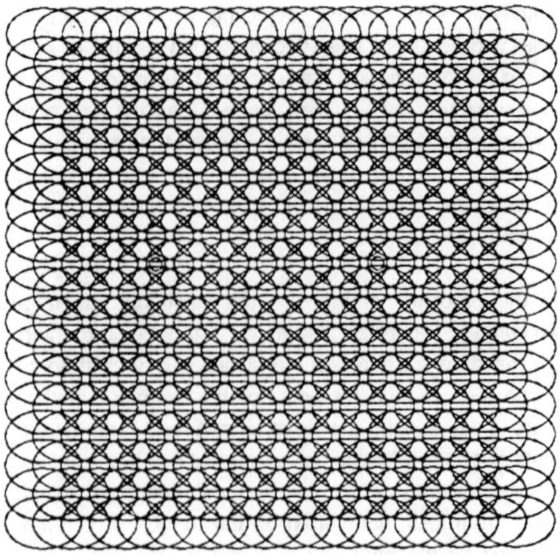

a

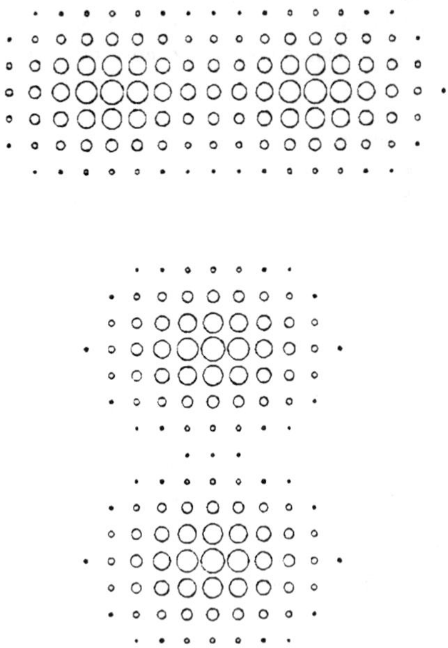

b

Figure 3

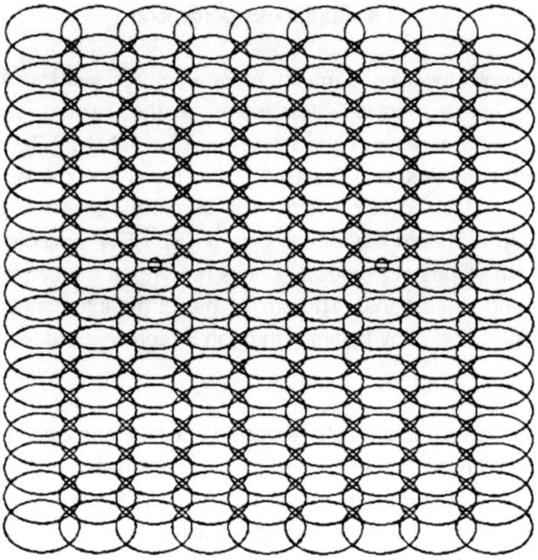

a

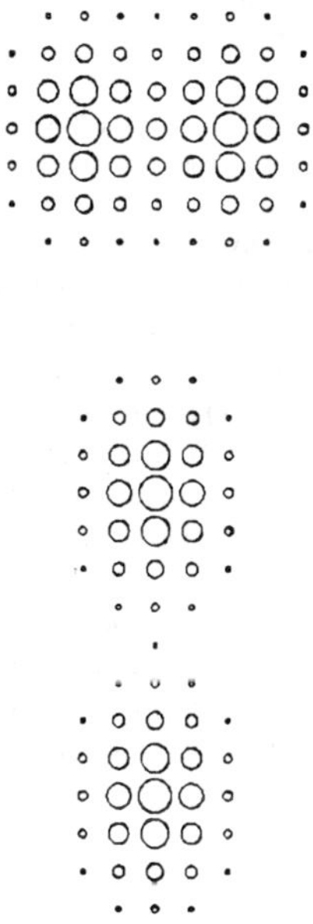

b

Figure 4

4. Brightness perception

The second example involves a much more complex system, which models achromatic brightness perception. For a detailed description of the system, mathematical specification, physiological motivation, and a number of simulations, see Grossberg & Todorovic (1988). The overall architecture of the model is presented in Figure 5. The model is composed of 6 levels, depicted by thick-bordered rectangles. Each level contains one or more sublayers, grouped into a boundary contour system (BCS) and a feature contour system (FCS). The symbols inside the rectangles are graphical mnemonics for the types of processing units residing at the corresponding model level, and will be used in the following simulations. The arrows depict the interconnections between the levels. The thin-bordered rectangles coded by letters A through F represent the type of transformations taking place between levels.

Level 1 models the retinal achromatic receptors. Level 2 contains two sublayers modelling the on- and off- ganglion cells. Level 2 on-units feed their excitation forward to level 3 and level 6. Level 3 contains twelve sublayers modelling the cortical simple cells. Each sublayer contains units tuned to detect edges of a different orientation and luminance polarity. Level 4 contains six sublayers modelling cortical complex cells, tuned to detect edges of six different orientations, regardless of luminance polarity. Level 5 contains a single layer with units that pool, after a thresholding step, input from all six level 4 units with coextensive receptive fields. Finally, complex interactions take place at the single layer of level 6. Somewhat simplified, level 6 units are excited by level 2 units, inhibited by level 5 units, and excite each other through lateral connections. The net effect is a filling-in process: activity induced by level 2 is blurred and averaged at level 6, but only within boundaries defined by level 5. Activity at level 6 is assumed to correspond with the brightness percept.

A notable feature of this system is that it contains 23 sublayers, and that the response of each of them to any reasonably differentiated stimulus is likely to be qualitatively different. For example, consider the responses of the system to the stimulus depicted in Figure 6a. It is a rather simple proximal stimulus with only two levels of grey, separated by a contour consisting of two horizontal and one vertical edge, forming two corners. Figure 6b depicts the response of the receptor surface, assuming to simply register the relative intensity values of the stimulus. As in the previous model, the size of the circles codes activity level. More interesting are Figures 6c and 6d, presenting the reaction of the level 2 on- and off-sublayers to the stimulus. The circular symbols represent the structure of the receptive fields. The structure of the stimulus is recognizable in these images, but it is distorted. The two-valued stimulus profile is transformed into multi-valued functional subimages. The on-image contains overshoots along the more luminant side of the edges, undershoots along the less luminant side, a peak corresponding to the bright convex corner, and a trough corresponding to the dark convex corner. The off-image is a dual of the on-image. The complementary relation of the two images is a consequence of the complementary relation of the receptive fields of the on- and off-units.

Figure 7 depicts several images from the level 3 sublayers, the simple units. As suggested by the circular symbols, Figure 7a presents the activity profile of the sublayer of units sensitive to horizontal (0 degrees) edges with a bright top side and a dark bottom side. The other images involve cells tuned to 30, 60 and 90 degrees, respectively, with the bright side in the top right direction. The orientation tunings exhibit some breadth, so that the units respond to a range of neighboring

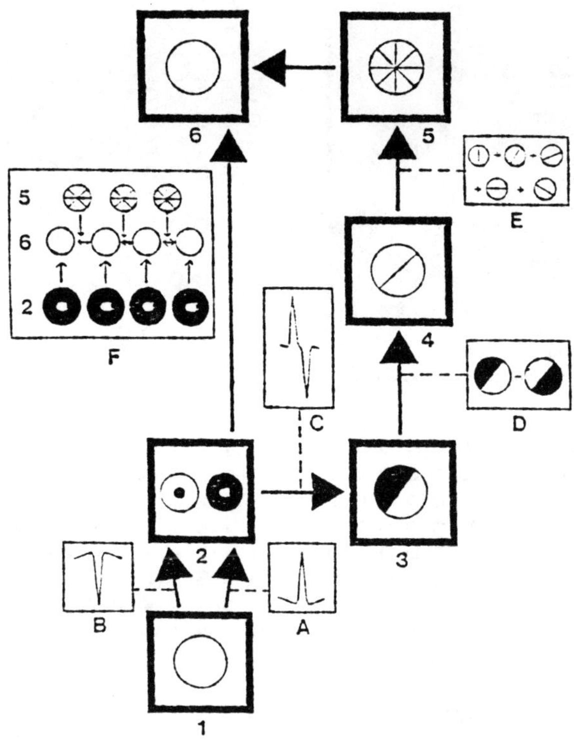

Figure 5

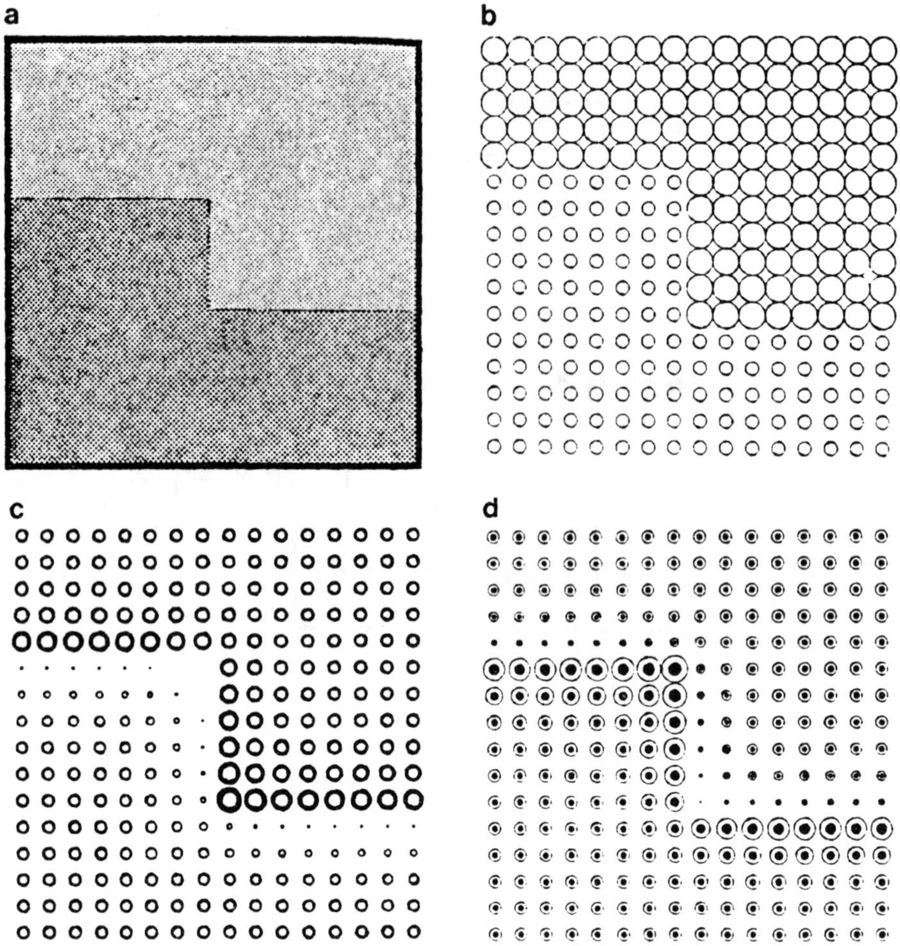

Figure 6

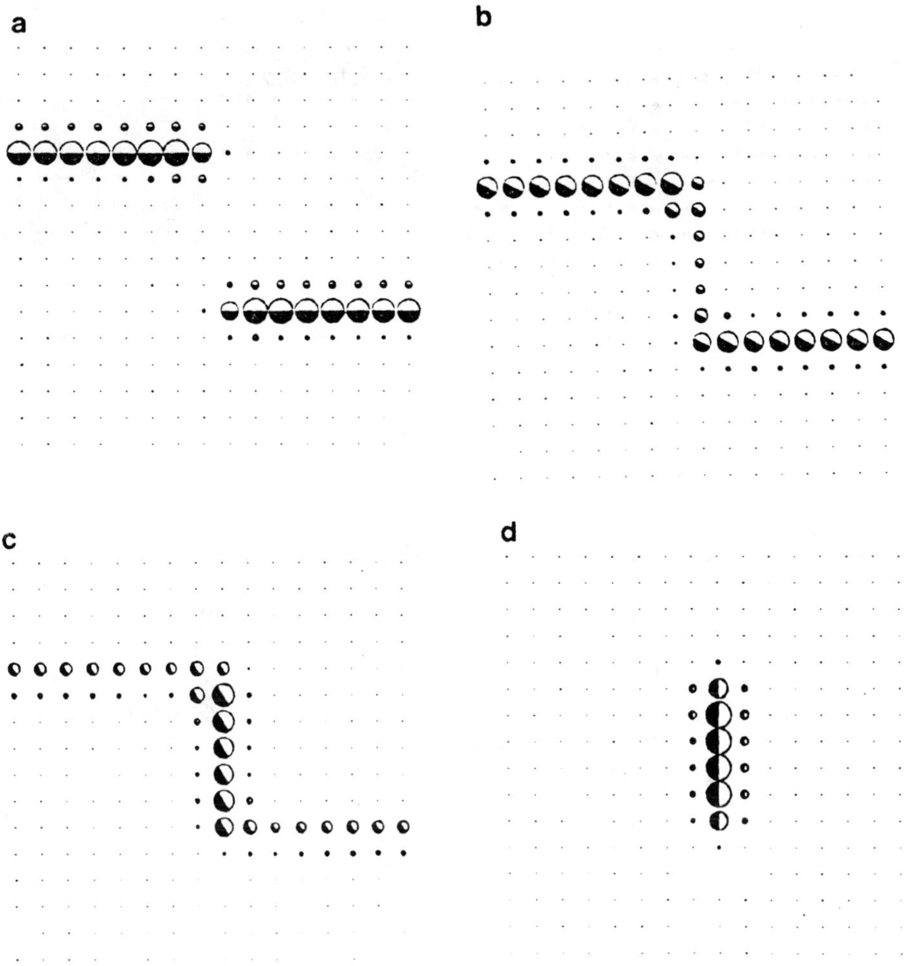

Figure 7

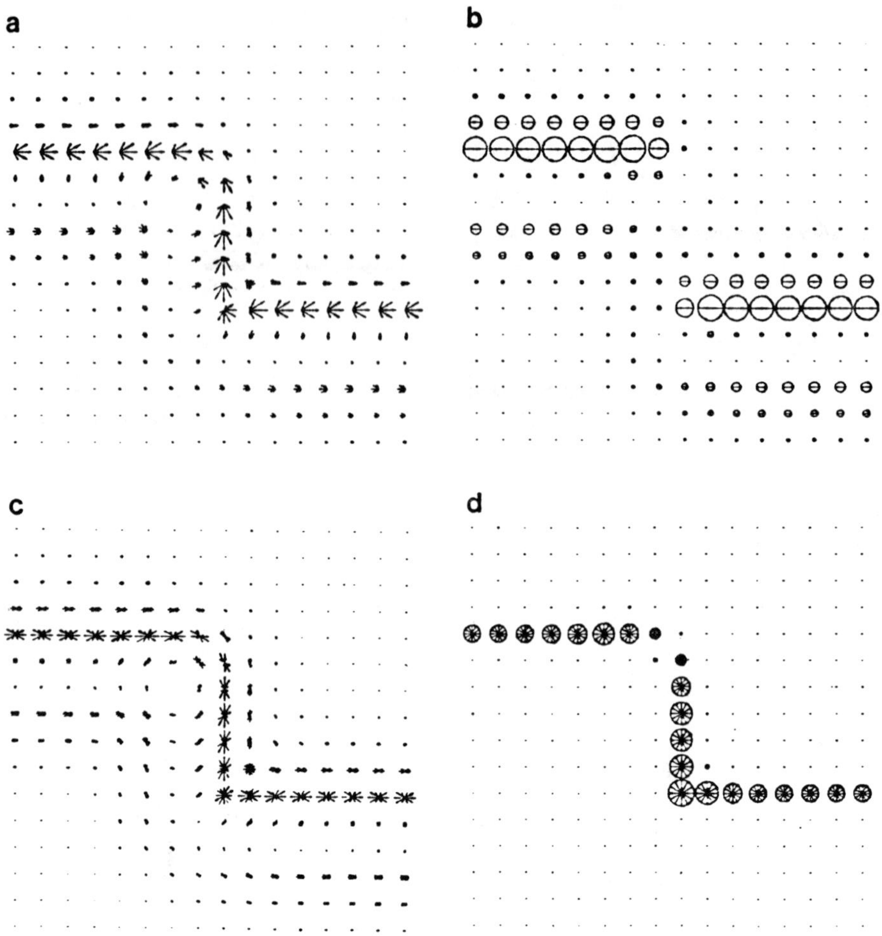

Figure 8

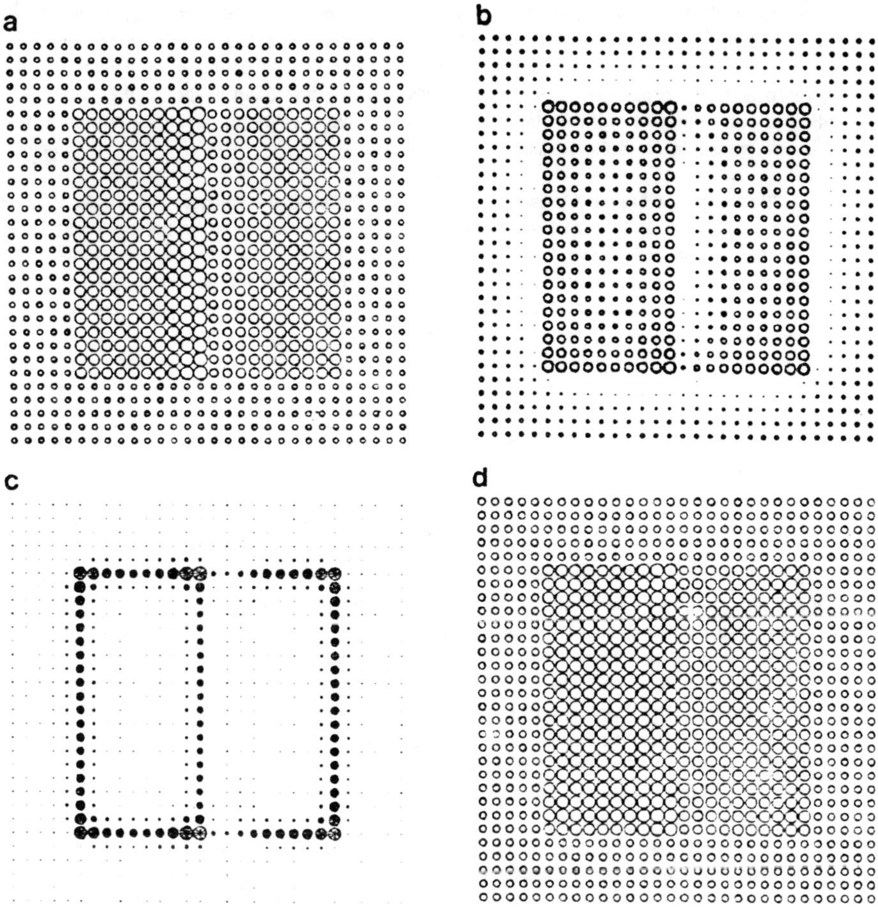

Figure 9

orientations, but with appropriately diminishing excitation. In contrast to the on- and off-images, in which most units exhibit positive activity, the simple unit images exhibit mainly zero activity, except in localized portions. This behavior agrees with the fact that on- and off-cells tend to be spontaneously active even in the absence of stimulation, in contrast to simple cells, which generally show weak or zero spontaneous activity (Hubel & Wiesel, 1968). The units in Figure 7a pick up only the presence of the horizontal edges, while the unit in Figure 7d register only the vertical edge. In contrast, units in Figure 7b and 7c, because of tuning breadth, although they are tuned neither to horizontal nor to vertical edges, manage to pick up the presence of both types of edges, and thus provide a more adequate representation of the stimulus.

The images in Figure 7 present only 4 out of 12 simple unit images. Figure 8a shows a composite image of activity in all 12 sublayers, but using a different code. In the composite image each star-like Figure represents the activity of 12 units. Each unit belongs to a different sublayer, but all have co-extensive receptive fields. Each line in the Figure codes the activity of one simple unit. Line length codes unit activity level, and line orientation codes orientation sensitivity. The next set of sublayers comprises Level 4 of the model. Level 4 units pool activity from simple units sensitive to the same orientation but opposite polarity. Figure 8b depicts the image of the sublayer of complex units sensitive to horizontal orientation. Figure 8c is another example of a composite image. It represents the activity of all six complex unit sublayers, in a code similar to Figure 8a. Figure 8d represents the image of the Level 5 units. It is the output of the BCS, whose activity generates the representation of luminance induced boundaries.

The final output of the system, the image of level 6, is not presented here, but it is very similar to Figure 6b, the initial input. Thus, in this case, the predicted structure of the percept is isomorphic to the structure of the stimulus. However, there are a number of other examples in which the final image is not isomorphic with the stimulus, but it is isomorphic with the percept. Figure 9 is a simulation of the Craik-O'Brien-Cornsweet effect (Cornsweet, 1970; Todorovic, 1987). Figure 9a represents the stimulus, which consists of two adjoining vertical rectangles on a dark background. The rectangles are identical in size and luminance, except for an inhomogeneity within a vertical strip along the common boundary, spanning 3 columns of units on either side. In the left rectangle, luminance increases from left to right, and in the right rectangle, it decreases from right to left, so that a luminance boundary is created. Figure 9b is the image at the sublayer of on-units (level 2), and Figure 9c is the output of the BCS (level 5). Figure 9d is the final image, and a correct prediction of the percept, in which the left rectangle looks brighter than the right one. In other words, two rectangles of inhomogeneous but mostly identical luminance are perceived as two rectangles with different but homogeneous brightness levels. Grossberg & Todorovic (1988) present additional simulations of cases of brightness constancy, brightness contrast, brightness assimilation, the Hermann grid, the Koffka-Benussi ring, an achromatic Mondrian image, and other classical and more recent brightness effects.

5. Discussion

The foregoing sections have provided examples of the physiological strategy in the construction of perceptual theories. Although the two models are quite different, they share one characteristics. In both models, there is a single sublayer, with its corresponding subimage, whose attributes are assumed to correspond to the attributes of the percept. In the somatosensory model it is the second level, and in the brightness model it is the single sublayer at level 6. An extreme form of this single final sublayer notion is the old idea that there is a single region in the brain, 'the bridge locus' (Mueller, 1896; Teller, 1980), whose activity corresponds to the conscious percept. However, reality may be more complex. The existence of the multiplicity of cortical sensory areas suggests that they may all participate in the percept. There are several schemes which depict the possible perceptual functions of various cortical areas, in accordance with their different sensitivity to color, motion, orientation, stereo processing, etc (De Yoe & van Essen, 1988; Livingstone & Hubel, 1988; Zeki & Shipp, 1988). These areas can be grouped into processing streams. Such a stream is an interconnected sequentially ordered set of structural sublayers, each belonging to a different anatomical layer, whose neurons have similar processing characteristics. For example, a stream might be formed by achromatic non-oriented neurons from the retina, LGN, and the striate cortex.

One possible arrangement of the roles of these sensory areas in the make-up of the percept is that each perceptual aspect of a sensory modality (such as color, motion, orientation, etc) is exclusively assigned to a single cortical area, which may be the final sublayer in a sensory processing stream. Another possibility is that all sublayers that belong to a stream contribute, to a larger or smaller extent, to the constitution of the conscious apprehension of the relevant perceptual aspect. A still more complicated possibility is that, although a significant degree of specificity cannot be denied, there is no exclusive assignment of perceptual aspects to processing streams. Each stream may contribute, to some extent, to more than one perceptual aspect. This is quite likely, since many sensory neurons are not exclusive detectors of a single stimulus attribute, but are sensitive to a range of influences, although with different responsiveness. For example, many visual neurons would respond to a large change in luminance level within their receptive field. Thus they may all, in principle, contribute to the corresponding change of the brightness percept in the appropriate portion of the visual field.

However, there are data that suggest that some sublayers, at least some of the time, may not partake in consciousness. In the phenomenon of stabilized vision, the proximal stimulus distribution, or some portion of it, is projected at fixed retinal locations for extended periods of time, with the help of various technical devices. If the contour of a region is stabilized with respect to the retina in this manner, the region takes on the color and the brightness of the surround. For example, if the borders of a red circle on a blue background are stabilized, the visual field quickly becomes uniformly blue, despite of continuous presence of longwave (red) stimulation (Gerrits & Vendrick, 1970; Yarbus, 1967). However, after the cessation of the stimulus an afterimage of the faded figure appears, which in this case is a green circle. This afterimage is very similar to the normal afterimage that appears after prolonged viewing of a non-stabilized stimulus, generally attributed to reduced neural activation due to fatigue after excessive stimulation. It is likely that a similar process of fatigue, at some level of the visual system, is the cause of the appearance of the afterimage after the cessation of the stabilized stimulation. However, and this is the main point, the activity of that level does not appear to influence the percept during stabilized stimulation. This can be shown by comparing the percepts in two visual situations. The first is the example of the stabilized red figure on the blue background that was just discussed. The second is the presentation, stabilized or non-stabilized, of the homogeneous blue background without any figure on it. In both cases the percept is identical - a completely blue image.

However, the state of the visual system must be different in the two cases, since a green afterimage appears after the cessation of the first stimulus, but not after the cessation of the second stimulus.

In conclusion, the physiological approach in the explanation of perceptual phenomena has a venerable history. However, the relevant physiological knowledge that could put this type of theorizing on a sound empirical basis has only been emerging in the recent decades. Even more recent have been the advances of the theory and simulation techniques in the study of biological neurosensory networks. Nevertheless, it is already clear that the application of neural network concepts in the study of perception is not only a promising line of attack at some classical problems, but may also be a forceful new paradigm for general perceptual theory.

References

BLASDEL, G. G. & SALAMA, G. (1986). Voltage-sensitive dyes reveal a modular organization in monkey striate cortex. **Nature, 321,** 579-585.

COREN, S. & GIRGUS, J. S. (1978). **Seeing is deceiving: The psychology of visual illusions.** Hillsdale, NJ: LEA.

CORNSWEET, T. N. (1970). **Visual perception.** New York: Academic Press.

DE VALOIS, R. L. & PEASE, P. L. (1971). Contours and contrast: Responses of monkey lateral geniculate nucleus cells to luminance and color figures. **Science, 171,** 694-696.

DE YOE, E. A. & VAN ESSEN, D. C. (1988). Concurrent processing streams in monkey visual cortex. **Trends in Neurosciences, 11,** 219-226.

GERRITS, H. J. M. & VENDRICK, A. J. H. (1970). Simultaneous contrast, filling-in process, and information processing in man's visual system. **Experimental brain research, 11,** 411-430.

GIBSON, J. J. (1950). **The perception of the visual world.** Boston: Houghton Mifflin.

GIBSON, J. J. (1966). **The senses considered as perceptual systems.** Boston: Houghton Mifflin.

GIBSON, J. J. (1979). **The ecological approach to visual perception.** Boston: Houghton Mifflin.

GREEN, G. B. (1982). The perception of distance location for dual tactile pressures. **Perception & Psychophysics, 31**, 315-323.

GRINVALD, A., LEIKE, E., FROSTIG, R. D., GILBERT, C. D., & WIESEL, T. N. (1986). Functional architecture of cortex revealed by optical imaging of intrinsic signals. **Nature, 324,** 361-364.

GROSSBERG, S. & MINGOLLA, E. (1985). Neural dynamics of perceptual grouping: Textures, boundaries, and emergent segmentations. **Perception & Psychophysics, 38,** 141-171.

GROSSBERG, S. & TODOROVIC, D. (1988). Neural dynamics of 1-D and 2-D brightness perception: A unified model of classical and recent phenomena. **Perception & Psychophysics, 43,** 241-277.

HUBEL, D. H. & WIESEL, T. N. (1968). Receptive fields and functional architecture of monkey striate cortex. **Journal of Physiology, 195,** 215-243.

HURVICH, L. M. (1981). **Color vision.** Sunderland, MA: Sinauer.

IGGO, A. (1982). Cutaneous sensory mechanisms. In H. B. Barlow and J. D. Mollon (Eds.), **The Senses.** Cambridge University Press.

JOHANSSON, R. S. & VALLBO, A. B. (1979). Tactile sensibility in the human hand: relative and absolute densities of four types of mechanoreceptive units in glabrous skin. **Journal of Physiology, 286,** 283-300.

KOEHLER, W. (1920). **Die physischen Gestalten in Ruhe und im stationaeren Zustand.** Braunschweig.

KOEHLER, W. (1947). **Gestalt psychology.** New York: Liveright.

KOFFKA, K. (1935). **Principles of gestalt psychology.** New York: Harcourt & Brace.

KUFFLER, S. W. (1953). Discharge patterns and functional organization of mammalian retina. **Journal of Neurophysiology, 16,** 31-68.

LIVINGSTONE, M. & HUBEL, D. (1988). Segregation of form, color, movement, and depth: Anatomy, physiology, and perception. **Science, 240,** 740-749.

MALLOT, H. A. (1987). Point images, receptive fields, and retinotopic mappings. **Trends in Neurosciences, 10,** 310-311.

McILWAIN, J. T. (1986). Point images in the visual system: new interest in an old idea. **Trends in Neurosciences, 9,** 354-358

MUELLER, G. E. (1896). Zur Psychophysik der Gesichtsempfindungen. **Zeitschrift fuer Psychologie, 10,** 1-82.

NOTHDURFT, H. C. & LEE, B. B. (1982). Responses to colored patterns in the macaque lateral geniculate nucleus: Pattern processing in single neurons. **Experimental Brain Research, 48,** 43-54.

PONS, T.P., GARRAGHTY, P.E., FRIEDMAN, D.P., & MISHKIN, M. (1987). Physiological evidence for serial processing in somatosensory cortex. **Science, 237,** 417-420.

REVESZ, G. (1934). System der optischen und haptischen Raumtauschungen. **Zeitschrift fuer Psychologie, 131,** 296-375.

ROBINSON, J. O. (1972). **The psychology of visual illusion.** London: Hutchinson University Library.

ROCK, I. (1975). **An introduction to perception.** New York: Macmillan.

ROCK, I. (1983). **The logic of perception.** Cambridge, MA: Bradford Books / MIT Press.

SUR, M., NELSON, R.J., & KAAS, J.H. (1982). Representation of the body surface in cortical areas 3b and 1 of squirrel monkeys: comparisons with other primates. **Journal of Comparative Neurology, 211,** 177-192.

TELLER, D. Y. (1980). Locus questions in visual science. In C. S. Harris (Ed.), **Visual coding and adaptability.** Hillsdale, NJ: LEA.

TODOROVIC, D. (1987). The Craik-O'Brien-Cornsweet effect: New varieties and their theoretical implications. **Perception & Psychophysics, 42,** 545-560.

TODOROVIC, D. (1989). Simulations of tactile spatial discrimination. In R. M. J. Cotterill (Ed.), **Models of brain function.** Cambridge: Cambridge University Press.

VAN ESSEN, D. C. (1985). Functional organization of primate visual cortex. In A. Peters and E. G. Jones (Eds.), **Cerebral Cortex (Vol 3).** New York: Academic Press.

WALLACH, H. (1948). Brightness constancy and the nature of achromatic colors. **Journal of experimental psychology, 38,** 310-324.

WALLACH, H. (1976). **On perception.** New York: Quadrangle.

WEINSTEIN, S. (1968). Intensive and extensive aspects of tactile sensitivity as a function of body part, sex, and laterality. In D. R. Kenshalo (Ed.), **The Skin Senses.** Springfield, IL: Charles C. Thomas Publishers.

YARBUS, A. L. (1967). **Eye movements and vision.** New York: Plenum Press.

ZEKI, S. & SHIPP, S. (1988). The functional logic of cortical connections. **Nature, 335,** 311-317.

6

A COMPARISON OF MLP AND FSCL-LVQ NEURAL NETWORKS FOR VOWEL CLASSIFICATION

by Stanley C. Ahalt, Tzyy-Ping Jung, and Ashok K. Krishnamurthy, Ohio State University*

1 Introduction

Neural networks are being widely used for pattern classification. Two commonly used neural network architectures for pattern classification are the Multi-Layer Perceptron [1] and the Learning Vector Quantizer [2]. However, these two architectures are different in a number of ways, and it is not always clear which of these models is appropriate for a particular classification task.

In this chapter we explore a number of issues related to the use of Multi-Layer Perceptron (MLP) and Learning Vector Quantizer (LVQ) neural networks. We examine and compare the use of both architectures in the context of three speech recognition tasks – vowel recognition, speaker recognition, and gender recognition. For each task, we compare the performance of the two architectures, and study the effects of different input features on performance. We also consider the effects of noise and, finally discuss the computational issues associated with the use of the two architectures.

Our major conclusion is that LVQ offers a number of advantages over MLP for many pattern classification tasks. For example, the MLP network trained using the Back-Propagation (BP) algorithm is restricted to one distortion measure – namely the squared error at the output. The LVQ architecture, on the other hand, has decided advantages in applications in which a more appropriate distortion measure can be used. We also show that the LVQ architecture allows common training, i.e., the net can be trained once for a

*This work was supported in part by a Cray Research Award

set of classification tasks and then incrementally trained for specific tasks in the set. In contrast, the MLP architecture requires complete re-training for each classification task.

The chapter is organized as follows. In the next section we develop the background information needed to compare the two architectures. We discuss the BP training algorithm and LVQ training. We also discuss the speech feature sets which were used in the experiments. The next section describes the experiments which were performed and compares the results for the two architectures. The following section discusses of the computational requirements of the architectures, specifically the number of iterations needed for convergence and the applicability of common training in a modular architecture. The final section summarizes our results and conclusions.

2 Background

In this section we describe the two neural net architectures which are compared with respect to the pattern classification tasks. We briefly describe the MLP, and give a more detailed account of the FSCL-LVQ architecture. The rest of the section is devoted to a description of the various speech feature representations which were used for the experiments.

2.1 Multi-Layer Perceptron

The MLP network is a supervised, continuous valued multi-input and multi-output feedforward multi-layer network which utilizes the back-propagation algorithm for training [1,3]. Each layer of the net is fully connected to its subsequent higher layer. For example, all of the nodes of the input layer (the first layer) are connected to the nodes of the second layer.

The back-propagation algorithm used to train the MLP network can be viewed as consisting of two phases: a feed-forward process and a back-propagation process. Learning occurs through the adjustment of weights associated with each neural unit. During the learning phase, an input vector is presented to the net and the vector propagates to the output layer. This is known as the feed-forward process. The output vector generated is then compared with the desired output vector, which is provided by an external "teacher". The back-propagation process, the second process of the learning phase, propagates the error back through lower layers so that the weight matrix of each lower layer can be adjusted. A complete description of the back-propagation learning algorithm can be found in [1].

The BP algorithm used in the experiments was a straightforward implementation of the basic algorithm described in the literature. More advanced algorithms can be used to improve the speed of convergence during training, and a discussion of these techniques can be found in [4].

2.2 Learning Vector Quantizer

The LVQ architecture is a continuous valued multi-input, single-output single-layer network which utilizes a combination unsupervised and supervised training algorithm [2]. The LVQ classifier attempts to determine the optimal decision boundaries between the classes so as to minimize misclassification error. Training occurs in two phases, the first of which is unsupervised training (similar to Kohonen's Self-Organizing Feature Maps [5]) and the second is a supervised training. We use the Frequency Sensitive Competitive Learning (FSCL) algorithm for the first phase and the LVQ training algorithm proposed by Kohonen [2] for the second phase. These two phases are discussed below.

2.2.1 FSCL Training

The FSCL training algorithm was developed to overcome the problem of under-utilization of codewords in Competitive Learning(CL) [6]. Under-utilization of codewords can occur when some subset of the initial codewords are repeatedly selected as the winning codewords during training and are updated. The remaining codewords are then "under-utilized" because they are infrequently updated.

Many Competitive Learning neural networks algorithms have some mechanism to solve this problem. Kohonen Self-organizing Feature Maps [5] maintain topological neighborhoods, forcing all of the codewords in a neighborhood to be updated. The counterpropagation network [7] solves the problem by temporarily withdrawing over-utilized codewords from the competition. This allows other codewords to be chosen and updated.

The method used in FSCL differs from both of the methods mentioned above. In the FSCL network, the distortion measure used to determine the winner unit is modified to include a count of how frequently each unit is the winner. Thus, the chance of winning for each unit is a function of both the distortion and the number of times it has been modified.

Specifically, let $d(x, w_i(t))$ be the distortion measure that we want to minimize during the quantization process, and let $n_i(t)$ be the number of times that neural i has been the winner during training. Then, the modified distortion measure is defined as:

$$d'(x, w_i(t), n_i(t)) = d(x, w_i(t)) \times f(n_i(t)), \tag{1}$$

where x is the input pattern in $\mathbf{R}^n$, $w_i(t)$ is the reference vector at time t, and $f()$ is the "fairness" function which determines how the count influences the modified distortion. In most circumstances, the fairness function can be set to $f(n_i(t)) = n_i(t)$.

After the training process, the weight vectors of the neural units will be roughly adapted to the statistical density function of the inputs vectors. Then we assign each weight vector to the same class as the majority of training vectors that are mapped to that weight vector.

2.2.2 LVQ Training

The second phase of FSCL-LVQ training is done using the LVQ procedure. The LVQ procedure, developed by Kohonen [5], assumes that there are a number of codewords, w_i, distributed in the pattern space. Each class can be assigned more than one codeword, and the class boundaries are decided by these codewords. However, it is not necessary to assign the same number of codewords to each class, since the number of codewords needed depends upon the requirements for linearly defining the class boundaries. In the FSCL-LVQ classifier, initial values for the w_i are defined by the FSCL unsupervised training, instead of the "topological map" method used by Kohonen [5]. During training with labeled exemplar data, each codeword is assigned to the class which has the most data mapped to the codeword during the training process. Afterward, the LVQ supervised training algorithm is used to optimize the vectors w_i which have been been assigned to each class. Let c be the winner node assigned to class C_i for training vector x belonging to class C_j . Update the codeword w_i as:

$$\begin{aligned} w_c(t+1) &= w_c(t) + \epsilon(t)(x(t) - w_c(t)) && \text{if } C_i = C_j \\ w_c(t+1) &= w_c(t) - \epsilon(t)(x(t) - w_c(t)) && \text{if } C_i \neq C_j \\ w_i(t+1) &= w_i(t) && \text{for } i \neq c. \end{aligned} \tag{2}$$

Here $\epsilon(t)$ is the learning rate ($0 < \epsilon(t) < 1$) which is decreased during training.

Combining FSCL unsupervised training and LVQ supervised training results in a classifier well suited to the classification of multi-dimensional data.

It should be noted that the BP learning rule and the LVQ learning rule differ in a fundamental fashion, particularly when used for classification tasks. The back-propagation algorithm uses a generalized Delta Rule [1] to minimize the squared between the actual and desired output values summed over all output units and all pairs of input/output pairs. This is in contrast to the LVQ learning paradigm which attempts to directly minimize classification error.

2.3 Speech Features and Distance Measures

2.3.1 Autocorrelation Coefficients

The first speech feature that we studied is the set of autocorrelation coefficients computed from short-time segments (usually 20 ms) of the speech signal. Let $X(\omega)$ and $Y(\omega)$ represent the spectrum of short-time segments of two speech signals. Let $r_{i,X}$ and $r_{i,Y}$ $i = 0, \cdots, p$ be the corresponding first $(p+1)$ autocorrelation coefficients. We examined two possible distortion measures can be used with autocorrelation coefficients: Euclidean distance and Itakura–Saito distortion.

- *Euclidean Distance:* The Euclidean distance between $X(\omega)$ and $Y(\omega)$ is defined as

$$d(X(\omega), Y(\omega)) = (\sum_{i=0}^{p}(r_{i,X} - r_{i,Y})^2)^{1/2}$$

- *Itakura–Saito distortion:* The Itakura–Saito (I–S) distortion measure is frequently used in speech coding and recognition applications, and is a spectral distortion measure. The I–S distortion between two spectra is defined as

$$d(X(\omega), Y(\omega)) = \int_{-\pi}^{\pi}[\frac{X(\omega)}{Y(\omega)} + \ln(\frac{Y(\omega)}{X(\omega)}) - 1]\frac{d\omega}{2\pi}.$$

Frequently, the speech signal spectrum is modeled as being all–pole using the Linear Predictive Coding (LPC) algorithm [8,9]. In this case,

$$X(\omega) = \frac{\sigma_X^2}{|1 + \sum_{i=1}^{p} a_{i,X}e^{-ji\omega}|^2},$$

$$Y(\omega) = \frac{\sigma_Y^2}{|1 + \sum_{i=1}^{p} a_{i,Y}e^{-ji\omega}|^2}.$$

It can be shown that for such all-pole models, the I–S distortion can be computed as [10]

$$d(X(\omega), Y(\omega)) = \frac{\mathbf{a}_{\mathbf{Y}}^{\mathbf{T}} R_X \mathbf{a}_{\mathbf{Y}}}{\sigma_Y^2} + \ln(\frac{\sigma_Y^2}{\sigma_X^2}) - 1, \tag{3}$$

where R_X is the $(p+1) \times (p+1)$ matrix formed from the autocorrelations $r_{i,X}$ of the signal $X(\omega)$, and $\mathbf{a}_{\mathbf{Y}} = (1\ a_{1,Y} \cdots a_{k,Y})^T$ is a length $(p+1)$ column vector. From (3), it is clear that the I–S distortion measure is very similar to a weighted inner product, with the weighting matrix R_X being signal dependent. Also note that the I–S distortion is not symmetric, i.e.,

$$d(X(\omega), Y(\omega)) \neq d(Y(\omega), X(\omega)). \tag{4}$$

In order to minimize the amount of computation, the I–S distortion is usually computed as [11]

$$d(X(\omega), Y(\omega)) = b_Y(0) r_{0,X} + 2 \sum_{i=1}^{p} b_Y(i) r_{i,X}, \tag{5}$$

where

$$b_Y(i) = \sum_{j=0}^{k-i} a_{j,Y} a_{j+i,Y}, \ a_{0,Y} = 1.$$

During both the training and testing phases of the classifiers when using the I–S distortion measure, each codeword was stored in the form $(r_{0,X}\, r_{1,X}\, r_{2,X} \cdots r_{k,X})^T$. In the training data file, each training datum was stored in two equivalent forms: as the vectors $(b_Y(0)\, 2b_Y(1) \cdots 2b_Y(k))^T$ and $(r_{0,Y}\, r_{1,Y} \cdots r_{k,Y})^T$. This allows the distortion for each neural unit to be computed using Equation 4 using the first form of the training vector. Once the winning unit is determined, the weight vector for the neural unit can be updated using the second form of the training vector. Storing both forms of the training datum thus allows us to use the simple inner product form of the I–S distortion measure, and also allows us to update the weight vectors easily, without the additional computation needed to change between the two forms.

2.3.2 Weighted LPC Cepstral Coefficients

In speech recognition applications, it is desirable to arrive at a representation of the speech signal that is robust with respect to variations in talker, speaking style and noise. Recent results indicate that weighted cepstral coefficients derived from the LPC spectrum of the speech signal are a suitable candidate [12,13]. Thus we used these as our second set of feature vectors.

Again, let $X(\omega)$ be the spectrum of a short-time segment of a speech signal, and let $F(\omega) = \log(X(\omega))$. Then the cepstral coefficients of $X(\omega)$ are defined as

$$c_{k,X} = \frac{1}{2\pi}\int_{-\pi}^{\pi} F(\omega)e^{j\omega k}d\omega.$$

If we assume that $X(\omega)$ fits an all-pole model,

$$X(\omega) = \frac{\sigma_X^2}{\left|1 + \sum_{i=1}^{k} a_{i,X}e^{-ji\omega}\right|^2},$$

then, the c_k coeffiecients are real and can be computed using the recursion formula [12]

$$-kc_{k,X} - ka_{k,X} = \sum_{n=1}^{k-1}(k-n)c_{k-n,X}a_{n,X} \text{ for } k > 0.$$

The cepstral coefficients derived this way are referred to as the LPC-derived cepstral coefficients. The weighted cepstral coefficients, $C_{k,X}$ are obtained by weighting the LPC-derived cepstral coefficients using a bandpass "liftering" window [12],

$$C_{k,X} = c_{k,X}w(k),$$

$$w(k) = 1 + 0.5L\sin(\frac{\pi k}{L}),$$

where L is the length of the LPC vector.

Given two speech segments with spectrum $X(\omega)$ and $Y(\omega)$ and weighted cepstral coefficients $C_{k,X}$ and $C_{k,Y}$, the distance between the two is defined as

$$d(X(\omega), Y(\omega)) = (\sum_{k=1}^{L}(C_{k,X} - C_{k,Y})^2)^{1/2}.$$

2.3.3 Formant Frequencies

The final feature set that we used to represent each speech sound was the frequencies of the first four formants. The formant frequencies were derived from the roots of the corresponding LPC polynomial [8,9]. A dynamic programming algorithm was used to smooth the formant trajectory [14]. Let $f_{i,X}$, $f_{i,Y}$ $i = 1 \cdots, 4$ be the first four formant frequencies of the speech signals $X(\omega)$ and $Y(\omega)$ respectively. Then the distance between the two is defined as

$$d(X(\omega), Y(\omega)) = (\sum_{k=1}^{L}(f_{k,X} - f_{k,Y})^2)^{1/2}.$$

3 Experimental Results

3.1 Experimental Conditions

The speech data used in this study was obtained from ten speakers, five male and five female[1]. Each speaker sustained the vowel in the words *beet, bat, boot, bought, bach, burt* for about a second. The recordings were made using an ElectroVoice microphone in a sound booth and directly digitized into VAX 11/750 computer at a 10 KHz sampling rate. Each sample was of 16 bits accuracy.

Each sustained vowel phonation from each speaker was divided into two equal parts. One part was used for the training of the recognizer, and the second part was used for testing the recognizer. Unless otherwise indicated, all recognition results reported here pertain to the test data set.

The analysis of the speech signal to extract the speech features was done using the ESPS Speech Processing Package [15]. A crude form of pitch-synchronous analysis [15] was performed; the average frame rate therefore differs from speaker to speaker and vowel to vowel. For each vowel and speaker, the following features were computed:

1. The first fifteen autocorrelation coefficients, $r_{i,X}, i = 0, \cdots, 14$;
2. The weighted cepstral coefficients, $C_{i,X}, i = 1, \cdots, 15$; and
3. The first four formant frequencies, $f_{i,X}, i = 1, \cdots, 4$.

3.2 Vowel Recognition Experiments

We performed a number of speaker–independent vowel recognition experiments to study the effects of the distortion measure, the input feature, and noise on the performance of the two classifiers.

3.2.1 Effects of Distortion Measure on Classifier Performance

The MLP classifier is typically trained using the backpropagation (BP) algorithm. The BP algorithm attempts to determine the weights in the network by minimizing the squared er-

[1]The data used in the study was provided by Dr. D.G. Childers of the Mind–Machine Interaction Research Center at the University of Florida. We are grateful for his assistance.

ror between the actual and desired outputs. The FSCL-LVQ network, on the other hand, allows any distortion measure to be used in the FSCL stage of the training algorithm. Next, in the LVQ stage, the probability of misclassification is minimized. Does this offer any special advantages for the FSCL-LVQ procedure? In particular, since the I–S distortion measure has proven useful in conventional speech recognition experiments, are there advantages to using the I–S distortion during the FSCL step of the training procedure?

To answer this question, consider Tables 1,2, and 3. These three tables show the percentage misclassification error for vowel recognition when the first fifteen autocorrelation coefficients are used as the input feature. Table 1 shows the results for the MLP, Table 2 for the FSCL-LVQ network when using the Euclidean distance measure, and Table 3 for the FSCL-LVQ classifier using the I–S distortion measure. In all three cases, the results are best when the training and testing sets match (i.e. trained on male+female data, tested on male+female data.) The very interesting result however, is that average errors for the FSCL-LVQ classifier using the I–S distortion measure are significantly lower than for the other two classifiers. This clearly illustrates the fact the choice of the proper distortion measure can have significant benefits. This also points out a potential advantage of the FSCL-LVQ classifier as compared to the MLP classifier, since FSCL-LVQ can be trained using any appropriate distortion measure, while MLP is typically restricted to squared error[2].

Table 1: Percentage Misclassification. MLP ($15 \times 16 \times 6$); Input data : Autocorrelation coefficients.

Testing Set	*Training Set*		
	5 Males	5 Females	Males + Females
5 Males	2.08	63.58	4.0
5 Females	54.00	15.92	25.67
Males + Females	28.04	39.75	14.83

[2]Strictly speaking, the requirement for the BP training algorithm is that the error measure be differentiable with respect to the network weights. Thus other error measures besides squared error that satisfy this criterion can be used. But using the squared error has the advantage that it leads to a simple procedure for updating the weights without requiring the storage of additional quantities. The squared error is the most common error measure used with MLP classifiers.

Table 2: Percentage Misclassification error. FSCL-LVQ (15 × 60); Input data : autocorrelation coefficients; Distortion measure : Euclidean.

Testing Set	*Training Set*		
	5 Males	5 Females	Males + Females
5 Males	11.17	70.25	11.83
5 Females	64.17	17.25	17.25
Males + Females	37.67	43.75	14.54

Table 3: Percentage misclassification. FSCL-LVQ (16 × 60); Input data : autocorrelation coefficients; Distortion measure : Itakura-Saito

Testing Set	*Training Set*		
	5 Males	5 Females	Males + Females
5 Males	1.50	59.33)	3.92
5 Females	54.00	3.83	9.25
Males + Females	27.75	31.58	6.58

3.2.2 Comparison of Different Speech Features

In this experiment, we wanted to study the effects of the input feature used on the recognition performance. To this end, we repeated the vowel classification experiments using three different feature sets: (1) the autocorrelation coefficients; (2) the weighted cepstral coefficients; and (3) the formant frequencies. An important point to note here is that all three representations contain the same amount of information, in that any one representation can be derived from the other. Thus any difference in performance has to be attributed to how well the representation partitions the input space and how well the particular classifier is able to take advantage of the partitions. The results are shown in Tables 1, 4, and 6 for the MLP classifier and in Tables 3, 5, and 7 for the FSCL-LVQ classifier. All classifiers except the FSCL-LVQ classifier using the autocorrelation coefficients as input were trained using a squared error measure. The results in these tables clearly show that the weighted cepstral coefficients lead to the best performance for both the MLP and the FSCL-LVQ classifiers. The performance with the formant input is slightly worse, while the performance with the autocorrelation coefficients as input is substantially worse. Thus, it appears that in speech recognition, the choice of the appropriate input feature can significantly affect recognition performance. In a later section, we will see that it also has a significant effect on the training time for the classifier.

Table 4: Percentage misclassification error. MLP (15 × 16 × 6); Input data : LPC weighted cepstral coefficients.

Testing Set	*Training Set*		
	5 Males	5 Females	Males + Females
5 Males	0.92	59.00	1.42
5 Females	58.00	2.25	1.00
Males + Females	29.46	30.63	1.21

Table 5: Percentage misclassification error. FSCL-LVQ (15 × 48); Input data : LPC weighted cepstral coefficients.

Testing Set	*Training Set*		
	5 Males	5 Females	Males + Females
5 Males	0.17	51.75	1.17
5 Females	49.42	1.67	2.58
Males + Females	24.79	26.71	1.88

3.2.3 Effects of Noise on Vowel Classification Performance

It is frequently the case that a speech recognizer is trained in a quiet room with high signal-to-noise (SNR) data, but has to be used in an environment where the noise conditions are substantially different. To see how this affects the classifier performance, we trained the MLP and FSCL-LVQ classifiers with features extracted from the clean speech signal, and tested their performance with noisy data. The noisy data was created by adding synthetically generated white Gaussian noise to the clean data. The variance of the synthesized noise was adjusted to yield the desired SNR.

Table 6: Percentage misclassification error. MLP ($4 \times 16 \times 6$); Input data : Formant Inputs.

Testing Set	*Training Set*		
	5 Males	5 Females	Males + Females
5 Males	3.42	53.67	3.33
5 Females	33.92	4.67	4.17
Males + Females	18.67	29.17	3.75

Table 7: Percentage misclassification error. FSCL-LVQ (4×60); Input data : Formant Inputs.

Testing Set	*Training Set*		
	5 Males	5 Females	Males + Females
5 Males	1.42	67.92	1.75
5 Females	59.17	0.08	4.75
Males + Females	30.29	34.0	3.25

The results showing the misclassification percentage are shown in Figs. 1, 2, and 3 for the cases of autocorrelation coefficients, weighted cepstral coefficients and formants as input respectively. While the misclassification percentage increases with decreasing SNR in all cases, it is seen that the MLP and FSCL-LVQ classifiers using the autocorrelation coefficients appear to be most robust with respect to noise. Thus, even though these do not represent the best classifiers in the noiseless case, their performance degrades much more slowly when noise is added than any of the other classifiers. Also, for the FSCL-LVQ classifier, the one using the I–S distortion measure does well; the FSCL-LVQ using the Euclidean distance does poorly.

It is not clear at this time why the MLP classifier using the autocorrelation coefficients and a Euclidean distance measure does well while the FSCL-LVQ using the same error measure does not. We are presently investigating this further.

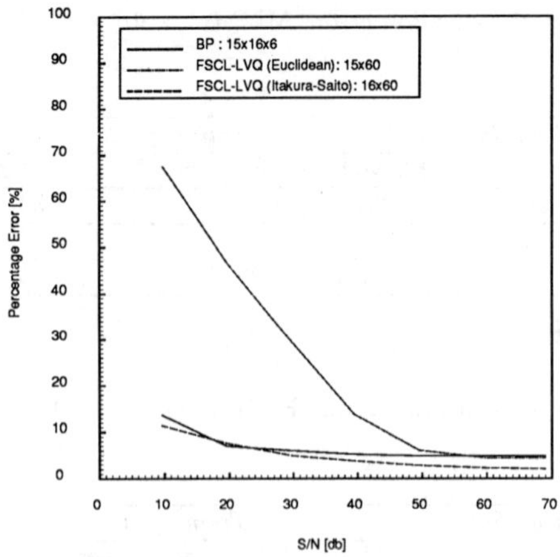

Figure 1: Noise performance using auto-correlation coefficients.

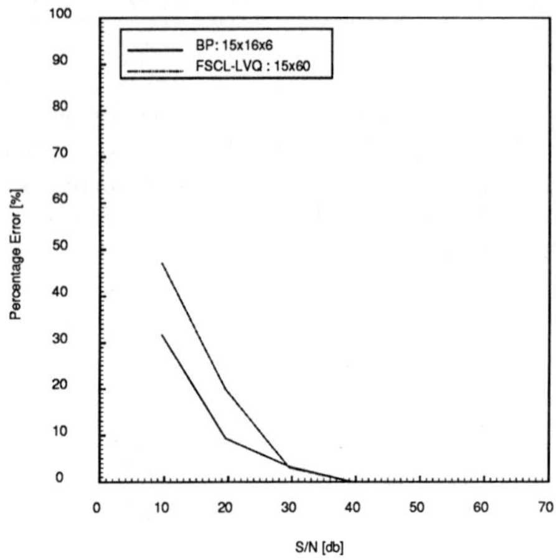

Figure 2: Noise performance using weighted cepstral coefficients.

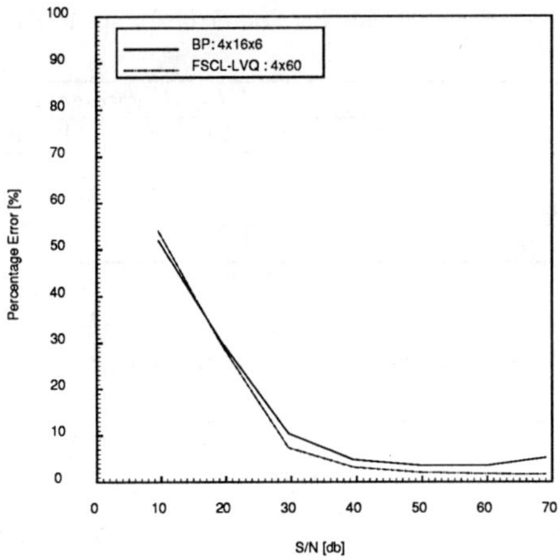

Figure 3: Noise performance using formant frequencies.

3.3 Speaker and Gender Recognition Experiments

We also performed speaker and gender recognition experiments using the same data and representation as for the vowel recognition task. The objective was to compare the effects of the input representation on recognition performance for a different task. Also, for the case of the FSCL-LVQ classifiers, the FSCL phase of the training is common across all tasks. We wanted to see if this would still yield good recognition performance.

The results are shown in Table 8 for the speaker recognition task and in Table 9 for the gender recognition task. The tables show the percentage of misclassification for the two network architectures and for the different input representations.

The speaker recognition results (Table 8) show that the FSCL-LVQ classifiers, in general, do better than the MLP. The best performance is achieved with the FSCL-LVQ network when using the weighted cepstral coefficients as the input, and the percentage misclassification is substantially lower in this case. The results for the gender recognition task (Table 9) show less difference between the MLP and the FSCL-LVQ classifiers, but again the best performance is obtained with the weighted cepstral coefficients as the input feature.

Table 8: Percentage misclassification error for speaker recognition.

Networks	*Input representation*		
	Auto-corr.	LPC weighted cepstral	Formant
Back-prop. net	25.0	16.08	26.54
FSCL-LVQ (Euclidean)	19.0	4.21	14.08
FSCL-LVQ (Itakara-Saito)	11.75	-	-

Table 9: Percentage misclassification error for gender recognition.

Networks	*Input representations*		
	Auto-corr.	LPC weighted cepstral	Formant
Back-prop. net	4.92	2.63	8.33
FSCL-LVQ (Euclidean)	4.88	0.88	4.83
FSCL-LVQ (Itakara-Saito)	2.42	-	-

The results indicate that the weighted cepstral coefficients form the best feature set for all three recognition tasks. We speculate that this representation results in a distribution of the training data in a way that allows the optimum decision surfaces to be easily formed.

3.4 Computational Issues

In this section we discuss the computational aspects of the neural network classifiers used in the experiments. We will show that the LVQ classifier converges with less training, and has the additional advantage of *common training.*

Figure 4 shows the rate of convergence for three neural classifiers – one MLP net and two LVQ nets. The percentage of misclassified vowels is shown as a function of the number of iterations, where an iteration is defined as one complete pass through the entire set of training vectors.

Note that the measured error displayed in the Figures begins at differing number of iterations for the various nets. For the experiment shown, the BP net was trained by

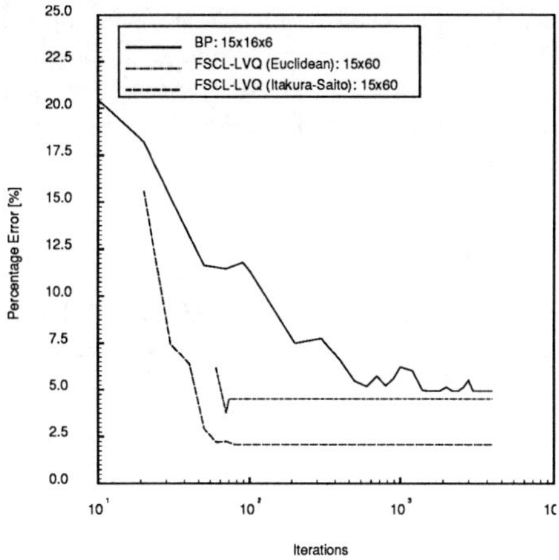

Figure 4: Convergence rates of three neural classifiers.

successive iterations through a set of 2400 auto-correlation coefficients, each labeled with the correct vowel classification. The desired output vector was a six element vector, where the correct vowel index was assigned a value of one and the others assigned a value of zero. Thus, classification errors can be measured with each pass through the data because the entire training process is supervised.

In contrast, as previously described, both of the LVQ classifiers undergo a training process which consists of two phases, an unsupervised first phase followed by a second supervised phase. The first phase of training effectively finds the cluster centers of the input distribution using the FSCL training algorithm, and assigns those cluster centers to the nodes of the neural network. During this phase, the classification of each training vector is ignored, since the clustering is a self-organizing process. The LVQ training algorithm is then used to adjust the classification boundaries. This entire process is labeled FSCL-LVQ to emphasize the two step training process.

The FSCL-LVQ net which utilizes Euclidean distortion required 60 iterations to find acceptable cluster centers, while the FSCL-LVQ net which used Itakura-Saito distortion required only 20 iterations. After the FSCL training was completed, the LVQ training phase was begun and classification errors measured. As the figure shows, the classification errors the FSCL-LVQ nets reached acceptable levels in approximately 100 iterations, while the BP net required significantly more training. It should be noted that [4] indicates techniques that can be used to speed BP training, but these techniques were not used. Nonetheless, the LVQ architecture yields significant improvements in the amount of training iterations required for convergence.

3.4.1 Common Training

An additional advantage of the LVQ architecture is that it allows the first unsupervised training phase to be used to perform a number of tasks, as shown in Tables 10 and 11.

Table 10: Training set iterations required for various tasks and networks. Feature sets comprised of auto-correlation coefficients collected from 5 males and 5 females. FSCL-LVQ nets used Itakura-Saito distortion.

Networks : Back-propagation ($15 \times 16 \times 6$)
FSCL-LVQ, Itakara-Saito distortion (15×60)

Tasks	Back-prop.	FSCL	LVQ	FSCL-LVQ
Vowel recog	3000	60 common for all tasks	13	73
Gender recog.	5400		6	66
Speaker recog.	12400		9	69

As can be seen from the tables, one phase of unsupervised FSCL training was used to develop cluster centers from the data for the tasks of vowel recognition, gender recognition, and speaker recognition. Then, for each task, a supervised LVQ training phase used the same training vectors but with an appropriate label to indicate vowel, gender, or speaker. This is in contrast to the BP architecture, in which a complete training process was required for the BP net for each of the tasks.

In some cases, this advantage was rather limited, since only limited training can be shared by the tasks. In some cases, 20 iterations through the training set was sufficient to develop cluster centers, but this was followed by substantial supervised training.

However, for some of the experiments, substantial saving of computation could be realized using the FSCL-LVQ technique. For example, Table 11 shows and example of a case in which very little supervised training was required after the cluster centers were formed, regardless of the classification task.

Table 11: Training set iterations required for various tasks and networks. Feature sets comprised of LPC weighted cepstral coefficients collected from 5 males and 5 females. FSCL-LVQ nets used Euclidean distortion.

Networks : Back-propagation ($15 \times 16 \times 6$)
FSCL-LVQ (15×60)

Tasks	Back-prop.	FSCL	LVQ	FSCL-LVQ
Vowel recog	90	20	3	23
Gender recog.	20	common for	1	21
Speaker recog.	1000	all tasks	3	23

The efficacy of common training seems to be dependent on both the input representation and the distortion measure utilized, but largely independent of the task. However; the amount of training required for the BP classifier seems to depend on the task and the input representation.

4 Conclusions

We have shown that the FSCL-LVQ architecture offers a number of distinct advantages over the MLP architecture. These advantages are:

- Arbitrary distortion measures: The FSCL-LVQ training algorithm allows the use of any distortion measure, while the BP algorithm attempts to modify weights in the network by minimizing squared error between the actual and desired outputs. Consequently, for some tasks, the LVQ architecture can perform more accurate classification. For example, for the vowel recognition task average errors for the FSCL-LVQ classifier using the I–S distortion measure are significantly lower than for the Euclidean distance. This clearly illustrates the fact the choice of the proper distortion measure can have significant benefits.
- Common training: For some tasks substantial computational savings can be realized using the FSCL-LVQ technique. In particular, some tasks require very little LVQ supervised training after the cluster centers are formed using FSCL training, regardless of the the classification task. In contrast, MLP architectures using BP training

require complete training for each task, and the amount of training seems to depend on the task and the input representation.

- Rapid training convergence: Our results show that the LVQ training algorithm requires less training iterations than the MLP/BP. Although there are more sophisticated MLP training algorithms which reduce the number of training iterations required, these usually require more computation per training iteration.

We have also shown that the feature set used in classification can have a significant difference in recognition performance in a variety of ways. For instance, the vowel recognition results clearly show that the weighted cepstral coefficients lead to the best performance for both the MLP and the FSCL-LVQ classifiers. Furthermore, the effects of noise are less pronounced with some feature sets than others. The experiment show that while misclassification percentage increases with decreasing SNR in all of the experiments, it is seen that the MLP and FSCL-LVQ classifiers using the autocorrelation coefficients appear to be most robust with respect to noise. Thus, even though these do not represent the best classifiers in the noiseless case, their performance degrades much more slowly when noise is added than any of the other classifiers.

Finally, the speaker recognition results show that the FSCL-LVQ classifiers, in general, do better than the MLP and the best performance is achieved using the FSCL-LVQ network when using the weighted cepstral coefficients as the input, and the percentage misclassification is substantially lower in this case. Although the results for the gender recognition task show less difference between the MLP and the FSCL-LVQ classifiers, again the best performance is obtained with the weighted cepstral coefficients as the input feature.

The results indicate that the weighted cepstral coefficients form the best feature set for all three recognition tasks. We speculate that this representation results in a distribution of the training data in a manner that allows the decision surfaces to be easily formed.

References

[1] D. E. Rumelhart, J. L. McClelland, *et al.*, *Parallel Distributed Processing.* Cambridge, Massachusetts: MIT Press, 1986.

[2] T. Kohonen, "Learning Vector Quantization," in *Abstracts of the First Annual INNS Meeting*, p. 303, Boston, MA, Sept. 6 - 10, 1988.

[3] D. C. Plaut and G. E. Hinton, "Learning sets of filters using back-propagation," *Computer Speech and Language*, vol. 2, pp. 35–61, 1987.

[4] P. D. Wasserman, *Neural Computing: Theory and Practice.* New York: Van Nostrand Reinhold, 1989.

[5] T. Kohonen, *Self–Organization and Associative Memory, 2nd Ed.* Berlin: Springer–Veralg, 1988.

[6] S. C. Ahalt, A. K. Krishnamurthy, P. Chen, and D. E. Melton, "Competitive learning algorithms for vector quantization," *Neural Networks*, 1989. (to appear in May 1990 issue).

[7] R. Hecht–Nielsen, "Applications of Counterpropagation Networks," *Neural Networks*, vol. 1, no. 2, pp. 131–141, 1988.

[8] J. Markel and A. Gray, *Linear Prediction of Speech.* New York: Springer–Verlag, 1976.

[9] L. Rabiner and R. Schafer, *Digital Processing of Speech Signals.* Englewood Cliffs, NJ: Prentice–Hall, 1978.

[10] D. O'Shaughnessy, *Speech Communication: Human and Machine.* Reading, Mass.: Addison-Wesley, 1987.

[11] A. Buzo, A. H. Gray, Jr., R. M. Gray, and J. D. Markel, "Speech Coding based upon Vector Quantization," *IEEE Transactions on Acoustics, Speech, and Signal Processing*, vol. ASSP-28, no. 5, pp. 562–574, October 1980.

[12] B. Juang, L. R. Rabiner, and J. G. Wilppon, "On the use of bandpass filtering in speech recognition," *IEEE Transactions on Acoustics, Speech, and Signal Processing*, vol. ASSP-35, no. 7, pp. 947–954, July 1987.

[13] B. A. Hanson and H. Wakita, "Spectral slope distance measure with linear prediction analysis for word recognition in noise," *IEEE Transactions on Acoustics, Speech, and Signal Processing*, vol. ASSP-35, no. 7, pp. 968–973, July 1987.

[14] D. Talkin, "Voicingepoch determination with Dynamic Programming," in *117th Meeting: Acoustical Society of America*, p. S149, Syracuse, NY, 1989.

[15] Entropic Speech, Inc., *Entropic Signal Processing Systems.* April 1989.

7

NEURAL NETWORKS FOR MODEL BASED RECOGNITION

by Gene Gindi,[‡] Eric Mjolsness,[†] and P. Anandan[†]
Yale University

1 Introduction

The minimization of objective functions is an attractive way to formulate and solve visual recognition problems. Such formulations are parsimonious, being expressible in several lines of algebra, and may be converted into artificial neural networks which perform the optimization. Advantages of such networks including speed, parallelism, cheap analog computing, the ability to support learning and biological plausibility have been noted [Hopfield-85].

According to a common view of computational vision, recognition involves the construction of abstract descriptions of data governed by a data base of *models*. Abstractions serve as reduced descriptions of complex data useful for reasoning about the objects and events in the scene. The models indicate what objects and properties may be expected in the scene. The complexity of visual recognition demands that the models be organized into compositional hierarchies which express object-part relationships and specialization hierarchies which express object-class relationships.

Here, we describe a methodology [Mjolsness-89a], [Mjolsness-89b] for expressing model-based visual recognition as the constrained minimization of an objective function. Model-specific objective functions are used to govern the dynamic grouping of image elements into recognizable wholes. Neural networks are used to carry out the minimization.

Previous work on optimization in vision [Barrow-71,Burr-83,Hummel-83,Terzopoulos-86] has typically been restricted to computations occuring at a single of level of abstraction and/or involving a single model. For example, surface interpolation schemes, even when they include discontinuities [Terzopoulos-86] do not include explicit models for physical objects whose surface characteristics determine the expected degree of smoothness. By contrast, heterogeneous and hierarchical model-bases often occur in non-optimization approaches to visual recognition [Hanson-86] including some which use neural networks [Ballard-86]. We attempt to obtain greater expressability and efficiency by incorporating hierarchies of abstraction into the optimization paradigm.

This work represents a departure from most neural-net applications to vision in two senses. Neural network formulations of vision problems have usually been applied to early vision problems where the style of processing is uniform; for example the computation of retinotopic dense fields such as as optical flow. Here, an attempt is made to formulate model-based visual recognition, in which the style of processing has typically been nonuniform, as a optimization problem to be carried out by a network. Another departure is the explicit incorporation of hierarchies in the model base. In this work, we also will introduce methods for obtaining improvements in programmability and efficiency by incorporating hierarchical organizations into the optimization paradigm.

2 Casting Model Matching as Optimization

Our approach to the use of optimization in vision involves matching some part of a database of models to perceived data. Because both the models and perceived data will be organized as graphs, our approach becomes an elaboration of graph matching. To this end, we first illustrate the approach for the simpler problem of exact graph matching. We then consider the transition from graph matching to model matching.

2.1 Model Matching as Graph Matching

Consider the following problem of pure graph matching (see Figure 1). Given two graphs each consisting of N nodes, let α $(1 \leq \alpha \leq N)$ index the nodes of one of the graphs, and i $(1 \leq i \leq N)$ index the nodes of the other. Let $G_{\alpha\beta}$ be the connection matrix of one of the graphs, i.e. $G_{\alpha\beta} = 1$ if the nodes α and β are connected by an arc; otherwise $G_{\alpha\beta} = 0$. Likewise g_{ij} is the connection matrix of the other graph. A sparse match matrix M $(0 \leq M_{\alpha i} \leq 1)$, of dynamic variables represents the correspondence between nodes α and i. Note that the entries in the graph connection matrices and those in the match matrix represent the pointers that are typically used in symbolic graph matching, but the numerical encoding has the advantage that it allows for concise expression of objective functions.

A simple objective function for this match matrix just maximizes the number of consistent rectangles[Hopfield-84a] (see Figure 1):

$$E(M) = -\sum_{\alpha\beta}\sum_{ij} G_{\alpha\beta} g_{ij} M_{\alpha i} M_{\beta j}. \tag{1}$$

This expression may be understood as follows: Given nodes α and i, the match value $M_{\alpha i}$ is to be increased if the neighbors of α match to the neighbors of i. If nodes β and j are neighbors of α and i, respectively, (i.e., $G_{\alpha\beta} = 1$ and $g_{ij} = 1$), then a nonzero $M_{\beta j}$ is evidence of such a neighborhood match, hence $M_{\alpha i}$ should be increased. By symmetry, a non-zero $M_{\alpha i}$ causes an increase in $M_{\beta j}$. As shown in Figure 1, nodes 2 and 3 on the model side and 1 and 4 on the data side form the corners of a "rectangle". For a binary-valued match matrix, E as defined in equation 1 merely counts the

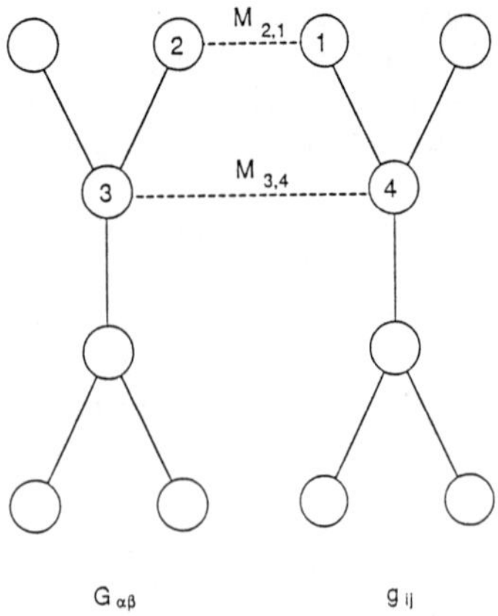

Figure 1: **Graph Matching** – The circles represent graph nodes, the solid lines graph arcs and the dotted lines matches between nodes in two different graphs. The nodes **1,2,3** and **4** form a consistent rectangle.

number of consistent rectangles in the system. Thus minimizing E is the same as maximizing the number of consistent rectangles.

Note that E as defined above can be trivially minimized by setting all the elements of the match matrix to unity. However, to do so will violate the syntactical constraint of having a one-to-one match between nodes. For the case at hand where the two graphs have equal numbers of nodes, such syntactic constraints can be expressed as follows:

$$\begin{aligned} \sum_\alpha M_{\alpha i} - 1 &= 0 \\ \sum_i M_{\alpha i} - 1 &= 0. \end{aligned} \tag{2}$$

In addition, we may also require that the elements of the matrix be binary-valued, i.e.,

$$M_{\alpha i}(1 - M_{\alpha i}) = 0. \tag{3}$$

In summary, the graph matching problem can be expressed as the problem of minimizing the objective function shown in equation 1, subject to the constraints given in equations 2 and 3.

A similar objective function for pure graph matching has been found independently by von der Malsburg and Bienenstock [von der Malsburg-86]. Also, Cooper and Hollbach [Cooper-87], [Cooper-88], [Feldman-88] have described a neural network expressing much the same graph-matching strategy,

The transition from pure graph matching to model matching is achieved by first identifying the graph $G_{\alpha\beta}$ as a model, and identifying g_{ij} as the data. However, to complete the transition the above graph needs to be augmented in a number of ways. To represent complex visual objects, the nodes of the data graph must include quantitative parameters that record information about shape, size, position, etc. In addition to checking the structural similarity between model and data graphs, the matching process should also measure the degree to which the data-side parameters satisfy the requirements imposed on them from the model side. Since object recognition must be independent of transformations such as translation, rotation, and scaling, parameters must be checked in a manner independent of these transformations. Although it may be possible to precompute and store the parameter checks in tables, geometric transformations (which typically occur in shape recognition) are sufficiently complex, and the incoming data may vary over a sufficiently wide range, that the table will be prohibitively large. This implies that the necessary arithmetic should be done dynamically.

As discussed above, we also require that nodes on the data side must be capable of representing objects at different levels of abstraction. To introduce the compositional hierarchy, there must be nodes representing wholes and nodes representing parts, and a special graph representing the relationship between parts and wholes. Since a single whole is usually connected to several parts, the part-whole graph is restricted to be a tree (or generally a Directed Acyclic Graph or DAG). Given a model node and a data node which matches it, all nodes which represent the parts of the data node must find unique matches among the parts of the model node.

In the simple graph matching example given above, the arcs between the nodes on the data side were provided as input. However, in most recognition and grouping problems, the dynamic determination of part-whole relationships and group membership is itself a significant and unavoidable task. The matching process should compute such relationships rather than assume them as input. The dynamic character of the grouping problem also implies that a node representing a group may not even exist until at least some of its parts have been determined. At that time the node may be allocated.

The motivation for incorporating specialization hierarchies includes the search efficiency provided by using a discrimination tree to index the models, and the notational convenience provided by the inheritance of properties from the general to the more specialized models. In particular, the addition of a specialized model requires only the verification of new properties not shared with the more general model; all the properties which are shared with the general model are automatically inherited. In order to achieve this, our model base should incorporate a specialization hierarchy (in the form of a tree or a DAG), the data nodes should be allowed to simultaneously match to a model and at most one of its specializations, and the match process should include property inheritance.

In summary, in order make the transition from pure graph matching to model matching and perceptual grouping, we have identified the following design requirements: parameter checks and arithmetic operations involving parameters, a compositional hierarchy with nodes representing objects at different levels of abstraction, dynamic allocation, and a specialization hierarchy with property inheritance.

2.2 Frames and Objective Functions

The introduction of compositional hierarchy to the pure graph matching problem is straightforward. We simply let the connection matrices represent part-whole relationships between objects and denote them as $INA_{\alpha\beta}$ on the model side and as ina_{ij} on the data side. The need for dynamic allocation of part-whole relationships implies that the data side ina values cannot be predetermined. This means that ina_{ij} will, in general, be a variable quantity. Also, the dynamic determination of "groups" implies that the parameters of the data node representing the group cannot be predetermined; hence, these parameters must also be variable quantities.

The addition of variable parameters to the data nodes suggests a natural organization: we package the parameters into "frames" which are bundles F_i of variable parameters F_{is}, where s indexes the different parameters (or "slots") of a frame. Frames can be regarded as representing visual abstractions or perceptual organizations in terms of a few parameters. The process of dynamically employing a frame to represent an abstraction is called "allocating" a frame. We will refer to such a network of frames and models as "Frameville". Our use frames is motivated by the conventional use of the same idea as established in [Minsky-75,Fahlman-79]. Our frames contain slots for parameters, and are connected to other frames via ina links. No information concerning the match criteria or information about the control flow is included in the frame. Our match criteria are expressed as objective functions while our control process is based on the particular choice of a technique for minimizing the objective function.

We introduce the necessary modifications to the objective functions and constraints in order to perform model matching with the aid of a Frameville example (Figure 2). The rectangle shown in Figure 2b is the extension of the rectangle shown in the pure graph matching problem (see Figure 1). Equation 1 becomes the "rectangle" rule:

$$E(M) = -\sum_{\alpha\beta}\sum_{ij} INA_{\alpha\beta} ina_{ij} M_{\alpha i} M_{\beta j}. \tag{4}$$

This expression may be understood as follows: For model α and frame i, the match value $M_{\alpha i}$ is to be increased if the neighbors of α (in the INA graph) match to the neighbors of i (in the ina graph). Note that $E(M)$ as defined above can be trivially minimized by setting all the elements of the match matrix to unity. However, to do so will violate additional syntactic constraints (discussed below) which are imposed on the optimization.

Whereas in the case of graph matching the sole syntactic constraint was that of one-to-one matches between data and model nodes, with the introduction of the compositional (and specialization) hierarchies, more complex syntactic constraints are needed. The new syntactic constraints will be discussed below. In Figure 2b, the ovals on the left represent the models while the triangles on the right are the data side frames. The circles inside the triangles represent the parameters

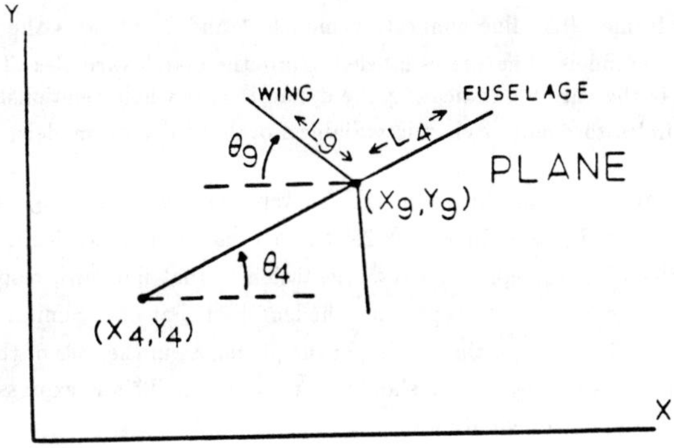

(a)

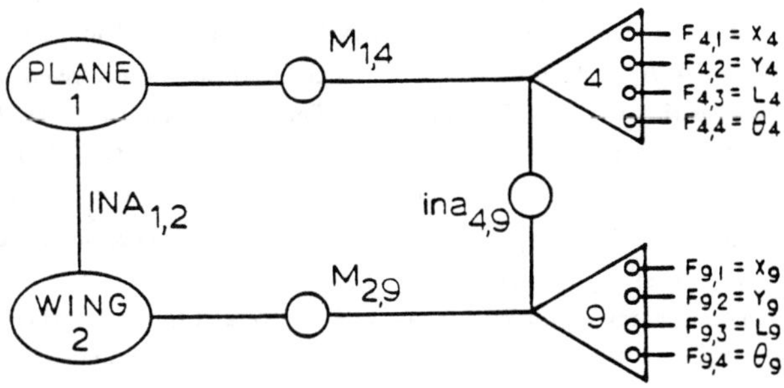

(b)

Figure 2: **Example of Frameville rectangle rule.** (a) Example object, a plane, consists of parameterized parts fuselage and wings. (b) shows the rectangle relationship between frames (triangles) representing a wing and the fuselage. The open circles symbolize dynamic variables that interact according to Equations 4 and 5. The ovals represent the models (plane and wing) and the arc connecting them represents the *INA* relationship between them.

(slots) of the frame. The line connecting models 1 and 2 indicates the part-whole relationship between the two models. The circles labeled M are the match variables. The circle labeled ***ina*** on the data side is the variable indicating the dynamic part-whole relationship between the frames. We will use circles to denote dynamic variables, ovals to denote models, and triangles to denote frames.

In this example, the parameters of the line representing the fuselage are also used as the parameters of the entire plane. In Figure 2a, the parameters (x_4, y_4) denote the coordinates of the end point of that line, θ_4 represents the orientation of that line with respect to an arbitrary but fixed coordinate system, and L_4 represents the length of that line. Similarly $(x_9, y_9, \theta_9, L_9)$ are the parameters of the line representing a wing of the plane. As in the case of the pure graph matching, the number of consistent rectangles should be maximized. This is expressed as the minimization of the term given above in equation 4.

Additionally, in order for the rectangle $(1, 4, 9, 2)$ to be consistent, the parameters F_{4s} and F_{9s} should satisfy the criterion indexed by models 1 and 2. Such a constraint generally results in the addition of the following term to the objective function:

$$\sum_{i,j,\alpha,\beta} INA_{\alpha\beta} ina_{ij} M_{\alpha i} M_{\beta j} H^{\alpha\beta}(F_{i1}, F_{i2}, \ldots, F_{j1}, F_{j2}, \ldots) \tag{5}$$

where the term $H^{\alpha\beta}(.,.)$ measures the deviation of the parameters of the data side frames from what is demanded by the models. Equation 5 expresses a general principle of Frameville, namely that objective functions can be model specific. This is an extension of the usual use of distance metrics in pattern recognition. Here the metric to be used is context dependent–indeed there is an entire database of metrics $H^{\alpha\beta}$. In the example in Figure 2 we specifically require that the end point of the line representing the wing should lie on the line representing the plane (fuselage), and that the wing should be at some reasonable angle for being a wing, e.g., the relative angle of the wing to the fuselage should be in the range $(45 - 90°)$. The term H can express coordinate transformation arithmetic (e.g. $H^{\alpha\beta}(x_i, x_j) = 1/2[x_i - x_j - \Delta x_{\alpha\beta}]^2$), and its action on a frame $\vec{F}_i$ is selectively controlled or "gated" by M and ina variables.

To illustrate the dynamic character of the matching variables M and the "allocation" variables ina we include an additional part (the tail) to our example (see Figure 3). We impose the additional constraints that a single frame (say 7) cannot match simultaneously the wing (model 2) and the tail (model 3), and that a single model (say 2) cannot match simultaneously two different frames (say 7 and 9) which are constituents of the same parent frame (say 4). More generally, two distinct parts of the same whole on the model side must match two distinct frames and vice-versa. To express the competition as shown in Figure 3, we have found the following formulation to be useful:

$$\sum_{\alpha} INA_{\alpha\beta} M_{\alpha i} - \sum_{j} ina_{ij} M_{\beta j} \;=\; 0, \;\; \forall \beta, i \tag{6}$$

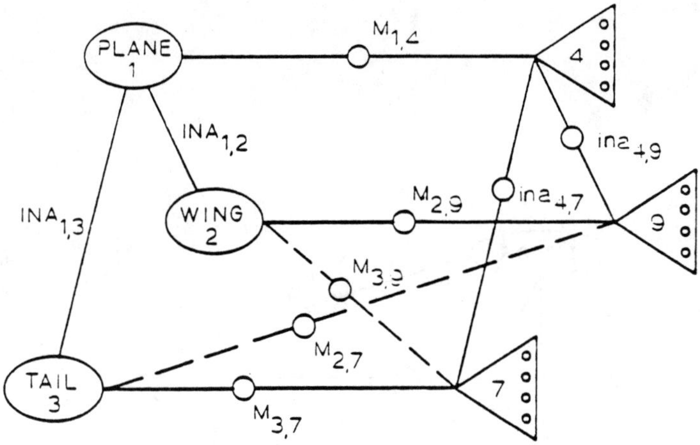

Figure 3: **Frameville sibling competition among parts.** The match variables along the dotted lines ($M_{3,9}$ and $M_{2,7}$) are suppressed in favor of those along the solid lines ($M_{2,9}$ and $M_{3,7}$)

$$\sum_i ina_{ij} M_{\alpha i} - \sum_\beta INA_{\alpha\beta} M_{\beta j} \quad = \quad 0, \ \forall \alpha, j \tag{7}$$

where the first sum in each equation is necessary when several high-level models (or frames) share a part. (It turns out that the first sums can be forced to zero or one by other constraints.) Obviously, the correct assignment of the frames to models will be determined by the most consistent parameter checks.

We illustrate the incorporation of a specialization hierarchy by modifying the example shown in Figure 2 to the one shown in Figure 4. Specifically, two competing specializations, "propeller-plane" and "jet-plane" are introduced, along with the corresponding specializations of the wing model. We incorporate a specialization hierarchy by introducing a link on the model side called $ISA_{\alpha\beta}$, a binary matrix equal to unity if model β is a specialization of a model α. A frame may simultaneously match to a model and at most one of its specializations. Thus, in this example we require that Frame 4, which matches to the plane (model 1) should also match uniquely to one of jet-plane (model 4) and propeller-plane (model 6). Similarly Frame 9, which matches the wing (model 2) also matches uniquely to one of models 5 and 7 (prop-wing and jet-wing respectively). In general, matches between ISA siblings compete for matches to a given frame; it is this competition which makes the network act as a discrimination tree, and is expressed as

$$M_{\alpha i} - \sum_\beta ISA_{\alpha\beta} M_{\beta i} = 0. \tag{8}$$

Note that property inheritance is automatically achieved by allowing the same frame to match to

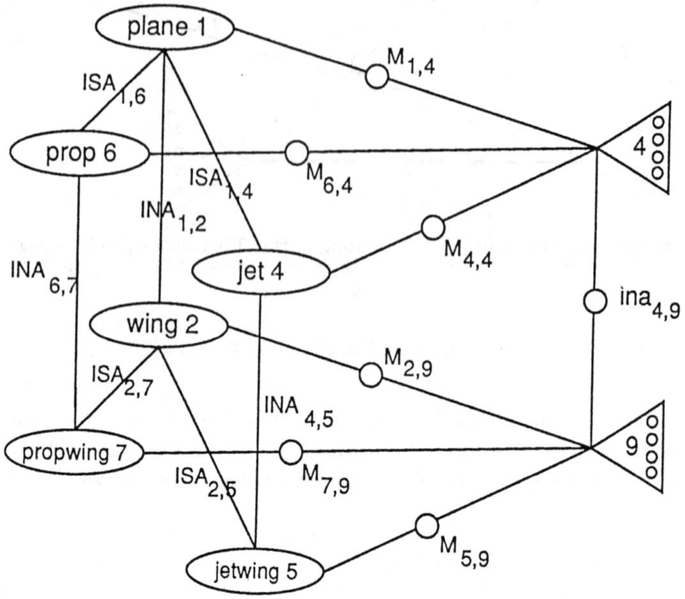

Figure 4: **Frameville specialization hierarchy**. The *plane* model specializes along *ISA* links to a *propeller plane* or a *jet plane* and correspondingly the *wing* model specializes to ***prop-wing*** or *jet-wing*. Sibling match variables $M_{6,4}$ and $M_{4,4}$ compete as do $M_{7,9}$ and $M_{5,9}$. **The winner in these** competitions is determined by the consistency of the appropriate rectangles, e.g. **if the 4-4-9-5** rectangle is more consistent than the 6-4-9-7 rectangle, then the *jet* model is favored over the ***prop*** model.

a model and its specialization. The additional verification of properties specific to the specialization is simply expressed as additional model-specific constraints involving the parameters. For example, in order for a plane to specialize to jet-plane, its wing must specialize to a jet-wing, which involves verifying more stringent constraints on the relative angle of the wing to the fuselage (e.g., that it should in the range 45-60 degrees). We need not reverify that the jet-wing satisfies all requirements for a general wing model, as this is verified by the plane-wing consistency rectangle (i.e., the rectangle involving models 1 and 2 and frames 4 and 9).

Figure 4 also illustrates a general syntactic requirement on the *ISA* and *INA* matrices. If, for example, three of the four links of the "diamond" formed by the plane, wing, propeller, and propeller-wing models are present then the fourth must also be present. Note that this is a syntactic requirement on the constant matrices of the model side and not a rule involving the dynamic variables.

Finally, we include the constraints that the match M and the ina variables should stabilize to binary values (0 or 1), although they may take intermediate values during the course of the optimization. Thus, we require the following:

$$\begin{aligned} M_{\alpha i}(1 - M_{\alpha i}) &= 0 \\ ina_{ij}(1 - ina_{ij}) &= 0. \end{aligned} \tag{9}$$

The parameters F_{is} should, however, be allowed to take real values; currently, we use an analog variable to represent such parameters. This contrasts with the value-unit representations used in [Ballard-86] and other traditional connectionist approaches. Our choice is motivated by the fact that complex arithmetic relationships, such as those involved in coordinate transformations, will be relatively inefficient if value-unit representations are used.

3 Optimization Techniques

Having outlined some of the basic objective functions and constraints involved in our optimization problem, we now consider various approaches for performing the optimization. The optimization problem at hand can be stated as that of minimizing $E(\mathbf{x})$, subject to constraints

$$h_i(\mathbf{x}) = 0, \ \forall i, 1 \le i \le m \tag{10}$$

$$g_j(\mathbf{x}) \le 0, \ \forall j, 1 \le j \le p \tag{11}$$

where $\mathbf{x}$ is the collection of all dynamic variables M, ina, and F_{is} in Frameville, and h_i are the previously listed syntactic constraints and g_j express the restrictions on the ranges of some of the dynamic variables.

3.1 Unconstrained Optimization – Hopfield Networks

One can generally approximate a constrained problem as an unconstrained problem by incorporating the constraints as additive "penalty" terms in the objective function. Each constraint results in a term of the form $c_i h_i^2(\mathbf{x})$ where c_i is a constant. For example, Equation 8 specifying the constraint of sibling competition in a specialization hierarchy becomes the additive term

$$c\,(M_{\alpha i} - \sum_{\beta} I\!S\!A_{\alpha\beta} M_{\beta i})^2. \tag{12}$$

Thus the Frameville objective function to be minimized consists of the original rectangle rule plus penalty terms to reflect constraints.

Hopfield [Hopfield-84b] has proposed a neural network implementation for unconstrained optimization problems similar to ours. In [Hopfield-84b] the dynamic variables are identified with neurons; the architecture (connection weights between neurons) follows from the form of the objective function; and a descent procedure specifies the update rule for each neuron. As discussed above, constraints are incorporated as penalty terms in the objective function [Hopfield-85], and, in addition, an "analog gain" term is added to constrain the dynamic variables to lie within a certain range. This analog gain term leads to a network which includes the familiar nonlinear sigmoidal mapping beween the internal state of a neuron and its output.

For a Frameville version, the resulting equations of motion are

$$\begin{aligned} \frac{du_i}{dt} &= -\frac{\partial E}{\partial V_i} \\ V_i &= g(u_i) \end{aligned} \tag{13}$$

where E is the objective function, and, for notational convenience, the dynamic variables M, ina, and F_{is} are identified with a singly subscripted variable V_i, the output of the ith neuron. Also, u_i is the internal state of the ith neuron and g is the sigmoidal mapping between V and u. It is interesting to note that Equation 13 can be recast as a form of gradient descent (in V) with a variable step size to ensure that V remains bounded [Utans-89]. In addition, an interesting interpretation of tha Hopfield dynamics Equation 13 as a continuous quasi-Newton method is described in [Utans-89].

Unlike the familiar quadratic objective functions used by [Hopfield-85] and others, our objective functions are of higher order (> 2) as seen from the form of the rectangle rule, Equation 4, and the constraints in Frameville. Also, the nonlinear analog gain term applies only to M and ina. Finally, it should be noted that for these types of neural nets, the objective function appears typically as polynomial combinations of dynamic variables in order that the objective function be easily mapped into a network. This is an unnecessary restriction as shown by Mjolsness and Garrett in [Mjolsness-90]; there techniques for compiling into networks objective functions consisting of nonpolynomial expressions, such as transcendental functions, are presented.

3.2 Constrained Optimization With Networks

The advantage of approximating the constrained optimization problem by an unconstrained problem is that it is possible to use descent methods to solve the unconstrained problems, and such methods naturally give rise to network implementations. However, sometimes we may wish to retain "hard" constraints, i.e., require that a constraint be strictly satisfied. In some cases, this may even be a requirement; for example, when performing arithmetic it may be useful to have intermediate variables which are related to other variables via hard constraints (see line grouping example in section 4).

A common method to solve a constrained optimization problem with "hard" constraints is the method of Lagrange multipliers. This involves the formulation of the Lagrangian [Luenberger-84]

$$l(\mathbf{x}, \lambda_1, \lambda_2, \ldots) = E(\mathbf{x}) + \sum_j \lambda_j h_j \tag{14}$$

where λ_j are the Lagrange multipliers. The necessary conditions for a solution to the original constrained problem are,

$$\begin{aligned} \nabla_{\mathbf{x}} l(\mathbf{x}, \lambda_1, \lambda_2, \ldots) &= 0 \\ h_j(\mathbf{x}) &= 0. \end{aligned} \tag{15}$$

A search technique, itself possibly an optimization, is generally needed to solve for these conditions.

Recently, a network implementation [Platt-87] has been developed for a continuous descent algorithm [Platt-87,Arrow-58] to solve the search problem given above. In addition to the original set of dynamic variables, the descent algorithm also updates the Lagrange multipliers. Thus, in Platt's implementation there are nodes denoted V_i in the network corresponding to each of the dynamic variables and other nodes denoted λ_j to the Lagrange multipliers. The equations of the motion are,

$$\begin{aligned} \frac{dV_i}{dt} &= -\frac{\partial E}{\partial V_i} - \sum_j \lambda_j \frac{\partial h_j}{\partial V_i} \\ \frac{d\lambda_i}{dt} &= h_i(V_1, V_2, \ldots). \end{aligned} \tag{16}$$

Platt [Platt-87] has demonstrated good results in applying this method to the solution of the Travelling Salesman Problem and an analog decoding problem. Since some of our examples involve the use of hard constraints, this may be a promising technique to consider.

4 Experiments

4.1 Recognition of Simple Stick Figures - Stickville

An early implementation these ideas was object recognition in Stickville, [Shumaker-89], a precursor to Frameville that contained many of its important aspects. Stickville is a domain of stick figures composed of connected assemblages of linear segments or "sticks". As shown in Figure 5 a model part at the lowest level corresponds to a single stick. Abstraction in Stickville is interpreted as representing a collection of parts by a single main part. Thus the "plane" model is abstracted by "fuselage", the main part of "plane". A summary of the domain definition and experiments follows, but the many baroque details can be found in [Shumaker-89].

An important restriction in Stickville is that the data groupings are not dynamic; they are precomputed. Thus ina_{ij} is a constant and not a dynamic variable. In Stickville, the *ina* matrix is defined so that $ina_{ij} = 1$ if data stick j is connected to (abuts) data stick i and is zero otherwise. Also, our input data was restricted to consist of a set of trees, i.e., each stick in a connected assemblage of sticks (except for one root stick) had the property that one of its ends abutted the side of one other stick. Hence, each stick has a natural beginning and end. Figure 5a shows the stick figure of a plane and its *ina* links, and 5b shows a model representation for a plane and its *INA* links. The tree structure may be observed in figure 5a.

Another important restriction involves parameters on the data side. Like *ina* links, parameter checks are also precomputed; hence there are no dynamic variables corresponding to frame slots. For Stickville, three quantities are precomputed for each pair of connected sticks i and j. These parameters, illustrated in figure 5c are: r_{ij}, the log ratio of length of stick j to stick i, θ_{ij}, the relative angle, and y_{ij}, the location of the attach point of stick j to stick i in a coordinate system whose y-axis ($0 \leq y \leq 1$) is coincident with stick i [Gindi-86]. It turns out that we need not consider the value of y_{ij} if stick i abuts stick j since the definition of *ina* filters any expression that would involve such a term. Thus in place of a frame with slots, a vector of fixed parameters is associated with each connected ($ina_{ij} = 1$) pair of data nodes.

A specialization hierarchy is included in Stickville. Figure 6 shows a model-base typical of the ones used in our simulations. In Stickville, specialization is achieved by the inclusion of new parts and by the restriction of allowed parameter ranges on pairs of other parts. For example, in order to specialize "plane" to "jet", four new parts (two engines, two tails) must be found, and the angle of the wing relative to fuselage must fall within a subset of the allowed wing-fuselage angle for plane, i.e the wings must be swept back. The specialization hierarchy is encoded in a binary matrix $ISA_{\alpha\beta}$ as described earlier.

The rectangle rule for Stickville becomes

$$\begin{aligned} E(M) &= -\sum_{\alpha,i,\beta,j} INA_{\alpha\beta} ina_{ij} M_{\alpha i} M_{\beta j} H^{\alpha\beta}(\mathbf{J}_{ij}) \\ \mathbf{J}_{ij} &= (r_{ij}, \theta_{ij}, y_{ij}). \end{aligned} \tag{17}$$

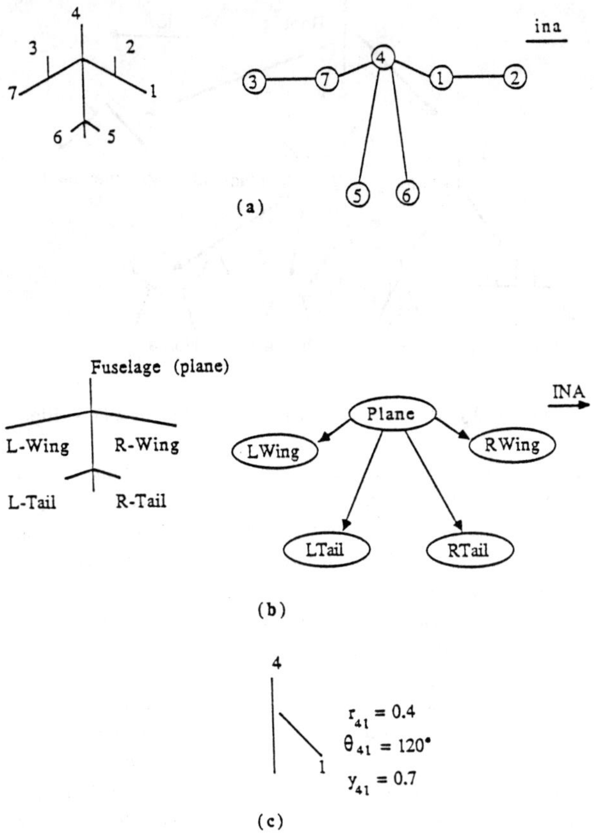

Figure 5: **Definitions in Stickville.** (a) A stick figure of a plane, and its representation as a graph with *ina* links (which are symmetric in Stickville). (b) A plane model and its representation as a graph with asymmetric *INA* links. (c) Parameters characterizing the relationship between two data sticks.

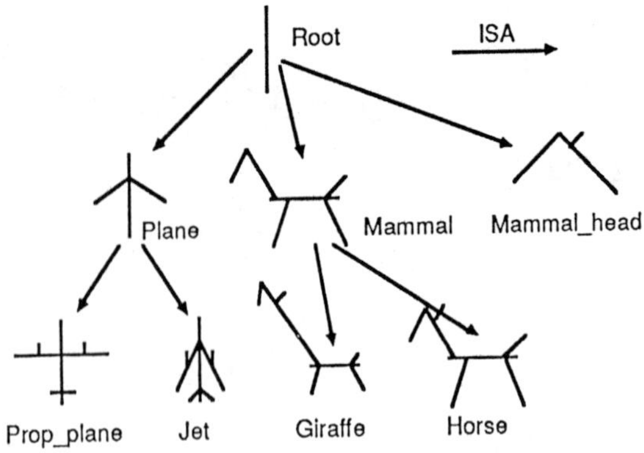

Figure 6: **Typical specialization hierarchy for Stickville.**

Note that the only dynamic variables are the match neurons M. Unlike Equation 17 where the parameters F_{is} depend on one frame i and a slot number s, the precomputed parameters J_{ij} here depend on two data sticks i and j. The parameter check term H is a stored function that evaluates the vector $\mathbf{J}$ and returns a large number if the data side parameters satisfy conditions specified by $H^{\alpha\beta}$ on the model side. Two forms for the "fit" term $H^{\alpha\beta}$ were employed. One was the sum of square deviations of the data quantites from corresponding reference quantities. The other form had H zero when the data quantity was within an allowed range of a reference quantity and unity otherwise.

Because the number of *INA* links to a model α may not equal the number of *ina* links to a stick i, a match between α and i cannot require a strict one-to-one match between the parts of model α and parts of stick i (i.e., those sticks connected to it). Thus in Stickville, where the data-side *ina* links are fixed *a priori*, Equations 6 and 7 cannot both be exactly satisfied. Instead, we have an ungainly situation in which we seek a best match between a generally unequal number of models and parts. An appropriate constraint in this case is:

$$\sum_{\alpha j}(\sum_{\beta} INA_{\alpha\beta}M_{\beta j} - \sum_{i} ina_{ij}M_{\alpha i})^2(\sum_{\beta} INA_{\alpha\beta}M_{\beta j}) = 0 \tag{18}$$

This term encourages a model to match to a unique part or to no part at all. A corresponding constraint encourages a given part to match to a unique model or no model:

$$\sum_{\beta i}(\sum_{j} ina_{ij}M_{\beta j} - \sum_{\alpha} INA_{\alpha\beta}M_{\alpha i})^2(\sum_{j} ina_{ij}M_{\beta j}) = 0 \tag{19}$$

Note that by retaining the possibility of no match, cubic terms in M are required. The original

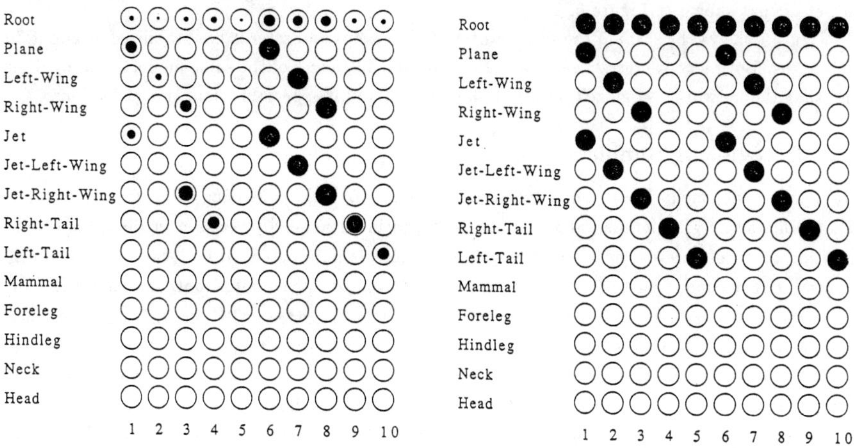

Figure 7: **Stickville results** (a) Stickville match matrix after 28 time steps. The circles represent the dynamic variables whose value is encoded by the radius of the shaded portion. The different columns represent the different data sticks, and the different rows represent different models. The model-base consists of plane, jet, mammal and their parts, and a root model. The data consists of two jets. (b)Stickville match matrix achieves the correct fixed-point after 70 time steps. Note that a stick matches to a model and all of its generalizations (more than one neuron on in a column) and that both the jets have been found (more than one neuron on in a row).

choose rule Equation 8, was also modified to retain the possibility of no match:

$$\sum_{\alpha i}\Big(\sum_{\beta} ISA_{\alpha\beta}M_{\beta i} - M_{\alpha i}\Big)\Big(\sum_{\beta} ISA_{\alpha\beta}M_{\beta i}\Big) = 0 \tag{20}$$

This form allows the possibilty that a general version of an object is found, but not enough evidence exists to instantiate a specialization.

For the result shown, we used the Hopfield neural net model, Equations 13, as an optimization method in our Stickville simulation. We used the forward Euler method to simulate the differential equations as a sequence of discrete time steps. Other results using the constrained optimization method are reported in [Shumaker 89].

An experimental result is displayed in Figure 7 in the form of the match matrix. Here, each circle is a match neuron $M_{\alpha i}$ and its value is proportional to the radius of the shaded portion. The rows are labelled with symbols corresponding to model parts (e.g. jet, jet-left-wing, right-tail, mammal, foreleg, etc.), and each column corresponds to a single data stick. For the results shown, the input consisted of 10 sticks comprising two separate jets, and the model base consisted of a subset of that shown in Figure 6.

Figure 7 shows the state of the system after 28 time steps and after it has stabilized at about 70 time steps. Both jets are recognized. Note that multiple instances of the same model are recognized and that the network recognized both the plane model and its specialization, the jet model.

4.2 Recognizing Simple Shapes

Frameville experiments were conducted in a domain, "TLville", consisting of a two-level compositional hierarchy. (A detailed account may be found in [Utans-89].) As seen in Figure 8(a), the input data at the lowest level are unit-length line segments parameterized by location x, y and orientation θ, corresponding to frame parameters F_{jp} $(p = 1, 2, 3)$. We allow only horizontal $(\theta = 0)$ and vertical $(\theta = \pi/2)$ orientations. There are two high-level models, "T" and "L" junctions, each composed of three low-level segments. The task is to recognize instances of "T", "L", and their parts, in a translation-invariant manner. The high-level models are abstracted by the parameters of a designated main part, in this case, the upper vertical segment of each model.

On the model side, there are seven low-level models indexed by β, as shown in Figure 8(b). These correspond to seven positional roles that a segment may assume in the context of a composite figure. These positions are illustrated iconically inside the model nodes in Figure 8(b) and correspond to the positions of segments in the familiar seven-segment LED display. The high-level models "T" and "L", indexed by α, are then specified by the appropriate set of *INA* links. We distinguish between high-level frames, indexed by i, that may match only high-level junction models, and low-level frames, indexed by j, that may match only low-level segment models.

For this domain, the parameter check term $H^{\alpha\beta}$ checks the location and orientation of a given part relative to the main part. For example, in recognizing a "T", if low-level frame 3 is matched to model 5, a "middle horizontal" segment, then its parameters $(F_{3,1}, F_{3,2}, F_{3,3} = x_3, y_3, \theta_3)$ must differ from those of an "upper vertical" mainpart by quantities $+1, -1$, and $\pi/2$, respectively. In our design the parameters of a high-level frame represent a best fit to the parameters of its mainpart. So if high-level frame 7 is matched to model 9, a "T", then an appropriate parameter check term is:

$$H^{9,5}(\vec{F}_7, \vec{F}_3) = (F_{7,1} - F_{3,1} - 1)^2 + (F_{7,2} - F_{3,2} + 1)^2 + (F_{7,3} - F_{3,3} - \frac{\pi}{2})^2. \tag{21}$$

The quantitities $+1, -1$, and $\pi/2$ are thus model information stored in the objective function. This kind of objective function also determines the best-fit high-level parameters $\vec{F}_7$, even if the low-level mainpart frame itself is missing. Note here that a limited form of invariance is achieved by analog computation of relative coordinates; instances of "T" and "L" are recognized in a manner invariant to translation. (Rotation invariance can also be formulated if a different parameterization is used, but no experiments have been done.)

We used the unconstrained optimization technique in [Hopfield-85] to minimize the objective function. We achieved improved results by supplementing Equations 6 and 7 with terms demanding

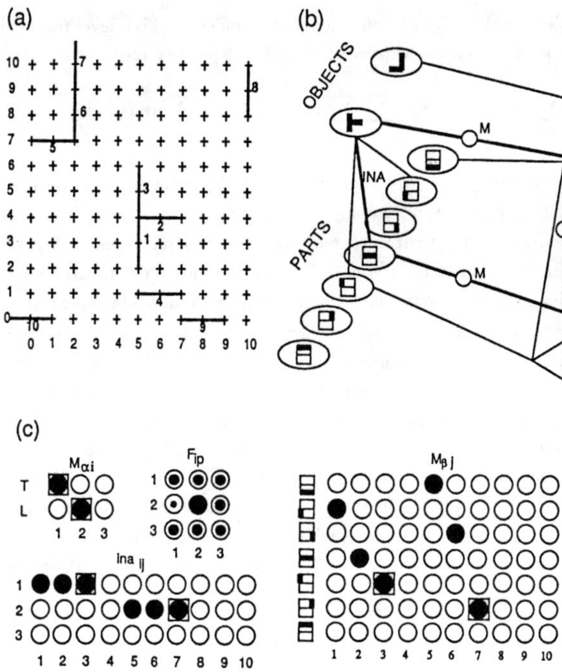

Figure 8: **(a) Input data** consists of unit-length segments oriented horizontally or vertically. The task is translation-invariant recognition of three segments forming a "T" junction (e.g. sticks 1,2,3) or an "L" (e.g. sticks 5,6,7) amid extraneous noise sticks. **(b) Structure of network.** Models occur at two levels. *INA* links are shown for a "T". Each frame has three parameters: position x, y and orientation θ. Also shown are some match and *ina* links. The bold lines highlight a possible consistency rectangle. **(c) Experimental result.** The value of each dynamical variable is displayed as the relative area of the shaded portion of a circle. Matrix $M_{\beta j}$ indicates low-level matches and $M_{\alpha i}$ indicates high level matches. Grouping of low-level to high-level frames is indicated by the *ina* matrix. The parameters of the high-level frames are displayed in the matrix F_{ip} of linear analog neurons. (The parameters of the low-level frames, held fixed, are not displayed.) The few neurons circumscribed by a square, corresponding to correct matches for the main parts of each model, are clamped to a value near unity. Shaded circles indicate the final correct state.

that at most one model match a given frame, and that at most one high-level frame include a given low-level frame as its part. These are expressed as additive penalty terms:

$$\sum_{i\alpha}\sum_{\alpha'\neq\alpha} M_{\alpha i}M_{\alpha' i}, \quad \sum_{j\beta}\sum_{\beta'\neq\beta} M_{\beta j}M_{\beta' j}, \quad \sum_{ji}\sum_{i'\neq i} ina_{ij}ina_{i'j} \tag{22}$$

In addition, we did not include the binary-value constraint (Equation 9). The linear analog neurons representing parameters in frames were not sigmoidally mapped.

Figure 8(c) shows results of attempts to recognize the two junctions in Figure 8(a). When initialized to small random values, the network becomes trapped in unfavorable local minima of the fifth-order objective function. (With only a *single* high-level model in the database, the system recognizes a shape amid noise given a random start.) If, however, the network is given a "hint" in the form of an initial state with mainparts and high-level matches set correctly, the network converges to the correct stable state. In particular, the linear parameter neurons settle to correct analog values corresponding to position and orientation of the mainparts of the junctions. Also, the proper dynamic grouping is accomplished as the *ina* neurons achieve the correct values, and the segment frames match the proper low-level models. Extraneous "noise" sticks remain unmatched.

There is a great deal of unexploited freedom in the design of the model base and its objective functions; there may be good design disciplines which avoid introducing spurious local minima. For example, it may be possible to use *ISA* and *INA* hierarchies to guide a network to the desired local minimum.

4.3 Line Grouping

An important problem in low-level vision is the extraction of long lines from an intensity image. We are interested in this problem because it is representative of a larger class of grouping problems. While the complexity of general shape matching is missing from this problem, it contains the essential aspects of grouping and abstraction. Line segments, which may be broken and corrupted by noise will have to be grouped into a longer structure, and abstracted into a single long line represented by a few parameters. Our approach follows the work of Boldt and Weiss [Boldt-87] in using a hierarchical structure relating lines at different scales.

The models in the line-grouping hierarchy are shown in Figure 9. The lines at various scales are represented as line models at various levels of this hierarchy, and correspond to the different scales of the edge hierarchy (i.e., Burt pyramid). The lines at different levels are defined recursively as follows: An L_l (a line at level l) line specializes to a two-part ($L2_l$) or a one-part ($L1_l$) line at level l. A two-part line model is composed of two lines at level $l-1$, while the one-part line model is made up of a single level ($l-1$) line. The two lines at level $l-1$ which form parts of the two-part line at level l are called "left" and "right" lines at level $l-1$ (LL_{l-1} and RL_{l-1}), while the single level ($l-1$) line which forms the one-part level l line is called a "single-part" line and is denoted

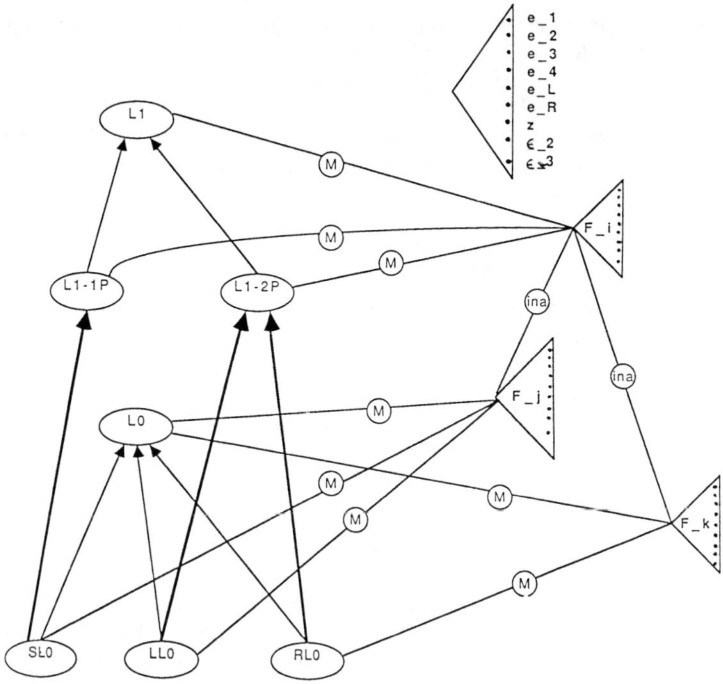

Figure 9: **The models for the line grouping problem.** The line model-base includes the level line models (denoted as $L1$ and $L0$), the one-part and two-part line models at level 1 ($L1 - 1p$ and $L1 - 2p$), and the left-, right-, and single-line models at level 0 ($LL0, RL0, SL0$). Each frame has slots for six two-dimensional vectors and three scalars, which are described in the text. The M and ina variables are represented by circles. The figure displays only the two lowest levels of the model base. The models and frames at higher levels will have similar relationships. Also, in order to maintain readbility, only a subset of the possible M and ina variables have been shown.

as SL_{l-1}. The *ISA* and the *INA* relationships between the various line models are indicated in Figure 9.

We also impose a pyramid architecture on the line-frames. The line frames at a particular level are organized as a two-dimensional array, and such planes of line-frames together form a pyramid. The choice of the pyramid reflects our intuition that there will be fewer longer lines, and that a locality constraint is inherent in the grouping process. Note that the existence of a line-frame at a specific location in the image does not automatically imply that a line exists at that location in the image. It simply reflects the possibility of such a line, whereas the actual presence of a line at a particular scale at that location is indicated by setting

$$M_{L_l,\mathbf{i}} = 1$$

where L_l denotes the line model at level l and $\mathbf{i}$ denotes an image location $\mathbf{i} = (i_1, i_2)$. If such a line is present, it should either be a two-part or a one-part line at that level (and vice versa). This is encoded by the following term in the objective function.

$$\sum_{l,\mathbf{i}} (M_{L_l,\mathbf{i}} - M_{L1_l,\mathbf{i}} - M_{L2_l,\mathbf{i}})^2 \tag{23}$$

where the summing over $\mathbf{i}$ and l indicates that such a term exists for each frame and level (within the architectural restrictions mentioned at the end of this section). Also, if a frame matches to a two-part line model at level l , then there should be other frames that match to the left- and right-line models at level $l-1$ that are allocated to that high-level frame (and vice versa). This is denoted by the following consistency terms in the objective function.

$$\sum_{l,\mathbf{i}} (M_{L2_l,\mathbf{i}} - \sum_{\mathbf{j}} ina_{\mathbf{ij}} M_{LL_{l-1}\mathbf{j}})^2 \tag{24}$$

$$\sum_{l,\mathbf{i}} (M_{L2_l,\mathbf{i}} - \sum_{\mathbf{j}} ina_{\mathbf{ij}} M_{RL_{l-1}\mathbf{j}})^2 \tag{25}$$

These constraints, together with the requirement that the dynamic variables M attain binary values, can be interpreted as "penalty" terms enforcing the following rule: If Frame $\mathbf{i}$ matches to a two-part line at level l, then there should be just one Frame $\mathbf{j}$ which both matches to the left-line (right-line) model at level $l-1$ and is a part of Frame $\mathbf{i}$. Similarly, the one-part line model gives rise to the following term:

$$\sum_{l,\mathbf{i}} (M_{L1_l,\mathbf{i}} - \sum_{\mathbf{j}} ina_{\mathbf{ij}} M_{SL_{l-1}\mathbf{j}})^2 \tag{26}$$

The specialization of the line model at level l to the left-, right- line and single- line models at the same level is expressed as,

$$\sum_{\mathbf{i},l} (M_{LL_l,\mathbf{i}} + M_{RL_l,\mathbf{i}} + M_{SL_l,\mathbf{i}} - M_{L_l,\mathbf{i}})^2. \tag{27}$$

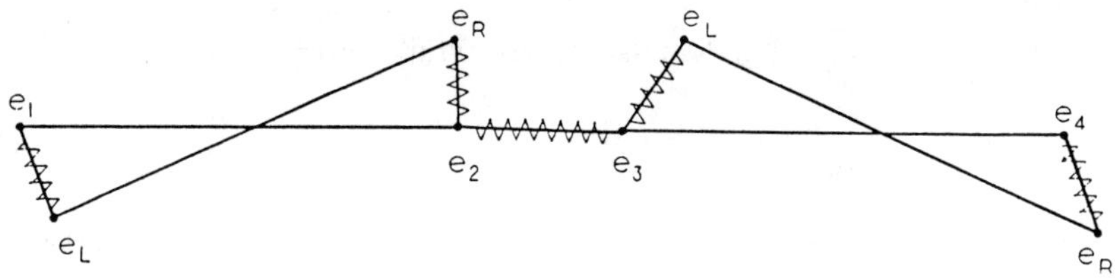

Figure 10: **The spring-stick mechanical model.** Each stick has two end-point vectors. In addition, the longer stick has two intermediate points constrained to lie on it. The outer end points of the small sticks attract the end points of the longer stick. The intermediate points on the longer stick move along that stick to be close to the inner end points of the smaller sticks, and close to each other. The resulting spring energies contribute to the objective function.

Finally, we also require that a lower-level frame can have only a single *ina* parent at the next higher-level. This is denoted as,

$$\sum_{l\mathbf{j}}(M_{L_l\mathbf{j}} - \sum_{\mathbf{i}} ina_{\mathbf{ij}} M_{L_{l+1},\mathbf{i}})^2 \tag{28}$$

Such a fan-out restriction implies that the same segment cannot be a member of more than one high-level group. For some other types of problems, it may be desirable not to impose this restriction.

To verify that the parts of a two-part line at level l are indeed aligned with each other along a straight line, we introduce what we call a "spring-stick" model, which is shown in figure 10. Each line frame contains six two-dimensional vector-valued parameters and three scalars. Although two points are sufficient to completely specify the line, the use of the additional parameters allows us to simplify the parameter-check terms in the objective function. In the description of the parameters below, we use vectors $\mathbf{e}_n = (x_n, y_n)$ to represent locations of points (numbered n) on the line. The meaning of the parameters and the constraints between them are illustrated by the spring-stick model shown in Figure 10. Four of the vector-valued parameters correspond to the four points marked $\mathbf{e}_1, \mathbf{e}_2, \mathbf{e}_3, \mathbf{e}_4$ on the higher level (longer) line in Figure 10. In addition, the end points $\mathbf{e}_3$ and $\mathbf{e}_4$ are also copied into slots $\mathbf{e}_L$ and $\mathbf{e}_R$, although possibly in the reverse order. This redundant representation is useful to allow the same line-frame to match to either the LL model or the RL model as necessary, i.e., a particular line segment may dynamically group with another line segment on either side of it. The points $\mathbf{e}_2$ and $\mathbf{e}_3$ are required to lie on the line joining $\mathbf{e}_1$ and $\mathbf{e}_4$. This is specified by hard constraints (described below). The scalar parameters ϵ_2 and ϵ_3 measure the distance along line of the points $\mathbf{e}_3$ and $\mathbf{e}_4$ from the end point $\mathbf{e}_1$. Finally, the binary-valued parameter z allows $\mathbf{e}_L$ and $\mathbf{e}_R$ to switch between $\mathbf{e}_1$ and $\mathbf{e}_4$.

The parameter-checks correspond to the energies associated with the springs shown in Figure 10, gated by the appropriate M and ina variables. Specifically, these are

$$\sum_{l,\mathbf{i},\mathbf{j}} a_l \; ina_{\mathbf{ij}} M_{L2_l,\mathbf{i}} M_{LL_{l-1},\mathbf{j}} (|\mathbf{e}_{1,\mathbf{i}} - \mathbf{e}_{L\mathbf{j}}|^2 + |\mathbf{e}_{2,\mathbf{i}} - \mathbf{e}_{R\mathbf{j}}|^2)$$

$$\sum_{l,\mathbf{i},\mathbf{j}} a_l \; ina_{\mathbf{ij}} M_{L2_l,\mathbf{i}} M_{RL_{l-1},\mathbf{j}} (|\mathbf{e}_{3,\mathbf{i}} - \mathbf{e}_{L\mathbf{j}}|^2 + |\mathbf{e}_{4,\mathbf{i}} - \mathbf{e}_{R\mathbf{j}}|^2)$$

$$\sum_{l,\mathbf{i}} b_l \; M_{L_l,\mathbf{i}} (\epsilon_{2,\mathbf{i}} - \epsilon_{3,\mathbf{i}})^2 \tag{29}$$

where a_l and b_l are scale-dependent spring coefficients (they decrease as l increases, which means a greater tolerance is allowed).

For the one part line, the spring-stick model is somewhat simpler. The e_1 and e_4 parameters of the higher-level frame are required to be "close" to the e_L and the e_R parameters of the lower-level frame. This is expressed as the following term in the objective function.

$$\sum_{l,\mathbf{i},\mathbf{j}} a_l \; ina_{\mathbf{ij}} M_{L1_l,\mathbf{i}} M_{LL_{l-1},\mathbf{j}} (|\mathbf{e}_{1,\mathbf{i}} - \mathbf{e}_{L\mathbf{j}}|^2 + |\mathbf{e}_{4,\mathbf{i}} - \mathbf{e}_{R\mathbf{j}}|^2) \tag{30}$$

As mentioned above the requirement that $\mathbf{e}_2$ and $\mathbf{e}_3$ should lie on the line joining $\mathbf{e}_1$ and $\mathbf{e}_4$ is expressed as a hard constraints. These are expressed by following equations which specify that the intermediate points should be an interpolation of the two end points. (We call such constraints "hard constraints" to indicate the fact that the solution to the minimization problem should be subject to the strict satisfaction of these constraints.)

$$\begin{aligned} \mathbf{e}_{2,\mathbf{i}} - \mathbf{e}_{1,\mathbf{i}} - \epsilon_{2,\mathbf{i}}(\mathbf{e}_{4,\mathbf{i}} - \mathbf{e}_{1,\mathbf{i}}) &= 0 \\ \mathbf{e}_{3,\mathbf{i}} - \mathbf{e}_{1,\mathbf{i}} - \epsilon_{3,i}(\mathbf{e}_{4,\mathbf{i}} - \mathbf{e}_{1,\mathbf{i}}) &= 0 \end{aligned} \tag{31}$$

where ϵ_2 and ϵ_3 measure the distance of $\mathbf{e}_2$ and $\mathbf{e}_3$ from the end point $\mathbf{e}_1$. Similarly, the switching of $\mathbf{e}_L$ and $\mathbf{e}_R$ between $\mathbf{e}_1$ and $\mathbf{e}_4$ are expressed by the following equations.

$$\begin{aligned} \mathbf{e}_{L,\mathbf{i}} - z_{\mathbf{i}}\mathbf{e}_{1,\mathbf{i}} - (1 - z_{\mathbf{i}})\mathbf{e}_{4,\mathbf{i}} &= 0 \\ \mathbf{e}_{R,\mathbf{i}} - (1 - z_{\mathbf{i}})\mathbf{e}_{1,\mathbf{i}} - z_{\mathbf{i}}\mathbf{e}_{4,\mathbf{i}} &= 0 \\ z_{\mathbf{i}}(1 - z_{\mathbf{i}}) &= 0 \end{aligned} \tag{32}$$

where the binary-valued parameter z encodes the switching mechanism. Besides these, hard constraints expressing the fact that M and ina are binary valued are also included.

The preference of two-part line grouping over one-part line promotion can be represented by a "length" constraint on the lines. Generally, one may expect the higher-level lines to be longer. This idea can be encoded as an explicit term which seeks to the maintain e_1 and e_4 to be separated by a resting length, which varies according to scale.

4.3.1 Simulations

We have performed simulations on small test-cases invoving a two-level line-grouping problem over 2×2 and 3×3 grids. We describe here the performance of our algorithm in a test case consisting of a 3×3 grid and a reduced model base.

The input data for this experiment consists of four line segments which group into two long lines in a 3×3 grid. The input data for our experiments is interactively specified. The user can input one line segment for each of the nine low-level frames or specify long lines that extend beyond a single grid element. For most of our experiments, the initial values of the M and ina variable were chosen to be a random number near 0.5. The initial values of the analog parameters of the high-level frames were chosen to be 0.

The higher-level models for this example included only the 2-part lines (thereby disallowing promotions). The resulting model-base and the set of terms in the objective function are therefore a subset of the more general model base described above. Simulations involving the more general model base are currently under way. All the line-grouping experiments involved the use of a network implementation of constrained optimization algorithm of [Platt-87,Arrow-58] that was described earlier.

Figure 11 displays the status of the network at the beginning, (a), at two intermediate stages, (b) and (c), and at the end of the experiment (d). The network initially appears to head towards an incorrect solution, but then moves to the correct course. In Figure 11b, each of the low-level frames has been allocated to a different high-level frame. This means that no grouping has taken place. However, as the z values are forced to go to 0 or 1, the network begins to perform proper grouping. This is evident from the status of the network in Figure 11c. By this time, two long high-level lines are beginning to form, and the match strength of the other two high-level frames to high-level frames is near zero. This can be interpreted as follows: The network has determined that there are only two long lines in the image, and has found the correct solution. Although the coordinates of the lines corresponding to the two unmatched high-level frames are non-zero, this information can be ignored, since the frames themselves are unmatched to any line. The presence of a small quadratic self-potential term associated with each analog variable forces that variable to zero in the absence any other forces. This is reflected in Figure 11d, which displays the lines after 7200 iterations.

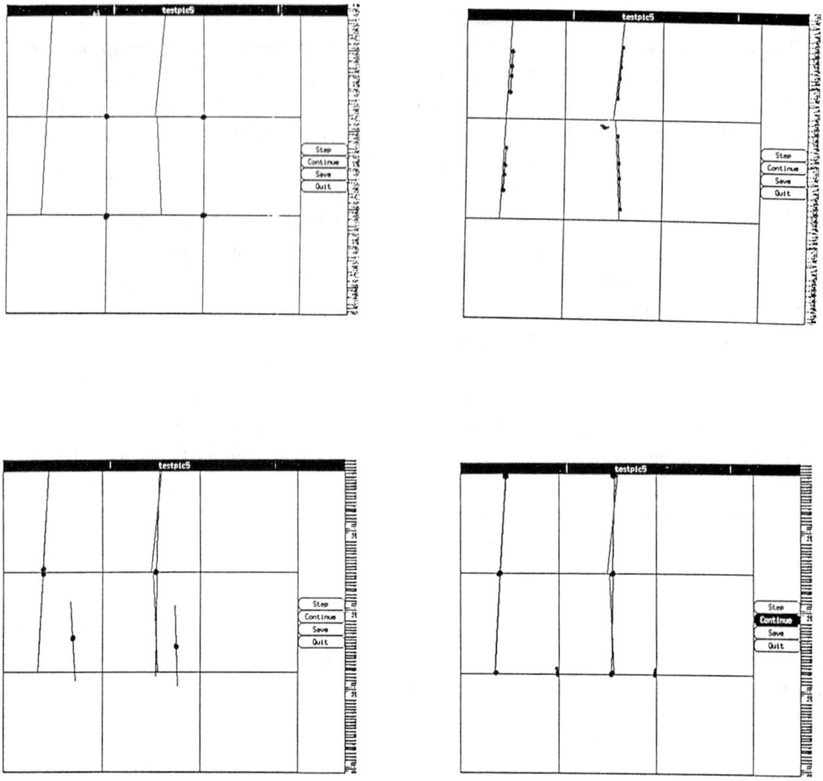

Figure 11: **The 3 × 3 line grouping experiment.** (a) shows the initial state of the network shows the input data containing four line segments. The black dots denote the four high-level frames. (b) shows the network at an intermediate stage. The shorter line segments correspond to the hypothesized high-level lines, the black dots indicate the location of the four points on the longer lines corresponding to the ends of their component data segments. (c) shows the network at a still later stage. Note that the grouping is well under way. Finally (d) shows the network converging to the correct solution.

5 Discussion and Conclusion

Frameville involves the design of objective functions whose fixpoints correspond to the solution of the complex coupled problems that arise in recognition and grouping and whose terms capture notions of hierarchy. (A related effort by P. Cooper [Cooper-89] uses estimation theory to derive in a principled way a method to solve matching and grouping problems in a domain of Tinkertoy objects, but no notion of hierarchy is included.)

The design of the Frameville objective function and constraints raises difficult questions of efficiency and functionality, some of which are addressed here. Full answers must await analysis and extensive experimentation with many particular cases such those outlined in section 4.

Optimization is easier when an objective function is quadratic or "second order" in its independent variables, but our objective functions are third and higher orders. Evaluation of such objective functions or its derivatives is expensive unless the interaction terms are very sparse or highly structured. Often, the high-order objective function may have a structure which allows it to be reduced to a lower order function with a reasonable number of additional dynamical variables [Mjolsness-90]. The expense also crucially depends on the sparseness of the dynamic M and ina matrices. If one enforces sparseness constraints during minimization, as well as at the final minimum, then large savings may result from using "virtual" matrix element variables which are created and destroyed dynamically. Such virtual neurons may be governed by objective functions and are related to "windows" of attention [Mjolsness-87].

Order reduction can also be achieved by setting subsets dynamical variables to constant values and simplifying the objective functions accordingly. Large gains in efficiency can result, at the expense of computational flexibility. For example, a frame F_i, whose match neurons $M_{\alpha i}$ are all fixed at definite binary values, is said to be "pre-typed". Likewise if its ina_{ij} variables are fixed then the frame is is "pre-allocated" to a particular position in the compositional hierarchy. Constant M and ina matrices may express efficient data structures for the recognition problem at hand.

Turning to questions of functionality one might wonder whether Frameville-style objective functions are restricted to high-level vision problems. But the inclusion of analog arithmetic for frame parameters means that one can construct low-level models such as fixed convolution filters, whose kernel is part of the model-specific objective function. Pretyped and preallocated pixel-frames and filter-frames may allow efficiency to approach that of an ordinary convolution. The Frameville version, however, could be integrated with intermediate-level vision.

It was noted in section 1 that various optimization techniques have been used to solve problems at single levels of visual abstraction, and it was argued that there should be cooperation between the processes operating at different levels. We have described how to express examples of high-level model matching problems (Stickville and TLville) and intermediate-level grouping problems (line grouping) uniformly in Frameville. Also, we have discussed the possibility of a Frameville version of low-level feature detection. The uniformity with which we have expressed these problems at different levels of abstraction immediately suggests a technique for integrating diverse visual processes. For instance, TLville and line grouping could be integrated simply by identifying the high-level line models as the low-level stick models in TLville. With minor modifications the objective functions for TLville and line grouping can simply be added.

Finally, the optimization paradigm within which we work may itself be questioned, especially when the objective functions are of high order in which case there will generally be many local minima. Of course our objective functions are not "general"; rather, the model-based objective functions are hand-designed and hand-evolved to favor unique correct image interpretations whenever the input data permits. It is not possible, yet, to say whether or not good design disciplines exist for the model base and its objective function which avoid introducing spurious local minima.

In defense of objective functions, one may also say that they form a notation, bordering on a language, of remarkable conciseness and perspicuity for many computations involving mixtures of quantitative and symbolic processing.

Acknowledgements

We wish to thank Joachim Utans, John Ockerbloom, Charles Garrett, Grant Shumaker, Volker Tresp, and Tony Zador for computer simulations. This work was supported in part by ONR grant N00014-86-0310, by AFOSR grant AFOSR-85-0344, and by DARPA grant DAAA15-87-K-0001.

References

[Anandan-88] P. Anandan, "A computational framework and an algorithm for the measurement of visual motion," *International Journal on Computer Vision*, 1988, to appear.

[Arrow-58] K. J. Arrow, L. Hurwicz, and H. Uzawa, editors, *Studies in Linear and Nonlinear Programming*, Stanford University Press, 1958.

[Ballard-82] D. H. Ballard and C. M. Brown, *Computer Vision*, Prentice Hall, 1982.

[Ballard-86] D. Ballard, "Cortical connections and parallel processing: structure and function," *Behavioral and Brain Sciences*, vol 9, pp. 67–120, 1986.

[Barrow-71] H. G. Barrow and R. J. Popplestone, "Relational descriptions in picture processing," in D. Mitchie, editor, *Machine Intelligence 6*, Edinborough University Press, 1971.

[Barrow-76] H. G. Barrow and J. M. Tenenbaum, *MSYS: A System for Reasoning About Scenes*, Technical Note, SRI – AI Center, 1976.

[Bienenstock-87] E. Bienenstock and C. von der Malsburg, "A Neural Network for Invriant Pattern Recognition," *Europhysics Letters*,. vol. 4, pp. 121–126, 1987.

[Boldt-87] M. Boldt and R. Weiss, "Token-Based Extraction of Straight Lines," COINS Technical Report, University of Massachussetts, 1987.

[Burr-83] D. J. Burr, "Matching Elastic Templates," in O. J. Braddick and A. C. Sleigh, eds., *Proceedings Of the International Symposium on Physical and Biological Processsing of Images* Springer-Verlag 1983.

[Cooper-87] P. R. Cooper and S. C. Hollbach, "Parallel recognition of objects comprised of pure structure," in *Proc. of DARPA IU Workshop*, Morgan-Kaufmann, 1987.

[Cooper-88] P. R. Cooper, Structure recognition by connectionist relaxation: formal analysis, In *Proc. of DARPA IU Workshop*, pages 981–993, Morgan-Kaufmann, 1988.

[Cooper-89] P. R. Cooper, Parallel object recognition from structure (The tinkertoy project) Technical report 301 , University of Rochester, Dept Computer Science 1988.

[Davis-79] L. Davis, "Shape matching using relaxation techniques," *IEEE Transactions on PAMI*, vol. 1, pp. 60-72.

[Fahlman-79] S. E. Fahlman. *NETL: A System for Representing and Using Real-World Knowledge.* MIT Press, 1979.

[Faugeras-81] O. Faugeras and M. Berthod, "Improving consistency and reducing ambiguity in stochastic labeling: an optimization approach," *IEEE Transactions on PAMI*, vol. PAMI-3, pp. 412-424, 1981.

[Feldman-88] J. A. Feldman, M. A. Fanty, and N. H. Goddard, "Computing with structured neural networks," *IEEE Computer*, pp. 91-103, 1988.

[Fischler-73] M. Fischler and R. A. Elschlager, "The representation and matching of pictorial structures," *IEEE Transactions on Computers*, vol. 22, pp. 67–92, 1973.

[Geman-84] S Geman and D Geman, "Stochastic relaxation, gibbs distributions, and the bayesian restoration of images," *IEEE Transactions on PAMI*, vol. PAMI-6, pp. 721–741, 1984.

[Gindi-86] G. R. Gindi and D. H. Delorie, Jr., "Indexing shapes for recognition," In *Proc of the SPIE: Fifth International Conference on Robot Vision and Sensory Controls*, vol. 729, pp. 28-35, 1986.

[Grimson-85] W. E. L. Grimson, "Computational experiments with a feature based stereo algorithm," *IEEE Transacations on PAMI*, vol. PAMI-7, pp. 17–34, 1985.

[Hanson-86] A. R. Hanson and E. M. Riseman, "A methodology for the development of general knowledge-based vision systems," in M. A. Arbib and A. R. Hanson, editors, *Vision, Brain, and Cooperative Computation*, MIT Press, 1986.

[Hopfield-84a] J. J. Hopfield, *Personal communication*, October 1984.

[Hopfield-84b] J. J. Hopfield. "Neurons with graded response have collective computational properties like those of two-state neurons," *Proceedings of the National Academy of Sciences USA*, vol. 81, pp. 3088–3092, 1984.

[Hopfield-85] J. J. Hopfield and D. W. Tank, "'Neural' computation of decisions in optimization problems," *Biological Cybernetics*, vol. 52, pp. 141–152, 1985.

[Horn-81] B. K. P. Horn and B. W. Schunck, "Determining optical flow," *Artificial Intelligence*, vol. 17, pp. 185–203, 1981.

[Horn-86] B. K. P. Horn, *Robot Vision*, MIT Press, 1986.

[Hummel-83] R. A. Hummel and S. W. Zucker. "On the foundations of relaxation labeling processes," *IEEE Transactions on PAMI*, vol. PAMI-5, pp. 267–287, May 1983.

[Lowe-85] David G Lowe, *Perceptual Organization and Visual Recognition*, Kluwer Academic Publishers, 1985.

[Luenberger-84] David G Luenberger, *Linear and Nonlinear Programming*, Addison-Wesley, 1984.

[Minsky-75] Marvin L Minsky, "A Framework for Representing Knowledge," in P. H. Winston, editor, *The Psychology of Computer Vision*, McGraw-Hill, 1975.

[Mjolsness-89a] E. Mjolsness, G. Gindi, and P. Anandan, "Optimization in Model Matching and Perceptual Organization," *Neural Computation*, Vol. 1, pp. 218–229, 1989.

[Mjolsness-89b] E. Mjolsness, G. Gindi, and P. Anandan, "Neural Networks for Model Matching and Perceptual Organization," in *Advances in Neural Information Processing Systems I*, pp. 618–626, D. Touretzky, ed., Morgan-Kaufman, San Mateo, 1989.

[Mjolsness-87] E. Mjolsness, "Control of attention in neural networks," in *Proc. of First International Conference on Neural Networks*, pages 567–574, IEEE, 1987.

[Mjolsness-90] E. Mjolsness and C. Garrett, "Algebraic Transformations of Objective Functions," To appear in *Neural Networks*, Fall 1990.

[Platt-87] John Platt and Al Barr. "Constrained differential optimization," *Proc. of Neural Information Processing Systems Conference*, 1987.

[Poggio-85] T. Poggio and C. Koch, "Ill-posed problems in early vision," *Proceedings of the Royal Society of London B*, vol. 226, pp. 303-323, 1985.

[Rosenfeld-76] A. Rosenfeld, R. A. Hummel, and S. W. Zucker, "Scene labeling by relaxation operations," *IEEE Transactions on SMC*, vol. SMC-6, pp. 420-433, 1976.

[Shumaker-89] G. Shumaker, G. Gindi, E. Mjolsness and P. Anandan, "Stickville: a Neural Network for Object Recognition via Graph Matching," Technical Report 8908, Yale University, Department of Electrical Engineering, Center for Systems Science, 1989.

[Terzopoulos-86] D. Terzopoulos, "Regularization of inverse problems involving discontinuities," *IEEE Transactions on PAMI*, vol. PAMI-8, pp. 413–424, 1986.

[Utans-89] J. Utans, G. Gindi, E. Mjolsness and P. Anandan, "Neural Networks for Object Recognition Within Compositional Hierarchies," Technical Report 8903, Yale University, Department of Electrical Engineering, Center for Systems Science, 1989.

[von der Malsburg-86] C. von der Malsburg and E. Bienenstock, *Statistical Coding and Short-Term Synaptic Plasticity: A Scheme for Knowledge Representation in the Brain*, pp. 247–252. Springer-Verlag, 1986.

[von der Malsburg-88] C. von der Malsburg, "Pattern recognition by labeled graph matching," *Neural Networks*, vol. 1, pp.141–148, 1988.

[Waltz-75] D. Waltz, "Generating semantic descriptions from drawings of scenes with shadows," in P H Winston, editor, *The Psychology of Computer Vision*, McGraw-Hill, 1975.

8

EMERGENCE OF BIOCHIP TECHNOLOGY
Interfacing Neurons and Computers

by Mitch Eggers, Ron McKay, and Dan Ehrlich, MIT*

0. ABSTRACT

Towards discovering and exploiting the collective principles underlying superior biological information processing, this report describes the multidisciplinary development of a microelectronic device (biochip) upon which living neural networks were grown and investigated. Specifically presented is the design, fabrication, and evaluation of multichannel microcircuit electrode arrays built to interface neurons and computers. Contributions supporting such technology included a detailed mathematical model of the electrode/electrolyte interface. With the resulting electrical characteristics mathematically modeled, an optimal microcircuit electrode design (in terms of maximum signal-to-noise ratio) was fabricated. Subsequent electrode impedance measurements were obtained with the electrodes submerged in electrolytic neural solution. Large sample results indicated a 7% discrepancy between theoretical and measured impedances. In addition to the engineering efforts, biological cell culturing techniques were developed to enable the growth of synaptically interconnected, electrically excitable cells on the biochip. Both dissociated invertebrate neurons and clonal mammalian cell systems were employed.

Together these contributions enabled microvolt signals to be recorded from *individual* neurons grown and synaptically interconnected on the biochip surface. Also recorded were neuronal responses to on-chip stimulation. Consequently the biochip technology provides a long-term, noninvasive, multisite electrical stimulation and recording capability necessary for extracting the mechanisms governing the way living neural networks connect, integrate, and self-organize.

*This work was supported by the Department of the Air Force under contract F19628-85-C-002 and the Pew Foundation. R. M. is a scholar of the Rita Allen Foundation.

1. INTRODUCTION

Today the study of biological intelligence constitutes perhaps the most challenging yet rewarding frontier of research. A most compelling notion attracting many researchers is that such complex intelligence originates from a vast interconnected architecture containing approximately 10^{12} relatively simple computational units or neurons. This massively parallel architecture, sporting approximately 10^{15} adaptable neural interconnectors, is responsible for the extraordinary pattern processing capabilities of the brain.

Among the pattern processing capabilities of interest to machine intelligence researchers pursuing engineering applications are fast pattern recognition by association, apparent infinite memory capacity, generalization, and robust, fault-tolerant performance. Furthermore, these system level capabilities are obtained biologically at modest expense — for the human brain consumes energy at a rate comparable to a single VLSI digital signal processing chip. Such efficiency arises from the rather conservative processing units, operating with 1 milisecond time constants and slowly communicating information (100 m/sec) along passive neuronal channels. Although the *components* are relatively sluggish (in comparison to conventional digital computers containing nanosecond processors performing millions of instructions per second) the nervous *system* is capable of quickly (10 miliseconds) recognizing patterns in environments that continue to elude conventional computing today. That is, biologically, a *fast reliable system emerges from numerous slow noisy components.*

In conjunction, quite profound are the recent neural network computing approaches to pattern processing, such as those proposed by Hopfield [1], Grossberg [2], Kohonen [3], Rumelhart and McClelland [4], which capture certain biological network properties including recognition by association, distributed parallel processing, and generalization. For example, Sejnowski [5] in months time demonstrated the associative memory capability of the multilayer perceptron by configuring a neural network to learn the phoneme transcription rules necessary to produce synthesized speech from text. A similar task accomplished by classical techniques employing specific parametric models and explicit expert rules required years. Other examples include computer simulations by Linsker [6] which suggest that neural networks with pattern processing properties as complex as those found in the mammalian visual system can evolve from simple adaptions in the neural interconnections during development. Such results imply that the nature of biological pattern processing systems can be understood (and imitated) if the rules governing neural architecture development are known. And from work conducted at Lincoln Laboratory [7-9] and elsewhere, many mathematical neural network models often perform similarly to classical approaches on established problems, yet do not require a-priori parametric models, statistics, or expert rules. Consequently these mathematical networks, adapted to given tasks through learning processes driven by available training data, seem to substantiate the ever prevailing wisdom acknowledging the suitability of neural-like architectures for pattern recognition and other random problems where algorithmic solutions do not exist [10].

Although recent neural network models offer an inspiring beginning, a vast performance gap remains fixed between these silicon implementations and their biological counterparts. Realizing the perpetuation of this vast difference is due to our limited knowledge of the system properties arising from neuronal architectures, the development of a biological/electronic technology is warranted, aimed at providing system level tools for exploring, modeling, and exploiting biological pattern processing capability.

1.1 Background

Basically, brain architecture development is a two-stage process. First, during *neurogenesis*, cells are rapidly generated and differentiate into specific neural types and are properly positioned within the developing brain. This first stage serves to build and position *all* the processing units (neurons) within the architecture. Next following neurogenesis, lifelong *synaptogenesis* serves to refine the architecture by adapting the interconnections among the processors. The adaption of the synaptic interconnections is dependent on electrical signaling from neighboring neurons. The importance of such network sensory stimuli in shaping the synaptic architecture of the nervous system is made clear by studies on both the visual and motor systems. In fact many neurobiologists believe the higher brain functions, including disposition, learning, and memory, reside in the actual geometry and adaption capability of these neural synapses [11].

Unfortunately, because of the lack of experimental techniques needed to monitor and regulate electrical activity during neural synapse development, the role played by electrical information on establishing synaptic architecture at the cellular and molecular levels remains a mystery. Specifically, conventional *single* cell *intracellular* recording and stimulation techniques are inadequate to characterize synaptic *network* phenomenon due to limitations in quantity and time. That is, micromanipulation requirements needed to bring conventional electrodes to the cells limit the number of electrodes (approximately three) placed into a restricted brain area containing thousands of neurons, thereby sampling only a mere fraction of the neurons involved in a given network. More recently, optical imaging methods have been developed with the potential of simultaneous monitoring of multiple cells in culture. However, these techniques cannot be used for stimulation — a crucial feature for detailed synaptogenesis study. In addition many molecular changes take place over long periods, often several days to weeks. With micromanipulation, keeping electrodes in good contact for more than a few hours is difficult. And finally intracellular recording can be a rather exhausting experience for both the experimenter and host neuron, since the 0.1 micrometer diameter glass micropipette electrode must be inserted just inside the 0.01 micrometer thick cellular membrane when experimenting with a typical mammalian (10 micrometer) neuron. Consequently, conventional cell recording techniques may be suited to the study and classification of single neurons, but are inadequate for providing system-level information necessary to describe the collective behavior of many neurons composing the network.

Towards extracting a more complete picture of network behavior, various multielectrode microcircuits have been developed for *in vitro* experimentation. Thomas *et al.* [12] are credited for the novel concept of bringing cells to the sensor rather than the sensor to the cells. Sheets of heart cells were grown on the surface of microcircuit substrates embedded with 30 electrodes. Although network behavior was observed from the spontaneous rhythmic contractions, no electrical recordings from single cells were obtained. Later Gross [13, 14] and Pine [15] successfully obtained electrical recordings from neurons clustered on substrates. A critical factor determined to govern the success of electrical recording was the impedance of the electrode. With low electrode impedances ($< 1M\Omega$), satisfactory recordings resulted with good signal-to-noise ratios (SNR). In efforts to reduce electrode impedance, Gross [13] developed a laser deinsulating technique which served to increase the effective area of the electrode, while Pine [15] plated the electrodes with platinum black to achieve similar results.

These multielectrode microcircuit contributions have demonstrated basic network phenomenon in vitro, including rhythmic activity and patterned bursting, although such properties were already known from single cell recording. However, quantitative network analysis necessary to support an understanding of biological pattern processing remains plagued by the extraordinary number of degrees of freedom, arising from cultures (of multiple neuronal types) that greatly exceed the size of the recording matrix. It is therefore important to reduce the complexity by more complete monitoring of smaller networks.

1.2 Biochip Concept

Inspired by the earlier microcircuit works cited, the report describes the development of a biological compatible microcircuit technology aimed at interfacing living neural networks and computers for network experimentation. The concept of the "biochip" is illustrated in Fig. 1. Basically, an array of microelectrodes embedded in a biologically compatible substrate is fabricated using conventional microfabrication techniques. Since the electrodes are embedded in the surface, neurons can grow in contact with the electrodes and their electrical properties monitored as they differentiate. The approach presented differs from those cited above because of the local stimulation capability introduced, detailed electrode modeling and optimization, and the reduction of neural network complexity by selectively choosing and placing neurons on the microcircuit, preferably one or more electrodes per neuron. Specifically, identified, individually harvested Aplysia neurons with known transmitters are placed over the electrodes that generate synaptic connections with neighboring neurons. Also, identical (cloned) immortalized precursors of neurons are placed on the biochip to obtain a stereotyped network, greatly reducing mathematical complexity. The potential exists for placing identical class neurons in columns on the microcircuit, where each column would represent a specific neural layer found in a portion of the brain of interest.

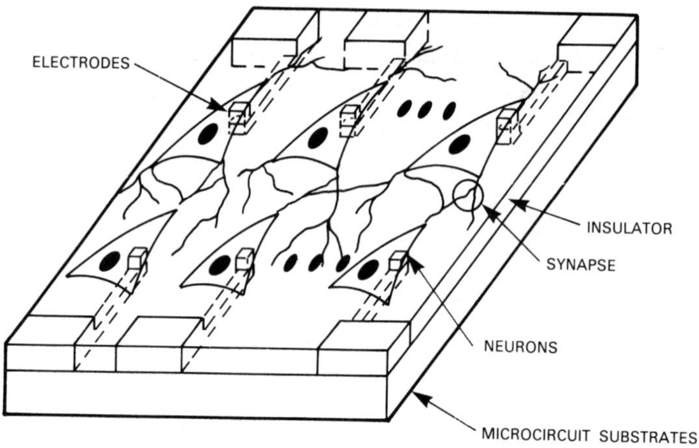

Fig. 1. Illustration of the biochip concept.

Moreover, the novel biochip stimulation capability facilitates even more controlled experimentation, enabling the analysis of how electrical stimulation influences synaptic architecture modification. Here both global and local (single neuron) on-chip stimulation techniques are described using customized electrodes. A significant contribution lies in the theoretical electrode modeling, design, and evaluation procedures presented with supporting calibration experiments.

Overall, the biochip technology presented describes the engineering, biology, and resulting measurements obtained from the microelectrode arrays suitable for electronically interfacing living neuronal networks. First, electrical engineering efforts are discussed including the characterization of the biophysical neural signals together with the design, fabrication, evaluation, and system integration. Next biological aspects are presented which describe both dissociated and clonal neural cell growth methods established using the biochip. And finally, the integration of both engineering and biology is reflected by the final neural measurements section that demonstrates both on-chip noninvasive recording and stimulation capability.

2. BIOCHIP ENGINEERING

2.1 Biophysical Signal Source

The neuron is a clever information processor that relies on electrical signaling for both short and long distance communication. Signal processing tasks performed efficiently by a neuron include the routine integration of approximately 1000 input signals. The low frequency (<100Hz)/low voltage (0.1 to 10 milivolts) transduced neural inputs arise from neighboring synaptically coupled neurons. Often referred to as postsynaptic potentials, these local transmission signals are either inhibitory or excitatory, as displayed in Fig. 2. A postsynaptic signal generated by an excitatory synapse contributes towards neural firing (emission of long distance communication), while conversely, an inhibitory synaptic connection suppresses the activity.

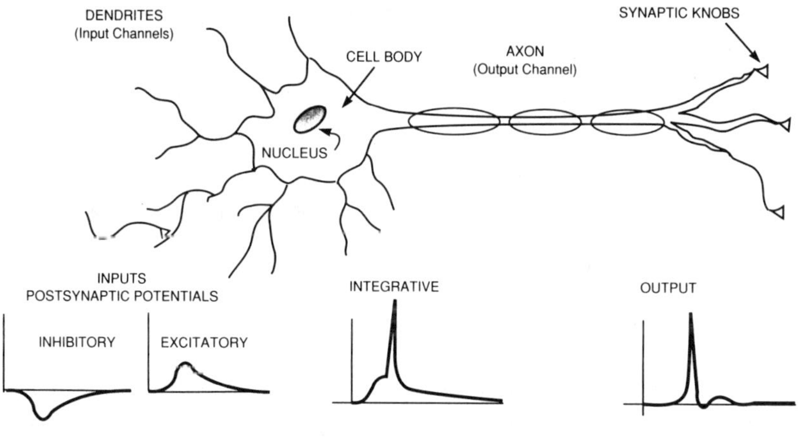

Fig. 2. Electrical signals processed by neurons.

Following signal integration, the neuron provides long distance communication by transmitting high frequency (1kHz)/high voltage (70 - 110 milivolts) pulses along the output channel (axon) as shown in Fig. 2. Since the initial intent is to investigate the collective properties of a neural network, these high frequency long distance signals that subserve network communication are of primary interest. Moreover, these pulses can be recorded via intracellular (conventional) or extracellular techniques as diagrammed in Fig. 3. The intracellular signal is known as the membrane potential, since the voltage signal is due to the electrical charge imbalance (among Na, K, and Cl ions) across the biological membrane. In fact the generation of the large membrane potentials for long distance transmission is due to a change in membrane permeability that effectively alters the distribution of these ions across the membrane. Conversely, the extracellular signal arises from the electrical charge imbalance near the outside of the biological membrane. In contrast to the intracellular potential, this potential is recorded *outside* the neural membrane with respect to the neutral extracellular fluid as diagrammed in Fig. 3. Moreover, the extracellular potential is typically in the microvolt range, while the intracellular potential is measured in milivolts. As a consequence, the three orders of magnitude decrease is signal strength warrants careful electrode modeling and design.

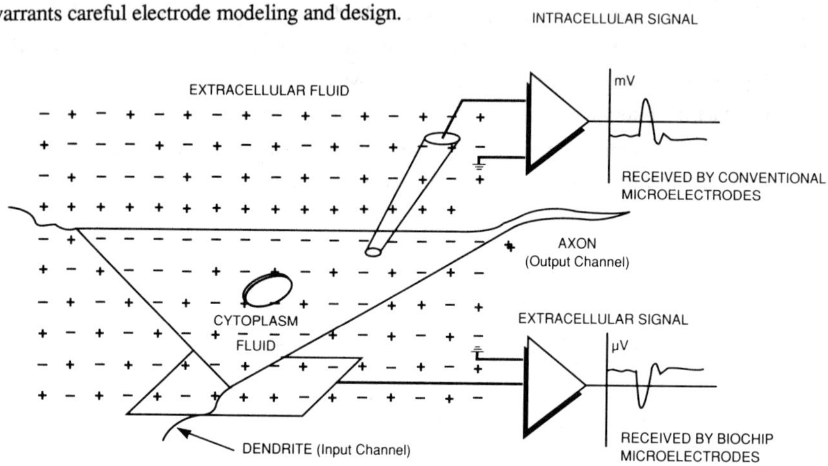

Fig. 3. Intracellular and extracellular recording methods.

2.2 Microcircuit Electrode Design

The ideal design objective is to specify the dimensions of an optimal microcircuit electrode for both extracellular recording and stimulation of interconnected neurons. The procedure entails specifying an objective (cost) function necessary to mathematically define *optimal* performance. By optimizing such function, a set of dimensions result giving rise to the optimal electrode design. Consequently, the design approach involves first expressing the electrical characteristics of the electrode in terms of the microcircuit dimensions, subsequently defining a cost function in terms of these electrical characteristics, and finally optimizing the cost function to yield the optimal electrode design.

2.2.1 Equivalent Circuit Components

The electrical characteristics of a microelectrode in a homogeneous conducting medium can be modeled as an equivalent circuit, with each electrical component expressed in terms of the fundamental electrode dimensions (see Fig. 4). These components are described and derived below. The general approach follows the treatment of Robinson [16] for conventional glass-coated wire electrodes, however, new techniques are presented where appropriate for the specific microfabrication application.

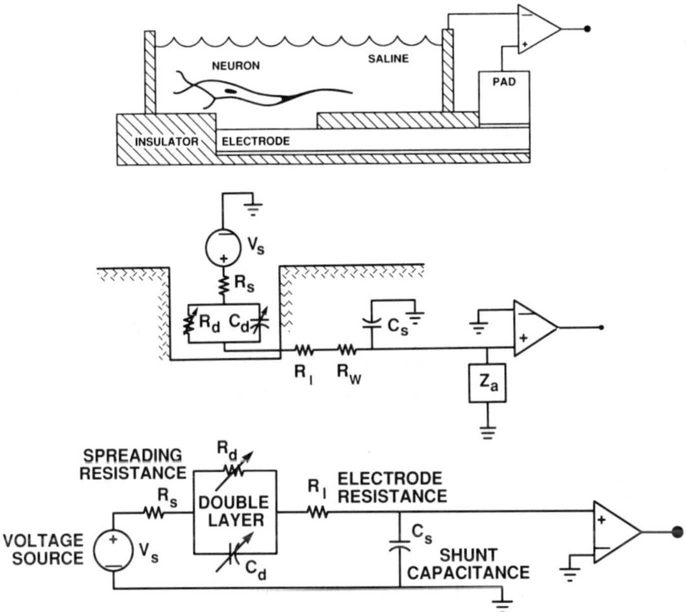

Fig. 4. a) Diagram of microcircuit electrode exposed to a homogeneous conducting solution for extracellular recording with accompanying b) electrical equivalent circuit, and c) reduced equivalent circuit.

V_S - Voltage Source

The neuron, for purposes of an equivalent electrode circuit, is modeled as an ideal voltage source. The voltage V_S is equal to the extracellular voltage that would be recorded immediately outside the axon wall and is referenced to the electrically neutral homogeneous conducting solution. Notice the voltage source is in series with the spreading resistance R_S such that removal of the neuron $(V_S = 0)$ results in the proper circuit depicting the current flow in a homogeneous conducting solution.

R_S - Spreading Resistance

The spreading resistance R_S is the resistance of the homogeneous conducting solution between the metallic electrode and the metal ground ring (designated infinity). The resistance can be derived by integrating the differential resistance along the current path according to

$$R_S = \int_{r_o}^{r_\infty} dR \quad . \qquad (1)$$

An expression is readily obtained providing the current path is perpendicular to the conducting surfaces. In such case, the differential resistance is

$$dR = \rho \frac{dr}{A(r)} \qquad (2)$$

where ρ is the resistivity $(\Omega \cdot m)$, dr is the differential current path, and $A(r)$ is the conducting surface area. Thus by slightly distorting the shape of both the electrode and ground ring (yet maintaining original surface area) as shown in Fig. 5, the current flow is perpendicular thereby resulting in the following expression

$$R_S = \rho \int_{r_0}^{r_\infty} dr \, / \, 2\pi r^2 \cos\phi_0 \quad . \qquad (3)$$

Moreover, r_0 and ϕ_0 are calculated by equating the surface areas amongst the distorted and actual conductive surfaces. For the square electrode surface

$$W_c^2 = 2\pi r_0^2 \cos\phi_0$$

$$\therefore \; r_0 = W_c \,/\, \sqrt{2\pi \cos\phi_0} \qquad (4)$$

and for the ground ring cylindrical surface

$$2\pi\left(\frac{D}{2}\right)H = 2\pi\left(\frac{D}{2}\right)^2 \cos\phi_0$$

$$\therefore \; \cos\phi_0 = 2H \,/\, D. \qquad (5)$$

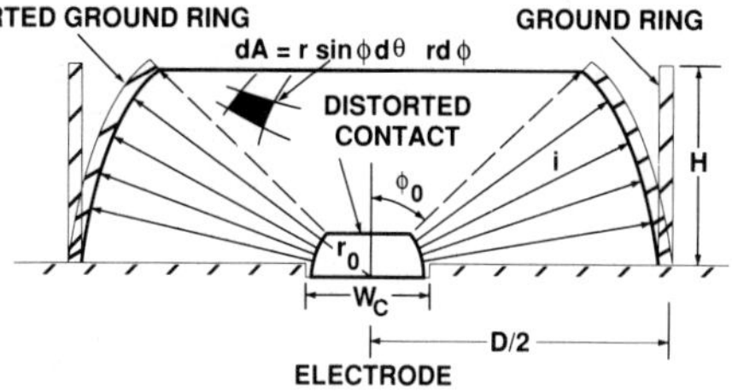

Fig. 5. Diagram of permissible current paths from electrode to ground ring.

Substituting (4) and (5) into (3) yields the spreading resistance

$$R_s = \frac{\rho}{W_c\sqrt{4\pi H / D}} \qquad (r_\infty >> r_0) \qquad (6)$$

where H and D are the height and diameter of the ground ring, while W_c is the width of the square electrode contact.

R_d, C_d - Double Layer Resistance and Capacitance

The complex electrochemical reactions at the interface of the metal electrode and electrolyte constitute an electric double layer, and is the most challenging phenomenon to model. The electric double layer arises from the potential difference that naturally exists at every metal-solution interface. The magnitude of the potential depends on the electronic work function of the metal, energy of absorption on the metal from components of the reaction, energy of chemical bonds between the metal and reactants, and the hydration energy. The net sum of these energies produces a chemical gradient that forces the charge transfer reaction in one direction as illustrated in Fig. 6a. As the reaction proceeds, an imbalanced distribution of charge (electrons for inert metal electrodes) develops across the interface, resulting in the formation of an electric field gradient that opposes the chemical gradient. Finally equilibrium is established when the electrical and chemical gradients are equal and opposite as shown in Fig. 6b. Here the reaction velocity reaches zero, preventing further charge movement. Consequently the trapped separation of charges at the interface (comprised of surface charge on the metal and diffuse counter charge of equal magnitude in the solution) constitute the high impedance electric double layer [17].

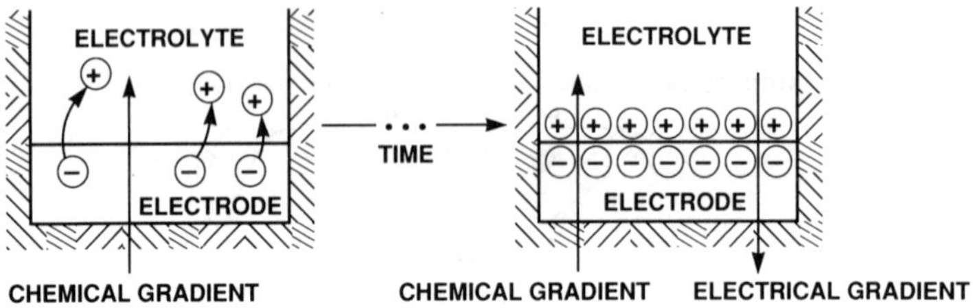

Fig. 6. Formation of the electric double layer from a) initial reaction to b) final equilibrium.

Numerous attempts have been made to rigorously explain and model the electric double layer. Helmholtz modeled the double layer as an electrolytic capacitor with the double layer potential given by

$$V(x) = \frac{\lambda}{\varepsilon}(x-a) \qquad 0 \le x \le a \tag{7}$$

where λ is the surface charge density, ε is the relative permittivity, and a is the width of the double layer (typically a few angstroms.) The voltage profile is shown in Fig. 7a. Notice the capacitor model yields a *linear* drop in potential, with a magnitude of $\lambda a / \varepsilon$ required to cross the double layer from the electrolyte to the electrode.

More complicated models allow for a diffuse distribution of charge about the interface. For example, the Gouy-Chapman model avoids the unrealistic homogeneous anion and cation planar charge sheets used in the Helmholtz model by purposing several charge sheets, each having both cations and anions but of varying concentration. As demonstrated in Fig. 7b, the charge sheets closest to the interface have a higher imbalance of charge, while those sheets furthest from the interface are electrically neutral. This double layer potential is obtained by utilizing Boltzmann statistics to characterize the charge density according to

$$\rho(x) = Z_+ F C_+^0 e^{-Z_+ F V(x)/RT} - Z_- F C_-^0 e^{-Z_- F V(x)/RT} \tag{8}$$

where Z_+ and Z_- are the charge valences, F is Faraday's constant, C_+^0 and C_-^0 are the concentrations of the cations and anions respectively in the bulk solution, and R is the ideal gas constant. Substituting the linear approximation of (8) into the Poisson equation

$$\frac{\partial^2 V}{\partial x^2} = -\rho(x) / \varepsilon \tag{9}$$

and solving the boundary conditions yields the double layer potential given by

$$V(x) = -\frac{\sigma e^{\kappa a} e^{-\kappa x}}{\varepsilon \kappa} \tag{10}$$

where

$$\kappa = \frac{F\sqrt{Z_+^2 C_+^0 + Z_-^2 C_-^0}}{\sqrt{\varepsilon RT}}. \tag{11}$$

Clearly, the length of the double layer depends on the ionic concentrations through κ, while the magnitude of the potential depends on both the surface charge and ionic concentrations. Notice the mathematical difference between the Helmholtz and Gouy-Chapman models lies in the double layer potential now being *exponential* in distance from the interface, as shown in Fig. 7b. Although more complicated double layer models exist, a complete understanding of the phenomenon and a corresponding precise mathematical model remain elusive.

Since a precise mathematical description of the double layer does not exist, empirical measurements are often incorporated into simple electrical circuit models to warrant an accurate representation of the electrochemical processes. Hence by first performing a calibration experiment to determine the necessary empirical parameters, the double layer can then be satisfactorily modeled for purposes of electrode design. The particular electrical circuit model employed consists of an electrolytic capacitor C_d in parallel with a leakage resistance R_d. Both components are allowed to vary with respect to frequency in order to conform with empirical findings. Certainly the capacitor intuitively follows from the idealized Helmholtz model. However by allowing the capacitor value to vary with frequency, together with the addition of the variable leakage resistor to account for the charge carriers realistically crossing the double layer, the parallel RC circuit is more representative of the Gouy-Chapman double layer model.

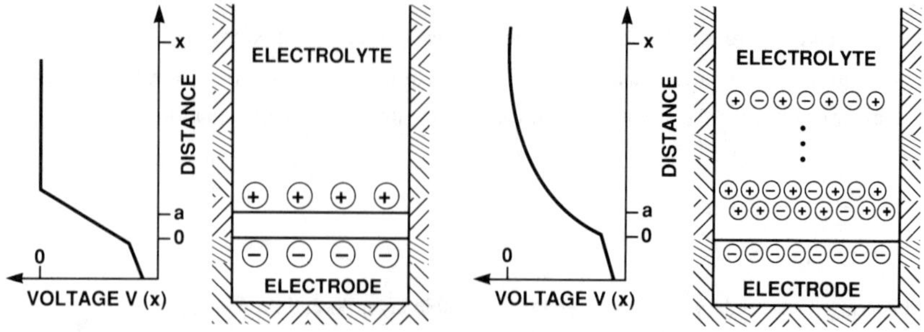

Fig. 7. Voltage profiles of a) Helmholtz and b) Gouy-Chapman electric double layer models.

Two methods can be used to obtain the double layer equivalent circuit components R_d and C_d. The first involves relying on published results for conventional glass-coated bright platinum microelectrodes calibrated in physiological saline solution. Under such circumstances, both R_d and C_d have been found to vary as $\omega^{-1/2}$, while the impedance phase θ_d remains near $-45°$ within the frequency band of interest (100 Hz-10kHz) [18,19]. Imposing these conditions upon the parallel RC model yields the relationships

$$\overline{Z}_d = \frac{R_d - j\omega R_d^2 C_d}{1+(\omega R_d C_d)^2} \tag{12}$$

$$\theta_d = \tan^{-1} - \omega R_d C_d = -45° \tag{13}$$

$$\therefore \quad R_d = 1 / \omega C_d \tag{14}$$

where C_d is determined from published empirical results ($20\mu F / cm^2$ [16]).

An alternative method for obtaining the double layer circuit components involves conducting an independent calibration experiment utilizing the actual physiological saline solution used for the biochip neural experiments. This approach also requires the calibration electrodes to be of the same metal and brightness as the microcircuit electrodes. As a consequence, when the conditions for employing the biochip differ from published experiments, the following calibration experiment is warranted to provide accurate double layer modeling.

The calibration experiment described enables isolation of the required circuit components R_d and C_d by providing a *macroscopic* environment where other electrical effects become negligible. The calibration tube utilized is displayed in Fig. 8a. The calibration *macro*electrodes are gold plated of similar brightness as the *micro*electrodes constructed in the biochip. These electrodes are connected to a precision impedance analyzer (HP 4284A) through a four-terminal pair configuration. Such configuration minimizes unwanted residual factors arising from self and/or mutual inductance between the individual leads. And since both open and short circuit measurements are made prior to the calibration, practically no stray impedance from the leads is introduced. Furthermore the glass tube is sufficiently long such that the electrode-to-electrode capacitance can be neglected. Consequently the circuit schematic shown in Fig. 8b provides sufficient representation.

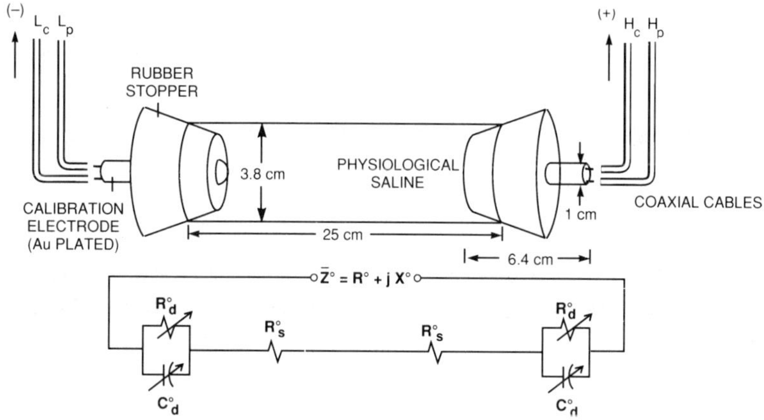

Fig. 8. Diagram of a) calibration experiment and b) equivalent circuit.

The specific objective of the calibration experiment is to calculate the calibration components $\overset{o}{C_d}$ and $\overset{o}{R_d}$ from the overall impedance measurements ($\overline{Z}^o$) performed at various frequencies of interest. This overall impedance can be expressed

$$\overline{Z}^\circ \equiv Z^\circ \angle\theta^\circ \equiv R^\circ + jX^\circ = \left(2\overset{\circ}{R}_s + \frac{2\overset{\circ}{R}_d}{\alpha}\right) + j\left(-2\omega\left(\overset{\circ}{R}_d\right)^2 \frac{\overset{\circ}{C}_d}{\alpha}\right) \tag{15}$$

where $\alpha = 1 + \left(\omega \overset{\circ}{R}_d \overset{\circ}{C}_d\right)^2$ and the spreading resistance for the calibration electrode is $\overset{\circ}{R}_s = \rho / 2\pi \overset{\circ}{r}$. Hence $\overset{\circ}{C}_d$ and $\overset{\circ}{R}_d$ are easily obtained from (15) in terms of the measured resistance and reactance according to

$$\overset{\circ}{C}_d = \frac{-2X^\circ}{\omega\left(\left(\overset{\circ}{R}_e\right)^2 + \left(X^\circ\right)^2\right)} \tag{16}$$

$$\overset{\circ}{R}_d = \frac{\left(\overset{\circ}{R}_e\right)^2 + (X^\circ)^2}{2\overset{\circ}{R}_e} \tag{17}$$

where

$$\overset{\circ}{R}_e = \overset{\circ}{R} - 2\overset{\circ}{R}_s. \tag{18}$$

In turn the microcircuit double layer component C_d is computed by

$$C_d = \overset{\circ}{C}_{d/A} A_c \tag{19}$$

where $\overset{\circ}{C}_{d/A} = \overset{\circ}{C}_d / 2\pi(r^\circ)^2$ is the capacitance normalized to the calibration *macro*electrode surface area and A_c is the *micro*electrode surface area. Finally the leakage resistance for the *micro*electrode is computed by

$$R_d = -\tan\overset{\circ}{\theta}_d / \omega C_d. \tag{20}$$

The results of the calibration experiment utilizing the specific neural growth solution employed in subsequent neural experiments are shown graphically in Fig. 9. Consequently, knowing both the double layer capacitance per area $\left(\overset{\circ}{C}_{d/A}\right)$ and the phase $\overset{\circ}{\theta}_d$, the necessary double layer components R_d and C_d are easily computed for the frequencies of interest.

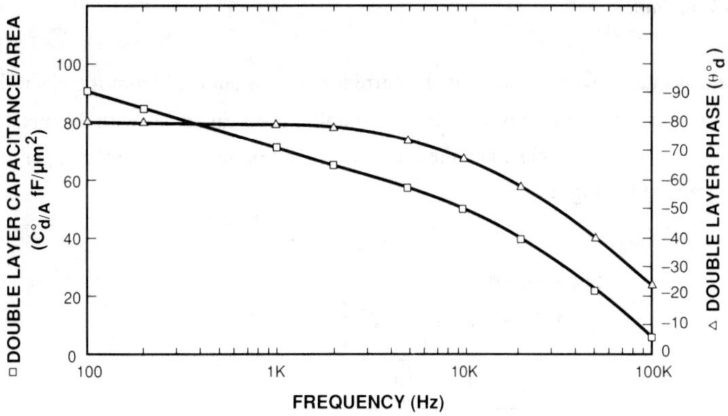

Fig. 9. Graph of experimental calibration constants.

R_l - Line Resistance

The resistance R_l of the metal conductor carrying current from the electrode to the microcircuit bonding pad is comprised of two components. The first resistive component is attributed to the adhesive metal (titanium), while the second is due to the primary conducting metal (gold) as shown in Fig. 10. Hence the line resistance for the double-layered conductor becomes

$$R_l = \frac{V}{i_1 + i_2} = \left(R_1^{-1} + R_2^{-1}\right)^{-1} = \frac{\rho_1 \rho_2}{D_{l_2}\rho_1 + D_{l_1}\rho_2} \cdot \frac{L_l}{W_l} \tag{21}$$

since

$$R_i = \rho_i L_l \,/\, W_l D_{l_i} \tag{22}$$

where ρ_1 and ρ_2 are the resistivities of the adhesion and conductor layers respectively, L_l and W_l are the length and width of the electrode line, while D_{l_1} and D_{l_2} represent the depth of the respective layers comprising the electrode line.

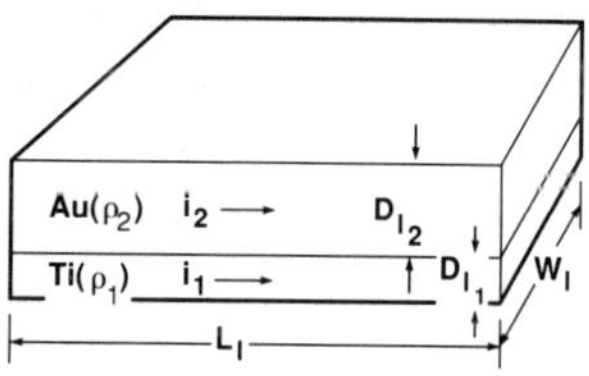

Fig. 10. Electrode line with conducting and adhesion layers.

C_s - Shunt Capacitance

The capacitance C_s accounts for the current which is shunted from the electrode line to ground. This shunt capacitance is modeled as a parallel plate capacitor, with the metal electrode line representing the bottom plate and the electrolyte solution representing the upper conducting plate as diagrammed in Fig. 11.

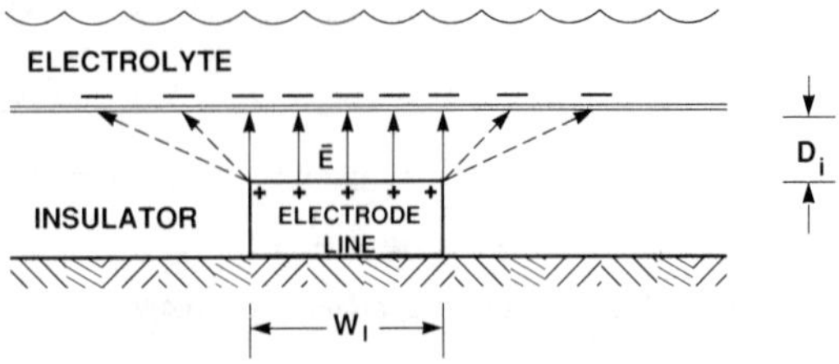

Fig. 11. Cross section of shunt capacitance between the electrode and electrolyte.

A first approximation for the shunt capacitance excludes the fringing effects due to the upper plate (electrolyte) exceeding the dimension of the lower plate (electrode line), thereby discounting the flux generated by the dashed electric field lines shown in Fig. 11. With such approximation, the shunt capacitance is

$$C_s = \frac{k\varepsilon_0 L_l W_l}{D_i} \tag{23}$$

where k is the dielectric constant, ε_0 is the permittivity, L_l, and W_l are the length and width of the electrode line under the electrolyte respectively, and D_i is the depth of the insulating dielectric. Although (23) is a first approximation, the model suffices since the shunt capacitance will be shown to be insignificant in comparison to the dominant double layer impedance.

The microcircuit electrode equivalent circuit is now complete and the components are summarized in Table 1 along with typical values calculated at a frequency of 1 kHz for a 50μm square electrode. The electrical characteristics are shown expressed as a function of the electrode dimensions labeled in Fig. 12.

MICROCIRCUIT ELECTRODE EQUIVALENT CIRCUIT

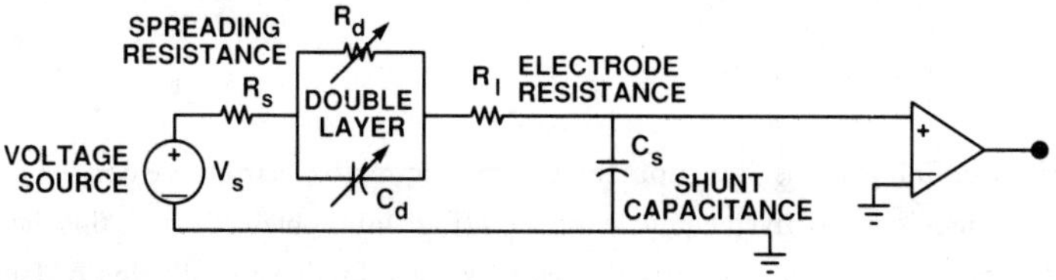

COMPONENT	MODEL	TYPICAL VALUES (1kHz)
SPREADING RESISTANCE	$R_s = \dfrac{\rho}{W_c\sqrt{4\pi H / D}}$	7.08 kΩ
ELECTRODE LINE RESISTANCE	$R_l = \dfrac{\rho_1\rho_2}{\left(D_{l_2}\rho_1 + D_{l_1}\rho_2\right)}\dfrac{L_l}{W_l}$	1.62 kΩ
DOUBLE LAYER CAPACITANCE	$C_d = C_{d/A}A_c \quad (\theta_d = 45°)$ $C_d = \overset{\circ}{C}_{d/A}A_c$ (calibration)	500pF 179pF
DOUBLE LAYER RESISTANCE	$R_d = 1/\omega C_d(\theta_d = 45°)$ $R_d = -\tan\overset{\circ}{\theta}_d / \omega C_d$ (calibration)	318kΩ 4.66MΩ
SHUNT CAPACITANCE	$C_s = \dfrac{k\varepsilon_0 L_{l_1} W_l}{D_i}$	3.84pF

Table 1. Microcircuit electrode equivalent circuit.

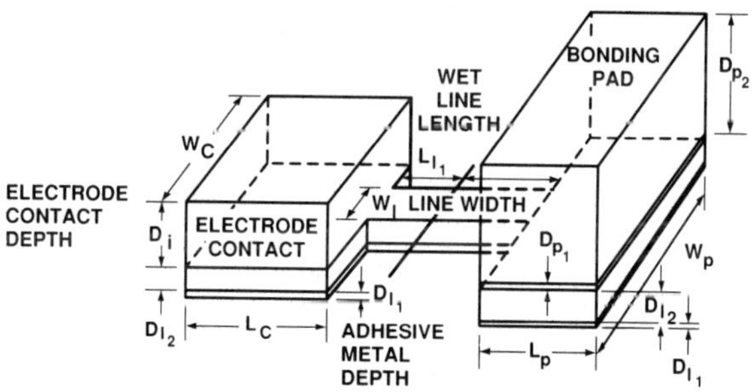

Fig. 12. Dimension labeling of microcircuit electrode.

Notice the double layer accounts for most of the impedance contribution. Therefore the area of the electrode tip, which in turn determines the double layer impedance through C_d and R_d, is a most influential factor in the electrode design.

2.2.2 System Impedance Calculation

Towards defining a cost function for the microcircuit electrode design, the system impedance of the previously derived equivalent circuit (Fig. 4c) is obtained. Also this theoretical impedance function serves as a convenient benchmark for subsequent evaluation of fabricated biochips. Hence the system impedance is instrumental in both design and evaluation.

The system impedance of the equivalent microcircuit electrode submerged in a homogeneous conducting medium is composed of two impedances in parallel. Combining these impedances

$$\overline{Z}_1 = R_s + R_l + \overline{Z}_d \tag{24}$$

$$\overline{Z}_2 = -j / \omega Cs \tag{25}$$

where

$$\overline{Z}_d = \frac{R_d - j\omega C_d R_d^2}{1 + (\omega C_d R_d)^2} \tag{26}$$

the system impedance becomes

$$\overline{Z} \equiv R + jX = \frac{\alpha R_e}{\beta^2 + (\omega C_s R_e)^2} - j\frac{\omega\left(C_s R_e^2 + \beta C_d R_d^2\right)}{\beta^2 + (\omega C_s R_e)^2} \tag{27}$$

or in polar form

$$Z = \left|\overline{Z}\right| = \sqrt{(\alpha R_e)^2 + \omega^2\left(C_s R_e^2 + \beta C_d R_d^2\right)^2} \Big/ \left(\beta^2 + (\omega C_s R_e)^2\right) \tag{28}$$

$$\theta = \angle\overline{Z} = \tan^{-1}\left(-\omega\left(C_s R_e^2 + \beta C_d R_d^2\right) / \alpha R_e\right) \tag{29}$$

where

$$\alpha = 1 + (\omega C_d R_d)^2 \tag{30}$$

$$\beta = 1 + \omega^2 R_d^2 C_d (C_d + C_s) \tag{31}$$

$$R_e = (R_s + R_l)\alpha + R_d \tag{32}$$

Consequently the system impedance (27) is expressed as a function of all relevant microcircuit electrode dimensions by substituting in the previously derived circuit component equations ((6),(19-21),(23)) summarized in Table 1. This net collection of equations can be computer programmed to provide an efficient system impedance calculation, given any microcircuit electrode dimensions. Moreover, the approximations to the system impedance function outlined below allow for rapid calculations in the absence of a computer.

In most practical microcircuit electrode designs, the double layer components dominate the system impedance. Hence by assuming $C_d >> C_s$ and $R_d >> (R_s + R_l)\alpha$, then the system impedance (28) reduces to

$$Z'' = \sqrt{(\alpha R_d)^2 + \omega^2 \left[R_d^2 (\beta C_d + C_s)\right]^2} \; / \; \left(\alpha^2 + (\omega C_s R_d)^2\right)$$

$$\cong \alpha R_d \sqrt{1 + \omega^2 C_d^2 R_d^2} \; / \left(\alpha^2 + (\omega C_s R_d)^2\right)$$

$$\cong \frac{\alpha R_d \sqrt{\alpha}}{\alpha^2}$$

$$= R_d \, / \sqrt{\alpha}$$

$$= R_d \, / \sqrt{1 + (\omega R_d C_d)^2} \tag{33}$$

with phase

$$\theta'' = \tan^{-1}\left(-\omega R_d^2 (\beta C_d + C_s) \, / \, \alpha R_d\right)$$

$$\cong \tan^{-1}\left(-\omega R_d^2 \alpha C_d \;/\; \alpha R_d\right), \qquad \alpha \cong \beta$$

$$= \tan^{-1}(-\omega R_d C_d) \tag{34}$$

Notice under this assumption, the system impedance function reduces to a mere parallel RC circuit where only the double layer components contribute.

Another reduction follows from assuming similar conditions supporting published results obtained from conventional glass-coated bright platinum microelectrodes calibrated in physiological saline solution. Here C_d and R_d also dominate the system impedance, but in addition the double-layer phase remains constant at $\theta_d \cong -45°$ [16]. Specifically assuming $C_d >> C_s$, $R_d >> (R_s + R_l)$, and $\theta_d = \tan^{-1} - \omega R_d C_d = -45°$, then the impedance (28) reduces to

$$Z' = \sqrt{4R_d^2 + \omega^2\left[R_d^2(2C_d + C_s)\right]^2} \;/\; \left(4 + (\omega C_s R_d)^2\right)$$

$$\cong 2R_d\sqrt{1 + \omega^2 C_d^2 R_d^2} \;/\; 4$$

$$= R_d / \sqrt{2} \tag{35}$$

with phase

$$\theta' = \tan^{-1}\left(-\omega\left(R_d^2 2C_d\right) / 2R_d\right)$$

$$= \tan^{-1}(-\omega R_d C_d) = -45°. \tag{36}$$

The original system impedance function (27) and the approximate forms (33-36), will be compared to actual biochip electrode measurements in the ensuing evaluation section 2.4.1.

2.2.3 Design Optimization

The optimization of the microcircuit electrode design proceeds by defining a cost function in terms of the previously derived equivalent circuit components. The cost function employed is the signal-to-noise ratio (SNR) defined across the microcircuit electrode bonding pad and ground terminal. Hence mathematically optimizing this cost function corresponds to selecting the electrode dimensions to ensure the largest received electrode signal given the present noise. The SNR is expressed as

$$SNR = P_S / P_N \tag{37}$$

where P_S is the average signal power and P_N is the average noise power, both derived below.

The limiting biochip noise source is thermal noise (Johnson noise), arising from the random motion of charge carriers. This noise is attributed only to the resistive component of the equivalent system impedance derived previously. Therefore the Nyquist thermal noise power expression for the biochip electrode is given by

$$P_N = 4kT\Delta_f R \tag{38}$$

where $k = 1.38 \times 10^{-23} J / {}^\circ K$ (Boltzmann constant), T is the operating temperature, Δ_f is the signal bandwidth, and R is the resistive portion of the system impedance (27).

Next the average signal power is easily expressed by realizing that the equivalent circuit (Fig. 4c) is a mere voltage divider, with the output signal voltage in phasor form given by

$$\overline{V} = \overline{A}\overline{V}_s \tag{39}$$

where $\overline{A}$ is the attenuation

$$\overline{A} = \frac{\overline{Z}_2}{\overline{Z}_1 + \overline{Z}_2} = \frac{1}{1 + j\omega C_s (R_1 + jX_1)} \tag{40}$$

and $\overline{Z}_1 \equiv R_1 + jX_1$. The attenuation magnitude is

$$A \equiv \left|\overline{A}\right| = \left[(1 - \omega C_s X_1)^2 + (\omega C_s R_1)^2\right]^{-\frac{1}{2}} \tag{41}$$

while the resistive portion of the system impedance can be expressed as

$$R = \text{Re}\left\{\frac{R_1 + jX_1}{(1-\omega C_s X_1) + j(\omega R_1 C_s)}\right\}$$

$$= \frac{R_1}{(1-\omega C_s X_1)^2 + (\omega R_1 C_s)^2}$$

$$= A^2 R_1 . \tag{42}$$

Consequently substitution of (39) and (38) into (37) yields the SNR expression

$$SNR = \frac{|\overline{V}|^2}{4kT\Delta_f R}$$

$$= \frac{A^2 V_s^2}{4kT\Delta_f A^2 R_1}$$

$$= \frac{V_s^2}{4kT\Delta_f R_1} \tag{43}$$

where

$$R_1 = R_s + R_l + \frac{R_d}{1 + (\omega C_d R_d)^2}$$

$$= R_s + R_l + \frac{R_d}{1 + \tan^2 \theta_d} . \tag{44}$$

Observe that optimizing the SNR design cost function (43) corresponds to minimizing the double layer resistance term $R_d / \left(1 + \tan^2 \theta_d\right)$, since typically $R_d >> (R_s + R_l)$ and both the temperature and bandwidth are fixed. In turn, minimization of the double layer resistance term corresponds to maximizing the electrode surface area A_c, because for the first method outlined for obtaining R_d (using a published value of $C_{d/A}$ and $\theta_d = -45$)

$$SNR' = \frac{2V_s^2 \omega C_{d/A}}{4kT\Delta_f} A_c \tag{45}$$

while the second method (based on the calibration experiment where $\overset{\circ}{C}_{d/A}$ and $\overset{\circ}{\theta}_d$ are measured)

$$SNR'' = \frac{\left(1+\tan\overset{\circ}{\theta}_d\right)V_s^2\omega\overset{\circ}{C}_{d/A}}{4kT\Delta_f\tan\overset{\circ}{\theta}_d}A_c \tag{46}$$

Notice the SNR is independent of the electrode line insulation depth D_i. Therefore the primary constraint governing the depth selection is the insulator breakdown voltage ($V_{bd} = 1.6mV / \mathring{A}$ for quartz). Also layering of the insulation layer provides additional immunity against migration of sodium ions.

As a consequence, an optimal microcircuit electrode design using *conventional* fabrication techniques simply corresponds to choosing the electrode surface area A_c large as possible. An upper bound for the area is determined by the density of the connecting neurons, for too large an electrode will invite crosstalk from neighboring neurons. Typically the electrode area is designed approximately the size of the neuron to avoid unwanted crosstalk in modest density networks (neuron to neuron spacing about 2-5 cell bodies).

Significant performance enhancement can be achieved by employing *unconventional* fabrication techniques. As observed from the SNR expressions (45) and (46), electrode design optimization employing conventional fabrication techniques requires maximizing the surface area of the electrode contact. However the footprint of the electrode contact is restricted to the size of the neural cell body to avoid crosstalk from neighboring neurons. Thus further increasing the SNR requires increasing the surface area while simultaneously maintaining a fixed electrode footprint of the order of the cell body size. An unconventional solution (borrowed from the biology community) to this *constrained* optimization problem entails electrically platinizing the microcircuit electrodes to create a rough porous surface several times greater in surface area. The enhanced effect of platinizing on the SNR can be formulated by considering the new platinized surface area to be

$$A_p = \gamma A_c \tag{47}$$

which results in the new SNR

$$SNR_{plat} = \gamma SNR \tag{48}$$

or in decibels

$$SNR_{plat} = SNR(dB) + 10\log\gamma \tag{49}$$

and hence an increase of $10\log\gamma(dB)$ in SNR results. For example, with a value of $\gamma = 100$, the SNR is improved by $20dB$.

Finally, it is important to realize that although mathematically optimal electrodes can be designed as discussed, the actual behavior of the electrode surrounded by neural tissue will vary from prediction. The deviation is attributed to the complex pattern of ionic currents that develop surrounding each of the current generating neurons. Consequently, the modeling and subsequent design optimization based on a homogeneous conducting medium (such as isotonic saline solution) offers much towards providing insight and general design guidelines, but should not be mistaken as an accurate representation of experimental conditions surrounding nonhomogeneous neural networks.

2.2.4 Bipolar Electrode Design

The previous design sections provide techniques for designing microcircuit electrodes which exhibit good recording performance (high SNR). However, additional considerations must be addressed to provide *both* extracellular recording and stimulation capability. Without such additional considerations, stimulation can be achieved only in a global manner using the previously designed recording electrodes. That is, the electric field developed when a stimulus voltage is applied across a single recording electrode and the ground terminal irradiates the entire electrode array. Thus all neurons within the network are significantly influenced when attempting to stimulate a single neuron resting above a given electrode. Consequently, to provide focused or localized stimulation whereby only a single neuron is effected, the following bipolar electrode design criteria are presented.

The first bipolar design shown in Fig.13a is simply a combination of two recording electrodes, one serving as the anode, the other as the cathode. This represents the simplest bipolar design. An alternative design is shown in Fig. 13b. Although more complex, this circular design yields an electric field that is radially symmetric from anode to cathode. Here the electric stimulation induced is uniform with respect to the neural cell body centered over the circular electrode, thereby contributing to more efficient stimulation.

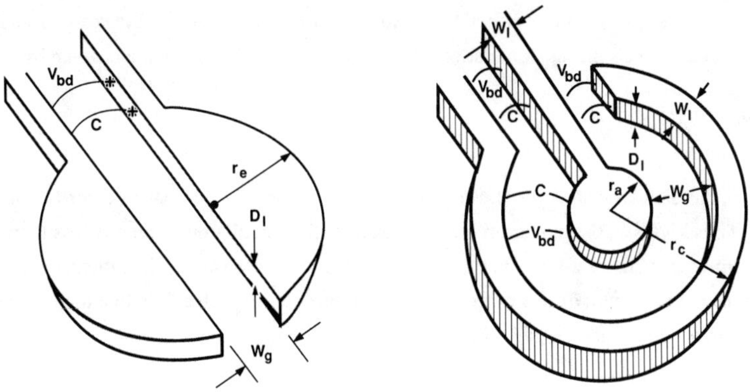

Fig. 13. Diagram of a) simple and b) circular bipolar electrodes.

Specifically, the additional design considerations center about the gaps between the anode and cathode, and between the paired electrode lines. These small dielectric gaps which separate two conductors can induce unwanted capacitance and cause dielectric breakdown if the stimulus voltage is excessive. Hence both of these adverse effects must be quantitatively addressed when designing bipolar electrodes.

The capacitance induced by the gap between the electrode lines is readily determined by assuming a parallel plate capacitor model. The resulting upper bound for the length of the paired electrode lines of depth D_l and separated by a gap of size W_g is

$$L_{\max} = \frac{W_g C_{\max}}{k\varepsilon_0 D_l} \tag{50}$$

where $C_{\max}$ is the maximum capacitance allowed (typically about 1pF). The additional capacitance between the anode and cathode for the circular bipolar design can be formulated by assuming an ideal cylindrical capacitor model. The resulting lower bound for the cathode/anode diameter ratio is

$$\left.\frac{r_c'}{r_a}\right|_{\min} = e^{2\pi k\varepsilon_0 D_l / C_{\max}} \tag{51}$$

where $r_c' = r_c - W_l$ is the cathode inner radius, r_a is the anode outer radius, and $C_{\max}$ is again the maximum capacitance allowable.

The remaining adverse effect to be quantized is the dielectric breakdown caused by excessive voltage levels during stimulation. The dielectric breakdown voltage is given by

$$V_{bd} = \xi d \tag{52}$$

where ξ is the dielectric strength ($1.6mV / \mathring{A}$ for quartz) and d is the distance across the gap of interest. Thus knowing the maximum voltage required for stimulation (typically less than 1 volt), the minimum gap distance allowable is easily computed. Notice several calculations must be made to determine the minimum distances for the electrode line pair gap, electrode line to electrolyte gap (D_i), and the anode to cathode gap (W_g).

2.3 Microcircuit Electrode Array Fabrication

Primarily conventional microfabrication techniques can be employed to fabricate the previously designed biochip electrode arrays. However, special biological driven requirements regarding material selection must be adopted to provide compatible and reliable biochips. These materials and the accompanying fabrication methods are detailed below. Also fabrication results for both unipolar and bipolar electrode arrays are displayed.

2.3.1 Material Selection

Special material considerations for interfacing fabricated microcircuits and living cells must be addressed to avoid cell contamination and biochip deterioration. Electrode deterioration can be minimized by choosing non-corrosive inert metals with good stable electrical conduction properties, such as gold. Moreover, the effectiveness of the insulator can deteriorate due to the persistent migration of sodium ions present in the physiological saline bath. Methods to curb insulator deterioration include choosing materials resistive to sodium migration such as silicon nitride, in addition to layering the insulator material to cover possible submicron pitts within each layer formed during fabrication. Although single layer silicon dioxide can be used, it is more permeable to sodium and hence eventually degrades within a few months.

Regarding materials compatible to cell growth, many of the common microfabrication substrates are suitable. Successful neural growth has been achieved on glass, silicon, and silicon dioxide (quartz). Quartz is favorable because the clear substrate enables viewing during neural experimentation using a transmission microscope, and is dimensionally stable at the high temperatures required for processing. Finally, by choosing 3 inch diameter quartz wafers, 4 biochips per wafer can be attained.

2.3.2 Fabrication Methods

Fabrication begins by cleaning the 15 mil. thick quartz wafers by ultrasonic agitation in a detergent bath for 15 minutes. Further cleaning is provided by a plasma etcher (97% helium, 3% oxygen) for one minute.

The basic procedure for biochip fabrication following cleaning is illustrated in Fig. 14. The electrode pattern is made by first treating the chosen substrate with an adhesion promoter. A solution of 50% hexamethydlisilazane (hmds) and 50% xylene is puddled on and allowed to sit for about 10 seconds. The substrate is then spun at 3000 rpm to remove all but a monolayer of hmds. One half micron of positive photoresist (Shipley S1805) is then spun onto the wafer and baked for 30 minutes at 90°C in flowing air. Next, the substrate is placed in vacuum contact with a 60 mil. thick glass mask bearing the electrode pattern in an ultraviolet (UV) opaque material. The photoresist is exposed to UV light through this mask. Subsequently, the substrate is dipped in developer to remove the photoresist which has been exposed to the light. This leaves photoresist everywhere except on the electrode pattern. Using an electron beam evaporator, 100 angstroms of titanium is then deposited onto the substrate followed by 500 angstroms of gold. The photoresist is removed in acetone "lifting off" the metal that has been deposited on the surface, hence leaving only the electrode pattern in gold.

Next the dielectric insulation layer is deposited. Depending on the design, 2000 to 4000 angstroms of silicon dioxide (SiO_2) is deposited using chemical vapor deposition. After covering the entire surface with SiO_2, holes must be cut to expose the ends of the electrodes. The substrate is coated with one half micron of photoresist and baked as before. Using a contact aligner, the photoresist is exposed with the hole pattern aligned to the electrode pattern. After developing, using the photoresist as a mask, the SiO_2 is etched through in a plasma etcher using a mixture of CF_4 and O_2. The photoresist is then removed in ACT-1 resist stripper at 90°C.

The outer ends of the electrodes need to be coated with 1 micron of gold for final package bonding. First, the substrate is coated with 3 microns of photoresist (Shipley 1375) and baked at 90°C for 45 minutes in flowing air. Next, the bonding pad pattern is UV exposed using a contact aligner and developed. Here 500 angstroms of titanium and 1 micron of gold are electron beam evaporated onto the substrate. The excess ti/gold is then "lifted off" by dissolving the photoresist in acetone.

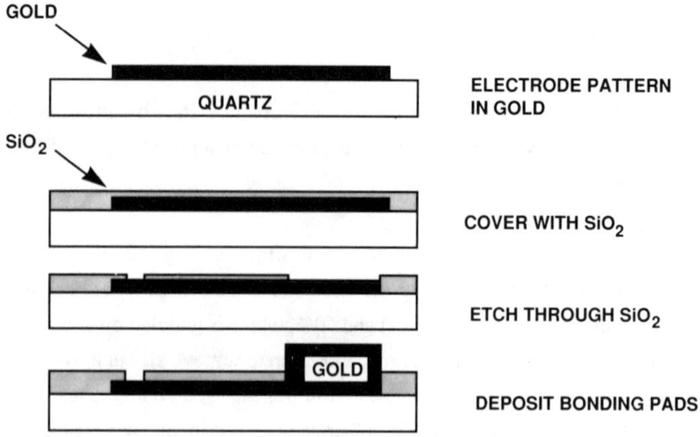

Fig. 14. Diagram of biochip fabrication procedure.

The microcircuit is now ready for packaging into a 72 lead package, with a hole cut in the back for microscopic viewing. The four circuits on a wafer are cut apart using a diamond saw. After being epoxied into the package, the package leads are wire bonded to the bonding pads using gold wire. A gold coated ring is then epoxied to the center of the circuit to isolate the growth solution, and act as the ground connection for the electrical measurements.

If platinizing is desired to further reduce electrode impedance and hence boost SNR, the following procedure can be performed. Platinization is conducted by passing a DC current through the electrodes while immersed in Kohlrausch's [20] platinum chloride solution. The magnitude and duration of the current controls the amount of platinum deposited. Here a trade-off is encountered since larger platinum electrode deposits do warrant lower impedances, yet are undesirably delicate. Hence the current is largely set by empirical findings that substantiate firm platinum deposits at the expense of higher impedance. Specifically the most favorable platinization conditions observed are shown in Fig. 15a. where a platinization current of $2\mu A$ for 30 seconds is sufficient to reduce electrode impedance by approximately two orders of magnitude, while simultaneously providing a firm platinum deposit as indicated by the electron micrograph shown in Fig.15b.

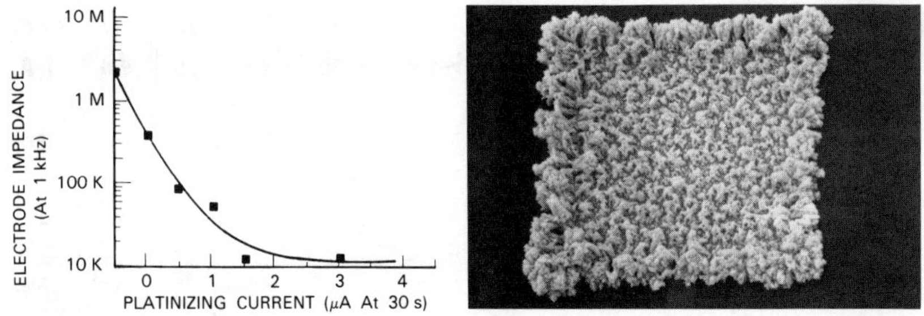

Fig. 15. Electrode a) impedance and b) colloidal surface layer following platinization.

2.3.3 Fabrication Results

Typical results from a good fabrication run are displayed. First a picture of the unipolar electrode array is shown in Fig. 16a. The outside dimensions are approximately one inch square with 18 bonding pads per side. The pattern of $5\mu m$ wide lines converges to the small electrode array shown in Fig. 16b. The array contains 72 electrodes spaced $50\mu m$ apart.

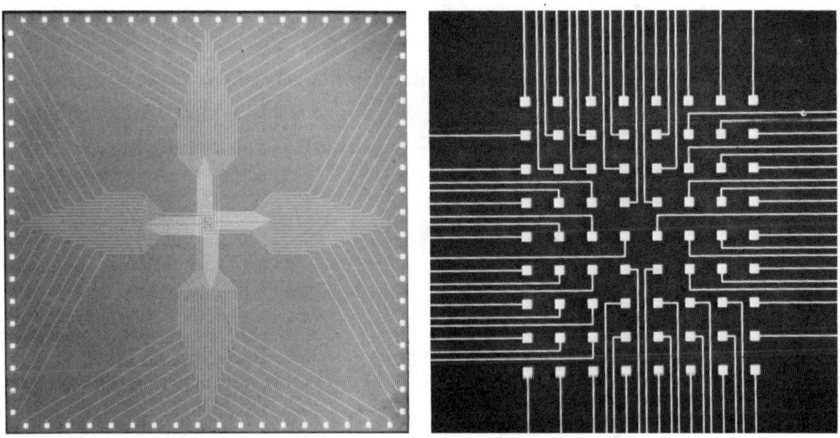

Fig. 16. Unipolar a) biochip with b) 72 electrode array.

The following picture, Fig. 17 shows the bipolar electrode array with similar outside dimensions and bonding sites. This array contains 34 bipolar electrodes spaced $250\mu m$ apart.

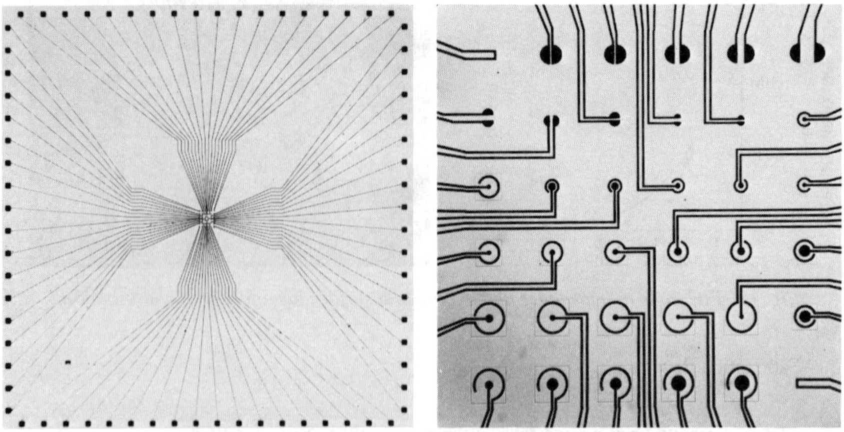

Fig. 17 . Bipolar a) biochip with b) 34 electrode array.

2.4 Microcircuit Electrode Array Evaluation

Once fabricated, the biochips are visually inspected and subsequently quantitatively evaluated based on the system impedance measurements. The evaluation consists of comparing the measurements, taken as prescribed below, to the theoretical impedance function (derived in Section 2.2.2). Finally, biochips with impedance values favorably correlated to theoretical prediction, and possessing low standard deviation across the 72 electrodes in the array are designated for neuronal experimentation.

2.4.1 Impedance Measurements

The measurement session begins by setting the test voltage amplitude and frequency, and conducting open and short circuit calibration tests using the precision impedance analyzer (HP 4284 A). Specifically, the sinusoidal test voltage level must be set low (approximately 25mV) to avoid insulator breakdown above the electrode lines. The frequency can be varied in the band of interest, however, the impedance values at 1 kHz are the most informative since such value is commensurate with the neural action potential bandwidth. Measurements are taken by filling the neural reservoir with neural growth solution, then clamping the ground test lead to the ground ring and the remaining lead to the biochip electrode channel of interest. The measurements are recorded in sequential fashion in the magnitude/phase form.

Evaluation results from the best fabrication run (565 electrodes were operable among 8 biochips) are shown in Fig. 18. Both theoretical and measured impedance values are shown. Notice the exact impedance function (28) and the approximation function that incorporates the calibration results (33) yields approximately (2%) the same values, while the other approximation method (35) based on published capacitance values is significantly different (74%). The discrepancy is attributed in part to the specific neural growth solution used and the gold electrode metal. Both are different from those substances used in the published calibration experiment from which $C_{dl/A}$ was obtained [16]. In regards to comparing the measured values to the exact and first approximation theoretical results, good conformance is displayed especially at 1kHz where less than 7% difference is reported. Notice the standard deviation among the 565 electrodes for the measurements taken at 1kHz is approximately 10%, while the deviation increases to 18% at 100 Hz. The difference in deviation is due to both the sampling size being smaller at 100 Hz (71 electrodes) and the credibility loss in the double layer model at low frequencies.

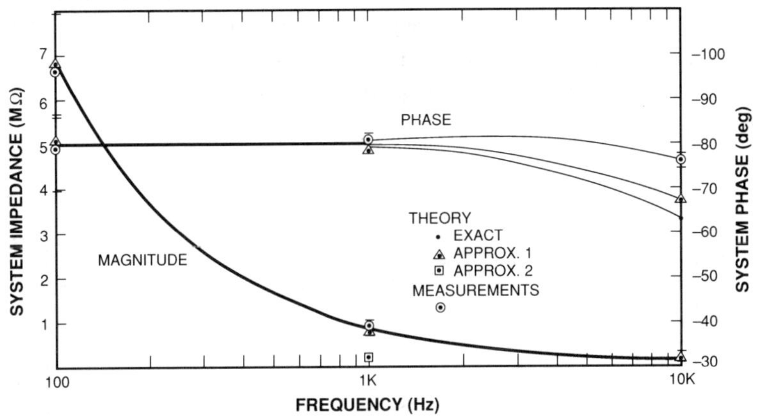

Fig. 18. Graph of theoretical and measured biochip electrode impedances.

Consequently, the evaluation results substantiate the particular electrode modeling approach introduced based on the calibration experiment from which the electrical double layer components are obtained. Also the use of the approximation impedance function (33) appears warranted.

2.4.2 Impedance Measurements of Platinized Electrodes

The measurement procedure for the platinized biochips is identical to the previously outlined approach. Since the effective electrode surface area is enlarged by a factor γ following platinization, and the impedance function is inversely proportional to such surface area, the best impedance reduction through platinization is expected to be γ^{-1}.

The results of the impedance measurements taken from a biochip (with 65 operable electrodes) selected from the previously evaluated fabrication run and platinized under the conditions specified are displayed in Fig. 19. Again the magnitude exhibits the $\omega^{-1/2}$ behavior. However, the phase varies substantially with frequency, unlike the unplatinized electrodes where the phase remains relatively constant for most of the bandwidth. In fact such phase variation may explain the frequency dependency of the impedance reduction, where the reduction factor γ achieved by platinization, is 46 at 100 Hz and diminishes to 8.5 at 10 kHz. Hence, the benefit of platinization is frequency dependent, with the greatest advantage experienced at lower frequencies. Another consequence of platinization is an increased deviation in the impedance values. This increase can be attributed to the nonuniform growth during platinization of the surface area among the various electrodes.

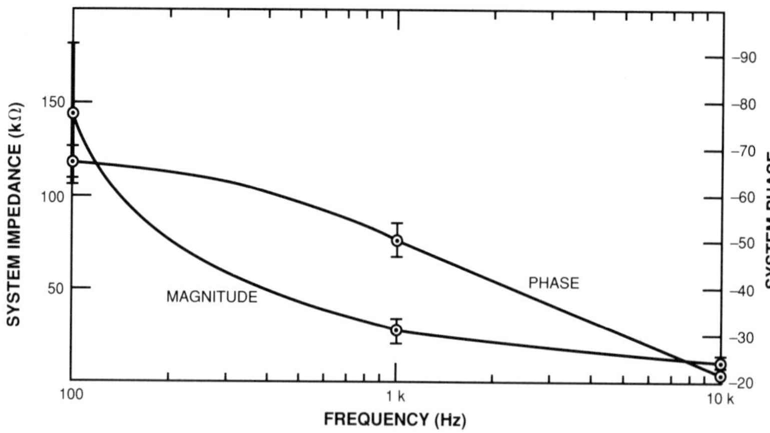

Fig. 19. Graph of theoretical and measured platinized biochip electrode impedances.

2.5 System Integration

The integration of the neural network signal processing system, ranging from the biochip (with microvolt analog signals) to the computer (with digital signals), consists of building custom instrumentation amplifiers and neuronal chambers to house the biochip. The specifications for the instrumentation amplifier are driven by the neural signaling properties, together with biological considerations. Regarding neural signaling, the extracellular action potentials may range from 50 to 400μV peak-to-peak and are embedded in 20-40μV thermal noise, while the bandwidth is generously selected at 7kHz. Therefore the amplification required is approximately 50,000. Considering the biology, the neuron must be isolated from the electronics to avoid induced behavior artifacts. Hence a very large amplifier input impedance is required. Moreover, a low bias current is necessary so that the high gain amplifier will not saturate when connected to the high impedance (MΩ) electrode source. The two-stage custom amplifier shown in Fig. 20a satisfying these constraints utilizes a Burr-Brown INA110 very high accuracy instrumentation amplifier and a subsequent conventional operational amplifier (AD711BQ) for additional gain. The front-end amplifier offers the desired high input impedance (1TΩ) by using dual precision FET buffers on the input. This design also affords a low DC bias current (50pA) to avoid saturation. Finally, the variable gain is set to 500 such that in combination with the second stage, the overall gain is near 50,000. The frequency response of the amplifier is shaped to provide a 3dB bandpass (see Fig. 20b) extending from approximately 170Hz to 8kHz .

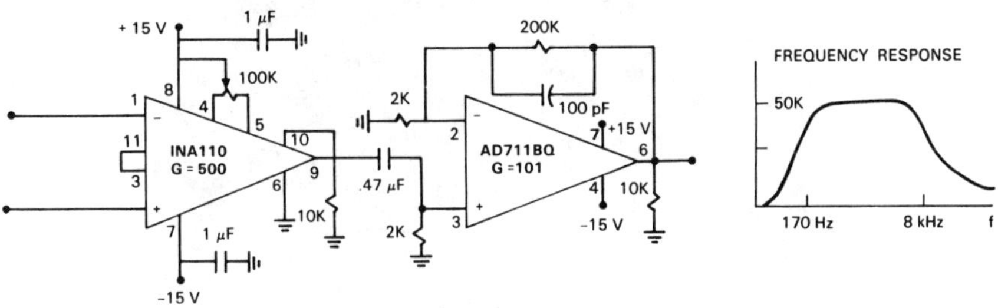

Fig. 20. Schematic of a) instrumentation amplifier and corresponding b) frequency response.

Regarding neuronal chambers, the specific chamber employed for the mammalian cells is displayed in Fig. 21. The metallic walls house a heating coil which is thermostatically controlled. Also the inner most sterilized chamber fits over the biochip package for easy assembly. The neuronal chamber designed for the invertebrate cells is shown in Fig. 22. Here a standard flatpack socket with matching carrier suffices since temperature need not be controlled.

Fig. 21. Mammalian neuronal chamber.

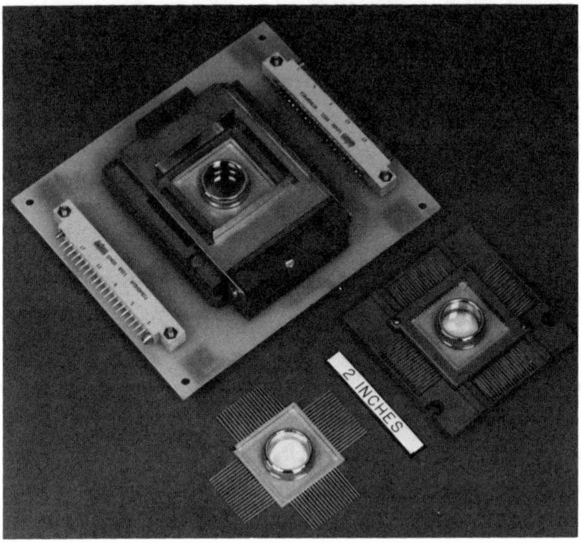

Fig. 22. Invertebrate neuronal chamber.

3. NEURAL GROWTH BIOLOGY

Electrically excitable cells from dissociated invertebrate and clonal mammalian systems are advantageous for neural network experimentation. Dissociated cell culture techniques are discussed first, followed by the cloanl cell methods.

3.1 Dissociated Cell Cultures

Neurons from dissociated invertebrate systems offer particular advantages for analyzing the response properties of the biochip. One major advantage is that the cells are large (approximately 50 micrometers), which permits easy handling and simultaneous recording from intracellular microelectrodes and extracellular biochip electrodes. Such simultaneous recording procedure is necessary for verifying the biochip recording capability. Also, such cells require minimal life support, unlike mammalian cells which require higher temperatures and elevated CO_2. In addition, these cells form synapses when grown in tissue culture and hence allow analysis of synaptic properties. The disadvantage with dissociated invertebrate cells is the large variation in cell types within a grown network, thus making the modeling much more complex.

Regarding specific dissociation and culturing methods, the ganglion of 2 to 10 gram sized *Aplysia califonica* sea slugs obtained from Howard Hughes Medical Facilities in Woods Hole and the University of Miami Aplysia Resources are dissected out and washed in incubation medium. Next the ganglia are incubated in dispase (Boebringer Mannheim 1%, pH7.4) in incubation medium for about 4 hours at 34°C. The base incubation medium consists of L-15 (Flow Labs) with the addition of NaCl (320mM), KCl (4.6mM), $CaCl_2$ (9.7mM), $MgCl_2$ (53.2mM), HEPES (5mM), glucose 1%, penicillin, and streptomycin. The solution is titrated to pH7.7 and sterilized by filtration. Following incubation, ganglia are washed with incubation medium and subsequently teased apart with fine forceps. The resulting dissociated neurons can be plated on the biochip by pipeting. The biochip culture medium consists of 0.5% methyl-cellulose in incubation medium and is kept at room temperature. Within 2 to 4 days synaptic connections develop with similar morphological characteristics of control cultures grown in conventional glass dishes.

3.2 Clonal Cell Cultures

To counter the added complexity inherent to dissociated cell cultures, where numerous cell types occur within a single network, clonal cell cultures can be employed. This approach allows the network to be tailored for specific experiments and applications. For example, identical cells can be networked on the biochip to provide a system amenable to mathematical analysis. Also since the cell line is immortal, a practically endless supply of cells can be obtained inexpensively. Although these tailored clonal neural circuits may well exhibit basic network properties, they are not expected to represent *in vivo* neural systems.

To produce the clonal cells, precursor cells are first extracted from fetal rat cerebellum. A temperature sensitive oncogene is then expressed into the precursor cell through a virus as illustrated in Fig. 23. Consequently the oncogene now within the precursor cell represents the control mechanism that causes the precursor cell to divide or differentiate. For at the lower temperature, the cell divides, while at the elevated temperature the cell differentiates into one of multiple fates.

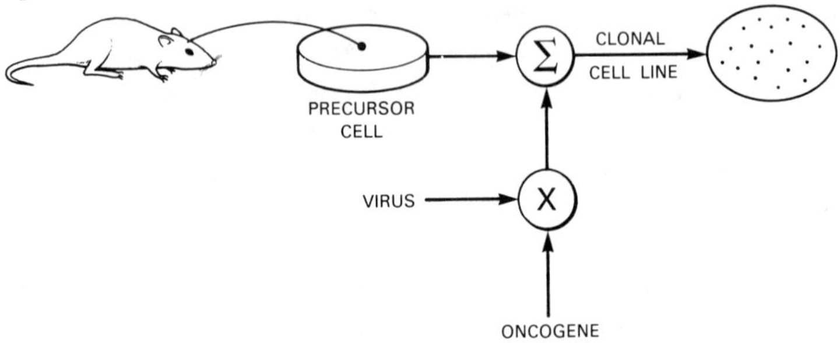

Fig. 23. Clonal cell generation.

Specifically, the ST15A cell line utilized can differentiate into cells with either neuronal or astrocytic properties depending of the serum conditions. These ST15A cells have been shown to differentiate uniformly into muscle cells [21] which are advantageous for microelectrode penetration due to the network growth in uniform, fused, syncitial sheets.

The ST15A culture procedure begins by trypsinizing cells which have been grown in 10% fetal calve serum (FCS) in DMEM at 33°C. These cells are then plated in the biochip culture well containing the same type of fluid. One day after the cells became confluent, the medium is changed to 10% horse serum (HS) in DMEM and the temperature is changed to 39°C. Five days later multinucleate cells are formed and ready for experimentation. The culture remains operable for at least one week without the change of medium. When the medium is changed, the fresh medium is first prewarmed in the culture incubator with the container lid loosely capped to equilibriate medium pH. The CO_2 is maintained at 5% in the incubator at all times. Only one third of the medium volume in the biochip culture well is replaced.

An alternative cell line, C2, proves easier to differentiate and grow on the biochip. Since the differentiated C2 muscle cells are rather long, intracellular stimulation is also easier. The C2 cell culture preparation is the same as ST15A cells, except that one day after the culture becomes confluent, the medium is changed to 5% calve serum (CS) in DMEM and the temperature held constant at 37°C.

4. NEURAL MEASUREMENTS

The neural measurements section demonstrates the capabilities offered through the integration of electrical engineering and biology. By combining the outcome of the preceding chapters, both neural recording and stimulation is achieved noninvasively utilizing the biochip.

4.1 Neuron Recording

The two measurement experiments described below demonstrate the ability to record from single neurons and a network of neurons grown and synaptically coupled on the biochip. The objective of the single neuron recording experiment is to verify the basic technology development and recording operation of the biochip. A conventional glass-coated intracellular microelectrode serves as the benchmark recording measurement. The $30M\Omega$ microelectrode is filed with 3M K-acetate and is made of glass tubing with 1.0 mm outside and 0.58 mm inside diameters.

The procedure begins by placing dissociated Aplysia neurons on the biochip surface per Section 3. An intracellular probe is inserted into a candidate neuron residing over an electrode as shown in Fig. 24. The neuron is subsequently stimulated by the intracellular probe with a current pulse which serves to depolarize the neuron. Recorded neuron signals from both the intracellular probe (Axoclamp-2 used in bridge-current clamp mode) and the extracellular biochip electrode are also shown in Fig. 24. The signals are displayed and recorded with a Nicolet 4049 digital oscilloscope in conjunction with a Nicolet XF-44 disc recorder. Notice both the intracellular and extracellular recordings display three action potentials with good correlation. Clearly the price for noninvasive recording is lower SNR, however, the SNR is sufficient to easily discern the microvolt-level extracellular neural response.

The second recording experiment serves to demonstrate that a network of neurons can be grown on the biochip. Specifically, the network is proven synaptically coupled by displaying highly correlated neural signals recorded from two connecting neurons. Both spontaneously active and artificially stimulated networks are employed.

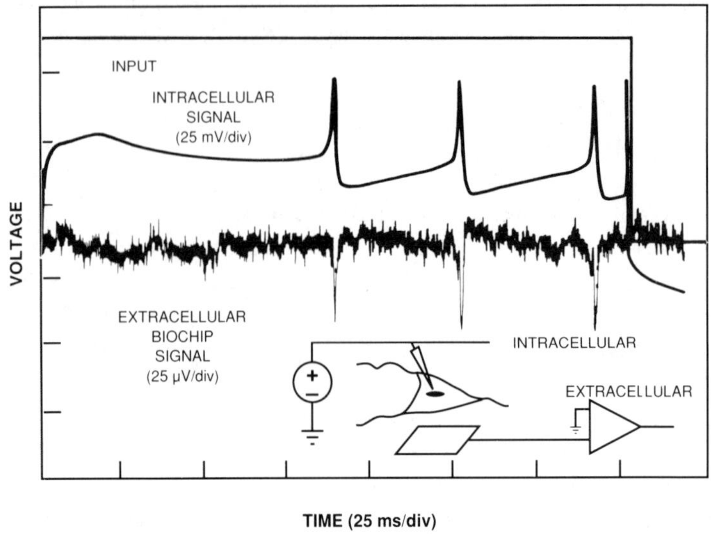

Fig. 24. Single neuron recording from conventional and biochip electrodes.

The experiment begins by growing Aplysia neurons on the biochip. Within days the neural processes grow to make connections with neighboring neurons. At approximately 3 days the network is mature and displays abundant convoluted connections as shown by the electron micrograph in Fig. 25. Notice most of the neural processes channel along the surface of the biochip, yet occasionally they are found suspended between neurons.

Conventional intracellular probes are then inserted into two neurons which appear visually connected. For the artificially stimulated network, one neuron (designated the presynaptic neuron) is stimulated with a positive pulse current, while signal records are taken of both the presynaptic and connecting postsynaptic neurons. Notice from Fig. 26, the signals display definite correlation, and hence substantiate the formation of a synapse. Specifically, the induced presynaptic neural action potentials are seen to promote postsynaptic neural action potentials in two of the three instances. On one occasion, the postsynaptic neuron responds with only a slight graded response, insufficient to warrant an action potential.

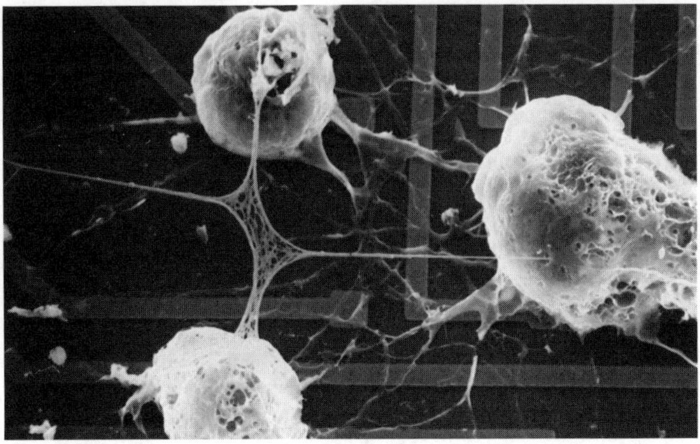

Fig. 25. Electron micrograph of synaptically connected neurons on biochip surface.

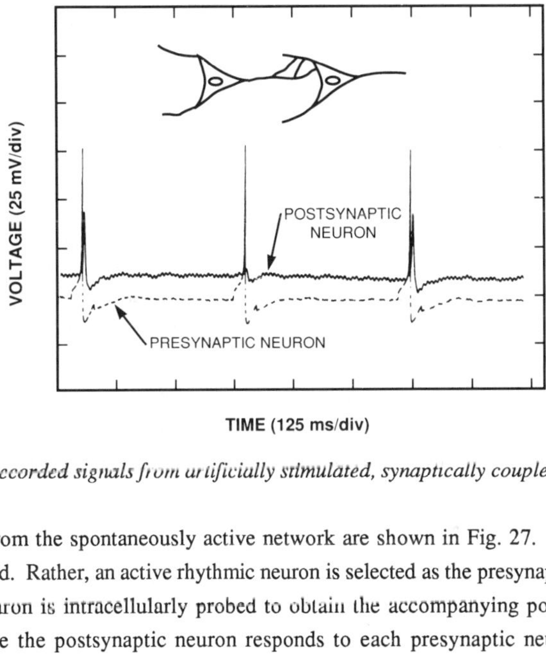

Fig. 26. Recorded signals from artificially stimulated, synaptically coupled neurons.

Results from the spontaneously active network are shown in Fig. 27. Here no external stimulus is applied. Rather, an active rhythmic neuron is selected as the presynaptic neuron, while a connecting neuron is intracellularly probed to obtain the accompanying postsynaptic neural response. Notice the postsynaptic neuron responds to each presynaptic neural input with a correlated graded potential. However, sometimes the graded potential is strong enough to elicit an action potential as displayed. Again strong correlation in presynaptic and postsynaptic neural signals confirm synaptic connection.

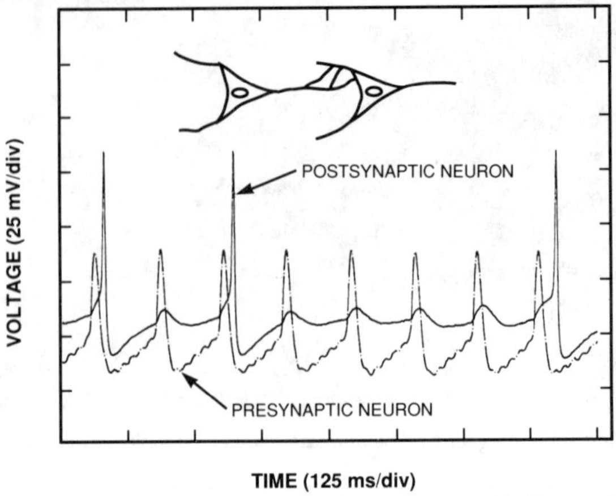

Fig. 27. Recorded signals from spontaneously active, synaptically coupled neurons .

4.2 Neuron Stimulation

To demonstrate on-chip stimulation capability with the electrodes, Aplysia neurons are placed on the biochip surface as described earlier. Next a candidate neuron residing over an electrode on the biochip is selected for stimulation. A conventional intracellular electrode is then inserted for recording purposes, specifically to verify that the on-chip stimulus signal promotes an action potential. The biochip unipolar extracellular electrode is subsequently driven by a symmetric voltage signal source as displayed in Fig. 28. The stimulation pulse generator consists of a WP Instruments interval generator 1830, pulse train module 1631, and a stimulus isolator 1850A. Also shown is the resulting intracellular recording that illustrates the successful depolarization of the neuron leading to the action potential. Notice further, the time between the stimulus ending and the beginning of the action potential response is almost 125 miliseconds. This time represents the maximum switching time for switching an electrode from stimulation (volt-level output) to recording (microvolt-level input) mode. Hence feasibility is established for employing a single biochip electrode for both global stimulation and subsequent local recording.

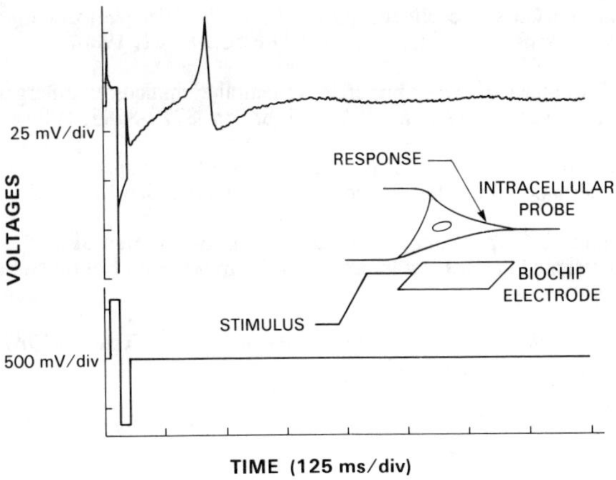

Fig. 28. On-chip neuron stimulation results utilizing biochip electrode.

5. CONCLUSION

In conclusion, the biochip technology presented provides a foundation for effectively interfacing living cells and electronics. Specifically, *long term noninvasive multisite recording and stimulation capability is achieved.* The continued multidisciplinary (electrical engineering, biology, physics) building of such interface is envisioned to be instrumental in both future information technology and medicine. For biologically inspired computer architectures that exploit the principles of superior biological information processing may become reality. In addition, the interface also supports medical prosthetic devices for restoration of nerve function.

6. REFERENCES

[1] J. J. Hopfield, "Neural networks and physical systems with emergent collective computational abilities," *Proc. Natl. Acad. Sci., USA*, vol. 79, pp. 2554-2558, April 1982.

[2] S. Grossberg, *The Adaptive Brain, Vols. I and II*, Amsterdam, North Holland, 1986.

[3] T. Kohonen, *Self Organization and Associative Memory*, Springer Verlag, Berlin, 1984.

[4] D. E. Rumelhart, G. E. Hinton, R. I. Williams, "Learning internal representations by error propagation", in D. E. Rumelhart, J. L. McClelland (Eds.), *Parallel Distributed Processing*, Vol. 1, 1986.

[5] T. Sejnowski and C. R. Rosenberg, *NETtalk: A Parallel Network that Learns to Read Aloud,* Johns Hopkins Univ. Tech Report JHU/EECS-86/01, 1986.

[6] R. Linsker, "From basic network principles to neural architecture: emergence of orientation columns." *Proc. Natl. Acad. Sci., USA* , vol. 83, pp. 8779-8783, 1986.

[7] R. Lippmann and B. Gold, "Neural-net classifiers useful for speech recognition", presented at IEEE 1st International Conference on Neural Networks, San Diego, CA, June 1987.

[8] W. Huang and R. Lippmann, "Comparisons between neural net and conventional classifiers", presented at IEEE 1st International Conference on Neural Networks, San Diego, CA, June 1987.

[9] R. Levine, *Neural Network Performance on the Stochastic Exclusive-Or Problem,* TR 808, MIT Lincoln Laboratory, July 1988.

[10] Y. S. Abu-Mostafa and D. Psaltis, "Optical neural computers", *Scientific American,* pp 88-95, March 1987.

[11] E. Kandel, "Small systems of neurons", in *The Brain, A Scientific American Book,* W. H. Freeman and Company, San Francisco, 1979.

[12] C. Thomas, P. Springer, G. Loeb, Y. Berwald-Netter, and L. Okum, "A miniature microelectrode array to monitor the bioelectric activity of cultured cells," *Experimental Cell Research,* vol. 74, pp. 61-66, 1972.

[13] G. Gross, "Simultaneous single unit recording in vitro with a photoetched laser deinsulated gold multi microelectrode surface," *IEEE Trans. on Biomedical Engineering,* vol. BME-26, no. 5., pp. 273-279, May 1979.

[14] M. Droge, G. Gross, M. Hightower, L. Czisny, "Multielectrode analysis of coordinated, multisite, rythmic bursting in cultured CNS monolayer networks," *The Journal of Neurosci.,* vol. 6, pp. 1583-1592, June 1986.

[15] J. Pine, "Recording action potentials from cultured neurons with extracellular microcircuit electrodes," *Journal of Neuroscience Methods,* vol. 2, pp. 19-31, 1980.

[16] D. A. Robinson, "The electrical properties of metal electrodes," *Proceedings of the IEEE,* Vol. 56, No. 6, June 1968.

[17] P. W. Davies, "The oxygen cathode," in *Physical Techniques in Biological Research,* Vol. 4, W. L. Nastak, Ed. New York: Academic Press, Ch. 3., 1962.

[18] R. Gesteland, B. Howland, J. Lettvin, W. Pitts," Comments on microelectrodes," *Proc. IRE,* Vol. 47, pp. 1856-1862.

[19] H. Schwan, "Determination of biological impedances," *Physical Techniques in Biological Research,* Vol. 6, W. L. Nastuk, Ed., New York: Academic Press, Ch. 6., 1962.

[20] H. Baldwin, S. Frank, and J. Y. Lettvin, "Glass-coated tungsten microelectrodes," *Science,* vol. 148, pp. 1462-1463, 1965.

[21] K. Frederiksen, J. Jat, N. Valtz, D. Levy, and R. McKay, "Immortalization of precursor cells from the mammalian CNS," *Neuron,* vol. 1, pp. 439-448, 1988.

9

STOCHASTIC ARCHITECTURES FOR RECURRENT NEURAL NETWORKS

by David E. Van Den Bout, Thomas K. Miller, III
and William B. Wike,
North Carolina State University

1 INTRODUCTION

Neural networks have been shown to be a powerful computing paradigm for many important problems. Thus, a great deal of effort has been expended searching for the best approach to implementing neural network computing models in hardware. This chapter focuses on an implementation approach for *recurrent* neural networks — those which employ feedback in their evolution towards the problem solution. Examples include Hopfield's network [11, 12], in which massive feedback is used to seek the minimum of an *energy surface* defined by the neuron connection weights, and Kohonen's self-organizing feature map [16, 17], in which feedback is used to adjust the connection weights during the competitive learning process. It will be shown that *stochastic architectures* are a practical and effective alternative to conventional analog and/or digital implementations of these recurrent networks, and two distinctly different examples will be described. The first is STONN (Stochastic Neural Network), an implementation of the Hopfield network. The second is TINMANN (The Integer Markovian Artificial Neural Network), which is based on the Kohonen self-organizing feature map.

1.1 Analog or Digital?

Artificial neural networks are massively parallel architectures that solve difficult problems via the cooperation of highly interconnected but simple computing elements. Such networks form a different paradigm of computing in the hopes of rapidly solving problems while adapting to a changing environment — qualities that are realized in von Neumann computers only with great difficulty. For example, vector quantization of images normally requires specialized programming to detect and encode the meaningful clusters of vectors, but a Kohonen self-organizing map can adaptively form the necessary codebook using a simple, general learning algorithm [23]. The speed advantage of this and other neural network approaches, however, cannot be realized without specialized hardware.

Unfortunately, the large number of processing elements (which we will refer to as *neurons*) and their highly interconnected nature makes the construction of neural networks challenging. A majority of implementations rely on analog electronics to provide compact neurons possessing the required computational primitives (usually the summation and non-linear transformation of signals from other neurons in the net). Analog chips have been fabricated containing 512 neurons and a 512×512 fixed-resistor matrix which can be programmed to solve a specific problem very rapidly [10]. However, variable resistors (or *weights*) are needed for the network to *learn* from previous experience. Such Hopfield neural networks have been built which store their weights on low-leakage capacitors [19] or in digital storage registers [27], while a Kohonen network is under construction which also employs adjustable analog weights [20]. The increased complexity and size of these adjustable weights greatly reduces the number of neurons which can be placed on a chip. Real-world applications will require many neurons, so finding a method of interconnecting these chips to form larger networks will be of primary concern. However, the large number of analog signals which must pass between chips will exceed the available input/output resources, while the noise and parasitic capacitances on the external I/O lines will distort the operation of the network and possibly lead to erroneous results.

The limitations of analog computing have led researchers of neural networks to rely upon digital simulation. Currently available high-speed ALUs excel at the inner product computations often found in neural network algorithms and have been used to construct a general-purpose neural network architecture [28] and a dedicated Kohonen network [14]. The size and I/O requirements of the digital logic limit the number of ALUs which can be placed on a chip, which in turn creates a computational bottleneck that prevents the system from taking full advantage of the parallelism inherent in neural computations. Attempting to remove this bottleneck by building systems with multiple single-chip digital signal processors [24] is only partially successful due to the overhead incurred when passing data between the processors.

1.2 Stochastic Processing

The use of *stochastic logic elements* [9, 21] permits neural networks to be constructed which avoid the problems of the preceding implementations. We have previously described a stochastic Hopfield neural network [4] in which the analog signals are replaced by binary

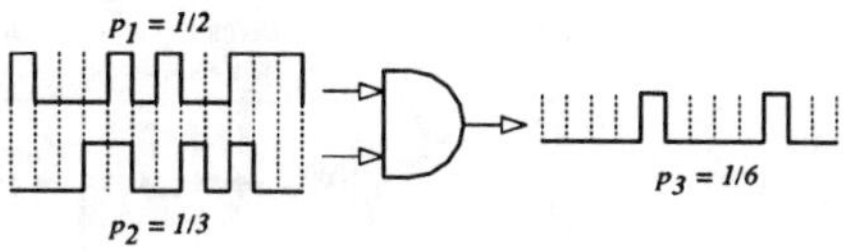

Figure 1: An example of stochastic multiplication.

signals that randomly assume either the value 0 or 1. The mean value of such a stochastic signal can be viewed as an analog signal in the range $[0, 1]$. This signal representation allows pseudo-analog computations to be performed using very space-efficient digital logic. Multiplication of independent stochastic signals, for example, can be done using only a simple AND gate as illustrated in Figure 1.

The space efficiency of stochastic processing elements is somewhat mitigated by the effective reduction in temporal efficiency — stochastically multiplied signals must be averaged over many samples to produce an accurate representation of the result. For this reason, stochastic architectures are poorly suited to applications in which the multiplicative product is the end result of the calculation.

Recurrent neural networks have the property that their feedback connections are *integrative*. In the Hopfield network integration occurs on the capacitors at the input of each neuron. In the Kohonen network integration occurs in the weight adjustment process during self-organization. Over time, both networks evolve to an equilibrium state which represents the solution of the problem. The networks are, in effect, finding the steady-state solution for a system of coupled, nonlinear differential equations.

When the output of a stochastic multiplier is integrated, the "noise" in the resulting signal is greatly reduced due to the low pass filter effect of the integrator. From another perspective, the temporal inefficiency of the stochastic multiplier is canceled by the temporal nature of the integration itself. These effects are clearly illustrated in Figure 2. (Note that the circuitry for integration of stochastic signals is simple as well — a binary counter serves the purpose.)

Stochastic processing provides a good compromise between analog and digital processing in recurrent neural networks. The pseudo-analog computations performed by the stochastic processing elements can be implemented with circuitry which is very compact as compared to conventional digital arithmetic circuits. At the same time, the stochastic signals preserve the benefits of digital systems, such as noise immunity in signal distribution and multiplexing in large, multi-chip systems, and ease of integration in the presence of long time constants. These factors combine to facilitate the construction of massively parallel, multi-chip systems.

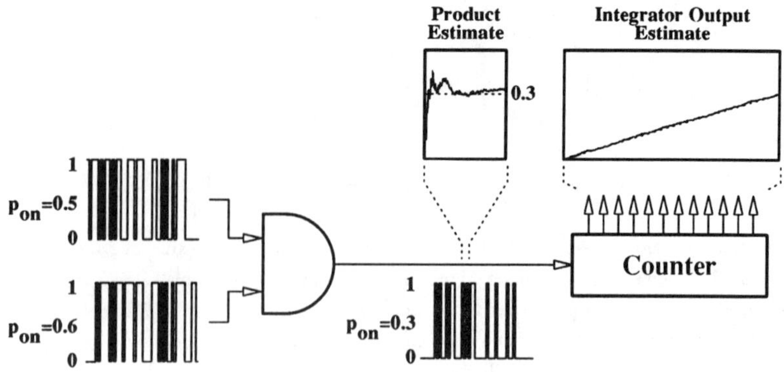

Figure 2: An example of stochastic integration.

2 StoNN— A STOCHASTIC IMPLEMENTATION OF THE HOPFIELD NETWORK

In an N-neuron Hopfield network, the charging equation for the voltage u_j upon the capacitor C at the input of the jth neuron is

$$\frac{du_j}{dt} = \frac{1}{C}\left[\sum_{i=0}^{N-1}\{v_i(t) - u_j(t)\}G_{ij} - \frac{u_j(t)}{R_j} + I_j\right] \tag{1}$$

where v_i is the output voltage of neuron i, G_{ij} is the conductance value or weight connecting the output of neuron i to the input of neuron j, R_j is a resistor which bleeds charge from C, and I_j is a bias current for neuron j. The nonlinear transfer function for a neuron j is *sigmoidal*, $v_j = [1 + \exp(-Au_j)]^{-1}$, where A is the *gain* of the neuron. Without loss of generality, C can be set to unity and the bias currents can all be replaced by a single bias neuron N with $v_N = 1$ that is connected to each neuron j through a conductance value of $G_{Nj} = I_j$. This gives

$$\frac{du_j}{dt} = \sum_{i=0}^{N} v_i(t)G_{ij} - u_j(t)g_j \tag{2}$$

where $g_j = \sum_{i=0}^{N-1} G_{ij} + 1/R_j$. Assuming $G_{ij} = G_{ji}$ and integrating the equations of motion in (2), it can be seen that the Hopfield neurons are performing gradient descent on an *energy surface* of the form

$$E = \underbrace{-\frac{1}{2}\sum_{i=0}^{N}\sum_{j=0}^{N-1} v_i G_{ij} v_j}_{combinatoric} + \underbrace{\frac{1}{A}\left[\sum_{j=0}^{N-1} g_j\{(v_j - 1)\ln(1 - v_j) - v_j \ln v_j\}\right]}_{monadic}. \tag{3}$$

E contains a *combinatoric* portion whose minima correspond to solutions of a complex problem involving many interacting 1–0 integer variables. E also possesses a *monadic* portion (due to the presence of the $u_j g_j$ term in (2)) which lacks such interactions. If $A \to \infty$ or $g_j \to 0$, the monadic term dies away and the combinatoric term dominates. As Hopfield explained in [13], increasing the gain in a neural network is similar to decreasing the temperature in the simulated annealing algorithm [15]. This similarity was used to advantage in [3, 5, 6] to improve the quality of solutions found by Hopfield networks.

The large number of calculations required to evaluate the coupled differential equations in (2) will require that special purpose machines be built before many practical applications can be solved in a reasonable amount of time using neural algorithms. The massive parallelism and simple circuit elements of Hopfield networks makes them attractive for analog VLSI implementations, but the large number of interconnections has limited the size of a neural system to the number of neurons that can be placed on a chip [10]. Multiple chip analog implementations will be plagued by parasitics and noise. Digital implementations require a large area for each neuron to house parallel multipliers or digital memory and associated logic for storing and evaluating interconnection weights [2, 22, 27].

In the remainder of this section, we will describe the design, implementation, and performance of STONN[4], a VLSI neural network which uses stochastic processing elements to solve optimization problems in a manner similar to simulated annealing.

2.1 Stochastic Theory of Operation

The basic stochastic computing element of the STONN is the AND gate [8] used as a multiplier to form the inner product of conductance values and amplifier output voltages (see Figure 1). The multiplication requires the multiplicands to be converted to single-bit, uncorrelated, probabilistic signals that are input to the AND gate. The mean value of the AND gate output will then be the product of the input probabilities. As shown in Figure 2, this method of multiplication does produce high frequency noise in the result. However, it has been shown in [2] and in our own research that noise injected into the network improves solution quality by helping to escape local minima.

In STONN, the network weights and neuron u_j values are stored in digital shift registers which are compared against random variables to produce the single-bit stochastic signals. These signals are then ANDed to produce another stochastic signal representing the charging current for each interconnection. The integration performed by the Hopfield neuron input capacitor is a summation of these charging currents. This summation operation can be implemented with a digital counter which is incremented by positive current pulses and decremented by negative current pulses. (The sign of the current is implemented with a sign bit associated with each conductance value which is directly connected to the counter.)

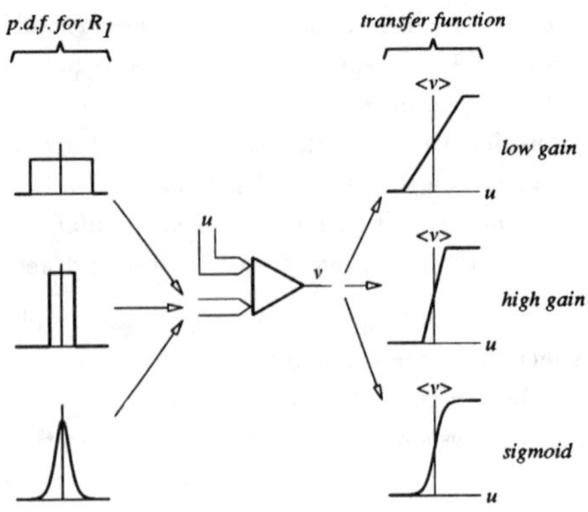

Figure 3: Changing the neural transfer function by altering the PDF.

Since the capacitor (or counter) acts as a low pass filter, the high-frequency noise of the stochastic multiply is removed. Thus, the counter output is very close to the ideal analog behavior as shown in Figure 2.

The digital comparison of a value, u, and a random number will produce a random binary signal with a certain mean value, $\langle v \rangle$. The transfer function relating the input value to this mean value is merely $\langle v \rangle = \int_{-\infty}^{u} p(x)dx$ where p is the probability density function (PDF) of the random number. By changing the PDF, the transfer function can be changed. For example, as shown in Figure 3, the neural gain can be lowered by widening the PDF, while a Gaussian PDF produces a sigmoidal transfer function. This method allows dynamic control of parameters such as the amplifier gain. In an identical manner, it is possible to store the weights as floating point numbers. The lower bits of the random number compared with the mantissa are given a uniform distribution, while the upper bits compared with the exponent are given an exponential distribution. In fact, any monotonic function can be realized with the appropriate PDF. This allows the use of a small number of bits in the weight storage registers without sacrificing precision or dynamic range in the values of the weights. Thus, stochastic processing allows STONN to dynamically alter its neural transfer function and precisely encode its weights without requiring a large silicon area.

2.2 Stochastic Architecture

In order to implement large, multi-chip neural systems, not only must the primitive computational elements be simple and easy to build, the interconnection between the elements

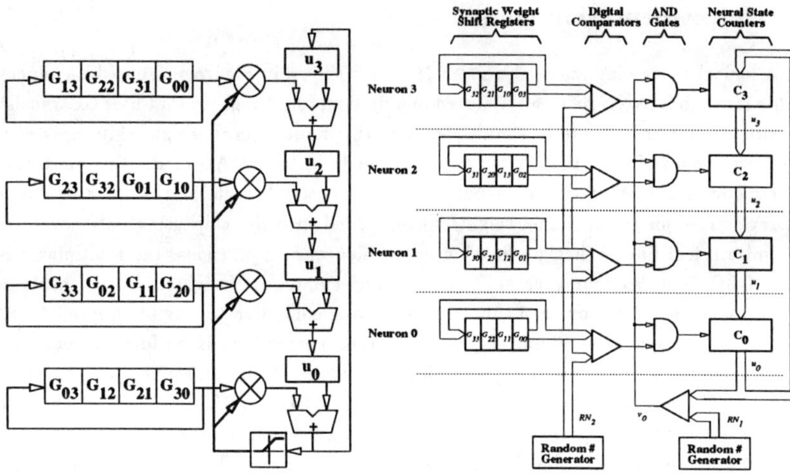

Figure 4: A systolic array and stochastic implementation for the Hopfield network.

must not exceed the practical limits on chip I/O. The StoNN architecture is derived from the Hopfield network characteristic equations and the computational data flow to minimize communication and control and allow expandability and pipelining.

The Hopfield network must distribute the outputs from N neurons to N^2 connections to compute the matrix-vector multiplication of (2) in a single cycle. Instead, if during every cycle each neuron accumulates the charging current that results from multiplying the output of a selected neuron by the weights connecting that neuron to every other neuron, then all the required multiplications and accumulations can be performed in N cycles. The data flow for this parallel implementation is shown in Figure 4. The weights and capacitor voltages circulate through shift registers. Note that the weights to each neuron must be distributed across all N memory arrays to align each connection with the proper capacitor voltage as data is cycled. (Similar arrangements were also proposed in [1, 18].) While this method reduces the order of parallelism from $O(N^2)$ to $O(N)$, it makes large networks possible since only the capacitor voltages and some control signals must be routed between chips regardless of the number of neurons simulated.

2.3 Implementation Details

A logical block diagram of the STONN chip is shown in Figure 4. The 7-bit connection weights for each STONN neuron are stored in a dynamic shift register that uses six transistors per shift register cell. There is a multiplexer at the input to each weight shift register that allows two modes of operation. With the multiplexer in the LOAD mode, the input of each shift register is connected to the output of the previous shift register, thus making one long shift register. This permits the weights to be loaded into the chip using only seven input pins and a select line. When performing actual neural computations, the multiplexer is in the CYCLE mode so that each shift register recirculates its weights. During each clock cycle, a weight is output by each shift register and is compared to a random number, RN2, using a 6-bit comparator. Simultaneously, a signed comparison is performed between the bottom capacitor counter and a signed random number, RN1, to produce the neural firing signal PV. PV is routed to all the neurons and is ANDed with the result of the weight comparisons to produce positive or negative neural charging pulses (depending upon the sign of the weight stored in bit 7) which update the counters. Then, the counters and the weight shift registers are all shifted one position and the process is repeated. In this manner, all the charging currents affecting each capacitor voltage are summed over time by the digital counters. Overflow circuitry is built into the counters to set an overflow bit and preserve the sign bit when a counter has reached its positive or negative limit. Convergence to a solution can also be approximately determined by detecting when all overflow bits of the neurons are set.

The regular flow of data in STONN allows the computations to be deeply pipelined down to the bit level. This bit-wise pipelining requires all weight and counter values to be stored in a skewed manner so that more significant bits reach a computation after the less significant bits have been processed. The skewed weights and counters with their associated pipelined comparison and incrementing operations are shown in Figure 5. As can be seen, the comparison result is computed six clocks after the shift register outputs the least significant bit of the weight, and the last bit of the counter value is updated after another 10 cycles. Due to the use of carry-save arithmetic, each comparator is simultaneously handling computations on different bits of 6 different weights, while each counter is concurrently updating 10 capacitor voltages. Thus, no clock cycles are wasted and the duration of a clock pulse is reduced to the time needed to perform a one-bit addition.

In order to save silicon area, counters which could only add 0, 1, or 2 to their contents were alternated with counters that could only perform subtractions of 0, 1, or 2. Such a pair of counters can perform the same computations as a pair of more complex increment/decrement counters. The setting and resetting of the overflow bit by the overflow protection circuitry is also simplified since a given counter can now only overflow in one direction instead of both.

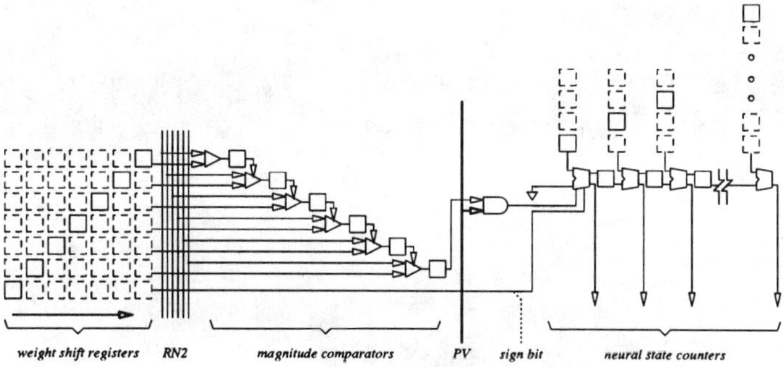

Figure 5: Bit-level pipelining in STONN.

In addition to the shift registers for storing the interconnection weights, another shift register is provided which stores the g_j decay weights for each of the neurons. By multiplying stochastic signals proportional to g_j and u_j, the capacitor counter associated with neuron j can be discharged toward zero. As was shown, this decay current gives rise to the simulated annealing properties of the Hopfield network. Annealing can be accomplished in STONN by 1) reducing the values stored in the g_j shift register, 2) decreasing the range of $R1$ (thus increasing the neural gain), or 3) reducing the probability that a decay pulse will reach the counter. The third option is by far the easiest to implement since it requires only the addition of a third stochastic signal, ANNEAL, to the AND gate which multiplies g_j and u_j. Annealing can then be performed as the neurons evolve by decreasing the probability that ANNEAL is high. As will be shown, the addition of the g_j weights greatly affects the quality of solutions found by STONN.

The current CMOS version of STONN contains 100,000 transistors organized into 20 neurons (see Figure 6), each of which can receive 100 inputs from other neurons (i.e. the weight shift register can store 100 weights). This allows a completely-connected set of neurons to be constructed using five cascaded STONN chips. Cascading chips requires that only the capacitor voltages, PV, and RN2 need be passed between adjacent chips. This reduces the pin count and is the key to building very large networks.

2.4 STONN **Advantages**

The use of stochastic arithmetic techniques greatly reduces the complexity of logic needed to perform the neural operations as compared to other digital implementations and begins to approach the computational density of analog techniques. Also, the stochastic

computing elements naturally accommodate the use of annealing techniques in Hopfield networks. By changing the PDFs of the random numbers input to the STONN chips, neural transfer functions can be easily altered and weights can be stored with high precision in registers containing very few bits.

By accepting $O(N)$ parallelism rather than $O(N^2)$, we have gained the ability to interconnect multiple chips to create networks larger than can be contained on a single chip. Other fully parallel implementations [2, 22, 27] are limited to a small number of neurons since the number of connections needed between two or more chips to maintain complete parallelism far exceeds the available I/O. The need to evaluate each connection during every cycle also increases the complexity and size of the circuitry needed to store the weights. The majority of STONN however, is composed of dense shift register cells since only one weight per neuron is processed each cycle.

With predicted speeds of the prototype STONN chips between 10Mhz and 25Mhz, the bit-level pipelining and $O(N)$ parallelism of STONN makes it several orders of magnitude faster than the fastest sequential processors. While STONN cannot solve problems faster than fully analog neural networks, our use of digital technology increases the system programmability and noise immunity while easing the difficulties of interfacing to host computers.

2.5 Experimental Results

STONN was applied to a combinatorial problem involving the partitioning a graph containing N nodes across two bins, $\{b_0, b_1\}$. An optimal solution for this bipartitioning problem minimizes the number of edges crossing between the bins while balancing the number of nodes in each bin. This is expressed by the objective function

$$E = \sum_{i=0}^{N-1} \sum_{j \neq i} E_{ij}(1 - v_j)v_i - r \sum_{i=0}^{N-1} \sum_{j \neq i} (1 - v_j)v_i$$

where the variables have been defined so that $v_i = 0$ if node n_i resides in bin b_0 and $v_i = 1$ otherwise. Each edge in the graph tends to attract the adjacent nodes n_i and n_j into the same bin with a force proportional to E_{ij}. Counterbalancing this attraction is r, an amorphous repulsive force between all of the nodes which discourages them from clustering together.

For the graph bipartitioning example, the performance of STONN was compared to directly solving the differential equations of (1) or finding an optimal solution using simulated annealing. The number of crossing edges are tabulated in Table 1. Over 1000 trials on a DECstation 3100, simulated annealing often found the optimal solution having 15 crossing edges. Solving the differential equations using predictor-corrector methods gave a solution having 20 crossing edges. (Since the neural network formulation enforces bin balance with

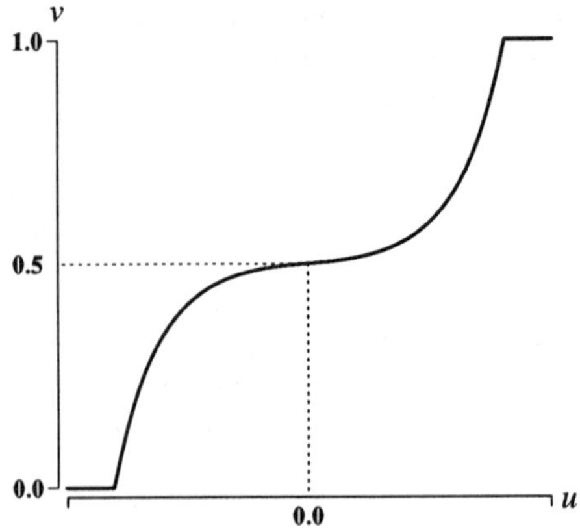

Figure 7: A neural transfer function with variable differential gain.

a soft constraint, a solution in which the bin contents differed by less than 5 nodes was considered balanced.) One hundred STONN simulations were run with 4 different operational settings. In the first 25 trials, STONN was simulated with $g_j = 0$ (i.e. the high gain case) and a linear transfer function which saturated at $v = 0$ and $v = 1$. In the next 25 trials, capacitor decay was enabled by setting g_j to a small value. This removed an average of 1 crossing edge from the solutions. For the next 25 trials, g_j was returned to zero and the neural transfer function of Figure 7 was used. The differential gain for this nonlinear function is small when $u \approx 0$ and grows as a neuron begins to saturate. This transfer function lead to approximately the same solution quality as annealing with g_j. For the last 25 trials, both annealing and the new transfer function were enabled, leading to the best solution quality found using STONN.

For execution times, simulated annealing required 1000 sweeps through the nodes to converge to a solution, consuming $\approx$ 2s on average on a DECstation3100. The predictor-corrector technique required 2000 sweeps through the 50 neurons, and evaluating each neuron required 700 floating-point operations. Thus, 70,000,000 floating-point operations were performed. The STONN neurons usually saturated within 4,000 sweeps through the 50 neurons. Assuming a clock speed of 10 MHz, convergence to a solution occurs within 0.02s. In order to reach the same speed, predictor-corrector techniques would require a computational engine capable of 3.5 GFLOPS.

Simulated Annealing	15.6 ± 0.712
Predictor-corrector	20.0
STONN $g_j = 0$, linear	20.2 ± 2.3
STONN $g_j > 0$, linear	19.4 ± 2.9
STONN $g_j = 0$, nonlinear	19.4 ± 1.9
STONN $g_j > 0$, nonlinear	18.6 ± 2.2

Table 1: A comparison of the number of crossing edges in a bipartitioning found using simulated annealing, predictor-corrector techniques, and STONN.

3 TINMANN — A STOCHASTIC IMPLEMENTATION OF KOHONEN'S SELF-ORGANIZING FEATURE MAP

In this part we describe TINMANN — a neural network implementation for competitive and Kohonen types of learning which employs large numbers of simple, all-digital neurons based on stochastic principles.

3.1 Learning Algorithms

In this section the algorithms used in competitive learning and Kohonen's self-organizing feature maps are restated, and a simplified fusion of these algorithms is presented which is amenable to VLSI implementation.

3.1.1 Competitive Learning

In the competitive learning algorithm [26], training vectors of length W, $\mathbf{v}= (v_1, \ldots, v_W)$, are presented to a winner-take-all network of N neurons. Each neuron i possesses a weight vector of length W, $\mathbf{w}= (w_{i1}, \ldots, w_{iW})$, and a winning neuron k is selected as the one whose weight vector is closest to the current training vector. The weights for neuron k are then slightly altered so as to reduce their distance from the training vector. The pseudocode for a simple competitive learning algorithm is shown in Figure 8.

If a neural network is trained using competitive learning with a set of vectors which are naturally clustered into N groups, then each neural weight vector will eventually reside in the center of a different group. Thereafter, an input vector applied to the network will activate the neuron which has been sensitized to the group containing the input, thus performing an encoding. Optimal 1-of-N encoding results if the neurons array themselves so as to divide the

```
/* initialize neurons with random weights */
for( i ⇐ 1; i ≤ N; i ⇐ i + 1 )
        for( j ⇐ 1; j ≤ W; j ⇐ j + 1 )
                w_ij ⇐ random()

/* apply training vectors */
for( v∈ {training set} )

        /* compute distance of neurons from vector */
        for( i ⇐ 1; i ≤ N; i ⇐ i + 1 )
                d_i ⇐ 0
                for( j ⇐ 1; j ≤ W; j ⇐ j + 1 )
                        d_i ⇐ d_i + |v_j − w_ij|

        /* find the closest neuron to the vector */
        k ⇐ 1
        for( i ⇐ 1; i ≤ N; i ⇐ i + 1 )
                if( d_i < d_k )
                        k ⇐ i

        /* adjust weights of winning neuron */
        for( j ⇐ 1; j ≤ W; j ⇐ j + 1 )
                w_kj ⇐ w_kj + ε · (v_j − w_kj)

        /* reduce the learning rate */
        ε ⇐ α_ε · ε
```

Figure 8: The competitive learning algorithm.

input vector space into regions which are sampled with equal probability. However, if some region of the input space is sampled more frequently than the others, then a single neuron usually begins to win all the competitions for this region. This leaves the remaining $N-1$ neurons to partition the less frequently accessed regions, thus giving a less than optimal encoding scheme. In order to counter this defect, each neuron i can record the number of times it has won, c_i, and add this to its computed distance from the current training input. Those neurons which win too often will have larger increases in their distance, which reduces their chances of winning the competition. The opposite effect occurs for neurons which seldom win, thus creating a kind of negative feedback which attempts to make all the neurons equally active. The addition of this *conscience* [7] to the competitive learning algorithm (Figure 9) greatly improves the encodings produced by the network.

3.1.2 Kohonen Learning

Kohonen's self-organizing feature maps [16] are trained using a generalization of competitive learning where each neuron i is provided with an additional X-element vector, $\mathbf{x} = (x_{i1}, \ldots, x_{iX})$, that defines its topological position with relation to the other neurons in the network. As before, neuron k of the N neurons wins if it is the closest to the current training vector, but the weight adjustment now affects neuron k and, to a lesser extent, nearby neurons as determined by a decreasing function f of their topological distance from neuron k and a threshold distance d_T. This function allows the winning neuron to *drag* its neighbors toward a given section of the input space so that topologically close neurons will eventually react similarly to closely spaced input vectors. The pseudocode for the Kohonen algorithm is given in Figure 10.

3.1.3 Integer Markovian Learning

The integer Markovian learning algorithm of Figure 11 combines and simplifies the previous two algorithms using the following observations:

- Kohonen's algorithm behaves identically to the competitive learning algorithm when

$$f(d_i, d_T) = \begin{cases} 1 & \text{if } d_i = 0, \\ 0 & \text{otherwise.} \end{cases}$$

- Floating-point numbers and operations can be replaced with their appropriately scaled fixed-point counterparts.

- The conscience mechanism of competitive learning can be added to Kohonen's algorithm in a straightforward manner.

```
/* initialize consciences and weights */
for( i ⇐ 1; i ≤ N; i ⇐ i + 1 )
        c_i ⇐ 0
        for( j ⇐ 1; j ≤ W; j ⇐ j + 1 )
                w_ij ⇐ random()

for( v∈ {training set} )

        /* compute distances with conscience offset */
        for( i ⇐ 1; i ≤ N; i ⇐ i + 1 )
                d_i ⇐ C · c_i  /* C = scaling factor */
                for( j ⇐ 1; j ≤ W; j ⇐ j + 1 )
                        d_i ⇐ d_i + |v_j − w_ij|

        k ⇐ 1
        for( i ⇐ 1; i ≤ N; i ⇐ i + 1 )
                if( d_i < d_k )
                        k ⇐ i

        for( j ⇐ 1; j ≤ W; j ⇐ j + 1 )
                w_kj ⇐ w_kj + ε · (v_j − w_kj)

        /* increase conscience of winning neuron */
        c_k ⇐ c_k + 1

        ε ⇐ α_ε · ε
```

Figure 9: Adding a conscience to competitive learning.

```
for( i ⇐ 1; i ≤ N; i ⇐ i + 1 )
        for( j ⇐ 1; j ≤ W; j ⇐ j + 1 )
                w_ij ⇐ random()

for( v∈ {training set} )

        for( i ⇐ 1; i ≤ N; i ⇐ i + 1 )
                d_i ⇐ 0
                for( j ⇐ 1; j ≤ W; j ⇐ j + 1 )
                        d_i ⇐ d_i + |v_j − w_ij|

        k ⇐ 1
        for( i ⇐ 1; i ≤ N; i ⇐ i + 1 )
                if( d_i < d_k )
                        k ⇐ i

        /* find neurons topologically close to winner */
        for( i ⇐ 1; i ≤ N; i ⇐ i + 1 )
                d_i ⇐ 0
                for( j ⇐ 1; j ≤ X; j ⇐ j + 1 )
                        d_i ⇐ d_i + |x_ij − x_kj|

        /* adjust weights of nearby neurons */
        for( j ⇐ 1; j ≤ W; j ⇐ j + 1 )
                for( i ⇐ 1; i ≤ N; i ⇐ i + 1 )
                        w_ij ⇐ w_ij + ε · f(d_i, d_T) · (v_j − w_ij)

        /* reduce the topological distance threshold */
        d_T ⇐ α_d · d_T

        ε ⇐ α_ε · ε
```

Figure 10: Kohonen's self-organizing map algorithm.

- The multiplicative scaling of the conscience can be replaced by adding C to the winning conscience.
- Three of the loops in the training section of Kohonen's algorithm contain noninteracting iterations which can be parallelized over the entire set of neurons.
- The neuron weights in both algorithms slowly *integrate* the effects of environmental stimuli, which can be done by updating the weights stochastically with a probability proportional to the strength of the input.

The stochastic update of the neural weights is accomplished by generating two uncorrelated random numbers on the interval $[0, d_T]$, R_1 and R_2, which each neuron compares to its distance from the current training vector and its topological distance from the winning neuron, respectively. A neuron will increment or decrement the elements of its weight vector closer to the training vector if the absolute value of the intervening distance is greater than R_1, thus creating a total movement proportional to the distance when averaged over many cycles. This movement is inversely modulated by the topological distance to the winning neuron k via a comparison with R_2. The total effect produced by these two stochastic processes is equivalent to that produced in the original competitive and Kohonen learning algorithms, but only simple additive operations are now needed.

Merely incrementing or decrementing the neural weights may cause the integer Markovian learning algorithm to converge slowly as compared to the original Kohonen algorithm. To see why, imagine a single neuron with a 1-dimensional weight vector initialized to zero is trained using a single example having a value of 1000. Obviously, it will take at least 1000 training cycles for the neuron to converge to the training example since the weight can increase by at most one after each cycle. A standard Kohonen neuron which decreases the distance between itself and the training example by $\epsilon = 10\%$ needs only 66 cycles to cover the same distance. The speed of convergence of the integer algorithm can be increased by allowing a neuron to update its weights with larger values than ± 1. This also coarsens the granularity of quantization achievable by the network, thus the size of the weight change should be decreased as the learning proceeds so that the fine-level quantization is regained.

3.2 Simulations

The following section presents the results from tests of the integer Markovian learning algorithm on a number of applications previously solved using the standard competitive and Kohonen learning methods.

```
for( i ⇐ 1; i ≤ N; i ⇐ i + 1 )
        c_i ⇐ 0
        for( j ⇐ 1; j ≤ W; j ⇐ j + 1 )
                w_ij ⇐ random()

for( v∈ {training set} )

        parallelfor( all neurons i )
                d_i ⇐ c_i
                for( j ⇐ 1; j ≤ W; j ⇐ j + 1 )
                        d_i ⇐ d_i + |v_j − w_ij|

        k ⇐ 1
        for( i ⇐ 1; i ≤ N; i ⇐ i + 1 )
                if( d_i < d_k )
                        k ⇐ i

        parallelfor( all neurons i )
                d_i ⇐ 0
                for( j ⇐ 1; j ≤ X; j ⇐ j + 1 )
                        d_i ⇐ d_i + |x_ij − x_kj|

        for( j ⇐ 1; j ≤ W; j ⇐ j + 1 )
                R_1 ⇐ random(d_T)
                R_2 ⇐ random(d_T)
                parallelfor( all neurons i )
                        if( |v_j − w_ij| > R_1 and d_i ≤ R_2 )
                                w_ij ⇐ w_ij+ sign(v_j − w_ij)

        c_k ⇐ c_k + C
        d_T ⇐ α_d · d_T
```

Figure 11: The integer Markovian learning algorithm.

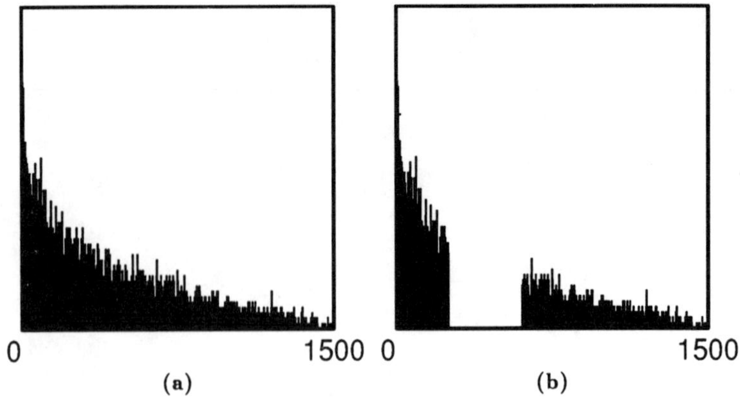

Figure 12: One-dimensional skewed training sets (a) distributed over $[0, 1500]$ and (b) with a gap on the interval $[250, 600]$.

3.2.1 1-D Competitive Learning

Our initial tests recreated the work found in [7]. Fifteen neurons were trained using competitive learning on two sets of one-dimensional training vectors distributed as shown in figure 12. The distance threshold was initialized to $d_T = 1500$ and was decreased to 90 over 20000 training cycles using $\alpha_d = 0.99986$. Since only competitive learning was being studied here, R_2 was held at zero and there was no need to initialize the topology vectors. When no conscience mechanism was used (i.e. $C = 0$), the weight vectors of only half the neurons evolved from their initial setting and there was much variation in the final firing frequencies of the neurons (Figures 13(a) and 14(a)). However, enabling the conscience (with $C = 2$) prevented any neuron from becoming dominant and winning too often, thus allowing all the neurons to evolve and achieve a near 1-of-N encoding in each case (Figures 13(b) and 14(b)) as was first seen in [7].

3.2.2 2-D Kohonen Learning

Following the initial success with one-dimensional training sets, several two-dimensional tests of integer Markovian learning were carried out. In each of these tests, the topological vectors of 100 neurons were evenly spaced over a 1500×1500 grid while the elements of the weight vectors were initialized to random values between 0 and 100. The distance threshold was started at 3000 and shrunk to 135 over 200000 training cycles using $\alpha_d = 0.999984$.

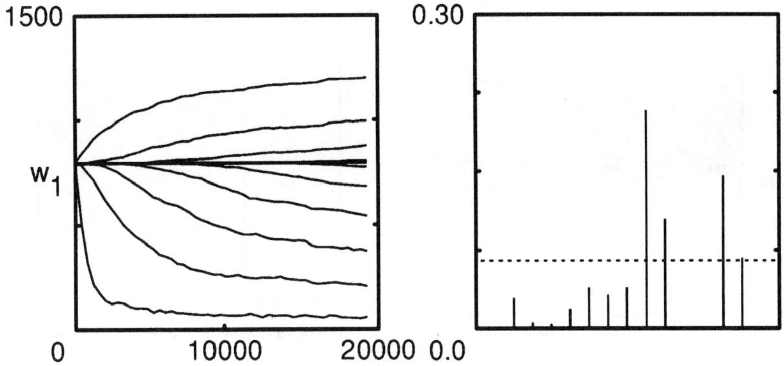

(a) No conscience

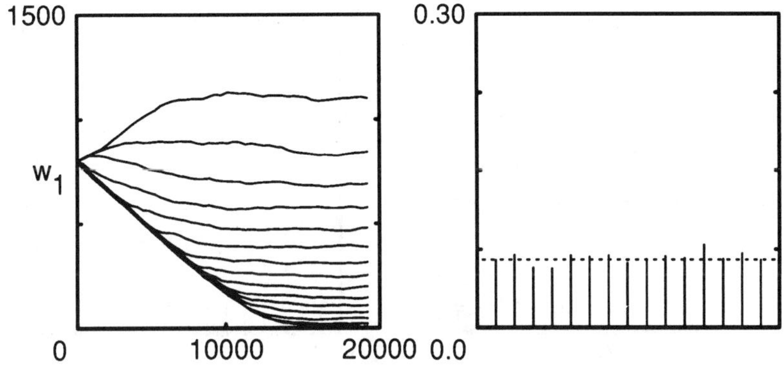

(b) Conscience

Figure 13: Evolution and final firing frequencies for a 15 neuron network trained (a) without and (b) with a conscience on the distribution of Figure 12(a).

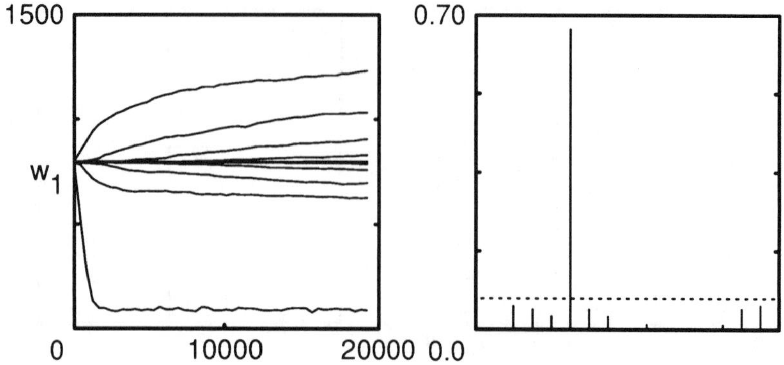

(a) No conscience

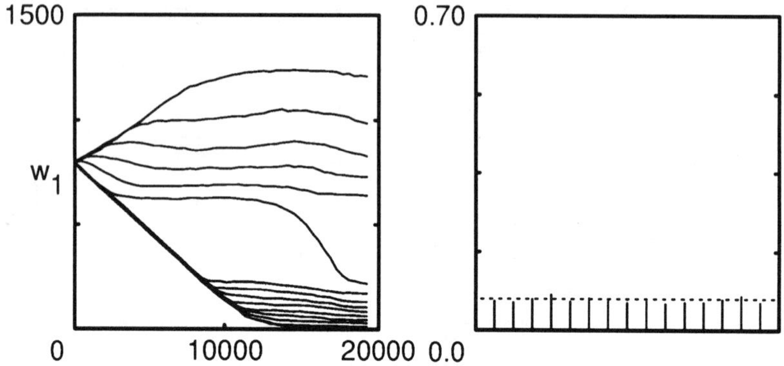

(b) Conscience

Figure 14: Evolution and final firing frequencies for a 15 neuron network trained (a) without and (b) with a conscience on the gapped distribution of Figure 12(b).

The first test used two-dimensional training vectors from a uniformly sampled 1500 $\times$ 1500 grid. The neural weight vectors evolved over 200000 training cycles from their initial position near the origin to evenly cover the grid while retaining their topological structure (Figure 15). This same problem was solved in only 22000 cycles using the standard Kohonen network with floating-point weights and operations. In a second trial, increasing the step size for the weight updates to ± 10 in the integer Markovian algorithm reduced the learning time to 29000 cycles without affecting the quality of the solution. Thus, the speed gained from massive parallelism need not be negated by an unacceptably slow learning rate as a result of using stochastic processing.

In another test, the network was shown a training set where each dimension followed the distribution of Figure 12(a), thus biasing the samples toward the lower-left corner. The network evolved into a configuration which was also biased toward the origin (Figure 16(a)), but the final firing frequencies of the neurons varied widely from the desired average of 0.01. By enabling the conscience with $C = 2$, the network settled into a configuration where the firing frequencies showed much less variation while still retaining the underlying neural topology (Figure 16(b)).

3.2.3 The Traveling Salesman Problem

In its last test, the integer Markovian learning algorithm was used to find optimal tours connecting a set of points [25]. The topological vectors of 100 neurons were evenly distributed around a square perimeter 4000 units in length, while the weight vectors were initially arranged evenly around a square perimeter of 1333 units centered in the set of points to be connected. The distance threshold was initialized to 2000 and shrunk to 36 over 200000 training cycles using $\alpha_d = 0.999979$.

When no conscience was used, the network nearly always evolved into a tour with a Manhattan length of 5926 (Figure 17(a)). By enabling the conscience ($C = 2$), much better tours were found, many of which were optimal with a length of 5658 (Figure 17(b)).

3.3 TinMANN Implementation

The integer Markovian learning algorithm is well suited for VLSI implementation since it is easily parallelized, the interneuron communications can all be handled using broadcast transmissions, and the neurons perform only very simple additive types of operations. The high-level architecture for such an implementation is shown in Figure 18. TinMANN consists of a global controller coupled to an array of simple neurons. The controller performs all the serial operations and coordinates the actions of the neurons. The neurons contain circuitry for comparing and updating their weights, and for enabling and disabling them-

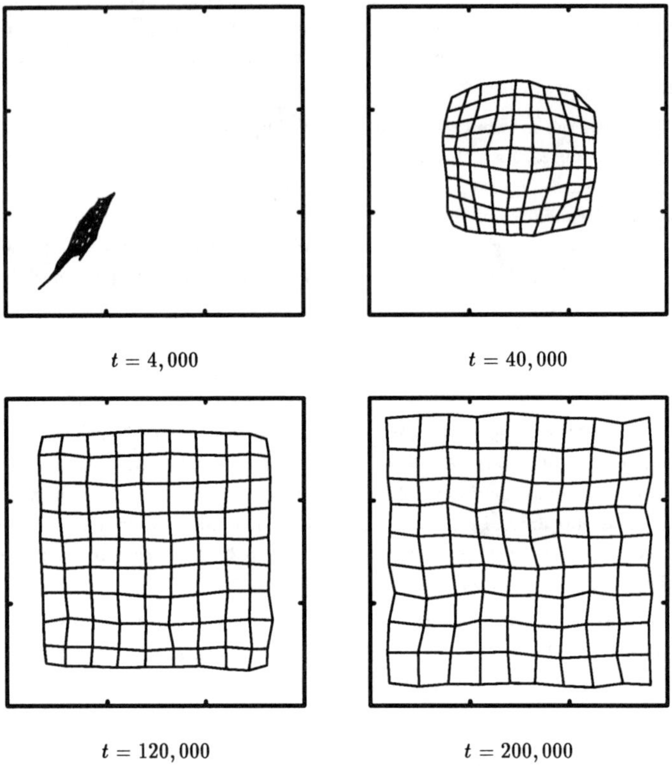

Figure 15: Evolution of a 10×10 network on a 1500×1500 uniformly sampled grid.

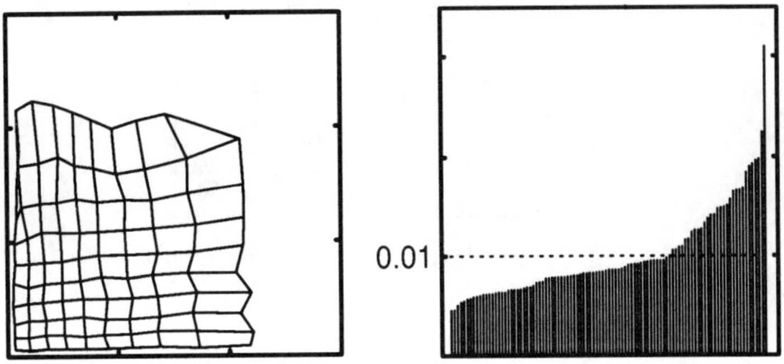

(a) No conscience

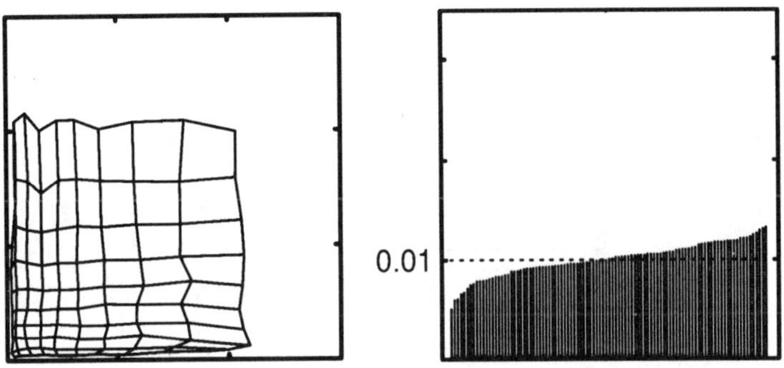

(b) Conscience

Figure 16: Final arrangement and firing frequencies for the neurons in a 10×10 network when trained on a 1500×1500 nonuniformly sampled plane both (a) without and (b) with the conscience mechanism.

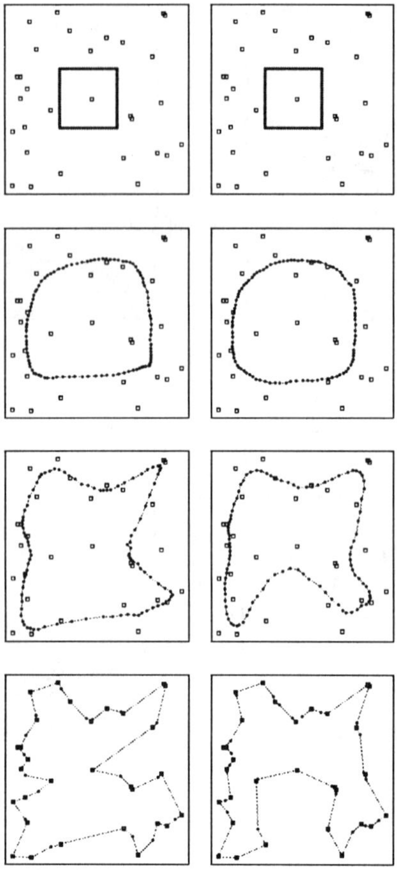

length = *5926*   *length* = *5658*

(a) no conscience   **(b)** conscience

Figure 17: Evolution of a 100-neuron network into a 30-city TSP tour on a 1000 × 1000 Manhattan grid both (a) without and (b) with the conscience mechanism.

selves during the conditional portions of the algorithm. It was also decided to encode the topological structure of the network by properly arranging the neurons in an X-dimensional space rather than attempting to represent a graph structure in the hardware. This allows the calculation of the topological distance between neurons using the same circuitry as is used in the weight calculations. Based on these decisions, each TINMANN neuron was built with the following components:

- A small RAM for holding the weight vector, topology vector, conscience counter, and some temporary values (T_1 and T_2) generated during the training computations;
- A gate, G, that allows the winning neuron to broadcast its topology vector to all the other neurons;
- A comparator for calculating the difference between an output from the RAM and a value on the broadcast bus;
- An accumulator, A;
- An adder/subtractor for accumulating values into A;
- A pipeline register, P, which breaks the computational critical path between the comparator and the adder/subtractor;
- Some logic which controls conditional operations of the neurons;
- A comparator flag, c, which is used by the conditional logic circuitry and also controls the adder/subtractor operation during absolute value calculations;
- An enable flag, e, which can be reset by the conditional logic so that certain neurons no longer participate in the calculations;
- A connection to a wired-OR status signal which is used to inform the global controller if all the neurons have been disabled.

As each training vector $\mathbf{v}$ is presented to TINMANN, the system performs the following operations:

1. The global controller broadcasts the W elements of $\mathbf{v}$ while each neuron accumulates and stores in T_1 the absolute value of the difference between the elements of its weight vector and those of the training vector.
2. The global controller does a binary search for the neuron closest to the training vector by broadcasting distance values bisecting the range containing the winning neuron. The neurons do a comparison with their stored distances and signal on the status

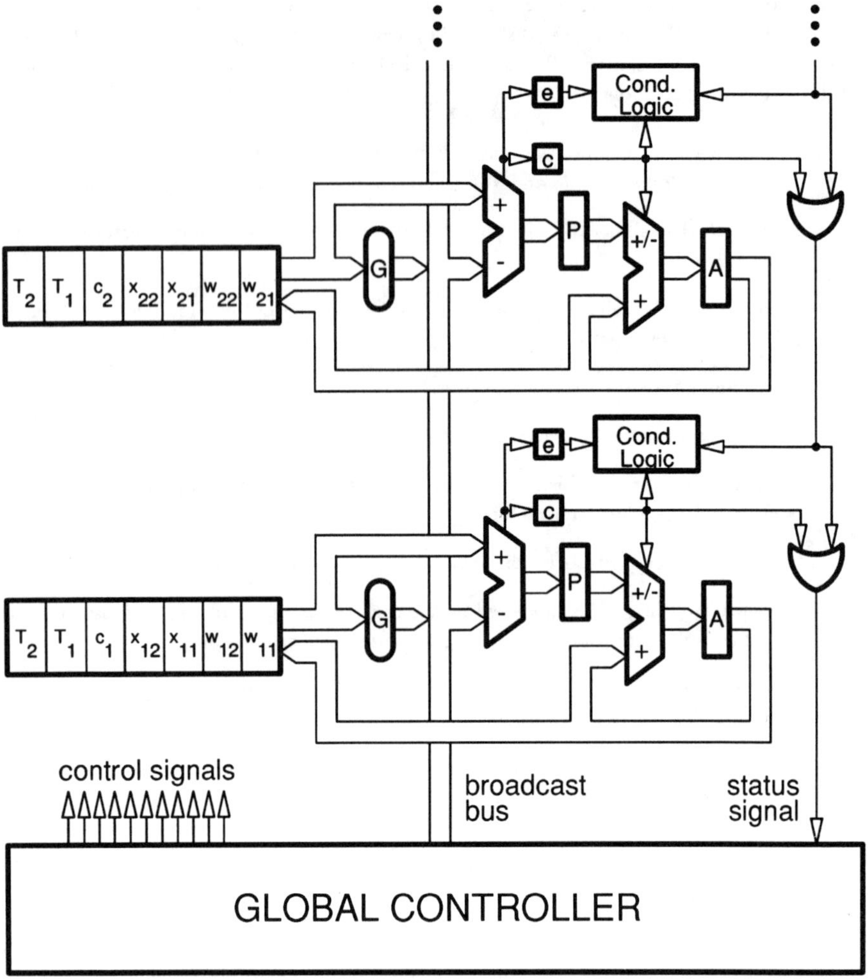

Figure 18: The TINMANN architecture.

line if a value exists which is less than the broadcast value. Neurons with distances greater than the broadcast value are disabled. However, if no neuron is left enabled, the global controller can restore the enable bits from the previous comparison and adjust its search region (this action is needed on $\approx M/2$ of the search steps, where M is the machine word length used by TINMANN).

3. The last neuron left enabled is the winner of the competition (ties are resolved by the conditional logic in each neuron). The winner adds C to its conscience c_k.

4. The gate for the winning neuron is opened so that it may broadcast the elements of its topological vector to the remainder of the neural array. The other neurons accumulate their topological distance from the winning neuron and store it in T_1.

5. Those neurons are disabled which have topological distances greater than the random number R_2 broadcast by the global controller. The remaining neurons each compute the distance between a component of their weight vector and that of the training vector broadcast by the global controller. For all neurons whose calculated distance is greater than another random number broadcast by the controller, the associated neurons increment or decrement their weight elements depending upon the carry bits left in the c flags during the distance calculations. All neurons are then re-enabled and this step is repeated for the remaining $W-1$ elements of the training vector.

The operations performed by TINMANN during a single training iteration are listed in Table 2 along with their duration in machine cycles. Since the neural weights are used only to compute the distance to a training example (which is independent of the number of neurons in the network), the machine word width can be determined by $M = \log_2(s/S)$, where s is the minimum separation between training vectors which must be quantized into different classes, while S is the maximum distance between training examples. For the examples in this paper, we chose $M = 12$ which provided more than sufficient precision for representing the [0,1500] range of the components in our training samples. A conservative 10 MHz clock should provide sufficient time to drive the global buses and perform the arithmetic operations. Assuming the above word size and clock speed, TINMANN can process a 2-dimensional training vector each 6.9 μs regardless of the number of neurons in the network.

The size of the circuitry for TINMANN is also reasonable as can be seen in Table 3. Assuming a machine word of 12 bits, and 10-dimensional weights and topology vectors (for handling higher dimensional spaces), a TINMANN with 1000 neurons could be built using one million transistors. Of course, such a network could be easily partitioned across several chips due to the small number of interconnecting wires used in TINMANN, but extra attention must then be paid to parasitic delays affecting the driving of the broadcast bus and the status signal.

Controller	Neurons	Cycles
Enable neurons	$e \Leftarrow 1$	1
Load conscience	$A \Leftarrow c_i$	2
Broadcast $v_1, \ldots, v_W$	$A \Leftarrow A + \lvert v_j - w_{ij} \rvert$	$W+1$
Store A	$T_1 \Leftarrow A$	1
Broadcast $2^{M-1}, 2^{M-2}, \ldots$	$e \Leftarrow c \Leftarrow T_1 \leq 2^{M-1}$	M
Check status line	$s \Leftarrow s$ **or** c	M
Reactivate neurons	$e \Leftarrow 1$	$\approx M/2$
Load conscience	$A \Leftarrow c_k$	2
Broadcast C	$A \Leftarrow A + C$	1
Store conscience	$c_k \Leftarrow A$	1
Enable G of winner k		1
Enable neurons	$e \Leftarrow 1$	1
Clear A	$A \Leftarrow 0$	1
Broadcast $x_{k1}, \ldots, x_{kX}$	$A \Leftarrow A + \lvert x_{ij} - x_{kj} \rvert$	$X+1$
Store topol. dist.	$T_1 \Leftarrow A$	1
Disable G of winner k		1
Broadcast R_2	$e \Leftarrow c \Leftarrow T_1 \leq R_2$	W
Broadcast v_j	$A \Leftarrow \lvert v_j - w_{ij} \rvert$	$2W$
Store vector dist.	$T_2 \Leftarrow A$	W
Broadcast R_1	$e \Leftarrow c \Leftarrow T_2 \geq R_1$	W
Load weight j	$A \Leftarrow w_{ij}$	$2W$
Update weight j	$A \Leftarrow A \pm 1$	W
Store weight j	$w_{ij} \Leftarrow A$	W
Enable neurons	$e \Leftarrow 1$	W
Total Cycles	$11W + X + 2.5M + 15$	

Table 2: Operations and machine cycles used by the TINMANN controller and neural array during a single training iteration as a function of the weight dimensionality (W), topological dimension (X), and machine word length (M).

Component	Transistors
RAM	$M(W+X+3)$
G	$2M$
P	$8M$
A	$8M$
Comparator	$20M$
Adder/Subtractor	$20M$
Conditional Logic	50
c flag	10
e flag	10
Total	$M(W+X+61)+70$

Table 3: Transistor counts for the components of a TINMANN neuron as a function of the weight dimensionality (W), topological dimension (X), and machine word length (M).

4 CONCLUSIONS

This chapter has presented two examples of neural network implementation based upon stochastic processing elements. In both cases, the recurrent structure of the networks allowed the benefits of stochastic integration to be exploited.

At the time of this writing, a 100,000 transistor, 20 neuron custom VLSI prototype of the STONN architecture is in fabrication. At a predicted speed of 10 MHz, a 50 neuron system based on this chip can solve a combinatorial optimization problem (minimum-cut graph bipartitioning) in 20 ms, roughly equivalent to 3.5 GFLOPS. The design can be easily modified using state-of-the-art VLSI technology to greatly improve speed and density.

The TINMANN architecture and the simplified fusion of the competitive and Kohonen learning algorithms upon which it is based were presented. A prototype implementation based on programmable gate arrays is currently under construction. Although a custom VLSI implementation of TINMANN has not been attempted, the architectural structure would lend itself well VLSI technology, and simulations indicate that the resulting hardware would be capable of accepting as many as 145,000 two-dimensional training vectors per second.

References

[1] A. Agranat and A. Yariv. A new architecture for a microelectronic implementation of neural network models. In *IEEE First International Conference on Neural Networks*, volume III, pages 403–410, 1987.

[2] J. Alspector, B. Gupta, and R. Allen. Performance of a stochastic learning microchip. In *Advances in Neural Information Processing Systems I*, pages 748–760, 1989.

[3] G. Bilbro, R. Mann, T. Miller III, W. Snyder, D. E. Van den Bout, and M. White. Mean field annealing and neural networks. In *Advances in Neural Information Processing Systems*, pages 91–98. Morgan-Kaufmann Publishers, Inc., 1989.

[4] D. E. Van den Bout and T. K. Miller III. A digital architecture employing stochasticism for the simulation of Hopfield neural nets. *IEEE Transactions on Circuits and Systems*, 36(5):732–738, May 1989.

[5] D. E. Van den Bout and T. K. Miller III. Graph partitioning using annealed neural networks. In *Proceedings of the IEEE International Conference on Neural Networks*, pages I:521–I:528, 1989.

[6] D. E. Van den Bout and T. K. Miller III. Improving the performance of the hopfield-tank neural network through normalization and annealing. Accepted for publication in *Biological Cybernetics.*, 1989.

[7] D. DeSieno. Adding a conscience to competitive learning. In *IEEE International Conference on Neural Networks*, pages I:117–I:124, 1988.

[8] B. Gaines. Stochastic computing systems. In *Advances in Information and Systems Science*, pages 37–172. Elsevier, 1969.

[9] B. Gaines. Uncertainty as a foundation of computational power in neural networks. In *IEEE First International Conference on Neural Networks*, volume III, pages 51–57, 1987.

[10] H. Graf, L. Jackel, R. Howard, B. Straughn, J. Denker, W. Hubbard, D. Tennant, and D. Schwartz. VLSI implementation of a neural network memory with several hundreds of neurons. In *American Institute of Physics Conference Proceedings No. 151*, pages 414–419, 1986.

[11] J. Hopfield and D. Tank. Neural computations of decisions in optimization problems. *Biological Cybernetics*, 52:141–152, 1985.

[12] J. J. Hopfield. Neural networks and physical systems with emergent collective computational abilities. *Proc. Natl. Acad. Sci, U.S.A.*, 79:2554–2558, 1982.

[13] J. J. Hopfield and D. W. Tank. Neural computation of decision in optimization problems. *Biol. Cybern.*, 52:141–152, 1985.

[14] M. Johnson, N. Allinson, and K. Moon. A digital realization of self-organising maps. In *Proceedings of the 1988 IEEE Conference on Neural Information Processing Systems — Natural and Synthetic*, 1988.

[15] S. Kirkpatrick, C. Gelatt, and M. Vecchi. Optimization by simulated annealing. *Science*, 220(4598):671–680, May 13 1983.

[16] T. Kohonen. Self-organized formation of topologically correct feature maps. *Biological Cybernetics*, 43:56–69, 1982.

[17] T. Kohonen. *Self-Organization and Associative Memory*. Springer-Verlag, 1984.

[18] S. Kung and J. Hwang. Parallel architectures for artificial neural nets. In *Proceedings of the 1988 IEEE International Conference on Neural Networks*, pages II:165–II:172, 1988.

[19] S. Mackie, H. Graf, and D. Schwartz. Implementation of neural network models in silicon. In Rolf Eckmiller and Christopher v. d. Malsburg, editors, *Neural Computers*, volume 41, pages 467–476. Springer-Verlag, 1987.

[20] J. Mann and S. Gilbert. An analog self-organizing neural network chip. In *Proceedings of the 1988 IEEE Conference on Neural Information Processing Systems — Natural and Synthetic*, 1988.

[21] P. Mars and W. Poppelbaum. *Stochastic and Deterministic Averaging Processors*. IEE, 1981.

[22] A. Murray and A. Smith. Asynchronous VLSI neural networks using pulse-stream arithmetic. *IEEE Journal of Solid-State Circuits*, 23(3):688–697, June 1988.

[23] N. Nasrabadi and Y. Feng. Vector quantization of images based upon Kohonen self-organizing feature maps. In *IEEE International Conference on Neural Networks*, pages I:101–I:108, 1988.

[24] P. Penz and R. Wiggins. Digital signal processor accelerators for neural network simulations. In *American Institute of Physics Conference Proceedings No. 151*, volume 151, pages 345–355, 1986.

[25] H. Ritter and K. Schulten. Kohonen self-organizing maps: Exploring their computational capabilities. In *IEEE International Conference on Neural Networks*, pages I:109–I:116, 1988.

[26] D. Rumelhart and J. McClelland. *Parallel Distributed Processing: Explorations in the Microstructure of Cognition*, chapter 5. MIT Press, 1986.

[27] M. Sivilotti, M. Emerling, and C. Mead. A novel associative memory implemented using collective computation. In *1985 Chapel Hill Conference on Very Large Scale Integration*, pages 329–342, 1985.

[28] G. Works. The creation of Delta: A new concept in ANS processing. In *IEEE International Conference on Neural Networks*, pages II:159–II:164, 1988.

10

OPIE—AN OPTICALLY PROGRAMMED NEURO-COMPUTER

by Cary D. Kornfeld, NEC Research Institute, Princeton, New Jersey

Introduction

Neural networks are attracting renewed interest within the scientific community. Loosely patterned after a simplified model of biological nervous systems, they have been proposed to yield *natural* solutions to a number of notoriously hard problems like computer vision and adaptive control. From the perspective of a computer architect, neural networks are an attractive alternative to traditional computer systems because they provide a fertile context in which to incorporate massive parallelism. In contrast to conventional parallel computing architectures, this ensemble of computing elements is neither explicitly configured nor programmed, but achieve their behavior adaptively in response to a training procedure in which their stimulated response is subtly adjusted until some measure of desired response is achieved to each of many stimulus patterns.

At the present time, research has focused primarily in three areas: the development of efficient methods for training such systems; a theoretical analysis of their behavior; and on the development of commercial application for this class of computing system. These studies have relied primarily on digital simulations of neural network models programmed on traditional computers. Digital accelerator boards are now commercially available for workstations but the speed of such systems permit only relatively small and hence simple neural systems to be simulated. In order to realize the emergent potential of these computing systems—their promise of massive, asynchronous parallelism—real, hardware embodiments of neural networks must be developed.

Practical realizations of large neural network computing systems require that a simple technique be found for implementing each of its principal components—neuron units and synaptic connections. There is some debate over the operational requirements for these components, but a number of characteristics are thought to be desirable. The programmability of these systems is enhanced when the synapses can assume a wide range of connection strength. Ideally, the synaptic connections should be continuously adjustable. It is also desirable that these synapses be dynamically programmable so that the neural system will be capable of adaptive behavior. Similarly, the neuron units should provide some mechanism for adjusting their activation threshold. Simulation results suggest that non-linear response characteristics within the neuron suppress noise within the machine and help stabilize system behavior.

Analog implementations of neural systems fall into two broad categories—optical and electronic. Optical implementations model neuron firing activity as a beam of light and use light modulators as synaptic elements [2-7]. Lenses and holograms are used to route neural signals (light) between neuron units. The basic neuron unit is typically composed of a photodetector, an electronic operational amplifier and a light emitting element. The use of electronic components in the neuron unit limits much of the speed potential promised by photonics.

Electronic implementations of neural networks often encode neuron firing strength as either a voltage or as the frequency of voltage pulses [8-13]. The synapses are modeled as either resistive or capacitive elements. A variety of proposals have been suggested for achieving variable strength resistive synapses in neural networks. These approaches suffer a number of problems. Some are relatively complex requiring Digital–to–Analog converters and a multi-bit memory be located at each synapse. Some approaches are sensitive to device parametrics and exhibit wide variations in operating characteristics. This is particularly true of CMOS implementations that map activating and inhibiting synapses to the transconductance of p-load and n-load devices. The use of floating gate memories (EEPROMs) as synaptic elements is being explored by a number of research groups [14-15]. The dynamic range in these devices is small and device characteristics can drift as a function of time, temperature and repeated cycling of the charge stored on the floating gate. Finally, there is an ironic mismatch between our ability to fabricate massive numbers of synaptic elements on a VLSI chip and the relatively small number of wire bond connections that can be made to VLSI chips. It is these wire bonds that determine the bandwidth of information that can pass into a VLSI neural chip and could become a critical design constraint that ultimately limits overall system performance.

This chapter describes a hybrid computer system that employs both optics and electronics for implementing a very large analog neuro–computer system. It employs a number of technologies developed for active matrix flat panel displays and for photovoltaics power cells. Each synapse can be programmably controlled over a continuous range of connection strength that can theoretically span more than five orders of magnitude. The arrays are relatively tolerant to variations in fabrication processing. Assembly and system integration are straight forward and provide considerably more information bandwidth than do many VLSI approaches.

The first section of this chapter describes the basic synaptic element—its structure and fabrication and reviews the rudimentary device physics that underlie its behavior. This enables us to meaningfully describe our experimental data.

The second section focuses on the neural computer constructed with these arrays and describes the system configuration, a variety of operation and application requirements. It discusses the implications of the device characteristics on the design and operation of the neuro-computer. It also describes in considerable detail many seemingly mundane issues like device mounting and analog circuitry and design. This section also describes the illumination subsystem and discusses possible trade-offs. The section concludes with a description of the user interface that controls the computer system.

Construction of a prototype "neuro-computer" enabled us to implement simple neural networks. These experiments helped delineate a number of problems with these synaptic arrays. The third section describes these device shortcomings and analyzes their cause. A new, enhanced photoconductive device is proposed that has better operating characteristics Early prototypes confirm the theoretical analysis that led to the refinements in these new optically programmed synaptic elements.

The final section of this chapter summarizes the many elements that contribute to the overall design and implementation of this computing system. It also suggests areas for continued research that will be required if these devices are to find wide use for neural computing applications.

1. Photoconductive Synapses†

One of the most seductive features of the neural computing paradigm is its facility to adapt its behavior in response to environmental feedback. Adaptation enables these systems to acquire knowledge and be capable of trained activity. In order to achieve adaptive behavior the synapses must be dynamically programmable during system operation. Ideally, the synapse weights should be continuously variable so that subtle adjustments can be made to achieve some notion of weight state balance. The dynamic range of synaptic weights should be as wide as is possible. Finally, if these systems are to find wide use they must be manufacturable at a relatively low cost. At the present time, no one proposal for building analog neural networks meets all of these requirements.

---

† I am indebted to C. Wong and R. Frye, my collaborators at A.T.& T. Bell Laboratories, without whom the design and development of these devices would not have been possible. My understanding of these devices is due in large measure to their teaching.

1.1 Device Structure and Fabrication

Our approach for building neural networks is based on fabricating large arrays of photoconductive synapses. Figure 1 shows a cross section of this device. Some liberties have been taken for clarity. The vertical scale of the diagram is highly exaggerated. For example, the Titanium/Gold (Ti/Au) metal electrodes are about 250 microns wide and two to three microns high; the hydrogenated amorphous silicon (a-Si:H) layer is typically only a few thousand angstroms thick.

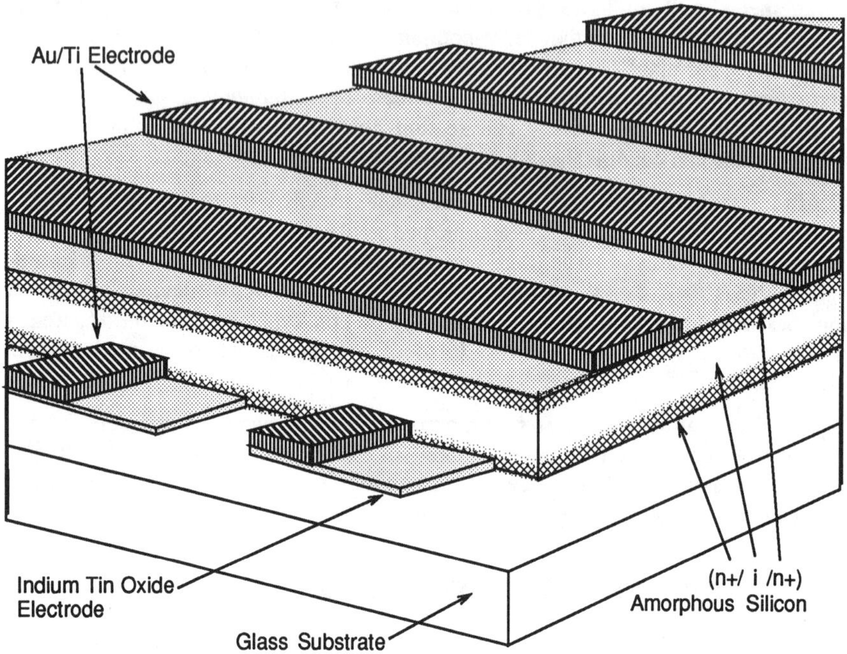

Figure 1 Cross section of a photoconductive synaptic array - overlapping electrode geometry.

The device is a three layer structure in which an amorphous silicon photoconductor is sandwiched between orthogonal electrode layers. Synaptic elements are created at the overlap of the row and column electrodes. The arrays are fabricated on glass substrates. This arrangement requires that one of the electrodes be transparent. We use Indium Tin Oxide (ITO), a transparent conductor widely used in calculators and flat displays. Unfortunately, ITO is a relatively poor conductor, so in order to eliminate the high series resistance that would be created by these long narrow ITO electrodes, we augment each with an additional strip (a parallel, but much narrower second electrode) of Titanium/Gold. During normal operation photomodulated current through each synapse is shunted into these auxiliary low resistance electrodes which then lead off the array.

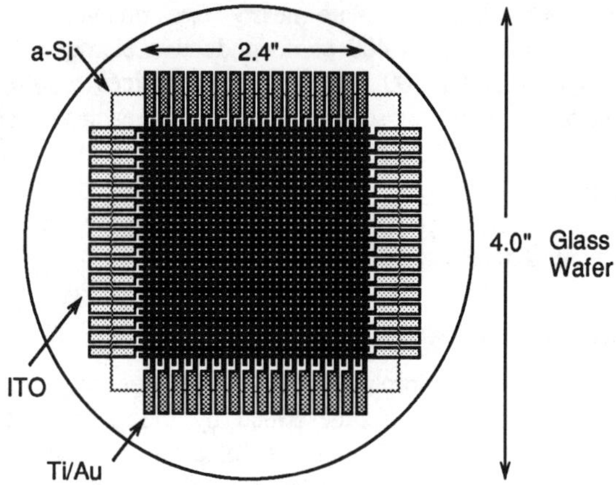

Figure 2 Synaptic array fabricated atop a 4 inch glass wafer.

The 14,400 element device array, depicted in Figure 2, occupy the center 2.4 inches of a 4 inch glass wafer. They are large by VLSI standards. We have chosen this size to facilitate making the 240 connections required to integrate the synaptic array to its neuron circuitry. The large size of the resulting synapses (approximately 35,000 micron^2) also relaxes some of the illumination and alignment tolerances required to optically program the $\mathbf{W}_{ij}$ matrix within the synaptic array.

The fabrication process for these arrays is surprisingly simple and requires very few process steps. The two electrode layers are patterned with the same mask. Since the synaptic elements are formed at the overlap of the top and bottom electrode structures, they are essentially self aligned. The auxiliary metal runners necessitate a second mask. This is the only aspect of the fabrication process that requires alignment, but since these structures are so large, alignment is easily achieved.

These devices use amorphous silicon as the photoconductor material. Our choice was predicated by our familiarity with the fabrication of amorphous silicon thin film transistors [15]. A variety of optically sensitive materials could also be used. The attraction of our approach lies in it simplicity. The arrays closely resemble flat panel displays both in size and construction. In contrast to the typical flat display in which each pixel is a light emitting or reflecting element, each pixel in our arrays has been transformed into a photoconductor in which the synaptic connection strength is directly proportional to the light flux falling onto it.

There are a number of fortuitous aspects to this approach. Our arrays require nearly the same fabrication technology as has been developed for flat displays[1]. Consequently, arrays with several million synapses can be made using existing

1 Actually, our devices are a bit simpler and hence easier to produce.

technology. Our prototypes are nearly five times larger than any previous implementation and have 14,400 photoconductive elements. The production cost of these arrays is under 100 dollars. Our devices employ the same physical phenomena used in low cost solar cells. In fact, each synapse closely resembles a photovoltaic cell both in construction and operation. Again, the underlying technology is well developed and mature[2]. Finally, because of the similarity to both solar cells and flat displays, we can employ the same assembly and connection technologies used by these products.

1.2 Device Characteristics

The operation of our amorphous silicon synapses rely on photoconduction in semiconductor materials. As described by the photoelectric effect, a photon captured by the semiconductor excites an electron into the conduction band of the solid and generates a hole in the valence band. When light falls on the synapse region of this device the population of free carriers increases. Since a voltage can be applied through this region, a proportional current will be generated. The particular properties of that current are influenced by a surprising number of factors.

In an effort to understand the properties of these a-Si:H photoconductive synapses a variety of simpler discrete device structures were fabricated and analyzed [16]. These structures are useful for measuring the photocurrent of our basic device structure. The data measured from an element within a large array is the product of many other factors as well. The discrete device illustrated in Figure 3 permits us to separate these effects. These discrete devices duplicate the behavior of the synapses formed within large arrays, but eliminate effects such as series resistance in the row and column electrodes, or effects like extraneous current paths between other elements within the array.

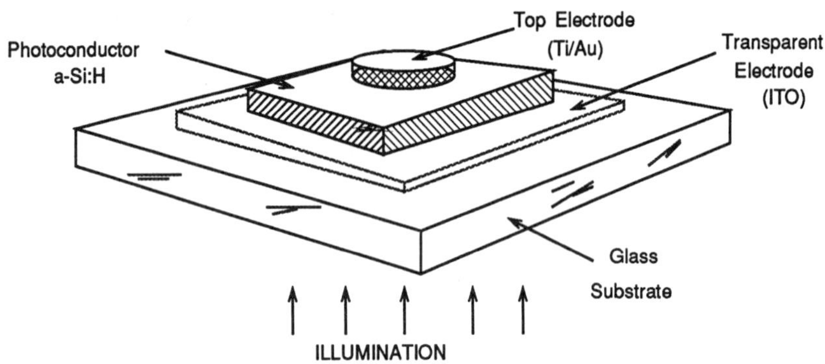

Figure 3 Discrete device for measuring fundamental properties of photoconduction in amorphous silicon films.

---

2 Small amorphous silicon solar cells are widely used in low cost pocket calculators.

The photoconductive behavior of amorphous silicon has been thoroughly studied [17]. Early research employed photoconductivity primarily as an indirect method for probing other material parameters such as carrier lifetime, density of states and to reveal the mechanism of carrier transport within the material itself [18-20]. In more recent years, a number of new devices have been investigated which directly employ the photoconductive properties of hydrogenated amorphous silicon (a-Si:H). One application that has much in common with our synaptic devices is the linear image sensor [21-22]. These devices typically consist of a linear array of several thousand photosensors that are uniformly spaced along a document sized bar of glass. This array is scanned down the length of a document converting the image into electrical signals. Amorphous silicon is particular well suited to this type of application because it can be deposited over large areas at moderate temperatures (250° C). This allows the use of relatively inexpensive glass substrates, and the process can easily accommodate areas larger than one foot. Studies of the properties of linear image arrays have shown the photoconductive response to be very uniform (approximately 5 percent over a 7 centimeter array), and variations in the conductivity of more than 5 orders of magnitude can be obtained with moderate light levels [23]. An additional advantage of amorphous silicon is that thin–film transistors can be incorporated into a photosensor array to provide peripheral circuit functions [24].

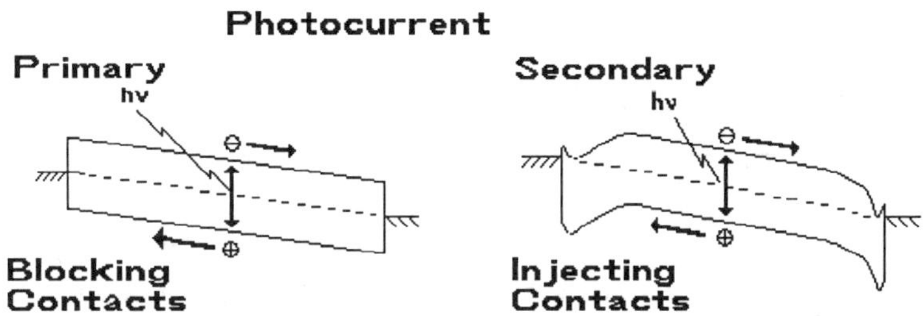

Figure 4 Band Diagrams of Primary and Secondary Photoconduction.

The response of such structures to light and applied voltage is strongly influenced by their contacts [26]. Examples of band diagrams for two extremes of photoconductive behavior are shown in Figure 4. In hydrogenated amorphous silicon, electrons have a much higher mobility than holes, and undoped films are generally **n** type, so the behavior of these devices is usually dominated by the electrons. If the electrical contact at the a-Si:H to metal interface is blocking to electrons, the photocurrent is limited to one electron–hole pair per absorbed photon. The time needed to respond to changes in illumination intensity is determined by the transit time of carriers across the device. This type of behavior is described as primary photocurrent. Since it is, in effect, counting photons, the current generated by primary photoconduction saturates at a constant value once a bias is established across the device sufficient to sweep out the carriers.

If, however, the contacts can inject electrons the photoconductive response is very different. When an electron is collected at the anode (the right hand contact in Figure 4), the charge imbalance causes the cathode to inject another. This process continues until the carriers recombine within the a-Si:H film, removing an electron–hole pair from the device. This kind of secondary photocurrent mechanism exhibits photoconductive gain. Many electrons can be collected per absorbed photon. This gain is proportional to the ratio of the electron lifetime (τ) to the transit time (T)

$$Gain = \frac{\tau}{T}$$

Since the transit time is inversely proportional to the field, the photocurrent is proportional to the applied bias. Secondary photocurrent is the mechanism that gives rise to the classical photoconductive effect in which the resistance of a material is changed by light.

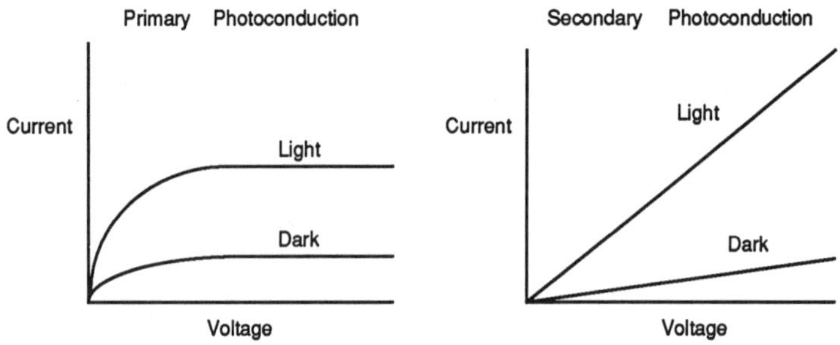

Figure 5 Current-to-Voltage characteristics of Primary and Secondary Photoconduction.

In most real photoconductors, both primary and secondary photocurrents are present to some extent. Generally, however, one of the two mechanisms dominates. Each has its relative advantages. The differences between the two (apart from the gain) are most readily apparent in the current-voltage characteristics shown in Figure 5. Primary photocurrent, as described above, saturates with applied bias. In this saturated region of operation, the device behaves like a current source, rather than a conductor. Because of its photon counting nature, primary photocurrent is dependent only on the incident light intensity and is very insensitive to other device parameters. Process related problems, like inhomogeneous contacts or spatial variations in trap density and lifetime have very little influence on primary photoconduction. Sublinear current—voltage characteristics are the typical hallmark of primary photocurrent mechanisms.

Secondary photocurrent, on the other hand, is indicated by linear current-voltage characteristics. Its linearity is one of its advantages. For applications that use the photoconductive array as an analog matrix multiplier, this linearity is very matrix multiplier, this linearity is very important. In addition, the increased photosensitivity from photoconductive gain may be an advantage in cases for which light intensity is at a premium. The disadvantage of secondary mechanisms, however, is that they are sensitive to all of the process induced inhomogeneities described above. Small variations in the injecting contacts or in the lifetime of the carriers show up directly in the photocurrent. Secondary photoconductivity, although desirable for its linear operating characteristics, is much more demanding from the point of view of device fabrication.

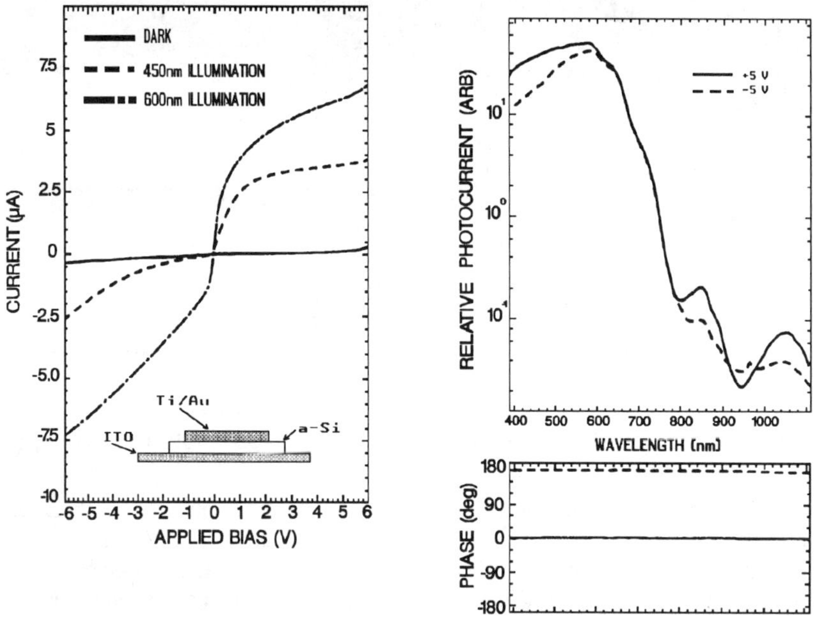

Figure 6 Photoconduction characteristics for a device with intrinsic interfaces at both the ITO and Ti/Au electrodes.

Figure 6 shows the current-voltage characteristics of a discrete device for which the photoconductive layer is formed from 6000 Angstroms of undoped a-Si:H. The area of the Ti/Au contact is 0.02 cm^2, and the applied bias refers to the Ti/Au, with the ITO layer held at ground. The illumination intensity is approximately 800 μWatts per square centimeter. The contact formed on both sides of the intrinsic layer is blocking to electron flow, so for both polarities of bias, primary photocurrent dominates. Note that the photocurrent tends to saturate at higher voltages, as expected for a primary mechanism. Figure 6 also shows the spectral response relative to a calibrated photodetector. The light, in this case, is modulated at 50 Hz. The difference in the short wavelength response is caused by the fact that blue light is strongly absorbed near the ITO contact, so this contact is a more efficient electron collector. The shape of these curves is mainly determined by the absorbency of the a-Si:H film.

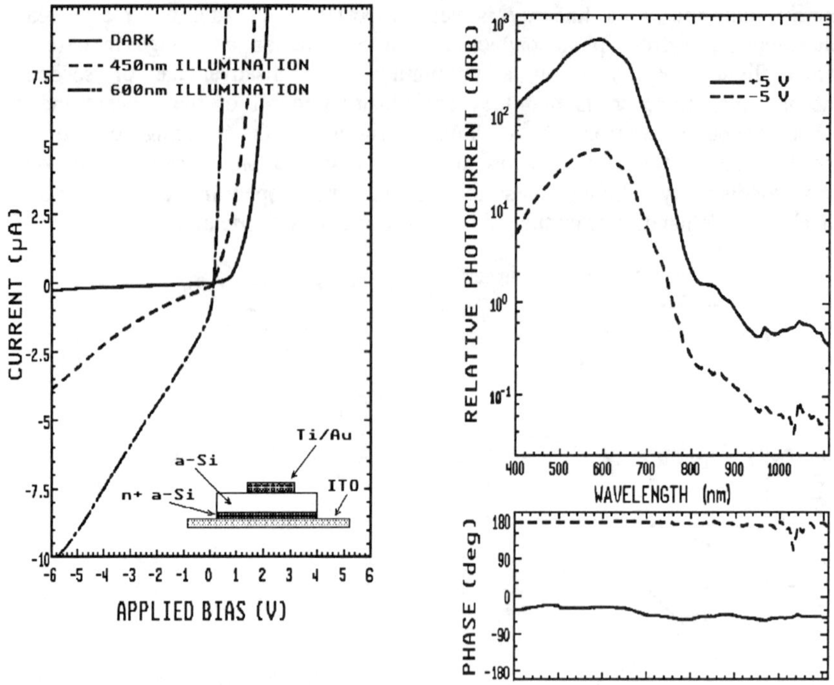

Figure 7 Photoconduction characteristics for a device with a doped a-Si/ITO interface and an intrinsic Ti/Au electrode.

Figure 7 shows the characteristics of similar devices, but the bottom 500 Angstroms of the film were heavily doped with phosphorous to form a thin **n+** layer. This layer eliminates the blocking potential barrier at the a-Si:H to ITO interface, forming an injecting contact. This causes increased photoresponse for positive bias. (Note that the negative bias characteristics are similar to Figure 6). The spectral response for these devices, also shown in Figure 7, shows the differences between primary and secondary photocurrent. For a negative applied voltage, the Ti/Au contact cannot inject electrons and the response is virtually identical to that of intrinsic silicon. The phase shift of 180° in the spectral response shows that the response quickly follows the 50 hz modulated light. (The 180° phase shift indicates that the sign of the current is negative for negative applied bias). For positive applied bias, however, the Ti/Au contact can easily pull electrons from the injecting ITO to **n+** doped a-Si:H contact, and the resulting secondary photocurrent is much larger. For this device the photoconductive gain is approximately fifteen. Note, however, that the phase of the photocurrent, which would ideally be zero for fast response, is instead about -30°. For the 50 Hz modulation frequency this corresponds to a response time of approximately 1.7 milliseconds. This illustrates another important trade-off in device design: the increased photosensitivity that can be achieved with a secondary photocurrent mechanism is invariably accompanied by a decrease in the speed with which the device can be optically programmed. This is a consequence of the population dynamics in two groups of carriers—those held in trapping sites and those free to conduct. If the illumination is suddenly turned off, the free carrier population will decay (with lifetime τ) by recombination. The population of carriers held in trapping sites will also decay in response to the reduced population of free carriers. This second decay phenomenon is many orders of magnitude slower and it is the trapping site de-population process which dominates the turn-off time response of these devices. Trapping effects such as these are characteristic of amorphous materials. They do not play as significant a role in the optical response characteristics of polycrystalline materials and are entirely negligible in crystalline materials.

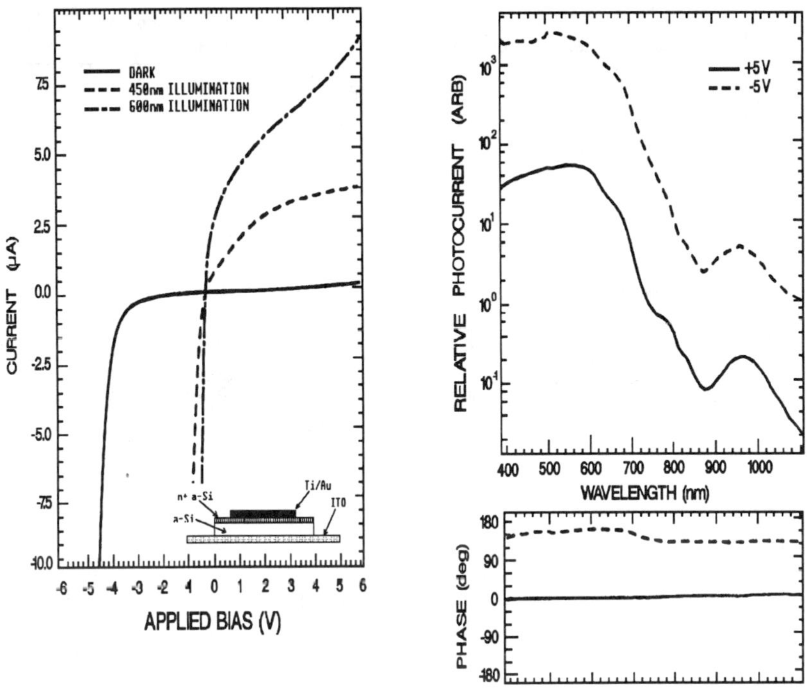

Figure 8 Photoconduction characteristics for a device with a doped Ti/Au and an intrinsic ITO interface.

Figure 8 shows equivalent data for devices with a heavily doped layer at the Ti/Au contact, and Figure 9 for devices with both contacts doped. It is clear from these results that in all cases, when the bias and contacts are in a configuration that results in electron injection, significant photoconductive gain occurs.

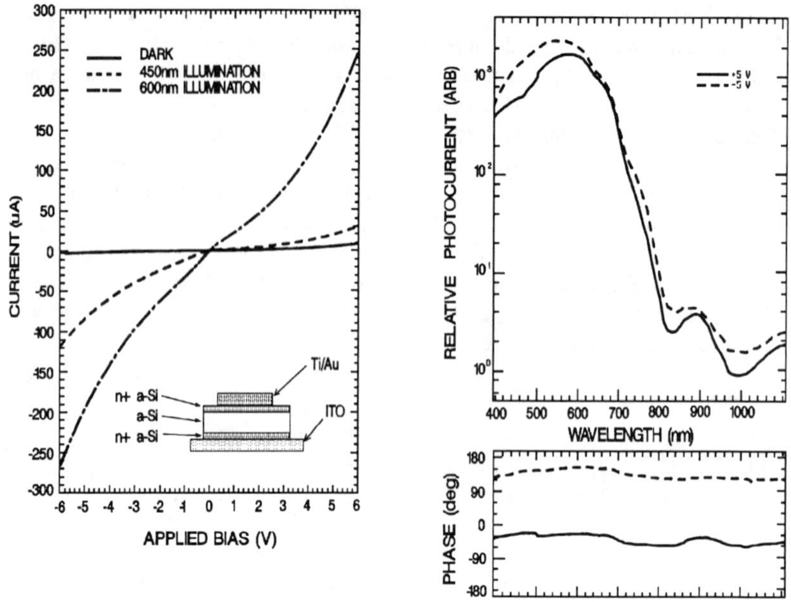

Figure 9 Photoconduction characteristics for a device with doped interfaces at both the Ti/Au and ITO electrodes.

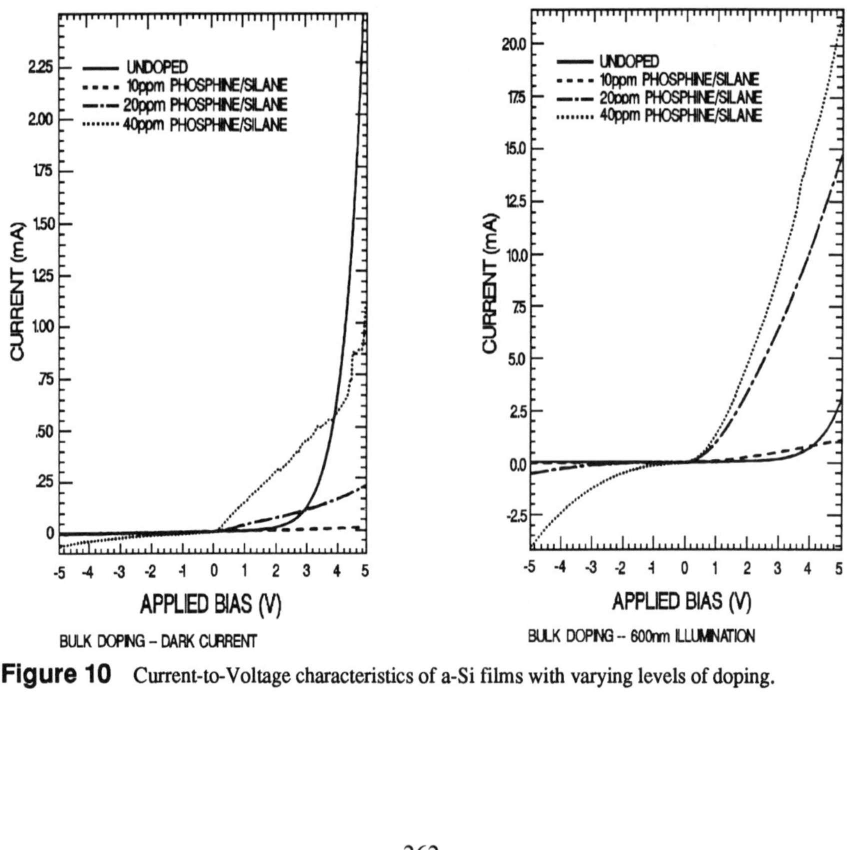

Figure 10 Current-to-Voltage characteristics of a-Si films with varying levels of doping.

Another important parameter in the composition of the photoconductive film is the doping level in the bulk of the photoconductive layer. All of the previous results concern the effects of variations in the doping levels at the contacts for devices in which the bulk is undoped. Figure 10 shows the dark and illuminated current-voltage characteristics for devices having an injecting bottom contact (as in Figure 7), and having various levels of phosphorous added during bulk film deposition. It is important to note, in comparison with Figure 7, the difference in the current scale in these figures. One of the effects of bulk phosphorous doping, even at low concentrations, appears to be the suppression of the knee of the forward (positive) bias turned-on. This is particularly apparent in the dark current, if we compare an undoped sample with a sample doped with 10 ppm phosphine in the gas phase. A second effect is a dramatic increase in secondary photocurrent. This possibly results from an increase in carrier lifetime as the Fermi energy moves above midgap. Whatever the origin of these doping effects, they give added processing flexibility in which to control the device properties.

One of the most important things that we've learned from this line of research is that the discrete device behavior that we've observed is unlikely to be useful for predicting the ensemble behavior of arrays of these devices. The discrete devices help elucidate the fundamental physics that govern the behavior of photomodulated synaptic elements, but there are a number of other factors that must be incorporated to accurately model large arrays of these devices. Even a very simple device array, like the one in Figure 2, requires many more processing steps than its discrete counterpart. Some of these steps, such as lithography and metal definition, require heating and exposure to various chemicals and etchants. These extra steps can have a significant impact on these devices, which are particularly sensitive to contact preparation conditions. The discrete device results are probably only useful for identifying the major features of photoconductive device behavior, and equivalent studies must conducted for a variety of array structures and other configurations.

Even small arrays like those with 120 by 120 electrodes have 14,400 individual photoconductive elements and the detailed testing of them can be a formidable task. Probing the characteristics of a single synapse within these arrays requires (at minimum) a six terminal measurement, so that each axon and dendrite can have the voltage on its immediate neighbors controlled. It has become clear that automated testing is the only viable solution. The problems of interconnection, signal generation, sensing, and illumination that must be solved in order to test the arrays are also encountered in operating them. For this reason, a general purpose computer system has been constructed that accomplishes both objectives.

2. Neuro-Computer Design

2.1 System Configuration

The system organization of OPIE (Optically Programmed, Interactive Execution), our optically programmed neuro-computer is shown in Figure 11. It consists of three computer subsystems—a SUN 3, a SUN 2 and an HP instrumentation controller. The SUN 3 generates the user interface and is responsible for implementing a software model of the neurons–thresholds, transfer function and activation level. It is the primary control and coordinating agent within the entire system. The illumination hardware is controlled by a SUN 2. The analog signal interface to the synaptic array is controlled through an HP instrumentation computer.

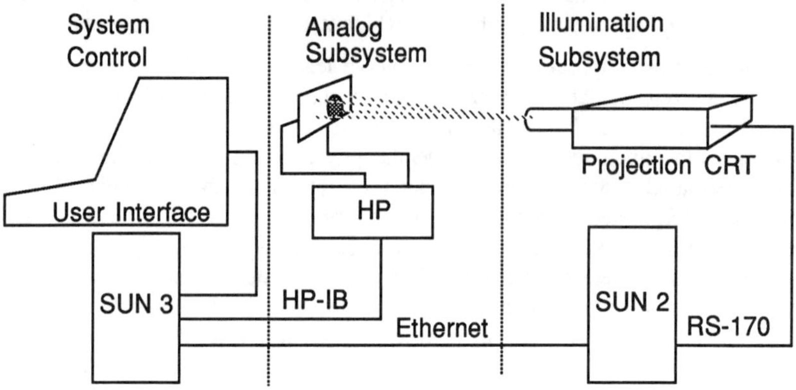

Figure 11 Block Diagram of the OPIE computer system.

This system serves the dual purpose of providing both operational and testing capabilities. Arrays of 120x120, although simple in design, comprise 14,400 individual photoconductive synapses. The task of testing so many devices clearly requires extensive automation. For the purposes of testing the arrays, voltage can be applied to one of the columns while keeping all others at ground. The output at each row is fed to a current-to-voltage amplifier (made from an operational amplifier) that has a virtual ground at its input, and in operation perform the current summing function on that row. A high speed FET scanner routes the output of each of these amplifiers into a voltmeter that passes the data onto the SUN 3 workstation.

This system does not operate in an optimal fashion as a neural network because we have interposed several computers into the loop between the output and the input of the synaptic array. Moreover, we use software to implement a model of the system's neurons. In contrast to a pure hardware implementation with analog neurons directly connected to the synaptic array, true asynchronous operation is not possible. This sacrifices much of the speed of the network, but offers in exchange enormous flexibility for research purposes. The array itself, together with its current summing amplifiers, constitutes a simple element performing the matrix multiplication that is a central feature of any neural network. With the computer, we are free to model the characteristics of the neuron elements as we choose, and to modify the input vector in an arbitrary fashion. Furthermore, since the mapping of the synaptic array's output to input is made via software, a number of neural network architectures can be implemented without rewiring the hardware.

2.2 Ilumination—Optical Programming

One of the most significant advantages of a photoconductive approach is that it offers a synaptic element whose connection strength can be programmed over a continuous range of values. The performance of the photoconductive synapse is determined by its inherent electrical properties. Even a perfectly ideal array, however, is limited by the system which illuminates it. The maximum useful size and density of these arrays may eventually be limited not by our ability to build them, but rather by our ability to generate high density patterns of light whose pixel intensities can be widely and independently varied. Moreover, the dynamic properties of the illumination system can directly determine the speed with which the network can be operated.

In many ways, we share similar illumination requirement with those who seek to build other kinds of optical computers. A number of proposals have been suggested for generating controlled illumination patterns. Typically these focus on generating binary images at very high speeds. Our system is driven by a somewhat different set of requirements. Unlike many other optical computers, the operational rate of our neuro-computer is not determined by the rate at which the illumination pattern can change, but rather its peak operational rate is determined by the time constants for electrical signal propagation through the photoconductive array and its peripheral circuitry. Illumination in our machine creates its internal configuration. It corresponds in some sense to the "*program*" within the machine rather than to the "*data*" passing through it. It is, of course, useful to be able to change the program[3], but at this stage in our research we feel that it is far more important that the illumination system have a wide dynamic range and be continuously variable because these factors determine the range of programs (or configurations) for the arrays and because they also dictate the ultimate size limit for building these arrays.[4]

There are a number of issues involved in the mapping of weight value to illumination intensity. The overall objective is to obtain a reasonably linear

3 It is not difficult to envision applications for neural networks in which they continuously change their internal configuration in response to new information or because they must continually adapt to a changing environment.

4 The dynamic range impacts the maximum number of sensors/synapses that can be tied together as a row of elements.

relationship between the weight value and the light intensity incident on the corresponding photoconductive element (synapse). But to do so requires that a number of system variables be controlled.

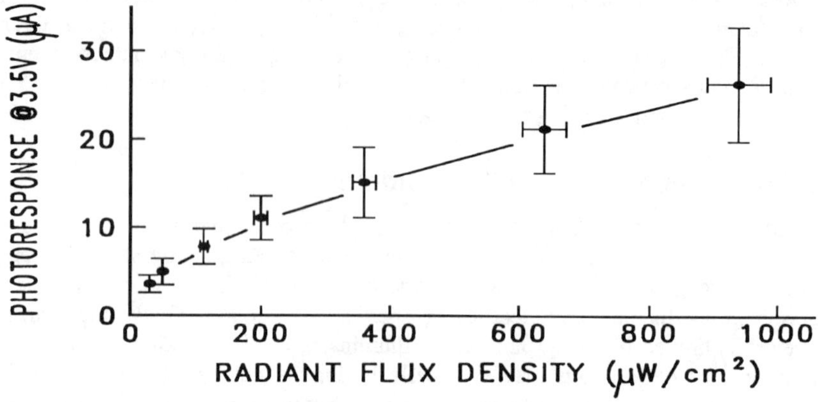

Figure 12 Photoresponse of a Synapse as a function of illumination intensity.

To begin, the photoresponse at each array element, as shown in Figure 12, follows a power law dependence.[5]

$$\sigma = \text{Gain} * \Phi^{0.55}$$

in which the conductance (σ) is a product of the optical flux (Φ) and the photoconductive gain of the device. The gain itself is dependent on a number of factors which include, for example, the density of traps in the amorphous silicon film. The situation is further complicated because the photoresponse/gain of individual elements varies widely among the 14,400 elements within each array.

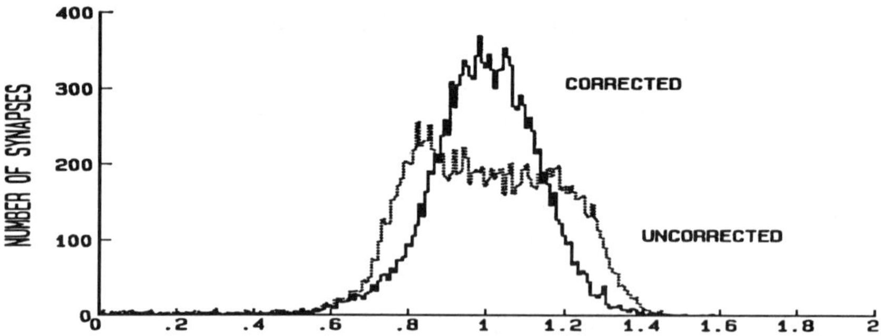

Figure 13 Photoresponse histogram of the 14,400 elements in a typical photoconductive array.

5 In retrospect, our use of Indium Tin Oxide as the transparent conductor may have adversely influenced the gain in our vertical geometry devices. Indium is known to diffuse into a-Si:H films and to increase its intrinsic trapping density. Future devices should use Tin Oxide.

Our measurements, shown in Figure 13, indicate nearly a 30% variation in optical sensitivity among them. In this figure we also show the distribution when the gain on each of the array's output current summing amplifiers is adjusted to remove line-to-line bias in the array response. This adjust distribution is labelled CORRECTED

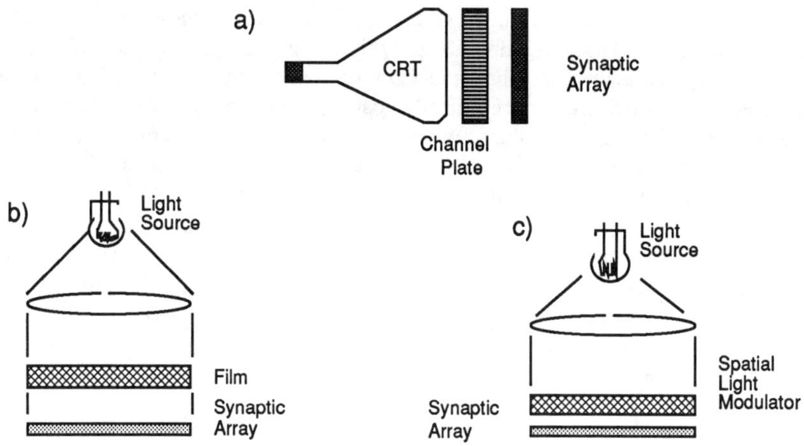

Figure 14 Illumination methods for controlling connection strength within synaptic arrays.

Figure 14 shows a variety of possible illumination alternatives. CRT display technology is, without doubt, the most widely used method currently available for generating high information content images. Because the light generated by the phosphor on a CRT faceplate is not collimated, and the glass is often thick, a CRT alone is not well suited for illuminating a small region of the array. For this reason, as shown in Figure14a, a fiber optic channel plate can be used between the CRT faceplate and the array to help minimize optical crosstalk between adjacent pixels.

CRTs have a number of attractive features. Each pixel can be independently controlled through a continuous range of intensities, and the peak illumination for some CRTs is exceptionally high. Moreover, this approach exploits a mature technology. The weighting matrix for the synaptic array is organized as a bitmap and manipulated by a sophisticated graphics computer system. This is a particularly attractive technique for applications that implement learning rules by interactively reprogramming the array.

CRTs are not, however, without problems. The illumination that they provide includes a periodic rastering component created by image refresh. The time at which peak illumination occurs for a particular pixel depends on its location in the display. If the photoconductive array and its peripheral electronics are faster than the refresh cycle of the CRT display, the system will track the dynamics of the refresh cycle. The only ways to overcome this problem are either to slow the network response time, compromising further its dynamic performance, or to resort to a high persistence phosphor in the CRT itself. The latter solution is preferable, since it only increases the time needed to reprogram the array. Other problems with CRTs include image misalignment and drift caused by stray fields or aging, and also limit the achievable density.

As shown in Figure 14b, a piece of photographic film or a shadow mask can be used to illuminate the photoconductive array. Theoretically, these can be made to the same tolerances used within the array itself, but in practice the film mask size can vary somewhat.. Since the film or mask can be pressed against or integrated into the device, exceptionally stable alignment can be achieved. A wide range of intensity values is possible over a near continuous range. Moreover, pixel crosstalk is very low when the mask is pressed against or integrated into the display. Unfortunately, this approach does not provide much latitude for changing the illumination pattern. Some versatility can be achieved by projecting the image onto the array since presumably the film within the projector can be changed. But this is at some loss in alignment precision, an increase in pixel crosstalk and system noise. Clearly, this approach is only valid for applications in which the resistive network need not be dynamically reconfigured during normal operation.[6]

Light valves offer a compromise solution that offers some of the better characteristics of both CRT and film based illumination systems (Figure 14c). An active matrix LCD display, like those used in pocket televisions, can be affixed to the front of the array or perhaps integrated into it. A uniform light source is used. The ensemble is not subject to the same alignment and drift problems as are CRTs—it is, like a piece of film, permanently aligned. It is similar to a CRT in the sense that its display image can be dynamically changed, but these too are also multiplexed displays and their pixel intensity exhibits periodic variations. At this time, LCDs provide very limited grey-scale and have poor contrast ratios.

The illumination falling on the array is surprisingly difficult to accurately control. The illumination source (either a photographic film projector or high light output CRT) is neither uniform nor linear. We estimate that the intensity of illumination varies by as much as 10% between the center and periphery of the illumination pattern. It is well known that linear increases in the beam current in a CRT do not necessarily generate equivalent increases in light output (hence one normally employs some form of gamma correction within the CRT drive circuitry itself). Moreover, significant increases in beam current can load the CRT's power supply so heavily as to subtly reduce the flyback voltages. This in turn causes the image to shrink slightly and to shift its position on the CRT's faceplate. These small changes in image size and position make the task of aligning the

6 The vast majority of neural network applications that we have examined fall into this category and do not require dynamic reconfiguration. Instead they require an initial *learning* phase in which the synaptic weights are adjusted, followed by an operation phase during which time the weights are fixed.

illumination pattern to the array extremely difficult to achieve. Similarly, the opacity variations of photographic film are strongly affected by factors like the illumination balance (was the image photographed under or over exposed) and by the conditions during film development (temperature, development time and chemical strength). For these varied and many reasons, the mapping of calculated synapse weight to the equivalent relative illumination level is difficult.

We explored a number of non-linear mappings like **(X-1)/X** and $\mathbf{(X\text{-}1)^2/X^2}$ to find an approximate mapping of weight to illumination without appreciable success. Considering the many factors at play in determining the exact mapping of synaptic weight to illumination level, we have generally concluded that it is preferable to employ an adaptive approach whenever possible. Improvements to the illumination subsystem are an important area of continued research.

2.3 Analog Subsystem

The photoconductive arrays themselves constitute only a portion of the neural network. They are, essentially, a passive, optically configurable resistive matrix. A useful system also requires active devices. Depending on the function of the network, these active devices may be, for example, current summing amplifiers or comparators or any other of a host of devices all of which provide the power gain[7] necessary to run the network The choice of a technology to build them is very closely tied to the methods that are used to interconnect these peripheral circuits with the array itself.

OPIE is a hybrid optical computer because light is used to modulate electrical signals that course through the array. It is also a hybrid computer in that sense that it employs both analog and digital components within its primary data path. The vector matrix product computation occurs within the photoconductive array via Ohms law and current summing. The input and output signals are digitally encoded and pass through digital/analog converters on entry and exit from the photoconductive array.

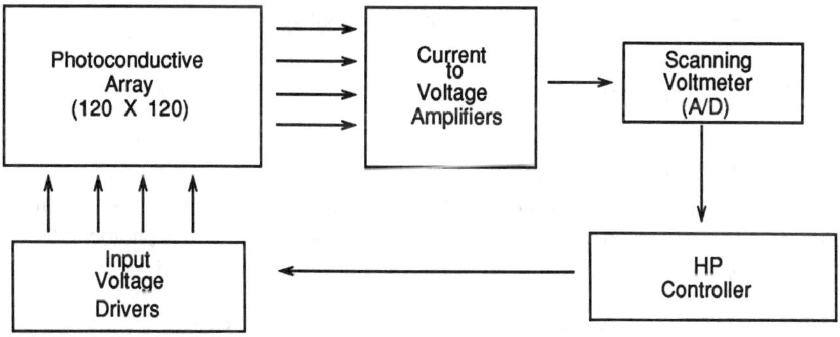

Figure 15 Block diagram of the components in the Analog Subsystem.

7 This should not to be confused with photoconductive gain.

An HP instrumentation computer is used to perform the analog to digital conversion. The analog subsystem is depicted in Figure 15. The input voltages are generated either by digital–to–analog voltage converters which enables us to implement neuron activity with a continuous range of analog depth or by digital I/O drivers (TTL), which can be set to one of two states—LOW (~0.17 V) and HIGH (~3.7 V). The digital I/O drivers are not capable of providing graduated neuron response but they do permit dual state neurons and provide reasonable functionality in some problem domains.[8]

The analog output from these arrays is a very small current (<10 μamps). We use current-to-voltage operational amplifiers with a gain of 10,000 to condition each of the 120 output signals. These are then sequentially measured with a fast voltmeter (100K samples/sec) which is digitally switched (by the HP computer) to each channel. A full sweep of the 120 output channels can be performed in as little as 1.2 milliseconds, but in practice the scanning rate is carefully synchronized with the raster rate of the illuminating CRT subsystem. One of the most annoying performance bottlenecks in this subsystem is not caused the sampling or capture rate of the scanning voltmeter, but is caused by the slow IEEE 488 bus interface that links the HP to the SUNs.[9]

One should not minimize the engineering challenges in the analog subsection of these neuro–computers. It is extremely difficult and surprisingly costly to work with the very low analog signal levels in each neuron. In our system this requires 120 identical channels of analog electronics each of which must be balanced and stabilized. The system is sensitive to power supply noise. Care must be taken when designing the wiring for the analog subsystem. In retrospect, the HP computer system enabled us to reduce many of these problems. It provided a very flexible analog subsystem that can be programmably controlled. It also simplified analog signal generation and measurement. But the incorporation of the HP instrumentation controller into the system also reduced the potential speed of the overall system.

2.4 Array Mounting

It is ironic that the size and density of our device arrays was ultimately determined not by limits in the fabrication process, but by peripheral issues like the physical attachment and support for the array and by illumination alignment considerations. The underlying technology permits fabrication of photoconductive junctions with feature sizes of only a few microns and could enable one to

8 The design of the output section of the synaptic array was determined primarily by cost constraints. There is a substantial cost difference (10:1) between the two types of voltage drivers.

9 The transfer rate is 120,000 bytes per second.

fabricate arrays with several hundred million elements. But to do so would require that the illumination pattern projected onto the array be aligned to the photo-sensors with exceptionally high precision. To maintain this alignment with micron tolerance across a very large number of elements requires a level of illumination control that is probably not attainable.

Fabrication of these arrays at the ultra high densities that are possible with VLSI technology requires that a method be devised for making the accompanying large number of electrical connections (e.g. 20,000) that must be made between the input (and output) electrodes of the array to the other components of the system (e.g. the neuron circuitry). VLSI chip wire bonding technology is capable of making only a few hundred wire bonds to a typical VLSI chip. New technology would be required.

These seemingly mundane issues eventually came to dominate and hence determine the final device feature size and element density. The arrays were designed to be press mounted to a simple printed circuit board. The input/output electrodes are placed at a 20 mil pitch: 10 mil electrodes and 10 mil inter-electrode spacing. As depicted in Figure 2 the electrode contact pads are larger and are inter-digitated from each side. This enables us to use the same Zebra strip elastomeric connector technology that is used in hand calculators, watches and flat panel displays.

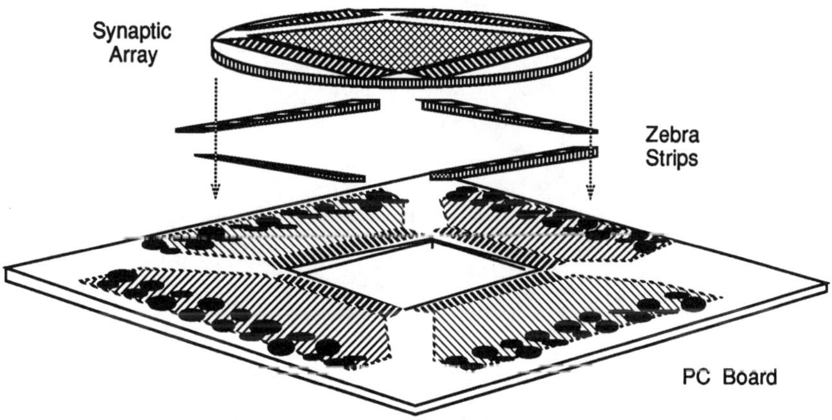

Figure 16 The Synaptic Array is press mounted to a Printed Circuit board.

A custom mounting structure is used to connect signal lines to the array. As shown in Figure 16, elastomeric connectors are sandwiched between the array and a specially designed printed circuit board. The mounting structure presses the entire ensemble together and maintains snug pressure on the array. Its design enables us to quickly disassemble it. Mounting a new array requires minimal alignment. This enables us to use a permanent electrically wired support structure but to easily change device arrays as new designs are fabricated.

2.5 System Operation

Fabrication of these synaptic arrays enabled us to begin construction of a simple neural computing system. There is very little previous work to provide guidance or direction for the architecture of analog neuro-computers. Consequently, our work was oriented toward building a flexible computing platform that would enable us to explore a variety of proposed neuro-computing paradigms. The computing system was also designed to allow us to obtain parametric data on these device arrays. This enabled us to continue the development of second generation arrays in parallel with our experiments in the neuro-computing.

The first arrays with a sufficiently low defect density to allow their use in neuro-computing were unusual both in their design and behavior. At that early point in our research we were uncertain about which characteristics to engineer into arrays. Seeking a comprehensive solution we fabricated arrays that had a mixture of characteristics. The a-Si:H under the top electrode was doped **n+** and the bottom was intrinsic. Our strategy was to build a device which would exhibit primary photoconduction when reverse biased, but when forward biased, secondary photoconduction would dominate. Indeed, the IV characteristics for that first array design, shown in Figure 17, exhibit a mixture of behavior.[11]

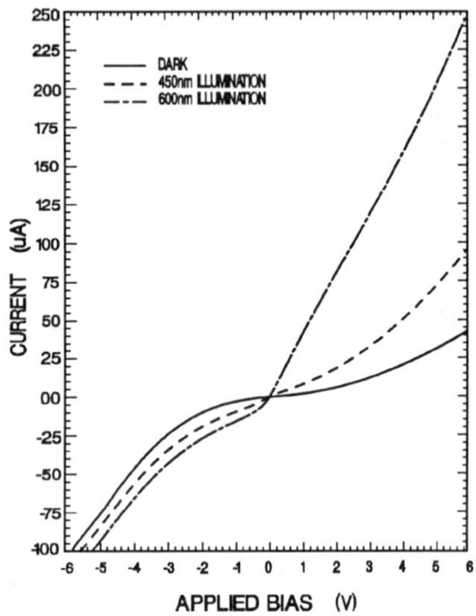

Figure 17 The Current-to-Voltage characteristics for a typical synaptic array used in early OPIE implementations.

---

11 These IV characteristics are measured for an element within a large array and differ somewhat from those seen in a discrete device like those shown in Figure 8.

From the perspective of a system architect, the resulting behavior creates a number of challenges if these devices are to be used for neural computing. The IV characteristics are asymmetric and non-linear. Moreover, under reverse bias the array has only marginal photoresponse.[12] These characteristics can have a profound influence on the resulting behavior of a complex neuro-computing system. The non-linearity in the current-to-voltage behavior causes sub-optimal stimulation between neurons. As the firing strength of one neuron increases, the stimulation through one of these synapses into the next neuron does not track properly. The stimulation increases but not by equal measure. Finally, there is an unusual spectral disparity in the photoresponse (particularly in the reverse bias regime). The photoresponse for this array follows a square law dependency. Fortunately, all of these characteristics are monotonically increasing. Because of this monotonicity, these nonlinear characteristics can be minimized by using adaptive weight assignment techniques during system's training.

It is certainly the case that these device nonlinearities make the task of optically programming these arrays more difficult than one would like, but these problems are relatively easily solved compared to the difficulties created by their highly asymmetrical forward and reverse bias current-to-voltage characteristics. These create serious obstacles to building a neural computing system with balanced behavior. The difficulty here is caused when trying to counterbalance activating and inhibiting stimulation. Earlier work [11] at Bell Laboratories had shown that unbalanced synaptic characteristics severely limit the type of activity that can be implemented and more importantly, the range of problems that can be addressed.[13]

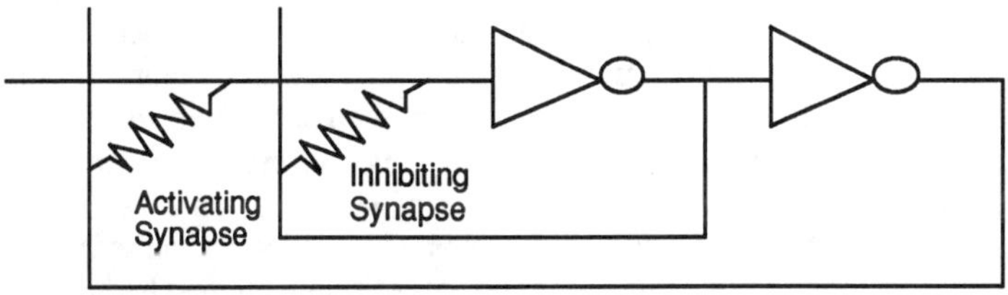

Figure 18 Traditional circuit used to implement analog neurons.

---

12 Note that the dark and illuminated characteristics closely track one another and differ by only 15 to 20 microamperes.

13 In this work, n-load and p-load transistors were used to implement activating (n-load) and inhibiting (p-load) synaptic elements. The carrier mobility in each of these transistor types is substantially different and the size of each transistor type was appropriately scaled (based on estimates of typical device characteristics from previous fabrication runs) to achieve balanced behavior. Ideally, activating and inhibiting synapses should be capable of cancelling one another. Unfortunately the particular fabrication run used to produce these CMOS arrays deviated from these estimates and the resulting device behavior was badly skewed. In these CMOS arrays there was a 6 to 1 difference between activating and inhibiting synapses and consequently balanced behavior was not possible.

The underlying problem caused by unequal synapse behavior occurs because the neuron circuit model relies on electrical current summing to determine the net neuron activation level. Figure 18 depicts a typical circuit for this type of neuron model. If we were to use this circuit with our device a number of compensations would be required. This neuron model requires that synapses be either current sources or sinks. If we assume that activating synapses are driven in forward bias and inhibiting are reverse biased then it is clear from the IV characteristics for these asymmetrical arrays that counterbalancing these two types of stimulation will be difficult, if not impossible to achieve. To do so requires that each synapse type be illuminated with its own rather skewed and unique set of illumination intensity to connection weight mapping. Moreover, considering the suppressed photoresponse of these photoconductive elements under reverse bias, we would be forced to operate the system within a very narrow range of both illumination and neuron firing strength. It is not clear that such measures could achieve balanced system behavior.

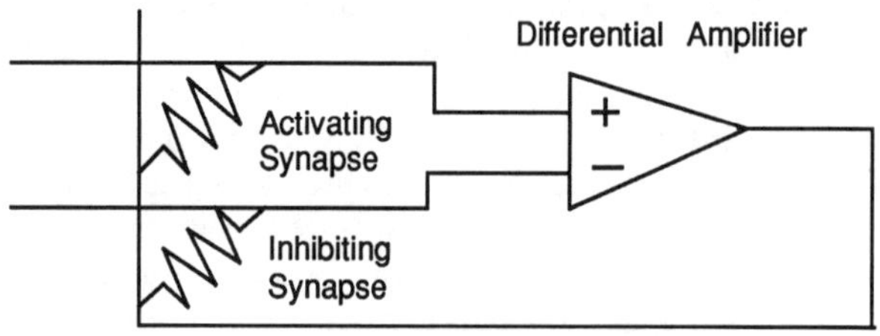

Figure 19 Comparator based neuron circuit used in OPIE.

Our solution to the many problems caused by the skewed device characteristics in these first arrays was to redesign the basic neuron circuit used in the system architecture (Figure 19). In contrast to the circuit shown in Figure 18, this circuit does not employ current summing along a common input line to the neuron. A differential amplifier is used to compare activating and inhibiting stimulation. The advantage in this approach is that both types of synapses can now be operated in the same region of the IV curves (in this case, forward biased). As such, balanced behavior is easily achieved. The same illumination schedule is used for both synapse types. Moreover since we are free to choose forward or reverse bias operation for synapse operation, we can select the region with the largest dynamic range and best photoresponse. This differential mode of operation means that the effective synapse strength and type is encoded as the difference between a pair of photoconductive junctions—one activating and the other inhibiting. As such, the resulting span of achievable connection strength can be easily controlled.

There are a number of advantages that result from the use of a differential amplifier as the neuron unit. The resulting system is more easily capable of achieving balanced behavior. In the simple neuromorphic model used in neural networks, an active neuron (one that is "firing") should be capable of simultaneously activating and inhibiting other neurons. The intensity of both types of stimulation should be more or less equivalent. If they are not then inhibitory stimuli are not capable of moderating neuron activity. For example, consider implementing synapses with zero connection strength (neurons which are not logically connected to one another). Ideally one requires a synaptic connection with infinite resistance, but this is not realizable in practice and typically one approximates such synapses with very large resistive values. These small but finite connections can create a small bias within the resulting system. In this context it is instructive to compare the two neuron circuit models. Since the circuit shown in Figure 18 relies on current summing along a single input line to combine activating and inhibiting stimuli, it requires that two conditions be met: first, the forward and reverse bias behavior of the synapses should be approximately equal and second, the dual outputs from the two inverting amplifiers in the neuron circuit should be balanced. The dual outputs from this circuit are potential sources of error within the system. The output from the operational amplifiers must balance so that their midpoint is held at ground. If this is not insured the system will have an inherent bias. In contrast, the differential neuron circuit outlined in Figure 19 has only a single output and hence there cannot be a difference between the output stimulation for activating or inhibiting other neurons. In this model the synapse between two neurons is implemented by using two resistive connections. The effective synaptic type and strength are encoded by the difference between them. As such, balanced activity and infinite resistance, are more easily achieved.

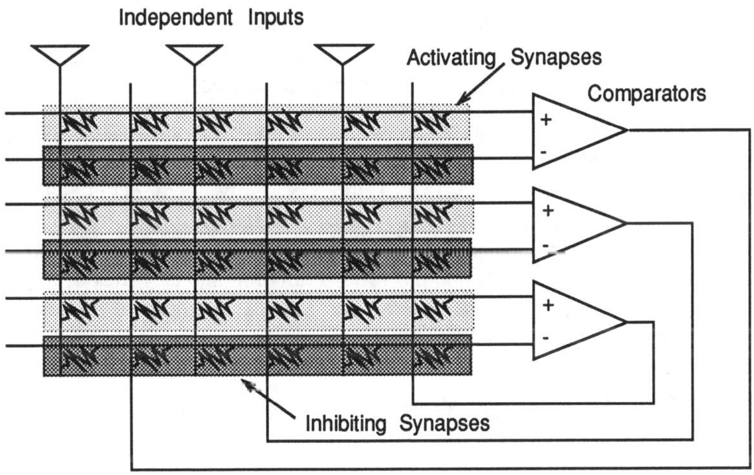

Figure 20 Partitioning of the synapses within an array for differential operation

There are other factors that influence the configuration of our neuro-computing system. Figure 20 illustrates the partitioning of these arrays into regions of activating and inhibiting connections. The drawing shows a logical partitioning. It is unlikely that this particular mapping would be used in an actual configuration. In practice the row pairings are chosen so as to find the closest match between device characteristics. Functional device arrays typically have a fairly large variation in characteristics across the 14,400 member population. The uniformity within these arrays (as shown in Figure 13) can have up to a 30% scatter in the photo-response among the individual elements[14]. Differential operation means that information is encoded not by the magnitude of each photoconductor's output signals, but rather by the difference between paired output elements. Not only does this tended to minimize many of the imperfections found in real devices, but it also decouples the system from changes in the absolute intensity of the illumination system.

Differential operation when used with our square *NxN* electrode arrays has one additional advantage. Since these arrays can be configured to form **N/2** neurons, each with two rows acting as its inputs (dendrites) and using a single column as its output (axon), an extra set of **N/2** column electrodes is available for other uses. We suggest that they be used as either independent input ports or as a means for biasing or annealing the computation.

As we acquired first hand experience with these devices and began to implement simple neural system applications, we came to understand that a number of other approaches might be taken for using these arrays in neural systems. The next section of this chapter describe a neural system capable of simple geometric pattern recognition and reconstruction. It uses a somewhat different method of operation. In that system each neuron is restricted to either **ON/OFF** operation. Synapses take on continuous values but are not easily classified as either activating or inhibiting. There is a one–to–one mapping of synapses to photoconductive elements. This enables us to implement 120 neurons and use a single photoconductive junction for each synapse connection..

Like many other neural systems, all of the inputs into a neuron are summed and compared to a threshold value. If the input exceeds threshold, the neuron is activated to fire and is switched into the **ON** state. Our approach differs somewhat because the stimulation signal is normalized to reflect both the actual device characteristics for each neuron and normalized to factor out the activity of other neurons in the system. Since the raw stimulation signal varies according to the number of neurons that are active, our system attempts to remove these fluctuations. In essence, it employs a dynamically varying neuron threshold. This dynamic threshold is unique to each neuron so as to reflect the actual device variations that are seen in these synapses.

---

14 There are a number of factors that underlie this non-uniformity. As described earlier, the photoconductive gain (and hence photoresponse of these devices is a function of the carrier transit time through the thickness of the amorphous silicon film. We use a plasma deposition process to create these films. It is difficult to control this deposition process with enough precision to ensure a uniform film thickness be deposited across an entire four inch wafer. Consequently, we see a strong spatial correlation to these non-uniformities.

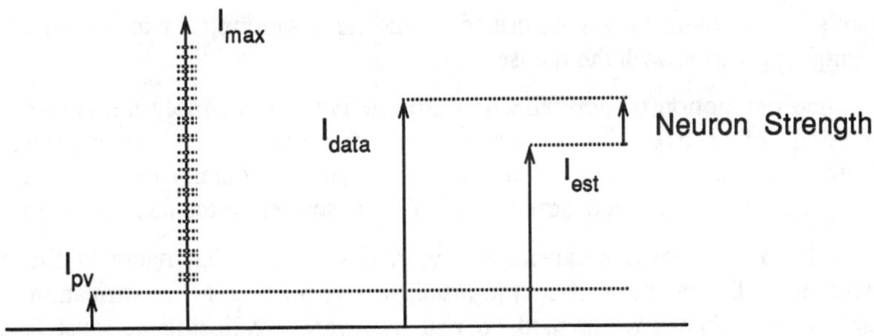

Figure 21 A number of calibration measurements are used to remove variations caused by device non-uniformities and variations in input drive levels.

Figure 21 depicts the many factors that are used to determine the activation threshold for the system. This approach relies on making two calibration measurements on the illuminated array. We first measure the current flowing out of each channel (electrode) when all of the input neurons are set to the **OFF** state. Theoretically the **OFF** state neurons are set to ground, but in practice our neurons used TTL drivers and typically averaged 0.16-0.17 Volts. Even if the neurons circuit drivers were held at ground we would still expect to see a small output current generated purely by photovoltaic mechanisms. In Figure 21, this output is labeled the Photovoltaic Current (I_{pv}). We then switch all of the neurons to the **ON** state and again measure the output current. This gives us the maximum possible output and is labeled I_{max}. The difference between these two measurements yields the dynamic range of the input to each neuron:

$$I_{dyn} = I_{max} - I_{pv}$$

This enables us to estimate the expected output value for each channel given the number of neurons actively firing into it. We estimate that any one neuron will generate 1/120th of the dynamic range. If **K** neurons are active, we estimate the average output value for a channel to be:

$$I_{est} = I_{pv} + (K * I_{dyn} * G) / 120$$

Where **G** is a user definable global scale factor that coarsely adjusts the sensitivity of the system. It is normally set to one, but when set to values less than one, the system tends to be more sensitive to input stimulation.

The estimated output value (I_{est}) is used to give a measure of the expected activation strength of the signal coming out of each channel (electrode) of the synaptic array. The neuron activation strength is defined as the difference between the actual and the estimated output from each channel:

$$\textbf{Neuron Strength} = I_{data} - I_{est}$$

It is this value that is displayed on the user interface and is used to determine the sliding threshold function. The actual threshold is determined by the placement of the red threshold bar across the graphed neuron strength for the system's 120 channels. As described in the next section, it can be adjusted by changing its position with the mouse.

In essence our notion of normalized neuron activation is simply a measure of the correlation of active (input) neurons to synapses with strong connection strength. Although seemingly complex, this approach actually behaves quite well in the geometric pattern reconstruction problem described in the next subsection.

It is clear to us from our experiences with this system that many of the neural network models that have been proposed will require some modification and/or enhancements when implemented on real hardware. Adjustments must be made to accommodate the many idiosyncrasies of real devices. The approach described above is but one of many different approaches for operating our system. This aspect of our research deserves further study and will undoubtedly result in changes and improvements to the basic design of our synaptic elements.[15]

2.6 The User Interface

One of the most useful components of this system is its graphical, highly animated user interface. It permits us to interactively control the operation of this neuro-computing system and to observe the activity of its many components. The user interface unifies the system, functionally and conceptually. It transforms the system from a large collection of complex, independent hardware elements (power supplies, illumination elements, analog signal generation and measurement equipment, etc.) into a unified comprehensive entity. This enables us to present the user with a view of the system which is not hardware oriented, but rather generates the abstractions of the problem domain. The user interface transforms the hardware into a computing system capable of useful and interesting behavior.

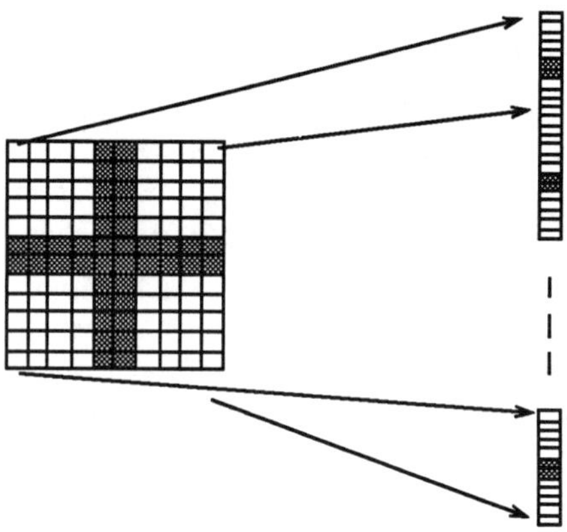

Figure 22 The 10x12 two dimensional patterns are linearized into a 120 element vector

15 The interplay between system development and device refinement is discussed in the third section of this chapter.

In one of the first demonstrations of the system a pattern reconstruction problem was implemented.[16] The system's 120 neurons were conceptually mapped as a 10 by 12 element two dimensional grid. Figure 22 shows a typical geometric pattern. The dark elements denote neurons that are firing (in the ON state) whereas the white elements are inactive or OFF state neurons. There is a simple correspondence between the two dimensional abstraction of a geometric pattern and its one dimensional counterpart. The system implements an associative memory capable of encoding and storing these 2-D geometric patterns and subsequently is capable of recognizing noisy, incomplete instances of these patterns and of reconstructing the original pattern. A Hopfield architecture was used[17] because it enabled us to generate an easily computable weight matrix which can be permanently encoded on a piece of photographic film[18]. The $\mathbf{W}_{ij}$ weight matrix is computed via:

$$\mathbf{W}_{ij} = \Sigma \mathbf{V}_i \mathbf{V}_i^T$$

We have used a computer generated optical program to implement the weight matrix.

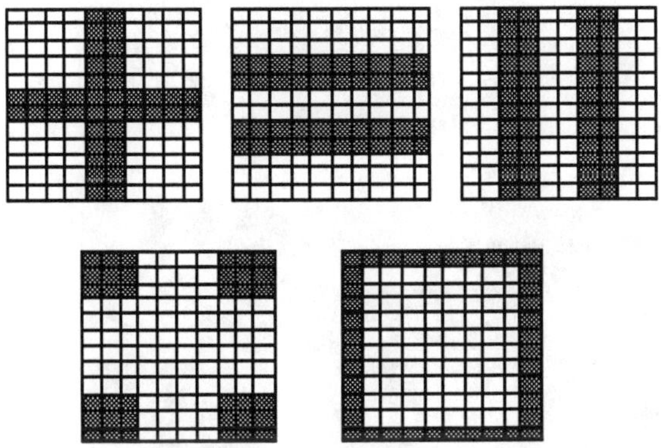

Figure 23 Five geometric patterns encoded into the synaptic weight matrix.

Figure 23 shows five typical geometric patterns. Figure 24a shows the weight matrix for these five geometric patterns. The grey scale value for each element of

16 A computing system of this size and scope is continually evolving as various aspects of the system are better understood or improved. Change is also inevitable as new applications and methods of operating the array and system are explored. In this section we describe one of these experiments.

17 The particular architecture created is implemented by a software mapping which determines the link between the array's inputs and outputs. In a Hopfield architecture the inputs are mapped one for one back onto the inputs. Layered networks, on the other hand, typically map the system's inputs to the first k elements of the input vector. The outputs from this first layer are then mapped to input elements k through k+t, etc.

18 At his early stage of the system's development, our CRT illumination system was not operational.

the optical pattern is determined on the basis of the optical response of the array and on the desired connection strength specified by the $\mathbf{W}_{ij}$ weight matrix. The cross product of each stored vector and its transpose are summed and the resulting values are mapped to gray scale to create the film mask.

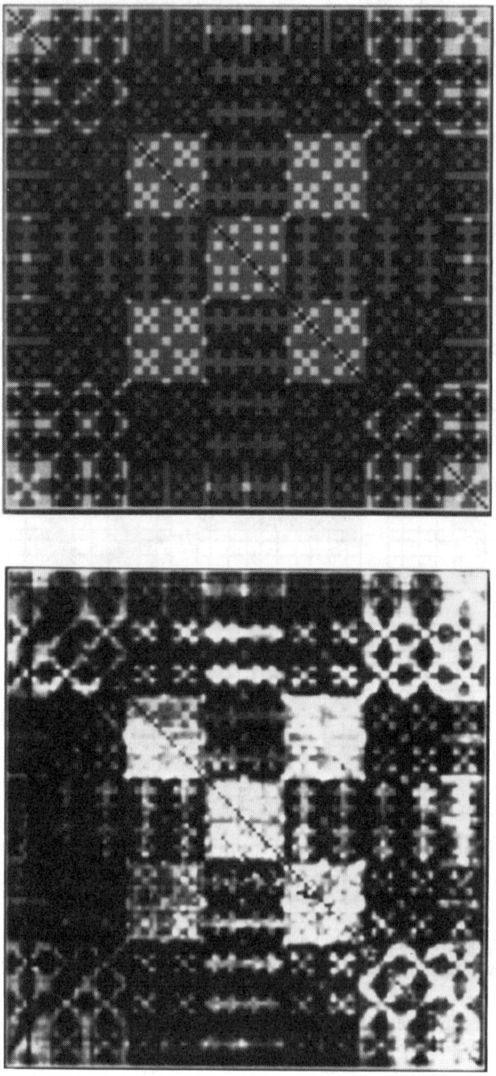

a

b

Figure 24 The response to the weight matrix illumination pattern (b) differs substantially from the actual illumination pattern (shown as a).

There is a striking contrast between the optical weight matrix encoded into the film mask, as shown in Figure 24,) and the response of the photoconductive array to that pattern of illumination. The array response is determined by driving one input (row) at a time into the array (the others are held at ground) and then measuring the output current at each column. Theoretically this gives us a measure of the optical response for each of the elements along that row (in practice, these measurements are a bit noisy). These values are then mapped to a 256 level grey scale and are depicted in Figure 24b.

As can be seen, there are a number of differences between the two images. Note for example that the right side of Figure 24b is brighter than the left. This indicates that the right side of the array is more sensitive to light than is the left. This is probably an artifact of the a-Si plasma deposition process indicating that the photoconductive film is slightly thinner on the left side of the array. A variety of other defects can also been seen. One entire column, near the left side of Figure 24b is non-responsive (defective). The image also shows a sprinkling of defective elements at the center, just below the major diagonal.

Some of the fuzziness seen in Figure 24b can be traced to our illumination system. In practice it takes some care to align the projected illumination pattern from the film mask to the synaptic elements on the array. If the aspect ratio of the film mask varies by more than 0.8% from that of the synaptic array, the pattern cannot be accurately aligned. These exceptionally tight tolerance could not be achieved when making the film mask. To compensate for this mismatch, the film mask was rotated by 11.5 degrees to achieve alignment. This causes the projected pattern to be slightly out of focus on the extreme left and right sides of the array. These errors can be seen in the somewhat fuzzy image shown in Figure 24b.

Despite the many problems evident in these images—a variety of point and line defects and a wide range of photoconductor response characteristics—these had little effect on the actual results of using the network for vector–matrix multiplication because the Hopfield encoding generates memory states that are distributed throughout the weight matrix. The eigenvectors for the film mask, shown in Figure 24a, which can be tested in simulation, are the same for the fuzzy image shown in Figure 24b. This behavior demonstrates the robustness of these networks. In some instances, the photoconductive array performs better than the idealized simulation, since it does not appear to demonstrate any metastable states.

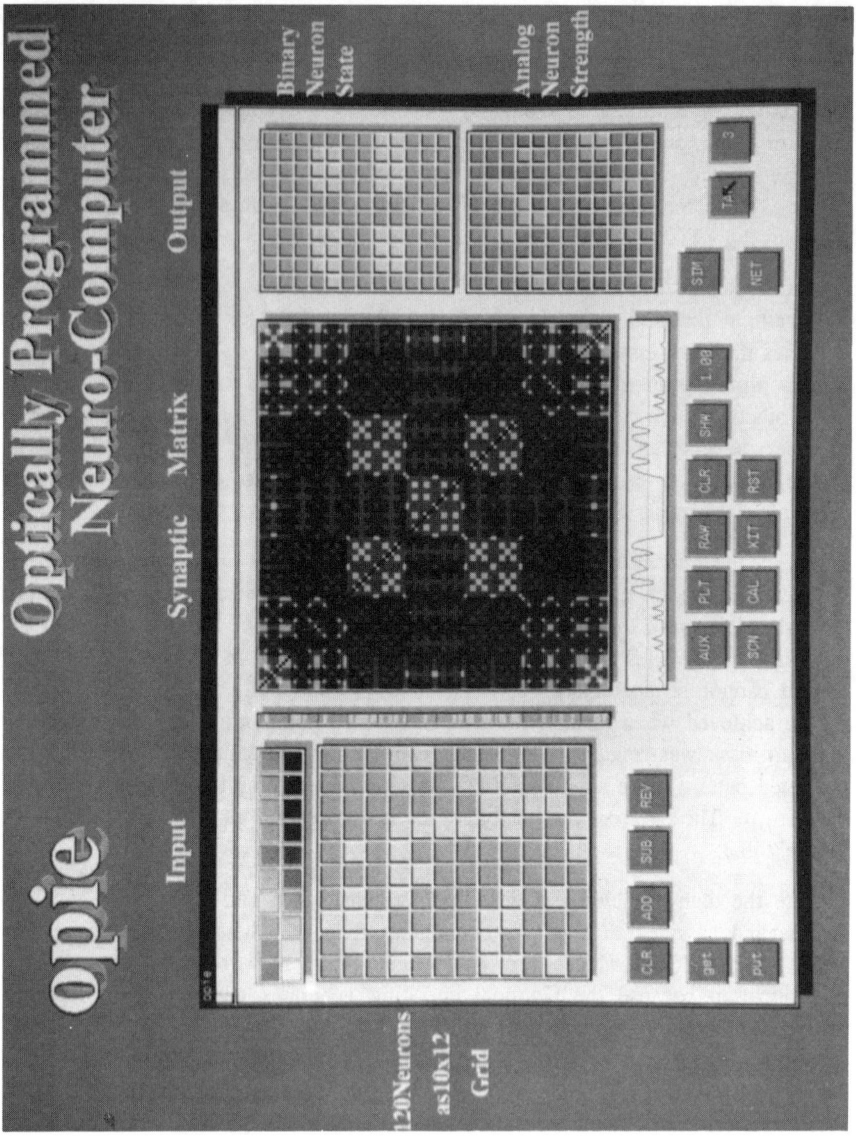

Figure 25 OPIE's user interface permits interactive control of system activity.

The user interface for this application, shown in Figure 25, enables the user to create geometric patterns, encode them in an optical weight matrix, generate the equivalent photographic film illumination pattern, align the illumination pattern, and finally to calibrate the entire system. The system is then capable of reconstructing corrupted versions of these geometric patterns either under simulation or via analog operation. The user interface generates and implements these abstractions.

Geometric patterns are input to the system using the mouse by drawing onto the large 10 by 12 element array on the left side of the user interface. The left mouse button turns elements/neurons ON (shown as white), the middle mouse button turns them OFF (shown in gray). The six buttons below the input pad control storage and recall of these patterns in the system's associative memory. ADD stores a pattern and SUB removes a pattern. REV allows the user to review the patterns currently stored. The CLR button clears the input pad (sets all elements to OFF state). GET and PUT enable a user to access a file of geometric patterns or to store the current collection of patterns to a user named file.

The center region of the user interface shows the 120 by 120 element optically encoded weight matrix. The gray and white vertical bar to its immediate left depicts the state of the current input vector. Active neurons are shown as white, inactive as gray. The graph just below the optical weight matrix represents a measure of the output strength of each of the 120 neurons.[19] The line across the middle of the graph indicates the activation threshold above which the neuron is switched into the ON state. The two smaller 10 by 12 grids to the immediate right of the optical weight matrix show the two dimensional encoding of the output activity of these 120 neurons. The bottom grid shows a color encoding of activity. The upper grid shows the firing activity of the neurons. All elements/neurons whose activity is greater than threshold (as measured by the height of the middle line in the output graph) are shown as white (ON), those below that threshold are shown as gray (OFF). This grid can also be viewed as the reconstruction pattern generated by the system.

The system operates by using the input pattern (the geometric pattern grid at left) as the seed input to the associative memory. The initial pattern is transferred to the input vector (the vertical bar to the left of the immediate left of the optical weight matrix) and is sent as a binary voltage vector to the photoconductive array. Conceptually, think of each element of this input vector/bar as attached to its associated row in the synaptic matrix[20]. Conceptually, any row connected to a white element (an ON state neuron) is

19 Please refer to section 2.5 (**System Operation**) for a more detailed discussion of this encoding.

20 In the user interface this mapping is shown schematically such that neuron 1 is linked to row 1, neuron 2 to row 2, etc., but in fact the actual mapping could be quite different.

driven at HIGH voltage (TTL high or about 3.7 volts). Gray elements (OFF state neurons) are held at ground. Only ON state elements/rows are meaningful. Any row which is driven at high voltage is capable of driving current into the output. Wherever that row passes through an illuminated region it passes current into a column electrode running vertically underneath. The intensity of the illumination determines the amount of current transferred. From the conceptual viewpoint, the 120 by 120 element matrix represents the synaptic elements—the brighter the synapse, the stronger the connection strength.

The graph at the bottom of the weight matrix shows a measure of this output current intensity but is normalized to account for the strength of the input vector. As mentioned earlier, the two smaller grids on the right are 2-D encodings of this output.[21] The threshold view (at the top) represents the partially resolved geometric pattern evoked by the associative memory. This is then used as the next input vector to the system. This cycle of activity is repeated until convergence is achieved (the output and input vectors are the same) or until a user definable number of machine cycles occurs.

The user interface is continually changing to reflect the current state of the system hardware. The hardware is capable of completing hundreds cycles per second, but to run the machine at that rate presents a chaotic view on the user interface. Typically the memory converges within half dozen or fewer cycles. Since the CRT display of the user interface is refreshed at 30 frames per second, the operator sees very little or no system evolution or convergence. For this reason, the system is deliberately set to run at approximately two cycles per second. At this running rate the user can watch the convergence of the associative memory and can better interpret its behavior. When the machine is operating, the user interface provides a fascinating graphical perspective of system activity.

The user interface incorporates a number of interesting features. It can (graphically) show the reverse mapping that relates a neuron's response to its input stimulus. One can graphically see the path of activation for each output neuron. Those synapses in the optical weight matrix that participate in the activation of a neuron are highlighted. This is particularly useful for detecting abnormal synapse activity. The system is also able to show the calibration curves for each of the 14,400 synapses. The mouse pointer is used to select a synapse (left mouse button) in the weight matrix and its calibration data is displayed in the output graph.

---

21 These are presented as two dimensional geometric patterns.

3.0 Device Enhancements

Our experience with these early amorphous silicon synaptic arrays provided us with valuable experience that led to a substantial re-design of the basic device structure. In these first generation devices we were plagued by a wide variation (approximately 30%) in the characteristics of elements within an array. Moreover, the basic IV and photo-response characteristics of these devices were asymmetric and highly non-linear. Finally, the RC time constants for propagation of signals through the array was disappointingly slow—milliseconds.

Many of the undesirable characteristics of these first generation devices can be traced to their device geometry. Each photoconductive element is formed at the intersection of orthogonal, overlapping electrodes. The attraction of this approach is that the synaptic elements are self-aligned and hence easy to produce. But incumbent in this design are limitations to its performance. In this overlapping electrode design one of the electrodes must be transparent to allow light to penetrate into the sandwiched amorphous silicon photoconductive layer. The asymmetry in the IV characteristics is probably caused by the use of different metals for each of these electrode layers—Indium Tin Oxide (ITO) and Titanium/Gold (Ti/Au). The work function associated with each metal is different.

In these first generation devices the synapse or photoactive region of each device is defined by the cross–sectional area of the overlap between the orthogonal electrodes. In these early devices, this region measures approximately 250 by 125 microns or 31,250 micron^2. This relatively large area creates a device with a very large overlap capacitance. This capacitance dominates the RC time constant for the device and seriously limits its speed.

Finally, the overlapping arrangement of the electrodes not only mandates that one of the electrodes be transparent but also creates a device in which photon generated free carriers move vertically through the thickness of the amorphous silicon film. This creates several problems. First, since the film is less than a micron thick the ratio of the metal–semiconductor interface area to the film thickness is highly skewed. The interface area is very larger and dominates the characteristics of the device. Second, since carriers move through the amorphous silicon film, many of the characteristics of the device (e.g. photoconductive gain) are determined by the film's thickness. It is likely that the wide distribution in device characteristics (non-uniformity) is caused by small variations in the thickness of the amorphous silicon film. Finally, the resistive characteristics of these devices (the effective length to width ratio) is proportional to the ratio of the cross-sectional area of the electrode overlap region to the thickness of the amorphous silicon film. Since the amorphous silicon film thickness is constrained within fairly narrow limits, the effective resistance of these devices changes as we scale the device geometries and increase the density of the electrodes.

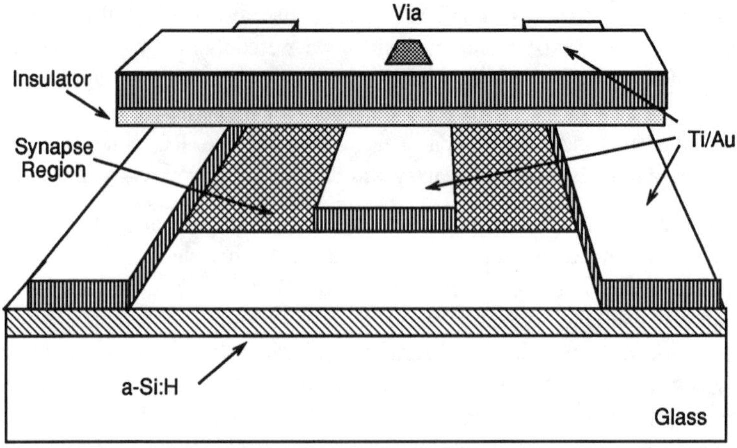

Figure 27 Lateral device geometries significantly improve device performance

Many of these problems can be overcome by changing the basic geometry of these devices. Figure 27 depicts the layout of the second generation (lateral) device geometry. The device is shown fabricated on a glass substrate. The optically active "synapse" region (the hatched area of the diagram) is defined by the area between a bottom runner electrode and one of the metal island structures. In this device, photon generated carriers traverse this region moving laterally across the surface of the amorphous silicon film. A second, top electrode runner is separated from the underlying amorphous silicon and metal layers by a layer of insulation. Note that a via is used to connect this top electrode layer to the island structure below.

This device is substantially different from the first generation "vertical" devices described in Section 1. Its geometry is more complex to fabricate. The addition of the via structure imposes more stringent alignment constraints on the photolithography process. Moreover, the use of two levels of metal creates topological variations that cause metallization and lithography difficulties.[23]

Despite its more complex fabrication, the new structure has many compensating advantages. Since the movement of free carriers is lateral, across the surface of the amorphous silicon film, the devices are no longer sensitive to the thickness of the photoconductor film and hence we would expect to see better device

23 Our measurements on early device arrays exhibit excellent device uniformity.

uniformity among the population of photosensors in the array. Moreover, because the optical region is defined by the intense field region established between an island and its neighboring bottom level metal runner electrode, the top level metal electrode size can be made arbitrarily small. This decreases the overlap capacitance by several orders of magnitude. Finally, the metal to amorphous silicon interface in this structure occurs at the edges of the metal electrodes and the optically active region and is orders of magnitude smaller than the equivalent interface region in the first generation devices. The device characteristics are now dominated by the properties of the amorphous silicon rather than by its interfaces.

Figure 27 shows the device fabricated on a transparent substrate with light passing through it into the a-Si film. This is not an essential element of its design. The device could also be illuminated from its top side (and hence be built on a non-transparent substrate). If illuminated from the top, a portion of the optically active region will be blocked by the shadow of the top, orthogonal electrode and hence reduce the optical efficiency somewhat. This may be more than compensated by improvements in carrier generation.

The dynamics of carrier generation differ somewhat in topside and backside illumination. In backside illumination, the preponderance of photon generated carriers occur at the bottom of the amorphous silicon film, near its glass substrate. Carriers must then migrate through the a-Si:H film to the overlying metal electrodes. In this case, the dynamics and efficiency are again a function of the thickness of the amorphous silicon film. When the photoconductive gain is large this is only a second order effect because it is only the primary, photon induced carriers that must traverse the amorphous silicon film thickness. Carriers injected into the a-Si by charge imbalance traverse only the top region of the film. Hence, as the photoconductive gain increases, the effect of film thickness (and its associated non-uniformity) are reduced[24].

The dynamics of carrier movement in the top illuminated devices is different. In this case, we assume that the majority of photon induced carriers are generated near the top surface of the a-Si film and move laterally across the film's surface. Even though a few carriers may be generated deep within the film, their number is small and the overall characteristics are not effected by the a-Si film thickness. The effect of variation in film thickness will only occur if the amorphous silicon film thickness is smaller than the extinction coefficient of the film and if some of the light penetrates through the film. In this case, variations in the thickness of the amorphous silicon film will only be seen as a clipping of carrier generation. Since generation falls exponentially with film thickness, these effects are likely to be immeasurably small.

24 The very thin vertical devices typically have photoconductive gains of about 15. We would expect that the lateral devices would have somewhat smaller gains.

We feel that the "lateral" device geometry is inherently superior to the first generation "vertical" geometry. The devices are better suited for scaling their size. The resistance in these devices is determined by the length to width ratio of the photoconductive region—the area directly between the bottom, metal electrode layer and the adjacent island. If the feature sizes are reduced, this bounded area scales proportionally and the effective length to width of the area is unchanged. Hence, scaling does not change the photoconductive properties of the device.

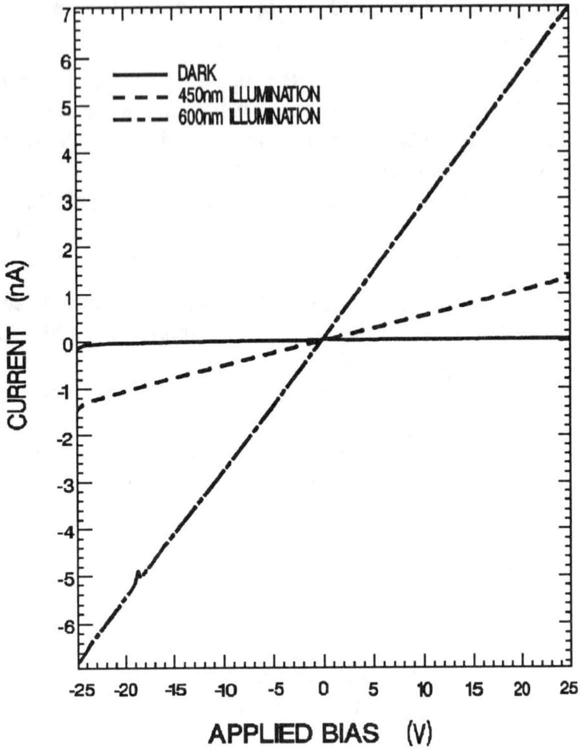

Figure 28 Current-to-Voltage Characteristics for the "lateral" device geometry.

Initial measurements from prototype "lateral" device structures support our optimistic projections of their behavior. The current–to–voltage characteristics for a discrete lateral device are shown in Figure 28. In contrast to the IV curves for "vertical" structures, the characteristics are both very linear and are completely symmetric. Moreover, preliminary measurements suggest that the RC time constants for these devices is about one thousand times smaller, approximately a nanosecond. Finally, the photoresponse of these elements is highly uniform. Variations are under 1% and are probably caused by variations in the illumination source.

We are encouraged by these measurements and look forward to building large arrays of these devices for even more powerful neuro-computing systems.

4. Summary and Conclusions

This research owes its genesis to our previous work building flat panel displays. [26] The central idea in that work involves fabricating large display panels with defect tolerant amorphous silicon, thin film transistors at each pixel. This project employs one very simple idea—the a-Si thin film transistor at each pixel in the display has been transformed into a light sensitive synaptic element.[25] The two arrays are built to the same scale and use the same basic suite of fabrication techniques as are used for active matrix flat panel displays. In retrospect, it is remarkable how far we have managed to pursue this simple idea. But of course the final system has evolved a great deal from this one simple idea. The neuro-computer system that emerged employs a number of other interesting ideas as well.

There are a number of fortuitous benefits that result from our use of amorphous silicon photoconductors as synaptic elements. Amorphous silicon has emerged as a cost effective, widely used technology for both photovoltaic power cells and in active matrix flat displays. The similarities between these devices allows us to use well established, commercially viable technologies both in the fabrication of these arrays and in their mounting and assembly.

The large area fabrication techniques now used to produce flat panel displays make possible the development of synaptic arrays with approximately one million elements (640x480x3). The manufacturing cost of these panels is rapidly falling. It does not seem unreasonable to expect that the manufacturing cost of these panels will approach a few hundred dollars within the relatively near future. These arrays are not only inexpensive to produce but provide a continuous range of connection strength that can span more than five orders of magnitude. There are no other approaches for constructing synapses that offer so many attractive features.

Our research explored a number of diverse issues. We began with a detailed study of the device physics that govern the behavior of these photoconductive thin film devices. We fabricated and characterized a large number of simple discrete devices in order to understand the influence of a variety of material compositions and geometries on the behavior of these devices. We learned that the semiconductor to metal electrode interfaces have a profound influence on the

25 The transition between these two ideas is rather natural. One of the unfortunate side effects of a-Si transistors is their sensitivity to light. A light shield is frequently included in their design. It is only a small step to use this unwanted secondary property to useful effect.

behavior of these devices. A range of device properties are possible that extend from simple primary photoconduction to more complex mechanisms like secondary photoconduction that exhibit gain. This range of behavior enables one to engineer device structures for particular application domains with unique requirements—from photon counters and light sensors to variable strength photoconductive elements. We believe that this flexibility is one of many benefits that this approach offers.

Our studies of the fundamental mechanisms that govern the behavior of these devices enabled us to fabricate large arrays of these photoconductive elements. Two different array densities were fabricated—1600 and 14,400 element arrays. As described, the device design enables us to create essentially self aligned structures. Early versions of these arrays exhibited excessive resistance. This was due primarily to the high series resistance associated with long ITO electrodes. Subsequent designs were modified to include a parallel runner of low resistance metal to offset the ITO resistance. A number of array types were fabricated including some with mixed electrode types in which either primary or secondary photoconductivity will dominate depending on the manner in which the arrays are driven—forward or reverse bias.

These arrays were used to construct a variety of neuro-computing systems. A number of interesting and challenging system issues arose in these systems. Some of these include techniques for illuminating the arrays; the design of an analog electronic support system and a variety of methods for operating these arrays. Illumination remains a difficult and as yet not totally solved aspect of these systems. Not only is it difficult to generate highly patterned illumination images with grey scale (variable intensity) pixels, but as was described, it is altogether non-trivial to align these patterns to the array and in some cases the illumination may have a temporally varying character caused by a rastered display device. In such cases, the analog subsystem must be closely synchronized with the illumination system to minimize these effects.

Our experience building these systems has taught us that real systems are quite different from digital simulations of neural network models. They are different because real synapses and real analog neurons exhibit a range of operating characteristics. These properties are non-uniform and can be highly non-linear. These factors have a significant impact on the methods used to run these systems. As described, a variety of normalization techniques were used to accommodate this variability in the real hardware.

The computing system described in this paper includes a sophisticated user interface that is graphically rich and highly animated. It transforms the system from a complex collection of interconnected components into a system that creates and maintains a number of abstractions that characterize its application domain. It adds immeasurably to the final system, giving it a sense of personality and identity.

Our experiences with these devices and systems taught us something about both the features of this approach and its shortcomings. The device arrays tended to be slow and to have a wide disparity in operating characteristics. We traced many of these problems to the vertical device geometry used in these first generation arrays. This enabled us to fundamentally redesign the basic device structure to minimize those properties. The new structure has a lateral geometry and as described in the third section of this paper has much better device properties. It is more than three orders of magnitude faster than the vertical structures. The IV characteristics are linear and has very good uniformity across the entire array. We look forward to using these new device arrays in a variety of unique applications. But our experience indicates that these new arrays are considerably more difficult to fabricate than were the first generation device arrays.

This chapter described the design, fabrication and operational characteristics of a new class of synaptic elements whose behavior is based on photoconduction in amorphous silicon films. Large arrays of these synaptic devices have been fabricated and characterized. Our studies indicate that their performance and characteristics can be engineered across a wide spectrum of behavior.

We also described a large, analog neuro-computing system constructed using arrays of photoconductive elements as synapses. Innovative computing systems of this type entail a number of interesting and essential engineering details which include mechanical support structures, illumination systems and analog electronic sub-system design. We have also described a highly graphical interactive user interface which enables interactive control of the computing system.

The experience that we gained in this work have led to a substantial redesign of the fundamental synaptic element. A handful of prototype devices of this type have been fabricated and indicate that this second generation device is three orders of magnitude faster and has much better uniformity and operating characteristics.

We have only begun to study and understand the temporal characteristics of these arrays. There are many challenges remaining to be solved in the control of the illumination for these systems. We are now investigating the implications of learning algorithms on the design of such systems. We are both encouraged and challenged by the promise of these synaptic arrays and look forward to exploring the many intriguing possibilities that they offer for building "real" neuro-computing systems.

References

1.. Psaltis, D. and N. Farhat, Opt. Lett., Vol. 10, pp. 98, 1985.

2. Farhat, N.H., et. al., App. Optics, Vol. 24, pp. 1460, 1985.

3. Fisher, A.D., C.L. Giles, and J.N. Lee, J. Opt. Soc. Am. Vol. 1, Vol. 1337, 1984.

4. Sofer, B., et. al., Opt. Lett., Vol. 11, pp. 186, 1986.

5. Anderson, D.Z., Opt. Lett. Vol. 11, pp. 56, 1986.

6. Yariv, A. and S.K. Kwong, Opt. Lett., Vol. 11, pp. 186, 1986.

7. G.D. Boyd, "Optically excited synapses for Neural Networks" *Applied Optics*, Vol. 26, pp. 2712, 1987.

8. H.P. Graf, L.D.Jackel, R.E.Howard, B.Straughn, J.S.Denker, "VLSI Implementation of a Neural network Memory with Several Hundreds of Neurons", *Neural Networks for Computing*, AIP Conference Proceedings 151, 1986.

9. M.A.Sivilotti, M.R.Emerling and C.A.Mead, "VLSI Architectures for implementation of neural Networks", *Neural Networks for Computing*, AIP Conference Proceedings 151, 1986.

10. J.P.Sage, K.Thompson and R.S.Withers, "An Artificial Neural network Integrated Circuit Based on MNOS/CCD Principles", *Neural Networks for Computing*, AIP Conference Proceedings 151, 1986.

11. H.P.Graf, W.Hubbard, L.D.Jackel and P.G.N. deVegvar, "A CMOS Associative Memory Chip", *IEEE First Intern"l Conf. on Neural Networks,* Vol. III, pp. 461, 1987.

12. J.I.Raffel, et al, "A Wafer-Scale Digital integrator Using Restructurable VLSI", *IEEE Journal of Solid-State Circuits*, Vol. SC-20, No. 1, 1985.

13. J. Alspector and R.B.Allen, "A Neuromorphic VLSI Learning System", *Advanced Research in VLSI*, proceedings of the 1987 Stanford Conference.

14. Ong,T.C., Ko,P.K., and Hu,C., "The EEPROM as an analog memory device", *IEEE Trans. on Electron Devices*, Vol. 36, pp. 1840-1841, Sept. 1989.

15. Card, H.C. and Moore, W.R., "EEPROM synapses exhibiting pseudo-Hebbian plasticity", *Electronics Letters*, Vol. 25, pp. 805-806, 1989.

16. C.D.Kornfeld, R.C.Frye, C.C.Wong, E.A.Rietman, "Device Properties of a-Si Photoconductive Synapses", Hardware Implementations of Neuron Nets and Synapses. A Workshop Sponsored by NSF and ONR, Jan 1988, San Diego CA..

17. J.I.Pankove Ed., "Semiconductors and Semimetals—Hydrogenated Amorphous Silicon", Vol. 21, Parts A-D, 1984.

18. P.G. LeComber, A.Madan, W.E. Spear, In *Electronic and Structural Properties of Amorphous Semiconductors*, P.G. LeComber and J. Movt Eds, Academic, New york, pp. 373, 1973.

19. R.S.Crandall, *Phys. Rev. Lett.* , 44, pp. 749, 1980.

20. R.S.Crandall, *Phys. RevLett.*, 2, pp.319, 1980.

21. G. Modell, D.A. Anderson, W. Paul, *Phys. Rev. Lett.*, Vol. 22, pp. 1918, 1980.

22. F. Evangelisti, P.Fiorini, G.Fortunato, A.Frova, C.Giovanella, R.Peruzzi, *J. Non-Cryst. Solids*, Vol. 55, pp.191, 1983.

23. T.Ozawa, M.Takenouchi, S.Tomiyama, *Mat. Res. Soc. Symp. Proc.*, Vol. 49, pp. 417, 1985.

24. S. Kaneko, Y.Kajiwara, F.Okumura, T.Ohkubo, *Mat. Res. Soc. Symp. Proc.*, Vol. 49, pp.423, 1985.

25. K.Rosen, G.Brunst, *Mat. Res. Soc. Symp. Proc.*, Vol. 70, pp.683, 1986.

26. J.J.Thompson, *Mat. Res. Soc. Symp. Proc.*, Vol. 70, pp.613, 1986.

27. A.Rose, *RCA Review*, Vol. 12, pp. 362, 1951.

28. C.D. Kornfeld, "A Defect–Tolerant Active Matrix Electrophoretic Display", *Tech. Digest of SID,* pp. 142-144, 1984.

Appendix

The Tables of Contents for Volumes I, II, III, and IV of *Neural Networks* are listed below.

VOLUME I

CONCEPTS

APPLICATIONS

IMPLEMENTATIONS

VOLUME II

CONCEPTS

APPLICATIONS

VOLUME III

CONCEPTS

APPLICATIONS

IMPLEMENTATIONS

APPLICATIONS

Index